The Rise and Evolution of Brazilian Jiu-Jitsu

From Vale-Tudo, to Carlson Gracie to its Democratization

Robert Drysdale

The Rise and Evolution of Brazilian Jiu-Jitsu
From Vale-Tudo, to Carlson Gracie to its Democratization
Copyright © 2023 Robert Drysdale

ISBN- 9798358633087

Independently published through Kindle Direct Publishing
https://KDP.amazon.com

Portions of this book were originally published on GTR:
Global-Training-Report
www.Global-Training-Report.com

Cover picture: Carlson Gracie is raised in the air by students from the Gracie Academy after defeating Waldemar Santana in 1956: Acervo Jornal O Globo
Back cover picture: 2016 IBJJF World Championships at the Walter Pyramind in Long Beach: IBJJF Archives

All images, unless otherwise noted,
© Robert Drysdale / Zenith BJJ, LLC

For more information about the film *Closed Guard: The Origins of Jiu-Jitsu in Brazil*, and the author's first book *Opening Closed Guard*, visit www.ClosedGuardFilm.com

*"This book is dedicated to my mother.
The strongest warrior I will ever meet."*

*"In memory of Ricardo Azoury, the official
photographer of the second-wave."*

"But, without insisting on the necessity of sumptuary laws, can it be denied that rectitude of morals is essential to the duration of empires, and that luxury is diametrically opposed to such rectitude? Let it be admitted that luxury is a certain indication of wealth; that it even serves, if you will, to increase such wealth: what conclusion is to be drawn from this paradox, so worthy of the times? And what will become of virtue if riches are to be acquired at any cost? The politicians of the ancient world were always talking of morals and virtue; ours speak of nothing but commerce and money. One of them will tell you that in such a country a man is worth just as much as he will sell for at Algiers: another, pursuing the same mode of calculation, finds that in some countries a man is worth nothing, and in others still less than nothing; they value men as they do droves of oxen. According to them, a man is worth no more to the State, than the amount he consumes; and thus a Sybarite would be worth at least thirty Lacedæmonians. Let these writers tell me, however, which of the two republics, Sybaris or Sparta, was overthrown by a handful of peasants, and which one made Asia tremble?"

Discourse on The Arts and Sciences - Jean-Jacques Rousseau

Table of Contents

Interviews with members from the second-wave: Sergio Malibu, Ignácio Aragão, Murilo Bustamante (1st half), Jean Jacques Machado, Marcelo Alonso (1st half), Royler Gracie, Luis Carlos Valois, Wallid Ismail (1st half), Richard Bresler and André Pederneiras (1st half)

The final days of Carlson Gracie. Interviews with: Carlson Gracie Jr., Antonio Rosado (2ⁿᵈ half), Murilo Bustamante (2ⁿᵈ half), Wallid Ismail (2ⁿᵈ half), Paulão Filho, Una Proença and Marcelo Alonso (2ⁿᵈ half).

Author's Note

The original title for this book was *"The Rise and Decline of Brazilian Jiu-Jitsu."* Thinking the title too pessimistic and perhaps even contradictory (after all, how can something that is at its height in terms of popularity, be declining?), I opted instead for the present title. Beyond this, I realized half way through writing this book that the theme of jiu-jitsu's evolution was more befitting the message I am attempting to get across anyway. BJJ is unlikely to ever "fall," but will rather continue to adapt (evolve) as it always has since the term first became associated with fighting in general. What was originally meant by "decline" is only in terms of what has been lost throughout this evolutionary process. Admittedly, much else has also been gained throughout this same process.

In many ways, this book is a sequel to *Opening Closed Guard* and focuses on a period that its predecessor almost completely ignored, other than the occasional observation and bridge to the present and the brief homage to Carlson Gracie at its end. Fittingly, the book picks up where its predecessor left off. After a brief description of the origins of *vale-tudo* in Brazil, it follows by placing Carlson as a bridge between that largely unknown and distant realm and the current world phenom that jiu-jitsu has become since Royce Gracie shocked us all in that first UFC.

Unlike my first book however, the one you are holding is not a travel journal of discovery. *Opening Closed Guard* was written as a diary belonging to a man completely ignorant about his roots and propelled by a hunch that something about our history was amiss. The present book attempts at being a history book instead (hence the excessive footnotes and sources, particularly in parts 1 and 2). Consequently, the book is not only more analytical than the first but also more revealing, even if as a result of this, it became a slightly heavier read.

Furthermore, and much like the book that precedes it, *The Rise and Evolution of Brazilian Jiu-Jitsu* makes extensive use of oral tradition in order to retell the events and atmosphere that give jiu-jitsu its current cultural and technical shapes. However problematic oral accounts may be, ignoring so many of these protagonists being alive and so willing to give their testimony, would be a disservice to jiu-jitsu and its history. And if I write "problematic" it is only because it truly is, as *Opening Closed Guard* taught me.

Whereas in my first book, I let the interviewees speak and only made a small effort to correct them (editing them less than I should have). In the present work I have been more careful when accepting their testimonies at face value. Since (unfortunately), I fear that ultimately the responsibility over the claims will fall on me, the author (or at least the perception that I am in complete agreement with their testimonies will). For this reason, I urge the reader to do the same and be skeptical toward all testimonies in this book. No exceptions.

Which is not the same as accusing anyone of lying (sometimes that can happen and we may never know when), but rather acknowledging that jiu-jitsu, like most things in life, has been highly politicized and memory (any memory) can't be trusted as a reliable source. Naturally, those who lived these events may exaggerate and aggrandize. Particularly in the case of themselves and those to whom they feel their allegiance is owed to. Even more common, interviewees forget or become contaminated by tales they have not witnessed themselves, but given their stature in the *jiu-jitsusphere*, are automatically granted ultimate authority simply due to this high-stature.

Simply put, the reader ought to be aware that, however old, credible, charismatic and well intentioned, people (all of us) can and do fall victim to their own biases. Since biases have an almost imperceptible way of crafting our judgement according to our own interests, conveniences and loyalties as these change over time. To this eye-opening insight, my own skepticism can't be credited. Between my lack of experience and accepting the authority of those who are ranked higher than myself in jiu-jitsu, the credit to this insight does not belong to me, but rather to Roberto Pedreira.

Off that same note, I would like to make it clear that I am not a professional historian. I have a BA in History and a lifelong passion for this discipline that has always coexisted in parallel with my love for the gentle-art. With that said, in historiographical terms, I did my best and still needed help. Over the last couple of years, and following the public acceptance of *Opening Closed Guard*, many of its readers granted me the reputation for being a better historian that I am. In truth, my "research" does not scrape the surface of what is out there when compared to what others have done before me. Whether it is acknowledged or not, there is such thing as rank in this world. This note is a brief reminder of it.

In regards to the organization of the book, I have decided to break jiu-jitsu down into waves whose swell begin and end with the events that most significantly mark its evolutionary transitions. Undoubtedly, many other markers were possible, but they would all be just as arbitrary as the ones I've elected here. Still, I believe that the ones I chose are reasonable enough and accomplish the job of mapping out the most relevant events, how they changed jiu-jitsu, when this happened and why it happened.

To help the reader to navigate so many names and events, I created a timeline for important events and the protagonists that bring these events to life. For the same reason, I have also created a name index and a glossary for terms specific to jiu-jitsu that may not be easily recognizable to all. Additionally, throughout the text I usually skip the titles of "Master" and "Grandmaster" and refer to these characters by their first or last names instead. Not out of disrespect, but rather to avoid being excessively repetitive given how often their names appear in the text. Lastly, all translations in this book are my own, excepting the ones from Japanese.

Acknowledgements

Considering that my competitive jiu-jitsu journey, as well as my interest in its history, are inevitably intertwined, to credit all those who have played a part in making this book possible would make this acknowledgement section at least as long as the book itself. Still, I find that some names standout in this journey as a competitor and in my daily life as a coach, while others standout in having assisted me in one way or another in order to help make this book a reality.

Unmentioned names are more likely to have been left out due to my own oblivion than to any intentional disregard for their assistance. Because again, memory can't be trusted, yet actions (of all brands and qualities), always make their way into the woven thread that is any history. Acknowledged or not.

Gratefulness, begins with our parents. Especially if they are good ones, and I have no complaints about mine. To my father, whose only fault is being too kind and to my mother who had I decided to become an intergalactic overlord instead of a fighter, would have supported me nonetheless. Also special thanks to Aunt Jill, for taking me in as her own son when Las Vegas was still new to me. Love and appreciation also go to my late maternal grandmother Estela, for instilling in me the passion (indeed, the necessity) for reading. But above all for first introducing me to critical thinking and to the notion that no one in this world is holy.

Back to the *jiu-jitsusphere*, to my first coach, Otávio de Almeida Jr., under whom I took my first steps in the gentle-art. Next, the kind of gratitude that lacks the right words to do all the memories justice is given to the coach who most invested his time and energy into me, Steve da Silva (also his wife Kris). For bringing a stranger into their home simply because me and Steve had jiu-jitsu in common. Moreover, for driving, feeding, training and trusting a stranger with his first real job as an assistant-therapist to their son, Marley. Beyond the lesson in trusting and helping a jiu-jitsu wannabe, Steve was instrumental in helping me believe in myself at a time where I was still in search for something to hold onto. During this same phase of my life, thanks are also due to Gustavo Dantas and John Lewis for being next to Steve, such great references early in my journey.

Yet all belief, having begun the slow process of taking root, requires constant nourishing. For this, I have my first wife, Michelle Nicolini to thank. Not only for pushing me, believing in me and trusting me as a coach, but primarily for raising a boy into manhood (sort of).

Moving forward along my journey, gratitude is due to Paulo Streckert and the Maromba crew in Indaiatuba, for showing me that those who are serious about jiu-jitsu, must compete and travel incessantly. That if they must sleep at bus stops, in cars, buses, vans and on the filthy gymnastics mats of the Caio Martins Stadium in Niterói, that they ought to do it while not only without complaining, but also having the time of their lives doing so. To them, I owe the priceless lesson that meaning is seldom found in luxury, but can be easily found among brothers in arms.

Thanks are also due to Fernando Terere, who was an outstanding coach to anyone who happened to be fortunate enough to live in that brief moment of jiu-jitsu history that gave rise to so many highly competent teams and athletes. Special thanks are also due to Leo Vieira and the Brasa crew, for giving me that boost of confidence every athlete needs in order to rise to the level their team expects of them. Having received my black-belt from someone whom I had always greatly admired, made that chapter of my life all the more meaningful.

Thinking my journey over, appreciation is due to Sean Rigo, for not only convincing me to move to Las Vegas to start anew, but also for giving so much of his time, resources and energy helping me operate my first jiu-jitsu gym in the USA. If it were not for Sean, there is a very good chance I would have never left Brazil for Las Vegas. On a similar note, thanks are also due to Jacob Cherrington for being such an exceptional cornerman during all these years, from the old J-Sect days all the way to today and never failing to be exceptional in that role. Despite our friendship, you two will die without ever earning your black-belts unless you both actually get back on the mats one of these days...

To those who have assisted with this book in one way or another, by providing sources, direction, instruction, pictures, advice and overall insight and knowledge regarding jiu-jitsu and its history, my deepest regards and gratitude are due to: Marcial Serrano and Elton Silva for their restless truth seeking spirits, José Tufy Cairus (with exceptional advice and support) and Pedro Valente, who never failed to promptly assist in any way he could.

Among those who assisted me, last but not least, gratitude is due to Roberto Pedreira whose books and personal correspondence were instrumental in giving shape to my own views as well as to the book you are holding. Without his insight and research, neither one of my books would have been possible. More than that, appreciation is due for his infinite patience (again) and for helping me learn how to read beyond words. But above all, for being a beacon of reason and intellectual integrity in a world that is lacking both.

Since this book is so reliant on oral testimonies, a note of gratitude for our interviewees is in order. For patiently and happily giving me their time and sharing their wisdom, thanks to Masters Carlos Antonio Rosado, Fernando Pinduka, Otávio Peixotinho, Ignácio Aragão, Arthur Virgilio, Sergio Malibu, Orlando Saraiva (and his son, Henrique who made the interview possible), Romero *"Jacaré"* Cavalcanti, Murilo Bustamante, Royler Gracie, Wallid Ismail, Paulão Filho, Una Proença, Luis Carlos Valois, André Pederneiras and Jean-Jacques Machado.

As for other jiu-jitsu *aficionados* whom I had the honor of interviewing, Marcelo Alonso from *Portal do Vale-tudo* for his efforts in helping record this history and whose video archives were immensely helpful in my own learning as well as for so willingly granting me so many great pictures illustrating our history.

Thanks to Richard Bresler, the original American jiu-jitsu practitioner, to wrestling legend Bob Anderson. Also a note of appreciation to the late and official jiu-jitsu photographer for the *second-wave*, Ricardo Azoury, to whom I was speaking to the day before the car accident that took his life. Also, thanks to Luca Atalla, to whom Ricardo also spoke to that day, giving me authorization to use the picture of Rolls Gracie that heads his chapter in this book as well as for having granted me permission for other pictures as well.

Speaking of this book and crafting it from vision and words into something readable, thanks to David Beasley who helped edit an early draft for this book. Thanks are also due to those who so eagerly took the time of reviewing the book for me before it went to print. They are: "Budo" Jake, Joe Silva, Roberto Pedreira, David Drysdale, Jill Drysdale, Shontai Zuniga, Danieli Bolelli, José Tufy Cairus and Paulo Guimarães. Special thanks to Jennifer Yang and Patricia Vandermeer for going above and beyond with their suggestions and edits. Moreover, thanks to Una Proença for so eagerly helping me uncover the man behind the legend.

Still on the subject of interviewees, special thanks to Carlos Gracie Jr., Marcelo Siriema, Andre Fernandes and Jon Medina of the IBJJF. Not only for their efforts in organizing jiu-jitsu and giving it a body that does its history justice, but also for so willingly granting me their time and insight. More than this, for patiently listening to me and my audacity in telling them what I think jiu-jitsu ought to look like moving forward (as if I could ever do their job better than them or achieve what they have).

A note of acknowledgment can never be complete without the names of those who are in one's life daily. The entire Zenith BJJ Team (affiliates and students), for believing and putting up with me (I am fully aware that I am not easy to deal with) and for sticking with me through the thick and thin of life's journey with all its many ups and downs. Your friendship, support, loyalty and love are appreciated more than you can imagine. I will always do my best to meet this love at the same level that all of you so willingly grant yours to me.

Speaking of that old and dying quality called loyalty, special thanks to my old-time student Marcelo Nunes. If the world had a hundred Marcelos, it would be a better place by that exact number. Lastly, love and thankfulness of the deepest kind to my two little angels and best friends. You two don't have to do anything. Your existence is enough to give me all the strength I need to keep going.

Timeline of Jiu-Jitsu events

1854 - Commodore Perry's armed fleet persuades the Shogun to open Japan's ports to commerce with the United States. Alongside commerce, the opening of the ports brought in ideas that would significantly impact the formation of judo.

1882 - Between 1882 and 1889, Jigoro Kano establishes a system of martial arts that comes to be known as *Kodokan Judo*.

Late 1800s and early 1900s - Stagnating economic conditions causing poor living conditions and high unemployment push Japanese people to search elsewhere for a better life. Many Japanese immigrate to the Americas.

1904-05 - Russo-Japanese War gives "jiu-jitsu" a marketing boost.

1908 - Judo/jiu-jitsu practitioner Sada Miyako arrives in Brazil.

1913 - Mario Aleixo is teaching jiu-jitsu in Rio de Janeiro. He claims to have learned the art from Sada Miyako. Later, in 1915, he would also claim to have learned the art from Mitsuyo Maeda (Count Koma).

1914 - Mitsuyo Maeda arrives in Brazil.

1916 - Mitsuyo Maeda begins to teach judo/jiu-jitsu in Belém do Pará in the Brazilian Amazon.

1920 - Mitsuyo Maeda awards rank to five Brazilians.

1921 - "Oscar" Gracie and Donato Pires dos Reis have a match. Both are referred to in the press as being students of Jacyntho Ferro.

1928 - Donato Pires dos Reis invites Carlos Gracie to be his assistant to the Police of Belo Horizonte. Geo Omori opens his school in São Paulo.

1929 - Carlos Gracie arrives in São Paulo and has a demonstration match, followed by a grappling match with Geo Omori.

1930 - Geo Omori and Carlos Gracie fight a second time. Carlos Gracie opens his first academy in São Paulo. In September, Donato Pires dos Reis opens the *Academia de Jiu-Jitsu* with Carlos and George Gracie as assistant instructors.

1931 - Donato and Carlos have a falling out, and Donato leaves the *Academia de Jiu-Jitsu*.

1932 - The *Academia de Jiu-Jitsu* is rebranded *Academia Gracie de Jiu-Jitsu*.

1933 - George Gracie and Tico Soledade fight in what is arguably the first *vale-tudo* (MMA) match in modern history.

1935-36 - Helio Gracie and Yassuiti Ono have two no-points matches that officially end in draws but that are dominated by Ono.

1951 - Helio Gracie fights Kato twice and Masahiko Kimura once, each time in front of a massive audience.

1954 - An in-house tournament at the Gracie Academy uses a point system that will become the foundation for the modern BJJ tournament system.

1955 - Former student of the Gracie Academy, Waldemar Santana, defeats Helio in a *vale-tudo* match.

1956 - Carlson avenges his Uncle by defeating Waldemar and redeems the academy's name in Rio.

1963 – Carlson fights Ivan Gomes to a draw. Oscar Santa Maria sues Carlos over property among various other accusations and jiu-jitsu loses its first major sponsor.

1964 – Carlson opens a gym in Rio alongside former opponent Ivan Gomes. The military take power in Brazil.

1967 - Establishment of the *Federação de Jiu-Jitsu da Guanabara*. Now rebranded *Federação de Jiu-jitsu do Rio de Janeiro* or *FJJRio*.

1968 – Euclides Pereira defeats Carlson Gracie in a *vale-tudo* match. The only loss in Carlson's career.

1970 – Carlson fights one last time against old rival/friend Waldemar Santana and defeats him once more.

1972 – Carlson opens the now legendary academy on the Figueiredo de Magalhães Street. Rolls joins him soon after.

1975 – Drastic changes in the jiu-jitsu ruleset of the Guanabara Federation making it more ground oriented.

1980 – Rickson fights and defeats Zulu for the first time.

1982 – Death of Rolls Gracie in a hand-gliding accident in Mauá, Rio.

1983 – Rickson fights and defeats Zulu a second time.

1984 – *Vale-tudo* event where Pinduka fights Marco Ruas and Marcelo Behring fights Flávio Molina, among other confrontations.

1991 – *Vale-tudo* challenge between luta-livre and jiu-jitsu is televised on national TV in Brazil.

1993 - Royce Gracie and the UFC make their debut.

1994 - Establishment of the *Confederação Brasileira de Jiu-Jitsu,* later known worldwide as the *International Brazilian Jiu-Jitsu Federation* (IBJJF). Carlos Gracie dies that same year.

2006 – Death of Carlson Gracie.

2007 – IBJJF moves its headquarters and most of its operations to California.

2009 – Death of Helio Gracie.

2010 – Instagram is created and becomes a dominant force in shaping jiu-jitsu's future.

Glossary of Terms

Carioca – Designation for a Rio de Janeiro native.

Casca-grossa – Term in Portuguese that literally translates as "thick-skinned." Meant to designate someone tough or strong.

Catch-wrestling (or simply "catch") - Style of fighting without a gi that is primarily focused on pinning your opponent down and/or submitting him to win and that is similar to BJJ in many ways. In Brazil, "catch" became known as "luta-livre" and it evolved in parallel to jiu-jitsu in Brazil.

CBJJ – *Confederagão Brasileira de Jiu-Jitsu.* Organization presided and founded by Carlos Gracie Jr. still in operation in Brazil.

Confere – Loosely translated as "check" or "to check." Term used to designate a practice that was meant to check the practitioner's adherence to the reality of combat. Despite taking place within an atmosphere of jest so typical of Brazilians.

Creonte – Term designated to refer to someone who is a traitor with no loyalty to their team, school or coach. The term was made famous in Brazil by Carlson Gracie.

First-Wave – Practitioners who began training between the early days of separation from judo in the 1930's and the foundation of the Guanabara Fedearation in 1967.

Firula – Term meant to describe excessive and superfluous movement or additions to something. I use the word in this book always in reference to anything that is unlikely to work in a real-fight or in MMA.

FJJRio – *Federação de Jiu-Jitsu do Estado do Rio de Janeiro* (formerly known as the Guanabara Federation). Organization run by Robson Gracie and still in operation in Rio today.

Fourth-Wave – Wave of jiu-jitsu practitioners who began training after the IBJJF moved its headquarters to California in 2007.

Guanabara – Name given to a city-state that included Rio de Janeiro when Rio was still Brazil's capital. It lasted from 1960 to 1975.

IBJJF – International Brazilian Jiu-Jitsu Federation. Organization founded by Carlos Gracie Jr. and operated by Marcelo Siriema and André Fernandes in California.

Kito-Ryu – Style of pre-Meiji *jū-jutsu* from which Jigoro Kano drew inspiration from.

Kodokan – The school founded by Jigoro Kano, understood to be the headquarters for judo around the world. Kodokan, in Japanese means "the place where the way is taught."

Kosen Judo – Style of judo practiced only in a few universities across Japan. It is known for its similarities to BJJ in terms of its sophistication on the ground, despite kosen judo being much older than BJJ. There is no direct connection in between these two styles of judo.

Luta-Livre – See "catch-wrestling" above.

MMA – "Mixed Martial Arts," previously known in the Anglo speaking world as "No Holds Barred" (or NHB) and in Brazil as *"vale-tudo"* or *"valendo-tudo."*

Machismo – In Portuguese, literally, "masculinist." Typically associated in Brazil (and as I use the term in this book) with values such as strength, courage and aspiration toward a position of leadership in relation to women and society in general.

Mundial – How the CBJJ referred to their biggest event of the year before rebranding it the "IBJJF World Championships."

Mutuca – Slang borrowed from cock-fighting that Carlson used to designate cowardly fighters that ran from a challenge.

Nutella – Slang term used primarily by *second* and *third-wave* practitioners to designate a softer approach to jiu-jitsu and life in general.

Paulista – Term to designate a native from the state of São Paulo.

Porrada – Term used to describe a "blow," "strike," or a "brawl."

Raiz – Literally "roots" in Portuguese. Term used to designate, "real," "tough," and often used in opposition to a "nutella" worldview.

Reality of combat – What is meant by this in the text is the practice of combat in a duel format and with few or no rules.

Rinha – Term used to describe a fight, normally in regards to cock-fighting (*rinha de galo*).

Savate – French style of kick-boxing.

Second-Wave – Consisted of practitioners who began training between the foundation of the Guanabara Federation and the rise of Royce Gracie and the UFC in 1993.

Taparia – Translates loosely as "slap-fest." Where practitioners are slapping each other with some moderation to remind the training partner to keep the practice of their jiu-jitsu as real as possible. Taparia is a form of "confere."

Tenjinshinyo-Ryu – Style of pre-Meiji *jū-jutsu* from which Jigoro Kano drew inspiration from.

Third-Wave – Made up of practitioners who began their jiu-jitsu journey during the post-Royce era of 1993 and before the IBJJF moved its headquarters to California in 2007.

Name Index

Carley Gracie – Carlos Gracie's son.

Carlos Gracie Jr. (aka Carlinhos) – Carlos Gracie's son, founder of Gracie Barra, CBJJ, IBJJF, owner of Gracie Magazine and current political leader of jiu-jitsu.

Carlson Gracie – Carlos Gracie's son and arguably the father of modern BJJ and MMA. He is credited by old-timers as the man who began the process of democratization in jiu-jitsu by removing it from the sphere of an elite practice and into a new one aimed at forging *casca-grossas* and more apt for evolution to take place.

Crólin – Carlos Gracie's son

Euclides Pereira – Next to Ivan Gomes and Carlson Gracie, one of the greatest *vale-tudo* fighters in Brazil prior to the UFC. Euclides was the only man to ever defeat Carlson in a fight and retired undefeated.

Eugenio Tadeu – Luta-livre representative and early rival to jiu-jitsu.

Geo Omori – Kodokan black-belt and highly influential in the spread of judo/jiu-jitsu in Brazil. Besides being an early adept of *vale-tudo*, Geo Omori held international fighting experience and cooperated with Carlos Gracie during his efforts to establish himself in São Paulo in the late 1920s.

George Gracie – Brother of Carlos, Oswaldo, Gastão Jr. and Helio. George, or the "red-cat" (*gato ruivo*) as he was known, was a leading figure in the early *vale-tudo* scene and the first champion in the Gracie family.

Helio Gracie – Youngest among the first generation of Gracie brothers, Helio is a central figure in the history of jiu-jitsu in Brazil and played a leading role during the "silent years" in which BJJ was under threat of either disappearing completely or being absorbed by judo. He became best known in Brazil for his fight against Masahiko Kimura in 1951.

Hugo Duarte – Luta livre representative and early rival to jiu-jitsu.

Ivan Gomes – Next to Euclides Pereira and Carlson, one of the greatest fighters of his era. He fought Carlson to a draw once, and with Euclides, a total of 5 draws. In 1964, he would become business partners with Carlson when they opened a gym to teach together in Copacabana.

Jigoro Kano – Japanese Grandmaster and the father of not only judo, but also of our contemporary understanding of martial arts as a form of education. Kano created judo out of two pre-Meiji *jū-jutsu* styles (*tenjin-shinyo-ryu* and *kito-ryu*) as well as sumo-wrestling and western-wrestling. His teaching methodologies and overall views for judo were heavily influenced by western ideas of sport and education.

King Zulu – *Vale-tudo* fighter from the north of Brazil. He was better known for his size, athleticism and aggressiveness than for his skills as a fighter.

Manuel Rufino dos Santos – Brazilian luta-livre practitioner who taught at the local YMCA. He was an opponent to Carlos Gracie inside the ring as well as outside of it.

– xxx –

Marcelo Behring – Son of Grandmaster Flavio Behring and also Rickson's student, he was one of the most dominant jiu-jitsu players in the 80s and early 90s in Brazil. Marcelo was killed by criminals in 1995.

Mario Aleixo – Brazilian martial arts pioneer who taught at the Brazilian Naval Academy. He can be credited with being an early visionary of martial arts syncretism by blending savate, capoeira and jiu-jitsu. He was teaching his own hybrid style of these arts in Brazil as early as 1913, a year prior to Maeda's arrival in Brazil.

Oscar Santa Maria – Arguably BJJ's first sponsor. Santa Maria is credited for having played a crucial role in financially assisting Carlos, Helio and the Gracie Academy's growth in general.

Oswaldo Fadda – Student of Luis França (former member of the Gracie Academy). He played a vital role in spreading jiu-jitsu away from the wealthier areas of Rio de Janeiro.

Oswaldo Gracie – Carlos and Helio's brother and one of the Gracies who played a much smaller role in the development of BJJ and *vale-tudo*.

Passarito – Wilson Oliveira, known as "Passarito" was a known *vale-tudo* fighter of his era.

Reylson Gracie – Carlos Gracie's son and first business visionary in the family.

Relson Gracie – Helio Gracie's son.

Rickson Gracie – Helio Gracie's son and likely to be the most dominant jiu-jitsu player during the 80s in Brazil. He became a legend in his own right based on the reputation he cultivated among the *second-wave* pracititioners.

Rilion Gracie – Carlos Gracie's son.

Roberto Leitão – Considered to be one of the founding fathers of Brazilian luta-livre.

Robson Gracie – Second son of Carlos Gracie and father to Renzo, Ralph, Charles and Ryan Gracie. Robson is the current President of the *Federação do de Jiu-Jitsu do Estado do Rio de Janeiro* or FJJRio (the organization that replaced the Guanabara Federation).

Rolls Gracie – Carlos Gracie's son raised by Helio. Rolls is best known for his charisma, skills and for working alongside Carlson at the Figueiredo de Magalhães Academy where they fostered the environment necessary to set jiu-jitsu on a more rapid evolutionary track.

Romero Cavalcanti – Also known as *"Jacaré"* (Alligator), Romero is one of the few people ever promoted to black-belt by Rolls. He is the founder of Alliance and one of the leading figures and coaches throughout jiu-jitsu history.

Rorion Gracie – Oldest of Helio's sons, founder of the UFC and largely acknowledged as the leading figure for opening the doors for the growth of jiu-jitsu in the USA as well as the flood of Brazilian immigrants that followed it.

Royce Gracie – Helio's son and the star of the early UFCs. Royce was the lead protagonist of what may be considered the second most important revolution in the history of martial arts, only behind the creation of judo by Jigoro Kano.

Royler Gracie – Helio's son and the most successful jiu-jitsu competitor among all of Carlos and Helio's children.

Sada Myiako – The first known Japanese practitioner to represent jiu-jitsu in Brazil in 1908. He is best known for losing to a capoeira practitioner called Cyriaco.

Takeo Yano – Highly influential judo/jiu-jitsu practitioner in Brazil who had close relationships with Roberto Leitão and George Gracie.

Tico Soledade - Alongside George Gracie, the protagonist of what is arguably the first *vale-tudo* fight in modern history.

Waldemar Santana – Former student and janitor of the original Gracie Academy. Later turned family's nemesis after defeating Helio Gracie in a *vale-tudo* fight.

Carlos Gracie's children: Carlson, Robson, Geisa, Rose, Sonja, Oneica, Reyson, Reylson, Rosley, Rolange, Carley, Rocian, Carlion, Clair, Rolls, Carlos Jr., Karla, Crólin, Reila, Rilion and Kirla.

Helio Gracie's children: Rorion, Relson, Rickson, Roulker, Royler, Royce, Rérika, Robin and Rici.

Preface

Helio Gracie was the size of a hobbit, but he could beat Kodokan black-belts, luta-livre champions and giants too—often, at the same time. He'd armbar one of them, get a rear naked on a second, and wrist-lock the third. He also single-handedly created jiu-jitsu, and was able to fly. If he were alive today, he'd hold the belt in every weight class in UFC, would create peace in the Middle East, and could cure cancer.

History in general, and the history of martial arts in particular, is filled with myths with only slightly more basis in reality than what I just outlined above. Since the dawn of times, people have loved stories where the lead characters are larger than life. So, not surprisingly, we have a collective habit of massaging the truth, and embellishing it with each retelling.

When it comes to the history of martial arts, this tendency is even more pronounced. Rigorous academic standards and martial arts have rarely been on friendly terms. This applies to all martial arts, and Brazilian jiu-jitsu is no exception. The result is that when it comes to Brazilian jiu-jitsu, what the average practitioner knows about its history is made of nine parts mythology and one part facts. In the present book and in his previous one, *Opening Closed Guard*, Robert Drysdale does his best to rectify this situation.

After reaching the pinnacle of the sport by winning both the ADCC World Championships and the IBJJF World Championships, and retiring from MMA after posting seven wins in as many fights, Drysdale has dedicated himself to teaching, coaching, and researching the history of the art. This is good news for anyone interested in separating facts from fiction when it comes to BJJ, since few are the reliable sources, particularly in the English language.

I teach history at the university level, and have trained in jiujitsu for over 20 years. It's also a safe bet that I have spent more time reading about the history of jiu-jitsu than the average person. And yet, I am blown away by the content Robert has unearthed and collected in this book. For example, most jiu-jitsu *aficionados* may be surprised by the fact that the curriculum and training methodologies at the Gracie Academy had little connection to the way most people train jiu-jitsu today.

Similarly, surprising to most would be the revelation that Carlson Gracie had a bigger impact on modern training methods than just about anyone else. Or what about the fact that the traditional story of Mitsuyo Maeda teaching the art to the Gracies may have never happened? Or that in the early days, BJJ was virtually undistinguishable from Kodokan judo and was developed within circus shows highly reminiscent of pro-wrestling? Or that for much of its history, the Gracie family was heavily divided in a virtual civil war between Helio and Carlson?

Keep in mind that what I just mentioned is barely scratching the surface of what Robert reveals in his work. As a true student of history, Robert didn't reach certain conclusions first, and then went looking for evidence to support them, but rather has let the evidence he dug up speak for itself. This is a treat for any jiu-jitsu practitioner interested in moving beyond the legends and into the heart of the reality of the history of the art.

Danielle Bolelli, PhD
History professor
Cal State Long Beach and Santa Monica College
Host of the podcast *History on Fire*
Back-belt in Brazilian jiu-jitsu and judo

Introduction

Sitting there, watching 8,600 tribe members move about, warming-up, competing, coaching, shopping, laughing and retelling old stories among old friends, brought back many memories. It also got me thinking about how jiu-jitsu's own life had at some point intertwined with the lives of some many people like myself, and how such an unlikely history had brought us all together, united under the same flag. The event we were witnessing was the 2022 World Master Jiu-Jitsu Championships, being held at the Las Vegas Convention Center. The man sitting next to me and starring at the crowd below us, was no other than the jiu-jitsu godfather himself.

The sheer size of the event was a celebration of sorts. A celebration that is made all the more extraordinary when we remind ourselves of its modest beginnings in what now seems like eons ago. It would be no exaggeration to call what I was witnessing next to Carlinhos (as Carlos Gracie Jr. is known in jiu-jitsu circles) an empire. Between clockwork matches, well trained referees, belt ranks, systems and hosting over 130 successful events every year, jiu-jitsu has come a long way and no one can deny that the IBJJF is the leading organizing body behind this effort. From the IBJJF onward, thanks to their logistical organization, the road was paved for the Brazilian version of jiu-jitsu to be permanently placed on a rapid evolutionary track of its own and away from judo, its parent martial art.[1]

What we were witnessing below, was nothing short of a victorious martial arts revolution started by Carlinhos' father almost a century ago. An unquestionable success, even if, according to Carlinhos at least, the

---

[1]   Although, to be fair, the road had already begun to be built back in 1967 (even if it would be another 30 years before the IBJJF turned the road into a highway). The year when Carlos Gracie, Helio Gracie, João Alberto Barreto, Hélcio Leal Binda, Carlson Gracie, Oswaldo Fadda, Robson Gracie and Orlando Barradas organized the first jiu-jitsu federation in Brazil, and called it the *"Federação de Jiu-Jitsu do Estado da Guanabara."*

war was far from over. Regardless of questions regarding its future, as it stands today, the Gracie family's version of jiu-jitsu achieved a world prominence and prestige that few, if any, could ever have imagined. That, no one can deny. This book is about this long winding path from total obscurity in the Carioca south-zone all the way to the celebration of jiu-jitsu today as a global phenomenon.

My interview with Carlinhos was over because I had asked him everything I wanted to learn about his father, Uncle, brothers and cousins as well the empire he had built among (in his own words), belligerent "feudal lords." With nothing else to talk about, Carlinhos' right-hand man and the mind largely responsible for executing his vision, Marcelo Siriema, had left the room to take care of some business. Left in that room sitting next to the most powerful man in the whole *jiu-jitsusphere*, contemplating through a glass window an army of *aficionados* below us, I was struck by a feeling that I wasn't only helping write history. More than this, I was witnessing it up close and in the VIP section. Certainly, a privilege as well as a responsibility.

With (apparently) nothing else to talk about, we both sat there alone, in meditative silence as if musing jiu-jitsu's past, present and future in that collective of people moving below us. Distracted in my own thoughts regarding jiu-jitsu and the interview itself, I can't say how much time had lapsed since we had been sitting there in silence, but it must have been a while.

Eventually, my awareness pulled me away from my deep thoughts and back into reality. Being fully awake and alert, I began to wonder with what thoughts Carlinhos (who seemed equally immersed), was busying himself with. It was right around then that Carlinhos, perhaps sensing that I had just snapped out of my own trance, decided to suddenly break the silence and reveal to me what had been occupying his mind:

"You know... when we were growing up, we would go to a tournament and there were Gracies everywhere. We were the tournament, we were jiu-jitsu. Now, walk around and see if you can find any Gracie

anywhere. There's not a single one. I'm the only one here. Why don't these guys support? Why can't they bring their students to compete?"

It had never occurred to me before what a great point that was. My own story in jiu-jitsu doesn't go nearly as far back as Carlinhos' did, but I recall going to the *Tijuca Tenis Clube* in Rio (where the World Championships were originally held) and seeing multiple members of the Gracie family in that arena. Running about, taking pictures with fans, arguing with referees, coaching, competing, getting into fights... Much like they always had throughout their history in jiu-jitsu. Carlinhos was right, for much of this history, the Gracies were the tournament, *they were jiu-jitsu's epicenter.* You could not even say the word *jiu-jitsu* in a conversation without automatically having the name Gracie mentioned in the following sentence. *What happened?*

What happened in between the Gracie family crafting a very specific system out of judo and *vale-tudo* during the first half of the 20th century all the way to its wide acceptance to the point of becoming a worldwide phenomenon? Certainly, a lot, but *how* and *why?* Much of what had shaped their original interpretation of jiu-jitsu would have to change and adjust itself to new realities. Including changes well beyond Carlinhos' observation in regards to his family's absence from that tournament.

Unlike the original question that had set me on the *Closed Guard* documentary quest (why I didn't have pictures of Mitsuyo Maeda, Carlos and Helio Gracie on my gym's wall), the book you are holding attempts to shed further light on questions that are far more complex. Perhaps because the focus of its inquiry is too recent and therefore harder to shed light on. Especially when we remind ourselves that historical distancing grants the sort of perspective that only a higher and more distant ground can offer. Without a doubt, the present is more contentious than the past. While the greater availability of information and testimonies, teach us that these testimonies are even more nuanced and politicized than those from a distant past. Which isn't surprising when we consider how invested in this past so many of these contemporary voices still are. Indeed, political affiliations can be found everywhere, while some wounds never fully heal.

Knowing of the problems I would run into, I began by asking myself simply, *if I were to explain to a jiu-jitsu student 100 years from now, all the changes that preceded me and that I had witnessed myself in the years immediately following the creation of the UFC and the CBJJ/ IBJJF in 1993-94, how would this hypothetical student in the future want this history to be explained to him as succinctly as possible?*

I decided to begin with some of the conclusions that were reached during the *Closed Guard* project itself. Namely, the departure from judo that the Gracie Academy underwent and that would ultimately culminate in what we now collectively refer to as "Brazilian Jiu-Jitsu" or, "BJJ" for short. I wanted to understand the evolution of their thinking, moving away from judo through their creation of the Guanabara Federation and the rules that preceded and followed its foundation.

Perhaps more importantly and starting where *Opening Closed Guard* had let off, I wanted to better understand the reasons for what seemed like, to me at least, the undervalued role attributed to Carlson Gracie in this history. Why is he so rarely celebrated? Even by his own family? Especially when the record makes it very clear that he was the family's greatest champion and coach?

Shortly after, I was realizing that the new questions were more complex than initially anticipated: Why did Carlson leave the original Gracie Academy to open his own? Was it because he felt financially underappreciated, or was there more to this story? Why open a gym with his former opponent Ivan Gomes and not with this brother Robson or with his Uncle Helio? By following in the footsteps of judo and creating the *Guanabara Federation* in 1967, did they create a competition framework that, once subjected to technical evolution, would ultimately be at odds with their original self-defense-based fighting system? If so, was the 1967 federation the beginning of a different version of their jiu-jitsu? One for competition and the other for real fighting? Why did Rolls Gracie also leave the original Gracie Academy and seek the instruction and mentorship from his older brother Carlson? Did he have a similar motivation to leave as Carlson did?

Eventually, Carlson and Rolls would end up being business partners in the now legendary Figueiredo de Magalhães Academy. They maintained this partnership by alternating the days in which they taught their own group of separate (but sort of mixed) students. But why separately and not one big group? Did Carlson and Rolls view and teach jiu-jitsu differently? Or were their differences only in terms of business practice? Is it an accident that the almost totality of today's leadership in jiu-jitsu, traces its lineage directly to the Figueiredo de Magalhães Academy? What made that place so special?

Was it by chance that two of Rolls' main students (Carlinhos Gracie and Romero *"Jacaré"* Cavalacanti), ended up becoming the two most dominant lineages in Brazil? Was it also by chance that Carlson's students ended up becoming such dominant *vale-tudo* fighters but who, at least in terms of the current competition circuit, weren't as successful as Carlinhos and *Jacaré* are today? Did the upbringing of 30 Gracie children in a competitive environment only help jiu-jitsu expand or did it also sow the seeds of discord that contributed to the lack of cohesion we experience today? Has the commercialization of jiu-jitsu been good or bad for the overall growth and integrity of the art? Who is responsible for this process, Americans or Brazilians?

I wanted to understand the current moment we are witnessing in jiu-jitsu so tracing this genealogy became a paramount task. I felt that these were questions worth asking but that they wouldn't necessarily be easy to answer. What did seem clear to me however, was that in 2022 jiu-jitsu can't be agreeably defined. What is equally certain is that whatever we are practicing today has changed remarkably from the more martially oriented practice of jiu-jitsu that defined most of its history in Brazil, both in technical and cultural terms. As for the questions above, could they be the right questions whose answers held the promise to explain the moment we find ourselves in? I think they are. Can we answer them conclusively? Probably not, but who said historical inquiry was ever *conclusive?*

Democratization and a World Undergoing Constant Change

The Gracie family is a very sensitive topic. In fact, just writing the preceding phrase already puts a political target on my back. And I write "political" because just 30 years ago the target would have been of a very different and less diplomatic nature... (yet another change jiu-jitsu has undergone beyond the absence of Gracies at the tournament noted by Carlinhos). Like any other family, it is full of endless quarrels and old grudges. The bigger the family, the more fertile the soil for these disputes to take root and flourish.

This is normal and expecting unity from a family with 30 children in a single generation (20 of them male) is a little bit too much to ask of any family. Particularly one where fighting is literally their business... Yet perhaps here we can gather a hint that might help explain Carlinhos' observation at the end of our conversation: How competitive with each other they always were and still remain.

Nothing is permanent. All things are in constant motion and jiu-jitsu, no matter how cohesive it may have been one day under the watchful eyes of its patriarchs, is no exception to this. The world changed and naturally, jiu-jitsu had no choice but to adapt to these rapid cultural changes. Among these societal changes, was the fact that, as observed by Carlinhos, jiu-jitsu is no longer solely in the hands of the Gracie family. It has been democratized, which had the upside of speeding its populational growth and evolution in a way that no family alone ever could (no matter how big the family). Along with democratization came some changes that were for the better, others for the worse. It was a process that, according to Carlinhos himself, began long ago, as a conversation he tells us he had with his older brother Rolls explains:

"So, Uncle Helio would say, 'be careful who you will teach!' I had that mentality too, it was a common way of thinking then, so I told Rolls 'your kids will lose one day! Be careful!' *Rolls looked at me dead serious and said,* 'you want to be good? better than others? Then train more than

them. The only way to be good is to train even more than they do, not by hiding jiu-jitsu from them.'"[2]

The political disputes that give background to this democratization is also a topic in this book. Beyond this, there were certainly many more changes that affected jiu-jitsu since Carlos and Helio began the gradual process of distancing themselves from judo and began crafting a universe of their own with their family at the center. Hence, these changes are much more than mere curiosities. They are instrumental to help us understand the swift process of popularization jiu-jitsu has undergone in the past 30 years.

With every passing day, the jiu-jitsu bug reaches more and more people, while there are fewer and fewer corners of the Earth that it hasn't yet reached, from young children and adults in Japan, Brazil, North America, Africa, Europe and Australia. We are dealing with a global cultural phenomenon here. Undoubtedly, Royce Gracie did more than his share by seducing us all with the elegance and efficiency of the art he represented. Having the UFC and its most renowned commentator and podcaster in our corner certainly helped too. The growing number of celebrities and people of all walks of life who are embracing jiu-jitsu as a lifestyle certainly increases its prestige, credibility and overall standing. Naturally, this success led to an increase in public interest who, in turn, demanded a steady supply of Brazilian instructors that were all too eager to get on a plane and actually live the American dream. An opportunity that up until Royce and the UFC, they had never even dared to entertain.

---

[2] This story is retold almost in the exact same words by Ignácio Aragão, one of our interviewees who witnessed the exchange. Although this democratizing mentality might have been passed on from Rolls to Carlinhos, it will become clear in this book, that Rolls is not the precursor to opening jiu-jitsu up to a wider audience. Carlson explains the thought process behind this democratization in his own words: *"My relationship with the rest of my family is great. I only fight with them over sportive issues, get it? The sports part. For example, if there is a tournament and many gyms enter, and everyone has their own gym, you will want to win. So just because a guy is a Gracie, am I supposed to tell my student 'look you have to lose to him because he is a Gracie.' What kind of coach would I be?"* See: *"Carlson Gracie Documentary"* https://www.youtube.com/watch?v=Sc634-syYcs

It was and remains a gold-rush of sorts and much of it is still up for grabs. Something its more voracious adherents are quick to note and take advantage of, regardless of the consequences for the integrity and cohesion of jiu-jitsu due to their rapaciousness. Indeed, this may be inevitable given the rise in jiu-jitsu's popularity, even if in this process we are all guilty of reshaping exactly what had first opened all these doors to begin with.

I began to think of the reasons for jiu-jitsu's rise even during the production of the *Closed Guard* project and the book that tells this story. What came out of that project was an understanding that what we now refer to as BJJ didn't captivate the world by accident. Its relaxed manners, its surf and açaí culture, its efficiency in combat and the sort of comradery that only struggling among brothers and sisters on the mats can bring about, were all key ingredients to this success. I was part of that rise; I had embraced its cultural values and eagerly celebrated every small victory jiu-jitsu underwent on and off the mats.

As I came to see these events, the victories belonged to all of us who were immersed in the Brazilian jiu-jitsu community. Since we had a mutual cause we understood ourselves to be fighting *to make jiu-jitsu the most practiced martial art in the world.* Still, I couldn't help but notice the changes it was going through in what was in reality a very short period of time since the events in 1993 catapulted the art into prominence during the 2000s and all the way to the popularity it enjoys today.

A notion perhaps best illustrated by a conversation I had not too long ago with my old-time friend, student and gym- manager, Marcelo Nunes, who casually and cynically suggested to me one day that *"jiu-jitsu has changed."* I had no other recourse other than to nod in agreement. The context of our exchange was the sudden realization on the mats that one of our blue-belts had just created her own logo with her name on it in order to begin promoting her own *brand* of jiu-jitsu. The sort of behavior that just 20 years ago no blue-belt would have had the audacity to even entertain, much less go through with.

This was a new reality that was met with nothing but cynical remarks because it didn't even surprise us at this point. Despite always having thought of jiu-jitsu as a bastion of strength and unity, I conceded long ago that certain cultural trends are unavoidable. Sadly, some of these trends made their way into the fabric of jiu-jitsu and contaminated what used to be (for most of its history at least), a fiercely hierarchical culture of merit, courage and strength. One with its eyes on learning how to fight *as real as it could get* and where competition was mostly a mat and ring business rather than a popularity contest saturated with typical money-grabbing appetite. This time, fully democratized and with a waning regard for either merit, hierarchy, or strength.

Nevertheless, despite Marcelo's remark being a common notion to anyone who began training jiu-jitsu before or immediately after the revolution ignited by Royce's victories in the UFC, it kept on ringing in my head as if demanding an explanation: *What has changed and why?* Do we even agree on *what jiu-jitsu is* and how it is changing? And in case we can't, doesn't that mean that jiu-jitsu was already fragmented even before its rise?

Before we can challenge its current trends that are steering it away from its fighting roots in technical and cultural terms, we must first understand *what* caused it to rise to prominence in the first place, *how* it made this far and *why* it has been so compelling to so many people to join the movement.

When Stubbornness and Resilience Win the Day

With all due respect to Carlos and Helio Gracie, it doesn't take much digging to realize that neither of them was in the position to have any idea of what pre-Meiji *jū-jutsu* looked like because neither of them (or any of their teachers), had any idea either. There is simply no way for them to have had any contact with whatever style they believed they were saving.[3] What is possible, was that they believed (erroneously) that the first Japanese immigrants coming to the Americas out of the Kodokan

---

[3] The 1967 manual for the Guanabara Federation, explicitly states that judo was a way of hiding "real-jiu-jitsu." Hence the belief Helio held that he was "saving" jiu-jitsu.

and other schools in Japan (during, more or less, the first 30 years of the 20th century) were practicing "real jiu-jitsu." Whereas the changes in rules Olympic judo was undergoing were a drift away from what they considered, or thought, "real jiu-jitsu" to be.

In other words, the times were changing for judo who was under strong directional selection toward the specific goal of reaching mass numbers. Nevertheless, Carlos and Helio remained unmoved throughout these transformations and for whatever reason(s) (pride, ambition, nationalism, love for the art, etc.), decided to stick to their own views of what they thought "real jiu-jitsu" was. All this while modifying it according to their personal preferences. Ultimately, it didn't matter what they believed or didn't believe. They were practicing their own modified version of Kodokan judo, even if they refused to call it that.[4]

Regardless of how we may feel about the multiple roles played by Gracies in all this, we must admit that they are a unique family. Not only due to their *patrician-ethos*, but also due to their insistence on doing things their own way, regardless of what the world thought of them and what they were doing.[5] And here lies the first major fork in the history of judo in Brazil.

---

[4]   An effort of separation that I don't think people fully appreciate in terms of audacity, stubbornness, ambition and determination. The base ingredients added by Carlos and Helio that, we could argue, allowed BJJ to even exist today. With that said, the departure from judo is difficult to pin because it was a gradual motion and it could be said, is even now still taking place. Loosely speaking, the rules and the culture are the dominant forces in terms of the practice of any martial art. In cultural terms, the warrior-ethos of the Gracie family could not have been more at odds with the culture of Kano's judo. In technical terms, the rules were the other facet of this separation. Helio's fights and rules disagreements with Yassuiti Ono in 1935 and 1936; the in-house tournament at the Gracie Academy in 1954 with a hybrid ruleset between judo and jiu-jitsu, the Guanabara Federation of 1967 and the foundation of CBJJ/IBJJF in 1994 are all good markers for this split.

[5]   The term *"patrician-ethos"* is borrowed from José Cairus Tufy's Phd. Dissertation and article (Cairus 2012a and Cairus 2012b). It is meant to describe the Gracie family's views of themselves as belonging into a higher place in Brazilian society. The *"Gracies were not originally from the ranks of the local middle class that emerged in Brazil during the first decades of the 1900s. Instead, they fell into the social category of the déclassé descendants of traditional families who were traumatically thrown into a middle class social limbo and struggled in a more competitive and complex social environment during the modernization period."* (Cairus 2012b, pg. 113). Later, I use a play of the term: *patrician-turned-warrior-ethos* to describe the addition of combat to their patrician spirit.

The more I understand this history, the more astounded I am by the resilience of sticking to something that wasn't working but that they stalwartly believed would eventually pan out. Come to think of it, that might have been Carlos and Helio's most important contribution to jiu-jitsu. It was, as Siriema commented during our interview, an article of "faith" more than of "logic". Even if Siriema was referring to the specific moment of the birth of the CBJJ, it is my understanding that it was this same sort of "faith" in what they were doing that had led Carlos and Helio Gracie, much earlier to stay the course by any means necessary. Noble or not.

In short, the Gracie brothers created a purpose, a way of thinking, principles to uphold and a belief system for their troops to defend, *"The Gracies created a local jiu-jitsu culture by refusing to abide by technical, philosophical and cultural aspects of the Japanese matrix. As a result, they laid the foundations for the future hybrid known as Brazilian jiu-jitsu."*[6]

This new martial arts universe they were creating was cohesive and strongly hierarchically stratified. Whereas mobility within this hierarchy was more of a familial and political question than a merit-based question. Under this worldview, *jiu-jitsu* and *Gracie* were designed to be practically synonyms with Carlos and Helio sitting at the top of this hierarchy as they continually defined and shaped the meaning of the art to their own shifting preferences.

To add to the social-glue that bonded and held their small army of warriors together, they even had a diet everyone had to follow. For all practical purposes, Carlos was laying out the foundation of something whose ingredients were *quasi-religious*. The only thing that was missing was the supernatural. Not that he didn't try to add that too, it is just that it didn't quite stick.

During this war of separation, the Gracies were practicing a version of judo that was increasingly centered around a more martial approach to it, more aimed at the reality of combat than it was to the reality of tournaments. Problem was, that this wasn't a sustainable model because

---

6   Cairus 2012a, pg. 92.

much like today, *vale-tudo* (MMA) is too brutal of a practice for the average person. Judo on the other hand, was family friendly and hence, more business friendly. But how do they keep a martial approach to judo alive in face of all the changes that the Kodokan was implementing in regards to adapting classical judo to a more sportive format to befit the public's expectation?

The answer is that the Gracies could not. They either had to abandon their more martial approach to fighting or they had to abandon judo. So they chose a middle-ground and began to craft a system of their own that was judo based, but heavily influenced by the fight scene in Rio of the 1930s and 40s which was becoming commonly known as *"vale-tudo"* (anything goes).

Of course, they could have given up and become part of judo as many other non-Kodokan affiliated Japanese had done.[7] But Carlos and Helio were too ambitious and stubborn for that. To submit to a hierarchy that they despised would not have been in accord with either of their personalities. They were going to do it their way. Perhaps they were right in doing so, as judo did indeed continue drifting toward a sportive practice and away from a more martially oriented one. With that said, it is obvious that the Gracie brothers didn't invent anything.

Surprisingly, and against all odds, (and to Sinatra's tune), *they did it their way* and survived to see the results at the other end of the very long and dark tunnel of obscurity which their choices relegated them to. But more than that, the seeds sowed by the Gracie Academy didn't simply survive, they never stopped growing. At the end of the day, it is

---

[7]   *"Amid the polemics that surrounded the fights between the Gracies and the Japanese martial artists, one aspect is noteworthy, Kodokan judo rose from the ashes after World War II to become a hegemonic style of jiu-jitsu worldwide. In France, for example, Kodokan black-belts encountered opposition from practitioners of pre-war jiujitsu schools. There, as occurred in Brazil, local styles developed putting emphasis on ground combat and preserving the pre-Meiji denomination 'jiu-jitsu.' These styles lasted through the 1950s, but they gradually vanished"* (Cairus 2012a, pg. 372). Others, took a hybrid approach in technical terms, remaining close to the Gracie interpretation of things, but eventually being absorbed by judo as well: *"In São Paulo, the Gracies pre-war rivals, the Ono brothers, also kept the name 'jiu-jitsu' and sought to balance the practice of standing and ground combat that contradicted the trend imposed by Kodokan judo. They only joined to Kodokan mainstream style in the 1960s through the symbolic adoption of the name 'judo'"* (Cairus 2012a, pg. 373).

their version of jiu-jitsu that would ultimately lead to the revolution set in motion by Royce Gracie and the UFC in 1993.

During much of their history however, they had little recognition or support outside the small yet borderline fanatical following they were nourishing in the Carioca south-zone. The Gracie brothers didn't have to invent anything to be central to this story. They played the leading role in keeping alive a crucial component of judo (ground-grappling or *ne-waza*), added what they saw fit (from the *vale-tudo* fight scene), and made it into a practice meant to teach you how to win fights, all while maintaining the "generic label" that was the word "jiu-jitsu."[8]

Their separatist civil war with judo was a success in the sense that they did succeed in separating themselves from its matrix. Not that anyone in judo cared. As its leadership saw it, judo was destined to grow with or without the Gracie brothers and their idiosyncratic technical preferences. Which judokas at the time understood to be simply bad judo. For judo, the Gracies could have been in or out and it would have made no difference whatsoever. As Pedreira notes: *"Judo was doing fine without the Gracies, in fact, was doing better without the Gracies. If the Gracies wanted to compete with judo, they were welcome to enter judo tournaments. They could not use their own rules obviously."*[9]

What judokas could not have foreseen (at least those who even knew that Carlos and Helio even existed) was that one day, this distinctive and Brazilianite version of judo, would become one of the most widely practiced martial arts in the world. Right next to judo itself.

Judo had a winning recipe that was clear for all to see. In fact, judo was developing so quickly throughout the 50s and 60s that eventually the Gracie brothers (with the help of others), decided to form a federation in 1967, that promised belt ranks, tournaments and legitimacy for their practice just like judo had done and continues to do.[10]

---

8   Cairus 2012b, pg. 116

9   Pedreira 2015a, chp. 6

10   Despite being founded in 1967, their federation would only receive formal government approval in 1973. See: Serrano 2016, pg. 290

With that said, this seems like a good place to ask a good question, *by following in judo's footsteps, was jiu-jitsu fated to abandon the martial elements the Gracie family valued at its core?* Namely, that the second they created a competitive practice away from the reality of combat, weren't they also creating a different version (or at least a new evolutionary track) from their original school of thought? And wasn't that school of thought (coupled with their ambition to be leaders rather than followers) that prompted them to depart from judo in the first place? Weren't they, by following judo so closely, at risk of making the very mistakes they had been so critical of?

For all practical purposes, what following in the footsteps of judo did was to create an entirely new evolutionary course for their version of jiu-jitsu to thrive under. Away from judo (in a technical and cultural sense), but toward it (in a logistical and organizational sense) as it intended to become a more sportive oriented practice (consequently, less martial).[11]

What the Guanabara Federation did in essence, was to create a second version of jiu-jitsu. One being their original fighting system carved out of judo and mixed with elements from various other styles and the second being the competitive format that decades later would become the brand of jiu-jitsu most people practice today.

The side-effect of this, even if those practitioners could not see it then, was that they had created not only a new evolutionary track for jiu-jitsu, they had also created an entirely new definition for it in practical terms, even if not in name. Even if still compatible early on, what competition under different rulesets tend to do is to decrease these compatibilities over time as the two arts evolve away from one another.

Carlos and Helio played their part in all this, but moving forward it was obvious that despite still being ahead of the governing body of jiu-jitsu, it would have been difficult for them to foresee the consequences of all this (that is what history is for). Moreover, neither would they be

---

[11] Regarding the long process of separation from judo, Tufy Cairus suggests *"that it took five decades to [sic] Brazilian jiu-jitsu to became a hybrid martial art. The 1980s marked the climax of a process of hybridization that started in the 1930s with jiu-jitsu's indigenization"* (Cairus 2012a, pg. 13).

ahead of jiu-jitsu when these changes became both obvious and unavoidable. The future of the version of jiu-jitsu they carved out of judo was now in the hands of their many children.

Ultimately, what the resilience of Carlos and Helio did was to give time and space for their children to mature and continue their legacy, not by necessarily always working together (although this did happen), but often in opposition, which also had its advantages for themselves and for jiu-jitsu, as we will see later on. The maturing led to more gyms, more instructors and, hence, more students. This coupled with the foundation of the Guanabara Federation which began to slowly organize a jiu-jitsu circuit for its new adherents. By doing so, jiu-jitsu began a process of accelerating its technical evolution away from judo and toward where if finds itself today.

What is Jiu-Jitsu?

Even today, do we even know or agree on *what jiu-jitsu is?* Have we ever? Is it self-defense? Or a skillset for domination in *vale-tudo* (now anglicized into "Mixed-Martial arts", or simply "MMA") like in the old-days? Is it a sport? Do we wear a kimono or do we train without one? Which ruleset do we follow? What are we training for anyway? To me, jiu-jitsu is all these things. Yet again, if it is all these things at once, is it really any of them at all? Another question worth asking here is, when did that division begin? Was there ever a moment where everyone agreed on what *jiu-jitsu was?* Or has it always been this way and all that popularization did was to highlight old divisions?

I'm sure that you, the reader, will have no problem coming up with answers of your own to all these questions, but that would miss my point. The greater issue here is, do we all agree on what these answers are, or do we all have our own custom answers as the age of individualism calls for?

What if we can't agree on a comprehensive and global definition of *what jiu-jitsu is*, what happens next? In this case, can we all claim to be practicing the same thing or do we concede to the times and continue to create and accept new meanings and practices until we all finally decide to come up with our own definitions and rulesets? Considering the complete disregard for any hierarchy as exemplified by blue-belts creating their own personal logos, this seems to be the next (and unfortunate) evolutionary step, no? Democratization is certainly good, but no one said it would be without problems.

The reality of this conversation is that "jiu-jitsu" is a word that has never been very descriptive of anything specific (remember, "jiu-jitsu" translates as "gentle-art"). In fact, throughout its history, *homogeny* and *jiu-jitsu* have always been antonyms. The term has always been malleable to the consumer's wishes and tastes. At least that was what the *original jiu-jitsu craze* of the first third of the 20th century was all about, when it meant to describe anything the Japanese sold to the West as exotic, the West in turn was all too eager to buy. Astutely, the Japanese adapted the use of the term according to the customers wishes. Then, as in now, popular demand has a way of shaping and reshaping things according to these preferences... Or, simply put, *money talks.*[12]

Fast-forward a few years and past Japanese immigration to Brazil, and you will find that the term was used to differentiate the Gracie family's version of jiu-jitsu from judo. Today, in the USA, the debate rages over whether it is still Brazilian or if it is now American, since Brazilians (much like the Gracies) no longer have a monopoly of either innovation or winning medals. There is a pattern here, whose only consistency is that the meaning attached to the kanjis *"jū"* and *"jutsu,"* have been undergoing consistent change over their long and cursive history from East to West.

Still, this simplistic observation misses the nuances of change and the variety of results they bring about. Despite the term "jiu-jitsu" only

---

[12] A problem that is, in fact, very old. In Craze volume 2, Roberto Pedreira addresses the issue of defining *what jiu-jitsu is* (or *was*) in the West as early as 1905: *"Jiu-jitsu simply served as the vehicle for conveying the message contained in the presupposition. He or anyone else could just as well have attributed these impressive qualities to tea ceremony or flower arranging. The confusion over what jiu-jitsu was, and whether it was better, worse, or the same, as judo intensified as more high-profile Kodokan judo men appeared."* For a deeper dive into the *original jiu-jitsu craze* see: Pedreira 2018; Pedreira 2019 and Pedreira 2021.

THE RISE AND EVOLUTION OF BRAZILIAN JIU-JITSU

doing what it has always been doing (to continue its evolutionary journey), I question whether or not our current evolutionary course is the best one, or if it is possible to think of improved ones instead. With these shifts in mind, I also question whether growth in numbers, rather than the longevity and credibility of the art, should be in the driver's seat of this discussion.

With these perspectives in mind, it is unquestionable that the jiu-jitsu landscape never ceased being in a state of change and since that is the case, then why should my friend and I be surprised that it continues to do so? Conversely, if change is inevitable, then shaping this change, becomes a commanding necessity. At least if jiu-jitsu is to survive into a distant future and not become completely dominated by trends and "likes" instead. Fashion, as we all know, comes and goes, while cohesion is durable and *the only thing that is immutable in all this, is the reality of combat.*

Jiu-jitsu today has evolved, that much is clear. Though not necessarily in the most desirable direction of being shaped with the focus on the efficiency of combat that gave jiu-jitsu its credibility inside a cage and sparked this whole revolution to begin with. It is my belief that other technical and cultural evolutionary courses were (and still are) possible for jiu-jitsu in order to keep its integrity and credibility intact with our eyes on the future.[13]

Jiu-Jitsu's Evolution from Warrior Code to Business Code

In the martial arts business, evolutionary change is shaped by specific environmental forces. On one hand, it is shaped by its technical canon (who in turn is a product of the rules of its practice); on the other, it is shaped by its cultural values (guided by its governing body as Kodokan does for judo, or by local cultural practices, such as in the influence of surf-culture in the specific brand of jiu-jitsu that grew out of the

---

[13] Evolution after all, does not equate linear progress toward superior forms (assuming we agree on what "superior" means), it only means adaptations to the reality around us, in our case here, the ruleset and culture.

south-zone in Rio for example). Unless these two are shaped for a very clearly defined purpose, evolution is blinded rather than guided. The book you are holding is an attempt to understand the changes I am describing beginning where I believe some of its roots can be traced.

On a personal level, since we are on the topic of definition (and as I make abundantly clear throughout this text), I am most interested in a specific interpretation of jiu-jitsu that is reality-based. Much as it was when jiu-jitsu was still under the control of the Gracie family. Particularly during what I refer to as the *second-wave* of practitioners. And I am less interested, though more concerned, with any form of jiu-jitsu that distances itself from the reality of combat in the name of fads, coolness, entertainment and ticket sales.

The lack of a clear definition of *what jiu-jitsu is* (or what it ought to be moving forward) is at the center of the debate within the Gracie family itself and much of the *jiu-jitsusphere* today. Is everyone on board with *what jiu-jitsu is* or ought to be? I don't think so. Carlinhos and Rickson, at least, seem to disagree on what jiu-jitsu's purpose and direction ought to be. The disagreement in terms of definition as well as the origin of this lack of clarity, are also part of the narrative of this book and the questions it will attempt to answer. But there is more that I hope the reader can take from it, if the reader can stay with me.[14]

Much of what made jiu-jitsu special and brought it into prominence in the first place is disappearing in this process of popularization. What changed was that it was in the gradual process of simultaneously moving itself away from judo (in technical and cultural terms), while also becoming more like it (as in an organized sports leagues) and further away from the distinctive reality-based warrior culture. The culture that had set it apart in the Carioca south-zone during its war of attrition with judo and

---

[14] Rickson has spoken extensively about this topic. See here for one example of many: *"How Rickson Gracie feels about modern BJJ, and why we should learn 'invisible' BJJ"* https://www.youtube.com/watch?v=e81X9R5yw_Y

other martial arts throughout most of the 20th century in Rio.[15] Were all these changes inevitable? Some of them perhaps, yet they are obvious nonetheless.

With the process of democratization, the reality-based approach to jiu-jitsu receded in face of financial pressures led by consumer demands as well as the pressures from a changing world that no longer tolerated a tough-love approach to jiu-jitsu or life itself. In effect, what this did, was to steer jiu-jitsu's technical evolution away from the Gracie family's original understanding of reality-based combat toward one that was more acceptable to consumers. Particularly in terms of its reception by freshly introduced demographics such as women and children. Simply put, jiu-jitsu, in technical terms at least, was and is undergoing rapid evolution. Which, in more than a few ways, has distanced it from the reality of combat (think wrapping your opponent's leg in a 50/50 guard with his own lapel or the practice of butt-scooting for example).[16]

Unsurprisingly, by sheer popularity and the money that followed it, jiu-jitsu was led into a phase of being at risk of what Pedreira refers to as its *Taekwondonization* (with all due respect to Taekwondo). In other words, jiu-jitsu is at risk of becoming exactly what it once criticized and had been at war with throughout most of its history in Brazil. Even if for the most part its rise in popularity has been beneficial, because it has brought positive change to the lives of millions of people around the world. Two non-mutually exclusive conclusions.[17]

---

[15]   Worthy of note here is that the Carioca south-zone was the cultural center of Brazil when all this was happening. Long story short, the geographical location of the Gracie family in Rio helped the democratization process of jiu-jitsu in Brazil tremendously. Also worthy of note is that the Carioca south-zone is also the birthplace of *bossa nova*. The musical style that blended jazz with samba and was Brazil's most known cultural export to the world until BJJ came about with its own unique mix.

[16]   "Lapel-guard" is the practice of trapping your opponent's legs with his own gi-jacket, while "butt-scooting" occurs when two practitioners fight to be underneath one another, rather than the more combat oriented approach for fighting to be on top.

[17]   To be clear, if throughout this text I seem critical of this process of democratization, is only in order to suggest that jiu-jitsu continues its growth instead of fragmentating itself by the loss of cohesion and credibility.

However beneficial all these changes may have been to so many people, particularly to those of us in positions to lead and shape jiu-jitsu, I can't help but notice that it changed the gentle-art in ways that I'm not so sure were positive. In some ways, jiu-jitsu was once more cohesive, stronger and truer to the reality of combat when it was still in the hands of the Gracie family prior to its democratization under the *third-wave*. Even if it was less organized then, it maintained an ethos that I can't help but admire (even if I don't admire some of the more unlawful and ego-driven expressions of this same ethos).

Those guys were there because they believed in something, not because there was any money to be made. Whether the prestige was enough I can't say for certain, but something tells me that it was more than prestige, or money, that these men were after, something more meaningful. Perhaps Jean-Jacques Machado was right and it was "pride" all along that kept them moving forward. Pride in their mutual belief that jiu-jitsu was the most efficient martial art in the world. Furthermore, popularization had the side-effect of blurring motivations and leading to the over-commercialization of jiu-jitsu. Which might have been an inevitable side-effect itself; and if this is the case, then the consequences of over-commercialization might be equally inevitable.

We are all making money, students are flooding through our doors without Rorion's Herculean efforts in the 1980s to promote jiu-jitsu by handing out flyers in parking lots at the local grocery store. This time it was the student who sought us out and we gladly took them in, (re)shaping jiu-jitsu to the customer's preference in consumerist style. In a motion that I like to call the *Americanization of Brazilian Jiu-Jitsu by Brazilians*.

I like money, you like money. *But what about jiu-jitsu?* Is what is best for me and you in financial terms necessarily what is best for jiu-jitsu and its future? Did jiu-jitsu not lose something in this process of commercialization? Did strength and cohesion give way to the most profitable strategies, even if that meant losing its warrior code? Exactly what made jiu-jitsu special and different from other martial arts in the first place?

While it would be easy to argue that some concessions were healthy and even necessary, I'm not so sure that can be said about other concessions and the placement of profits as the highest mark on the horizon. As they say, *money corrupts everything*, even something seemingly as strong and cohesive as jiu-jitsu. Admittedly, and to be fair, this isn't necessarily the norm. But can anyone deny that money is one of the strongest human motivations?

Conversely, is love for jiu-jitsu and the craving for money mutually exclusive? If not, then *who is and who ought to be* in the drivers-seat? A question I don't think any of us who make a living from jiu-jitsu (and hence the most obvious beneficiaries of its popularization), are prepared to answer honestly. As the reader may have noticed, this book is equally concerned with the threat of its culture being continuously shaped by economic pressure and worries that this pressure may corrupt the art, if it hasn't already.[18]

A Fresh Look at Jiu-Jitsu's History

Carlinhos Gracie is a man who does not lack vision or ambition. Much like his father before him, his purpose is clear and unrelenting. If it is left to him, jiu-jitsu will continue to expand to every corner of the earth. Not slowing down until it reaches a total global audience of 7 billion people, as Carlinhos intends to do, according to himself at least.

A proposition that may seem delusional, preposterous and overly ambitious to the less credulous. Still, Carlinhos is a man hard to doubt. His confidence, energy and natural leadership skills are contagious. When he first proposed to host a *"Mundial"* (as the World Championships were called then) in 1996 at the now nostalgic *Tijuca Tenis Clube* in Rio, he

---

[18]   On a side-note, I hope the reader doesn't get the impression that I am opposed to entertainment, monetization, technical sophistication or any other "ation" regarding the evolution of jiu-jitsu. What I am opposed to however, is the placement of entertainment, over the reality of combat; of monetization over the maintenance of high-standards; and of technical-sophistication over technical-efficiency. I only suggest that we give some thought as to how we structure our priorities moving forward, once we identity what the bigger issues are. This because I strongly believe that whatever shape the future of jiu-jitsu takes, it is fastened to this hierarchy of priorities.

was ridiculed (more on this later in Part 3). Now, almost 30 years later, it is his success in having "tamed the ogres" that jabs and ridicules the non-believers.

At any rate, and if I understand him correctly, being seen as a jiu-jitsu dreamer doesn't seem to bother Carlinhos in the least. In fact, I suspect that it is precisely this doubt that nourishes his ambition. It is what keeps him moving onto the next conquest, to prove the competition (Gracie or not) wrong once and for all. Dreamer he may be, but I will say this, after spending some time with Carlinhos, as well as seeing why those around him follow him with such zeal, I believe that Carlinhos and his plans for jiu-jitsu have only just begun.

Yet, despite everything that Carlinhos has proven to be right about, he was wrong about at least one thing. There was another Gracie in the arena that day. It's just that he was one of the quieter ones. Perhaps because he didn't achieve the same prominence on the mats as other Gracies achieved, or perhaps because he had a more modest nature. Regardless of the reasons for his silence over the years, this time around, he had a lot to say. Particularly in regards to his father, the man who is (as I will argue in this book and no matter where the trajectory begins) the gravitational center in the history of BJJ. Despite never expecting, demanding, or receiving the credit we all owe him.

As the reader may already suspect, this book is largely centered around Carlson Gracie and the leading role he played in shaping the specific brand of jiu-jitsu that would captivate the world. This book doesn't only place Carlson as the center of the history of jiu-jitsu, but also credits him with being the father of modern BJJ and MMA. Which, as I argue throughout the text, doesn't mean he did it alone (clearly no one accomplishes such enormous tasks alone) or that he was the only one working for this. What I mean by such a seemingly outlandish assertion is that Carlson is the central figure and a vital point of evolutionary departure from the previous form of jiu-jitsu that was taught inside the original Gracie Academy.

Accordingly, few (if any), are as well positioned to speak of him with as much authority as his only son, Carlson Gracie Jr. Who fortunately for us, felt it was time to break the silence in regards to the infighting and political disputes within his family in order to place his father exactly where he belongs. And breaking the silence is exactly what he did in what is perhaps the most revealing interview in this book (and next to the one with Carlinhos himself, possibly my favorite one).

Had it been left to other more prominent members of the Gracie family, Carlon's name would have been a footnote in the history of jiu-jitsu rather than its center. An obscuring that I can't help but to see as intentional and a notion perhaps best explained by Carlson Jr. himself when I interviewed him for this book:

"Everywhere you read up on these guys and they never have anything good to say about my father. Why? Are they scared? This reminds me of that movie, The Lion King. Have you seen it? Remember when the name Mufasa was mentioned and everyone just trembled in fear? That's it, it's the same with my father. And because no one ever says anything, unless I say something, no one will ever hear the truth."

I couldn't help but agree with what Carlson Jr. had to say in regards to the severely underappreciated role his father played in this history. Rorion and Rickson (through interviews and his autobiography respectively) skipped him almost entirely.[19] As for Carlson's sister, Reila, she did the fairest of jobs in placing Carlson where he belonged, but still fell short in my opinion.[20]

Sticking to my initial warning that no testimony is holy in itself, nor should it be taken at face value, I further advise the reader to apply a rigorous and skeptic criterion to all interviewees. Again, with no exceptions.

---

[19] See: Gracie 2021; Helio's interview here: http://www.global-training-report.com/helio2.htm ; Rorion's interview here: *"Rorion Gracie Playboy interview"* http://onthemat.com/rorion-gracie-playboy-interview/ ; See also Gracie 2008, chp. 35 and 38.

[20] Although this is perhaps easily explained by the fact that the book wasn't about Carlson, but rather their father, Carlos.

With that said, I strongly believe that Carlson Jr. is spot on in his interview.[21]

Curiously, the now primarily American led Gracie fan base, normally places Helio at the helm of the revolution or maybe Carlos, or even both.[22] Yet none, other than perhaps a few schools out there who trace their lineage directly back to Carlson, have his picture up on the wall or even acknowledge his importance in placing jiu-jitsu on a competitive evolutionary track. *But why?* It is also the purpose of this book to attempt to answer this question.

The proposition above might strike some as absurd, which if we are honest here, only goes to show the extent of the success of Rorion's marketing efforts in the post-Royce era and perhaps also the extent of how heavily politicized jiu-jitsu has become. To the martial arts world, the history of jiu-jitsu in Brazil was told with a very specific set of lenses.

It wasn't until recently that historians and researchers began to question the official narrative based on the facts that have become known, primarily through the digitizing of the Brazilian National Library and the efforts made by these historians and researchers. Thanks to their works, we now have an insight that we simply didn't have before. Naturally, a refreshing of our understanding of jiu-jitsu history is long overdue.

---

[21] To be fair and being heavily contaminated by a specific narrative throughout most of my life in jiu-jitsu, Carlson's preeminence as the center piece of jiu-jitsu history was something I had initially completely missed myself. It was during private correspondence with Roberto Pedreira that he made a comment in passing that opened the door to this understanding. The comment was in regards to most of Choque volumes 2 and 3 being about Carlson. Knowing that Choque had been written according to the availability of historical records (rather than political leanings), Carlson's prominence in Choque was not by design, but rather inevitable. It was that comment that got me rethinking the role and importance of Carlson Gracie in all this.

[22] Largely thanks to Rorion's remarkably successful marketing plots for popularizing jiu-jitsu in the USA and placing Helio at the center of this revolution. Interestingly, since Rorion's explanation of the history of jiu-jitsu took place mostly in the USA, Brazilians in general display a healthy degree of skepticism in regards to Rorion's views. On another note, due to lack of historiography during much of the development of jiu-jitsu in Brazil, Kano and Maeda often also find their way up on gym walls all over the world when in fact Maeda was not a student of Kano (Pedreira 2019, pg. 57) and neither was Carlos a student of Maeda, at least according to the evidence available (Drysdale 2020, pg. 239).

With that said, and as I will argue here, when it comes to giving BJJ the technical and cultural shape that captivated the hearts and minds of millions, Carlson is at the center of this story and I just don't see any way around that. This book is written in the hopes that by the end of it, we will agree.

An Architect and his Apprentice

Carlson left the Gracie Academy to open his own academy in 1964 with, out of all people, his former opponent, the legendary Ivan Gomes, with whom he had fought to a draw the year before.[23] Why did Carlson choose Ivan Gomes as a partner rather than a family member?

Finances, more oft than not, are behind these disagreements, but in case of Carlson and Helio it was clear that there was more to it. It was clear that they became increasingly estranged from one another over time and that their differences weren't only a simple family feud. As I will argue, their differences are at the heart of the events regarding the changes jiu-jitsu was about to undergo in the following decades.

The competitive atmosphere created by Carlson and Rolls inside the Figueiredo de Magalhães Academy would, as we will see in part 2 of this book, give shape to our current understanding of *what jiu-jitsu is* (at least in terms of how most of us practice jiu-jitsu today). It is to their brotherly-rivalry and the environment they nourished together that those who train a competitive version of BJJ today, owe their heritage to.

Interestingly, the more I spoke to those who had trained under Carlson and Rolls, the more I came to realize the significance of the Figueiredo de Magalhães Academy to the history of jiu-jitsu. It would become clear to me, that that building wasn't just a space where they shared and alternated days, it was the beginning of something new, a place where a whole new jiu-jitsu culture and methodology would grow out of. The Figueiredo Academy became the environment that gave jiu-jitsu space and time for a whole new evolutionary course to take shape.

---

[23]   Pedreira 2015b, chp. 3

What happened there would have long term repercussions for jiu-jitsu. As the evidence and testimonies suggest, there was a subtle split of sorts, not quite perceptible at the time, but that would become increasingly visible as time went on and these views drifted apart. It is true that both Carlson and Rolls took their first steps inside the original Gracie Academy, but their vision and methodology was not the same as Carlos or Helio's. Far from it in fact.

Accordingly, what they practiced in that building might have been born out of the original Gracie Academy on the Rio Branco Avenue, but was on its way to becoming something new, something more befitting the times as Brazil moved away from authoritarian military rule and toward democratic government. Brazilian society was fed up with authoritarianism, I am sure many jiu-jitsu practitioners from that era felt the same way. For his part, Carlson and Rolls personified the changes a younger crowd was so eager for.

Carlson certainly knew how to fight and teach it. But more than that, he was also modest, loved and liked, and enjoyed going out for dinner with his students. Rolls, much like his oldest brother, was also charismatic, loved and knew how to fight. By the time of his tragic and premature death, Rolls had already established himself as the family's new champion, replacing Carlson after his retirement. Between their charisma and chill attitudes, the surf, and the laid-back culture and manners that are as defining of BJJ today as armbars and chokes are, a new jiu-jitsu was born. The brand of jiu-jitsu that is in essence the one that would take the world by storm once Rorion, Royce and the UFC popularized it in the mid 90s.

From the beginning of their partnership in the Figueiredo de Magalhães Academy and well beyond Rolls' death in 1982, that academy dominated the jiu-jitsu landscape in Rio. In fact, if you are reading this and train BJJ, there is a very (very) strong possibility that your lineage traces directly back to that building.

BJJ, Politics and Karate Chops

Needless to say, much of this will also strike modern readers as well as old-timers as outlandish, particularly when we consider the past 30 years of repeating a narrative that placed either Carlos or Helio (or both) as the sole birth givers to the Brazilian version of jiu-jitsu. But before any premature judgement is given to any of this, I first ask the reader to read the answers these old-timers themselves give very carefully, and see if they don't confirm what I am proposing here.[24]

To be clear, this book does not postulate that Carlson invented anything in technical terms, but rather that he played the leading role in cultivating the sort of competitive environment for BJJ to evolve in. An effort that was years later given structural shape by his younger brother Carlinhos.[25]

I write this because I am aware of the political games that frame jiu-jitsu's landscape (then and now). Money and power matter and, accordingly, those who prize them above facts and reality, have an almost instinctive attachment to whatever narrative best suits their own standing. As addressed in the author's note of this book, a notion that all oral tradition inevitably suffers from. To address this issue, critical thinking free of politics, feelings and personal preferences becomes a necessity.

There are many things you notice when interviewing some of those who lived this history. One of those is that, from the times in which jiu-jitsu was still an idiosyncratic tough-guy practice from the beaches of the south-zone in Rio, all the way to becoming a global phenom, there are politics and allegiances everywhere. You will also notice that these allegiances often prevent people from either acknowledging or telling history in a forthright manner.[26]

While the politics may benefit individuals, jiu-jitsu and its history are all the less for it. It is my stance throughout this book, that this history is incredible as it is, and there is no need to elevate or obscure anyone

---

[24] Readers interested in a deeper dive, would also do well in reading the referenced sources in this book.

[25] Although Carlinhos, in more than a few ways, continued Rolls' legacy with Gracie Barra and its many offshoots, Carlinho's gifts as a coach should not be overlooked because of his prominence as a political leader.

[26] A common theme throughout these interviews, were the requests that many of the interviewees made to keep things *"off the record."* Presumably due to concern over political backlash.

or anything. The facts are good enough and, in this case at least, they reveal a far more interesting tale than the more fictional or politically driven accounts.

Those who insist on narratives that are politically loaded and inclined toward self-aggrandizement and other advantages may think that they are defending jiu-jitsu and its history. But I don't think they are, to the contrary in fact. By cultivating a political stance, these zealots are inviting opponents to do the same. And politics is by its very nature divisive while at the same time possessing a remarkable tendency to lead to dishonest, distorted or at least incomplete accounts of the events in question.

When I began to discuss and promote the *Closed Guard* project, I was initially accused of being secretly anti-Gracie. This, even before anyone knew what the project was about because neither the book or documentary had been out yet. Later, when the book was released, the stigma lingered. A notion that seemed to confuse those who read the book carefully. While others thought that I was either impartial or even that I had a Carlos-Helio centric view of jiu-jitsu's history.

The first assertion (of me being an anti-Gracie) somehow managed to miss all the many flattering remarks I made about George, Carlson, Royce and Carlos Gracie Jr. throughout the text. The second remark, in regards to my Carlos and Helio-centric view on jiu-jitsu, I concede more and more to it having been the case. With that said, I am perfectly willing to acknowledge that I may be unaware of my own biases, just not willing to acknowledge that I don't try to correct them as I become aware of them. A lesson that remits me to college in what might have been my most important lesson in historiography to date.

I recall that during one of our classes, a discussion broke out about whether or not a "theory" was needed in order to truly comprehend historical events.[27] The discussion about all this was raging lively until it

---

[27] As the reader may or may not know, in the Humanities, a "theory" isn't necessarily what it is typically understood to be in other fields of research, a hypothesis that has been upheld by good-quality evidence and preferably peer reviewed. In the humanities a "theory" can be a specific set of lenses (normally of political orientation) one uses to see clearer (or be blinded, depending on your cup of tea) and to better interpret the past and the world around us.

came time for the quiet-guy to speak... And every classroom has one of those, the quiet one who never has anything to say, but when he does finally decide to open his mouth, even the professors paid attention.

When it came turn for the quiet-guy to give his take on the matter, it didn't disappoint and I never forgot what he said, nor the motion of his arms coming down on the table, *"I think you should just interpret the data head-on just as it is."* Which he followed with a karate chop to his desk... The chop might as well have been to my brain.

It is strange that such a seemingly insignificant gesture could be so impactful. How could something so simple cut through so much theorizing and get straight to the point? It was perhaps even too simple. Of course, being objective and impartial is only simple in a sense that we should *"interpret the data head-on just as it is"* and nothing more. Still, the objectivity he was calling for required a good degree of self-awareness to our own biases as well as honesty, and neither of those are easy marks. As I will argue in Part 4 of this book, *simple* and *easy* are not the same thing, neither in jiu-jitsu nor when it comes to writing about highly politicized topics.

Despite my attempts at bypassing these political swamps, I achieved only mixed results. It didn't matter how many times I spoke about my intentions in interviews or what I had actually written in *Opening Closed Guard*. It is an unfortunate feature of our behavior, but with enough repetition, perception becomes reality, while most people don't bother learning before they draw their conclusions. Because the *need* for conclusions, often precedes the *need* to learn. Which in turn leads to the clutching of fragments of information and concluding that those fragments are sufficient to make sense of the puzzle.

As for the missing chunks of the story, they aren't normally completed with skepticism, thinking or learning. But rather filled by the preconceived prejudices and biases that were already beginning to frame the conclusion well before any fragment was made available. As a result of this flawed feature of our human behavior, I have received over the years no shortage of direct messages on social media about the book and project. Some of these interactions were quite entertaining so I'll share a couple of them here.

Perhaps my favorite one, was what I initially thought to be just a regular internet troll picking a fight with me.[28] To my dismay, the "troll," wasn't a troll at all, he was a 5th degree black-belt from the northeast of Brazil. He belonged to a well-known jiu-jitsu team, had a school, many students and a family. He even seemed like a really good guy, so I was surprised when he came after me as he did. The tale is quite comical.

His direct-message on my social-media account was a very long and detailed explanation as to why I was such a piece of crap and why my book should be burned. Curious as to which part of my book had upset him so much, I politely requested his reasons. He proceeded to explain to me why I was such an ungrateful traitor for promoting *"American Jiu-Jitsu"* and attacking the legacy of everything Brazilians and the Gracie family had done for all of us, including myself. Next, he followed with a rhetorical question, *"why didn't you interview Grandmaster João Alberto Barreto so he could tell you the true history of jiu-jitsu?"* Which I thought was strange because *I did* interview Grandmaster Barreto in the book...

Adding to the quite tall pile of ignorant remarks he was making, he again asked rhetorically, *"why didn't you interview Robson Gracie so he can explain to you the true origins of jiu-jitsu?"* At that point, his non-sense had already left the Earth's atmosphere. Robson Gracie had also been interviewed for the project... So finally I just asked what I already knew the answer to, *"did you even read the book?"* He fired back, *"I didn't and I won't because it is a piece of crap and so are you!"*

To my own detriment, I tend to have an uncanny like faith in the human spirit and always feel an obligation to reply to people who take the time to write me first, even if they are incoherently attacking me. I

---

[28] At first, I thought of the possibility of it being a Russian troll who read my book and was now attempting to politically arouse and radicalize me. But I quickly dropped that hypothesis as it would be highly unlikely that an internet troll working out of Macedonia or Kosovo would have read my book.

think I do this out of respect or hope that if given the time, they will see my point. Not sure why I insist on this, but I do. So, as I normally do in these situations, I decided not to quit on my new prospect of a friend and instead offered to mail him a copy of the book as a gift, in hopes that it would change his mind in case he actually took the time to read it. But even that was met with more insults. Exhausted from pointless arguing, I finally dropped it.

My second favorite story is less entertaining, but still pretty shocking. It basically consisted of a critical review of my book by a known member of the jiu-jitsu community. It was critical, not because the reviewer had made a reasonable and careful critique of my book (I am sure that attack can indeed be mounted), but rather because the reviewer somehow managed to make a number of points and arguments I had in text, *against* the text itself. As if I had not made that point beforehand in the text he was critiquing. That coupled with the complete lack of any elementary understanding what evidence is (not that I am a wizard in that department) made the episode memorable to me. Some of these events are comical, some border on illiteracy.

With the above in mind, I am not emotionally attached to any particular narrative, whether anyone in this story is Christ's vicar on Earth or the reincarnation of Josef Stalin; whether Carlson really was the worst referee in the history of jiu-jitsu (and soccer apparently) or not; whether some of these guys can tap you out with the power of their minds, or not; whether freestyle wrestlers are overall better cage-fighters than jiu-jitsu folk are, or not; I don't even care whether a Brazilian-French or two American brothers invented the airplane.

I entered this with no loyalty to the Gracie family (or against them), no loyalty to Brazil (or against it) nor any loyalty to the USA (or against it either). Regarding my efforts in telling this history, my allegiance is to accurate history telling to the extent of my ability (which, admittedly, isn't that great). As I see it, historical objectivity cannot, by definition, be political nor (pseudo) patriotic. And those who prefer politics over facts, aren't doing anyone any favors, other than perhaps themselves.

This Book's Division

As a sequel of sorts to my first book, the present book seeks to further explore the technical and cultural evolution of jiu-jitsu in Brazil. From almost complete anonymity in Brazil all the way through its triumphant rise by the hands of Royce Gracie and the UFC in 1993. To tell this story, I make use of the scholarly literature available as well as the many testimonies of the members of the *second-wave* that laid out the blue-print for our current definition of *what jiu-jitsu is*.

"The Rise and Evolution of Brazilian Jiu-Jitsu" is divided into four parts (or four waves) that are symbolic of this evolution. The *first-wave* (1930s-1967) looks at the rise of fixed-fighting as a circus act all the way to the creation of what they first referred to as *"valendo tudo,"* later *"vale-tudo."* It discusses the impact these fights had on the Gracie fighting system as the Gracie brothers blended what was coming out of that world with the judo they knew. Part one also discusses the struggles the Gracie brothers had in promoting their brand of jiu-jitsu as well as their strategies to overcome these challenges.

Part two continues with the Carlson Gracie era, where Carlson poses as the new family champion and how he essentially became a bridge of sorts, between the old tradition of *vale-tudo* in Brazil all the way into its revival in the mid-90s. Furthermore, part two examines the "civil war" between its two leading generals, Helio and Carlson Gracie and how this political backdrop played a vital role in shaping the *jiu-jitsusphere* of the south-zone during that era. Next, our first collection of interviews with some of the older members from the *second-wave* that lend support to this book's claims.

After this, we take a dive into the many rulesets that the Gracie brothers were exploring in order to craft what we now refer to as "BJJ." Additionally, part two of this book also analyzes the relationship between Carlson and Rolls Gracie and their brotherly-rivalry as a much-needed engine for jiu-jitsu to evolve. After this, we discuss the elevation of the Figueiredo de Magalhães Academy as the birth-place of the brand of jiu-jitsu that came to captivate the world. The political division that marked the early 90s and the end of the Carlson Gracie era are also a subject of part two. Lastly, our second batch of interviews with more members from the *second-wave*.

From part three onward (beginning with Royce and the UFC in 1993 all the way to IBJJF's move to California in 2007), the chapters become less dependent on secondary literature, relying instead on interviews as well as on my own observations as someone who witnessed the rise of BJJ in both, Brazil and in the USA, during the post-Royce era. Part three also deals with the exportation of jiu-jitsu to the USA thanks to the struggles of Rorion in not only creating the UFC, but also opening the doors for thousands of Brazilian immigrants in what would definitely come to be Brazil's number one cultural export to date.

This section also discusses the birth of CBJJ, as told by Carlos Gracie Jr. and his right-hand man, Marcelo Siriema, and their struggles in organizing jiu-jitsu at a time when the art was dominated by "ogres" and fighting "feudal-lords." Additionally, part three deals with the death of the last expression of hooliganism in jiu-jitsu in the shape of the *pit-boys* that helped make jiu-jitsu infamous in Brazil. Also included here is my analysis of the changing times away from a tough-love worldview toward a softer approach and how this shaped jiu-jitsu beyond its culture and as far as its technical canon.

In this section, we also discuss how Brazilians began to reshape jiu-jitsu according to the client's preferences as the demand for instructors in the USA increased alongside its popularity. A process that I refer to as *"The Americanization of Brazilian Jiu-jitsu by Brazilians."* Lastly, part three consists of interviews surrounding Carlson's final days as well as my thoughts regarding Carlson's overall neglected importance to jiu-jitsu.

Part four, consists of points I have made in various articles written for GTR (Global-Training-Report.com) and are synthetized here. These articles represent my overall stance and analysis of the *forth-wave* of practitioners (from IBJJF's move to California in 2007 to the present). The decline jiu-jitsu has undergone in terms of its performances inside cages as well as how fads and moves with no grounding in reality have come to replace the efficiency of combat jiu-jitsu was meant to embody. Lastly, part four discusses how the fragmentation led by jiu-jitsu's democratization coupled with the internet continues a long tradition of (re)shaping jiu-jitsu in new and unexpected ways. Much like in a not so distant past, this time around also camouflaged by a veneer of (pseudo) nationalism and shrewd marketing tactics.

Some of these changes, as I argue, threaten to further fragment our practice and to transform jiu-jitsu into exactly what it once criticized and away from what made its rise possible in the first place.[29] The book closes with my thoughts and hopes for the future of jiu-jitsu.

Some Final Remarks

Writing this book, brought back many memories, but above all, it reminded me of a process of personal transformation under the wings of the cultural practice I do my best to describe here. Jiu-jitsu changed my life as well as the lives of millions of people the world over.

To many like myself, it became what Siriema referred to me once as the *third place*. The *first* one being home (we all have to go home at some point); the *second* being work or school (no way around those two either); but the *third place* is the place you choose to be, it is the tribe you *choose* to be part of. The place where we can choose our extended family, get our endorphins and have a good laugh at the end of class. For most of us, simply having a place to belong in this world is enough to justify any effort.

I don't really know *what jiu-jitsu is* or ought to be to anyone else, I only know what it has meant and still means to me and it is much more than simply a place to belong. It means more to me than that because it has been an amazing coach in my life, teaching me that if we want to improve on ourselves, then our first step must be to confront reality

---

[29] At the risk of being guilty of the sin of false equivalence, an interesting comparison to be made here is between Elvis Presley and Joe Rogan. In their respective times, both are among the highest expressions in pop-culture and they both helped popularize the art they loved (karate and BJJ). Popularization (commercialization) is good, but it carries problems with it in terms of the loss of credibility when the art attempts to reach all demographics by sacrificing its technical intergrity in terms of the reality of combat. After all, from a practical standpoint and with a real-fight in mind, what is the difference between wearing a red gi and bandana while breaking a thin wood board; and wearing a flashy trendy gi and drilling lapel-guard sweeps and berimbolos?

head-on. And in case we aren't too happy with what reality has to teach us, that it remains nonetheless. Proving us wrong, again and again and always unscathed by our most sincere wishes.

Everything considered, it is fair to say that *"The Rise and Evolution of Brazilian Jiu-Jitsu"* is somewhat ambitious. Not because it presents the reader with any new facts, but because it attempts to convince the reader to rethink jiu-jitsu history with a whole new set of eyes and based on what we have learned in recent years. This, in the hopes that the past may help us comprehend the present and enlighten our future so that we don't fall into the same errors of our forbearers. History does suffer from that penchant after all.

The past matters not as a curiosity to be resolved by a google search. It matters as an exercise to teach us how to think and understand our current standings so that we may plan our future with purpose in sight. No one seems to disagree that *what goes around, comes around.* Yet few of us are willing to heed the lessons of the past and we seem instead intent on repeating the same missteps, rather than applying this knowledge when in search for direction.

Why is that? Why is it that despite knowing perfectly well that it will happen again that we are so hesitant to learn from the only trustworthy guide to human behavior that we have? Why do we seek instead our lessons from self-proclaimed gurus, influencers and charlatans of the most various brands with their prepackaged cheap wisdoms? Doesn't jiu-jitsu teach us to think ahead and learn from past mistakes?

During more pessimistic moments, I often think to myself that the observer of history (any history, including our own little favorite pajama game here) is like an *impotent idealist*. Always hoping that this time around it will be different, while knowing perfectly well that it won't. That our role in this drama may not be fated, but it is certainly framed by the only thing that is even more consistent than the history it authors: human nature. And the closer we observe the author, the clearer it becomes that self-gain typically wins the war within us. Accordingly, acute history telling is only granted its turn when the time comes to speak of narratives that are long dead and can no longer trouble the self-interest of the living.

Bitter as it may be to the pious and credulous among us, history is the sort of trade that spares us little choice but the one between the roles of an *impotent idealist*, or of the *impotent cynical*:

"*Read enough history, and you'll want to be a villain yourself. It pays better. If it hadn't been for the great Hannibal, we would never have heard of Carthage, but the retched place banished him, confiscated his property, and razed his dwelling to the ground! There's nothing new under the sun (...) The whole of history is one unmitigated fuck-up. It's every man for himself and the devil take the hindmost. There's neither truth nor error, no progress, no future.*"[30]

History may be the craft of villains and its abuse, filled with pay offs. Its composing, nonetheless, does not demand it to be written exclusively by the hands of deception. The road for truth-seeking is always open and inviting new travelers. And while this road may be bumpy, challenging and its explorers too imperfect to match the roads ambition, at the very least its wandering teaches us to identify villainy when we see it.

Lastly, because the complete lack of faith is too frightening of a prospect, this book is instructed by the methods of the indispensable believer for whom impotence is merely another giant begging to be slayed and for whom a more truthful world will always be worth the effort,

"*(...) because historians should and must be precise, truthful and unprejudiced, without allowing self-interest or fear, hostility or affection, to turn them away from the path of truth, whose mother is history: the imitator of time, the storehouse of actions and the witness to the past, an example and a lesson to the present and a warning to the future.*"[31]

---

[30] Solzhenitsyn, Aleksandr: *In the First Circle*. Chapter 15

[31] Cervantes, Miguel de: *Don Quixote de la Mancha*. Chapter 9

PART 1

The First-Wave and the
Vale-tudo Era - 1930s-1967

*"The thing that hath been, it is that which shall be;
and that which is done is that which shall be done:
and there is no new thing under the sun."*

Ecclesiastes 1:9

Chapter 1

From Circus Act to Victory Under the Trials of Reality

George Gracie ahi está em plena ação treinando com Jayme Ferreira para o combate com Geo Omori

George Gracie applies an unusual throw to his student Jayme Ferreira. Photocred: Brazilian National Library.

"Clowns of the Ring!"[32]

In the early 2000s the former UFC matchmaker, Joe Silva, came up with a slogan that perfectly described the rules that set the foundation

---

[32] *"Palhaços do Ring!"* See: Pedreira 2015a, pg. 244

for the organization he was helping grow, the UFC is "as real as it gets." A powerful slogan that perfectly personified what *vale-tudo* (now MMA) was all about. But more than that, the slogan was also descriptive of the mindset of a generation of jiu-jitsu practitioners whose practice was not only influenced, but in some ways, even shaped by the mentality this slogan condenses so well.

The now world-renowned slogan hit the nail on the head because it essentially gave all other martial arts a kick in the behind while also embodying exactly what *vale-tudo* was meant to become back in 1933, when it made its debut in the fight between George Gracie and Tico Soledade.[33] But before George and Tico went at it with chokes, knees, head-butts, elbows and whatever else would get their hand raised at the end, the fight scene in Brazil was already picking up momentum. In short, the birth of *vale-tudo* did not take place in a vacuum.

At the turn of the 20th century in Brazil, entertainment was the business of circuses. It was in those arenas that curious spectators sought to amuse themselves after a hard day's work. Unsurprisingly, to entertain a wide audience with diverse tastes, a number of different acts were necessary. Some wanted more than clowns for a good time and the promoters reacted to this with a business approach.[34] It was in these circuses that these early fans would be introduced to the concept of coordinated fighting from various styles from all over the world (greco-roman; catch-wrestling; boxing; savate; judo/jiu-jitsu; and of course, capoeira, the Brazilian *"luta nacional"* descended from Africa that made its way to Brazil through the slave trade).

---

[33] See: Cairus 2012a, pg. 85; and Pedreira 2015a, chp 12, pg.91 and 103.

[34] What is important to acknowledge in this chapter, is that in terms of fighting and show-business, both entertainment and reality are in a constant struggle for balance and can even coexist in strange ways. The great question we need to ask when attempting to analyze this balance is, *which one of the two is the leading force behind the evolution of the art: reality or entertainment?*

In the name of entertainment, anything would do, even fake fights.[35] As long as the fighters and promoters received their shares and customers were satisfied at the end of it all, everyone was happy. It was a typical business approach to combat, guided by larger-than-life marketing (more often than not filled with lies and exaggerations to impress a gullible audience) and the need to entertain the fans to cash in the proceeds.

The problem with the fake fights was that... well they were fake, and it doesn't take long for people to figure that out.[36] Which doesn't bother some fans (then and now) who are willing to place coordination and fancy tricks above the ghastlier, and perhaps sometimes more tedious, reality of combat. Nonetheless, the business model worked. In fact, the marriage between showbusiness and fake fighting was working so well that it would even grow beyond a circus act and warrant the development of a professional fight scene of its own. A whole new business-model that didn't bother with any coordination and instead sought to entertain in a more realistic manner with an ambitious and revolutionary promise to blend reality to amusement.[37]

Brazilian fight fans, promoters and fighters alike, all wanted to know the answer to the age-old question of *who is the best?* A question that

---

[35] The concern for the consequences of professionalization, entertainment and show business in general was one Kano had for judo early on. *"Kāno explained that jujutsu was once a noble warrior art that had recently become enfeebled by people who did not understand its true meaning but instead were engrossed in superficialities (i.e., looking impressive) and performed public shows for money in order to maintain a hand-to-mouth existence. He describerd them as shabby, coarse vulgar, crude, vile side-show exhibitions similar to sumō or acrobatics"* (Pedreira 2019, pg. 134).

[36] Even if the audience misses that the reason one party may want to throw a fixed fight is because that party knows perfectly well that it didn't stand a chance that day. Choosing to save face and "fix" the fight instead of getting humiliated publicly. Knowing how to play "the game" well is key to "success" I suppose.

[37] A business model, that I should add in passing, wasn't exclusive or even original to Brazil, but was widely used in a similar manner across circuses and other arenas worldwide. In fact, many of the wrestlers and Japanese judokas involved in these acts did not make their debuts in Brazil, they had come from previous experiences in Europe and the US. *What was unique to Brazil, was the development and survival over the decades of a more realistic approach to combat that would slowly evolve out of these fixed circus fights.* For more on fake fights and interdisciplinary matches in circuses and other arenas around the world, see: Pedreira 2018; Pedreira 2019; Pedreira 2021

promoters in Brazil were eager to answer, as long as it would draw people in and sell tickets. A fact made even more distinct by the notion that fighting, real-fighting (also then as in now), isn't for just any kind of appetite. So, naturally, its social acceptance over the years varied.[38] But despite this growing interest in a more realistic approach to combat, its evolution away from fake fights wasn't without any snags.

Firstly, organizing such fights posed a bit of a problem for the fighters, managers and promoters. Namely, that all these various martial arts styles differed significantly from one another in their technical scope. On their own, these styles couldn't possibly meet the standard of reality and fans couldn't really learn which style was the most efficient one or what would or wouldn't work in case opponents were not only resisting your offense, but also coming up with unpredictable offense of their own. A proposition to which, up to then, these limited styles had no way of preparing for in an empirical manner. They couldn't do this precisely because these fighting styles were limited by their many rules and as a consequence, limited by their lack of exposure to reality free of any rules.

As one would expect, every fighter wanted a ruleset that favored their area of specialization, while insisting on a ruleset that protected them from the exploitation of any potential weaknesses inherit in their styles (which is essentially and admittance of the style's limitations). Boxers had good hands and wanted nothing to do with being taken down to the mats, while wrestlers prepared for exactly that and neither wanted to wear a Japanese gi to give judokas any advantage. Needless to say, the lack of a universal ruleset for these cross-style matches created endless arguments about the rules that would govern these fights.[39] The not-so-perfect-solution was a case by case one in which the fighters, managers and promoters all had to agree beforehand what the specific rules were for each event.

---

[38] In those days, in Brazil at least, this question was likely to have been given wind by the typical Latino *machismo* of the time in solving disputes by pitching "man vs. man" (*homem-contra-homem*) in the most competitive and primal of ways. This cultural feature playing its part in the social acceptance of *vale-tudo* over time

[39] Although arguments over rules existed well beyond *vale-tudo* rules and were common in judo/jiu-jitsu circles as well. For a few examples, see: Pedreira 2015a, pg. 30 and 51; Pedreira 2015b, pg.91 and 103. And Cairus 2012a, pg. 95.

Secondly, cross-style fights that didn't involve fixing, had the potential to be incredibly violent in a way no promoter could predict, jeopardizing the entire business venture due to public backlash in case it became *too violent*. The problem was that no one really knew what would happen if they were pitched against one another with a bare minimum of restrictions, so they had to find out gradually. Obviously, some boundaries were warranted, but which ones?

It wasn't until 1933, that promoters, managers and fighters reached what in hindsight seems to us today as the obvious solution: *let them do and wear whatever they want*. For the first time in modern history, a fight would be *valendo-tudo* (anything goes).[40] Which in essence meant knees and elbows to the head, takedowns, head-butts, chokes, joint-manipulations and anything else that worked, short only of the most menacing of fouls such as biting and eye-gouging. From that point onward, the only thing they had to agree on was the number and length of rounds and the breaks in-between them. And just like that, the seeds of a martial arts revolution were sown.

For all practical purposes, *vale-tudo* set out to pitch style vs. style free from any limitations and rules of either style. The idea was to create an arena where violence had the least amount of restrictions possible. By inviting all styles to prove themselves in this real-life version of the video game Mortal-Kombat, Brazilians gave birth to a format that indeed was as real as it could get without getting anyone killed in the process.

Fundamentally what *vale-tudo* was proposing to do, was to expand the potential of the testing lab for effective techniques and put them all under empirical trial. This in order to get to the bottom of the matter of what fighting was really all about, *victory under the trials of reality*.

My point is that by evolving into an open lab for testing, *vale-tudo* rings became the most inclusive, far reaching and efficient fighting arena, because it assimilated the best of all worlds in an empirical manner. Its

---

[40] To be fair, cross-style and real-fighting had been going on in Brazil for many years. What distinguishes the George vs. Tico fight here, is that for the first time all strikes were allowed. This event, in essence inaugurated what would become known as *"vale-tudo"* in Brazil. See: Pedreira 2015a, pg. 242.

format necessarily put all the various techniques of various martial arts on trial. The slogan "as real as it gets" might have been invented by Joe Silva in the early 2000s. But the idea of fighting as realistically as possible and with a minimal level of safety, was much older.

Brazilians then, had no idea, but they had just planted the seeds of something that would take the martial arts world by storm in the mid-90s and later become a worldwide fever. Even if these events are unbeknownst to the average MMA fan today.

At any rate, this story would not have survived the trials of time from circuses to the UFC if it were not for a truly unique Brazilian family of Scottish descent. They would not only play a role in the development and survival of *vale-tudo* in Brazil, but would also in parallel to all this, play the leading role in crafting what we now collectively refer to as Brazilian jiu-jitsu. It is to their involvement in this early fight scene in Brazil that we turn to next.

Chapter 2

A Hard Sell

Carlos Gracie é o instructor de seus Irmãos, que sob suas vistas se preparam para os combates, de que têm sahido sempre vencedores. Nesta gravura apparece Carlos em um treino com Helio, o "caçula" da familia

**Carlos [playing guard] trains with Helio [standing] in a ring in 1934.
Photocred: Brazilian National Library.**

*"My friend, it was not easy, first because implementing Jiu-Jitsu here
in Rio de Janeiro, in Brazil, was not an easy thing. It was a give and
take kind of business. No one believed in the Jiu-Jitsu of Carlos, of Hélio,
of George, of Oswaldo Gracie."*[41]

Grandmaster Robson Gracie

---

[41] Drysdale 2020, pg. 200

From the beginning, *vale-tudo* knew what it was and never pretended to be anything else. It required obsessive determination as well as
exceptional skill and endurance. But above all, it was brutal and bloody,
so it evidently required enormous levels of courage. Long story short,
if *vale-tudo* wasn't even for all audiences to watch, it certainly wasn't
something for all to practice.

The violence so inherent in *vale-tudo*, was in reality, a double-edged-
sword. To some, that was exactly its appeal, while to others, it was exactly
what repelled them from it. In fact, a problem that *vale-tudo* (MMA)
never really managed to solve and still struggles with today (because it
can't be solved). Its sheer aggressiveness bound it to the very specific
and smaller demographic of young and competitive men who were not
only willing to tolerate higher levels of violence, but were attracted to
it precisely because of the promise of violence. Simply put, *vale-tudo*
(then and now) was a business model exclusive to professional arenas
for very specific paying spectators, not for a wider clientele of paying
practitioners.

All this was happening in open contrast with a rapidly expanding Japanese martial art called judo. While *vale-tudo* was created
to find out *who the best really is,* judo on the other had been envisioned to be open to all demographics, fashioned by Japanese eti-
quette and Western ideas of education and sport. It was designed
*"to be learnable with a reasonable amount of consistent effort, and
no more painful or dangerous than most other sports and forms of
gymnastics."*[42]

As such, judo carried in its DNA a far greater appeal to parents,
schools and society alike. Judo was a combat practice for all and that
promised to teach its students to defend themselves efficiently without necessarily hurting their aggressors and whose mission statement was the development of healthy citizens as its ultimate purpose.

---

[42] Pedreira 2018, pg. 115

Certainly, a far drift from *vale-tudo's* quest to discover *who the best really was.*

Due to the fact that one of them clearly wasn't for everyone, while the other had been created exactly for such a purpose, they developed different paradigms for growth. As time went on, it became increasingly clear that one of them was a reality and entertainment-oriented market with a very specific spectator in mind, while the other was a student-oriented sport, where essentially every person was a potential new member of the tribe.

Carlos, George and Helio were well in the midst of these early developments in Brazil. Initially, Carlos Gracie, the man who later would become known as the godfather of *Brazilian jiu-jitsu*, had a foot in both these worlds. One, as fight manager to his younger brother George (and for a brief moment, to Geo Omori as well), while the other, also next to his brother George at the *Academia de Jiu-Jitsu* in Rio de Janeiro. The academy where both Carlos and George worked under Donato Pires dos Reis as assistant instructors.[43]

The eventual fallout with his up-for-any-challenge brother George, left Carlos with an even smaller roster and without a poster-boy for the

---

[43] Carlos would have a short-lived partnership with both these characters. The relationship with Geo Omori went south at some point, possibly due to Carlos accusing Omori of fixing a match against Fred Ebert in 1932 (Pedreira 2015a, pg. 233). This event was possibly what led Geo Omori to retaliate and come clean in the press to state that himself and Carlos, by suggestion of Carlos' father Gastão Gracie, had fixed their matches in 1930 (see: Cairus 2012a, pg. 66) in order to boost ticket sales (Pedreira 2015a, pg. 257). As for Donato, he had three moments of interaction with Carlos. Once when they fight in Belém do Pará in 1921 (Drysdale 2020, pg. 262); again, in Belo Horizonte in 1928 where Carlos acted as an assistant instructor to Donato at the Polícia Civil headquarters (Gracie 2008, pg. 54 and Pedreira 2015a, pg. 131); and lastly in Rio de Janeiro in 1930 as assistant instructor to Donato at the *Academia de Jiu-Jitsu* (Pedreira 2015a, pg. 142). In the last two of these events, Carlos acts as an assistant instructor under Donato, suggesting a hierarchy that was either technical in nature or simply due to the fact that Donato, being also a government tax-collector, held more social prestige (in the case of the job at the Polícia Civil of Belo Horizonte) and/or financial status over Carlos (in the case of the *Academia de Jiu-Jitsu* where Donato was the academy's director and presumably held the lease on his personal credit).

academy he was now in charge of running after Donato left it in 1931.[44] Despite this, not all was lost because Carlos was a crafty man. Losing George hurt his managing career tremendously, but Carlos was quick to resort to his younger and less experienced brothers Oswaldo and Helio to replace George as the family's new poster-boys.[45] A solution of sorts, but considering Carlos' strong personality, building a roster beyond his brothers wasn't going to be easy. What this meant in essence was that there weren't too many options left for the young and ambitious Carlos Gracie in the fight world.

But what about judo/jiu-jitsu? Its credibility was steadily growing, not to mention the enormous potential for a mass-based audience, as judo was demonstrating through its methodology and the political maneuvering that helped fuel its growth. Plus, judo/jiu-jitsu had the added benefit of not being so bloody and brutal, nor did it require enormous courage to practice. In other words, judo/jiu-jitsu was for everyone, exactly as Kano had intended it to be.

Over time, Carlos kept a foot in both these worlds, but it was through his academy (now rebranded the Gracie Academy in 1932) that

---

[44] The reason(s) for Carlos' fallout with George are unclear but it is possible that it had something to do with the Manuel Rufino dos Santos episode in 1931. Note that George is not mentioned as one of the aggressors of Rufino, only that he was present alongside Carlos and Helio (Serrano 2019, pg. 74). George, is widely described in the Gracie family as a "rebel", (see interviews with members of the Gracie family (Drsydale 2020)). As far as Donato goes, him and Carlos had a fallout for unknown reasons. Following this, Carlos (according to Donato) ordered his brothers to attack Donato at the Hotel America in Rio where the latter lived (Pedreira 2015a, pg. 235). The fallout led Donato (the most qualified person to speak on the matter since he was also from Belém do Pará) to also claim in the press that Carlos had never even met (*"que nem ao menos o conhece"*) Mitsuyo Maeda (Drysdale 2020, pg.239) the man whom Carlos claimed to have learned judo/jiu-jitsu from (see also Pedreira 2015a, 126 and 159 and Pedreira 2015c 479-480). The attack essentially cemented the end of their relationship leaving the *Academia de Jiu-Jitsu* in Carlos' hands while Donato left Rio shortly after (Diário de Noticias 27-Jun-1931). At this point, Carlos rebranded the academy the *Academia Gracie de Jiu-Jitsu*.

[45] A crucial distinction between George and Helio is necessary here. George fought anyone, anytime, anywhere, under any ruleset, even in fake-fights as long as it got him paid. Unlike George, Helio was very specific about the rules and requirements he would fight under (him and Carlos in general, wanted longer rounds, short-sleeves and no points), but also unlike George (and according to George himself) Helio never conceded to fake-fights (Pedreira 2015a, pg. 244; 427 and 428).

he would begin to build the empire he was so intent on leading. Yet our protagonist had a lingering problem at hand. Carlos wasn't Kano and neither was he a Kodokan graduate. In fact, he didn't hold a black-belt or even any certification under any other style. According to the evidence available, his real teacher was a famed sportsman of the Brazilian Amazon called Jacyntho Ferro.[46] And in the age where the Japanese were immigrating to Brazil by the thousands, coupled with the world-wide spread of judo around the world, learning judo/jiu-jitsu from a Brazilian that had learned it from another Brazilian who in turn had learned it from a Japanese judo/jiu-jitsu expert and prize-fighter, was a *hard sell*.

Carlos Gracie had found a medium for his ambition through martial arts, he just lacked sufficient credibility in either *vale-tudo* or judo/jiu-jitsu to grow his brand the way he wanted to. But what he did have was determination. He also had his brothers Oswaldo and Helio who could not only fight, but would also remain loyal to Carlos and his vision, in both words and actions. Even if Helio, according to himself at least, had no previous experience in jiu-jitsu (or judo) and had in fact never even heard of it until the time he was 15 years old.[47]

At any rate, some circumstances did work in Carlos' favor. Rio was Brazil's capital at the time and was filled with business opportunities. Moreover, Rio also had a young and small but thriving fight community filled with prospect fights for his brothers. The leader of the emerging Gracie clan would use the social momentum of both judo/jiu-jitsu and *vale-tudo* to begin crafting a new universe with judo/jiu-jitsu as its foundation while adding some of the more fight ready moves and ideas that were being popularized in the promising Carioca fight scene.

[46] See: Drysdale 2020, pg. 239; Gracie 2008, pg. 39; Pedreira 2015a, pg. 130 and Serrano 2013.

[47] Helio Gracie, according to his own testimony, had never even heard of jiu-jitsu up to the time he was 15 years old (he was born on October 1st, 1913). It wasn't until Carlos' match with Omori in 1929 that that would change. Which discredits any possibility for any training the Gracie brothers may have been undergoing among themselves throughout the 1920's. The article reads: *"Helio Gracie, who had never before heard of jiu-jitsu, saw Carlos jump into the ring to challenge Omori, surprising everyone, including his own family."* See: Pedreira 2015b, pg. 44.

By borrowing from all these styles and coupling them with his family's *patrician-ethos*, Carlos began to breathe life into what we know call "Brazilian jiu-jitsu," but that should more accurately be referred to as "Brazilian judo," because there was no jū-jutsu in it other than the two styles (*tenjinshnyo-ryu* and *kito-ryu*) that had already been absorbed into Kano's judo anyway.[48] Leaving a meaningless nomenclature debate aside, jiu-jitsu might have been the same as judo then, but it wouldn't be for long. Carlos and his younger brother Helio would make sure of that.

Truth be told, Carlos was an outstanding manager and businessman who consistently got Helio and the Gracie name in the press. This was a kind of prelude to what would become a staple of the marketing machine that would make sure that as many events as possible were recorded with the Gracie name under a positive light. Many decades later, this same crucial marketing component would help give a rebirth of sorts to both *vale-tudo* and jiu-jitsu through Rorion Gracie's cunning use of his younger brother Royce in the UFC, (much like Carlos had made use of his younger brother Helio years earlier to promote the family's name). Again, "there is no new thing under the sun..." and Rorion certainly had good teachers to learn from and learn he did, to the benefit of all UFC fans today.

As the years went by, things were beginning to pan out for the Gracie brothers and their academy, Helio made a name for himself by fighting Kimura in 1951, the Gracies enjoyed wide prestige in Rio, they had powerful friends and owned multiple properties. Plus, Carlos was intent on passing his vision on to his many children and create a family legacy. He would go onto have a total of 21 children, while his younger brother Helio had a total of 9.

To their benefit in later expanding their brand around the world, most of them turned out to be boys (20 boys in total). Together, they would single-handedly create the largest martial arts dynasty (if not the largest sports dynasty) the world had ever seen. Not a bad outcome for an ambitious man from the Brazilian Amazon with little ring experience.

---

[48] Curiously, the same could be said about Kano and the term "judo." Kano only continued to use the word "judo," since the style that most influenced the one he was crafting from others (*kito-ryu*) was already known by that name. Kito-ryu had been known as "judo" at least since 1741. Source: Pedreira 2018, pg. 135.

Chapter 3

Toward a New Jiu-Jitsu (or Judo)

George, Helio and Carlos Gracie.
Photocred: Brazilian National Library.

"In any movement, the second generation is likely to be dissatisfied with what it has inherited, including the confused state of affairs produced by the pioneers. The urgent duty is to create a system, a single doctrine, that will exclude the new dissenters, rally the uncertain, and make one flock of the faithful."

Jacques Barzun, From Dawn to Decadence, Part 1.

During the first half of the 20th century, the Gracie Academy's fighting methodology was taking a somewhat new shape away from judo. Unquestionably influenced by all these styles and the practice of pitching them against one another.[49] It is within this eco-system of various

---

[49] It is worth noting here that I am not suggesting that what I am calling here the "Gracie fighting system" was as influenced by *vale-tudo* as it was by judo. It is clear that this hybridization took place only in the sense that they were practicing a modified version of judo and only added elements of *vale-tudo* to it. What they practiced was judo all along. A quick look at Helio's movements in the videos available strengthen the view that they were indeed judokas with a growing leaning toward fighting on the ground. In his match against Kato here, notice how Helio does not pull-guard and it isn't until 7 minutes when Kato takes him down that he begins to use the guard to choke him. See: *"Gracie Jiu Jitsu in Action- Old School Never Before Seen Fight Footage!!!"* https://www.youtube.com/watch?v=N2j0u4AQrIE

styles that the Gracie fighting system was born. An environment where George Gracie trained with judokas; where Mario Aleixo, as early as 1913 mixed savate, capoeira and whatever jiu-jitsu he claims to have learned from Sada Miyako to form his own system; and where Helio Gracie left the Gracie Academy in order to cross-train with capoeira and luta-livre stylists.[50]

Certainly not a small sample of styles and techniques for the Gracie Academy to choose from. But how many of all those techniques from all these styles had actually been tested in the lines of fire, that is the inside of a ring where anything goes? There was only one way to find out.

Despite Brazilians having created a lab for all this to be tested out, this didn't mean that evolution took place instantly or in a definitive manner. The exact same problem all martial arts initiates deal with today of not knowing what works, what doesn't, and what is a full out swindle, are the exact same problems martial artists dealt with then. *Trial and error are crucial for this process of selection.* The more of it, the faster the evolution. Which is to say, that even though *vale-tudo* was the best lab ever devised for all these trials, the lab was still very young and small as it took shape in Brazil throughout most of the 20th century.

The Gracies were deeply immersed in this fight scene and for all practical purposes successfully created a hybrid system between these various trending martial arts. Over time their tradition in mixed-fighting and *vale-tudo*, had the unquestionable upside of shaping their practice and maintaining a strong foothold in the reality of combat. Unlike other martial arts, which over time became excessively exposed to commercialization as a side-effect of their popularity. Which, we should note in

---

[50] While all this cross-training might seem outlandish and at odds with the official narrative, it is important to remember here that in the absence of large-scale competitions, instructional series and cameras, face to face interactions were the only medium for the dissemination of information during that era. Naturally, those who wanted to learn new techniques, had to resort to in person exchanges. See: Pedreira 2015a, pg. 221.

passing, gave the Gracie version of jiu-jitsu the technical edge over these styles whenever they met in the ring.[51]

Their interpretation of judo was one in which they managed to incorporate a martial element into this vision of what real-fighting was and what it was meant for. An incorporation that could even be seen in how they organized their curriculum, centered around the practice of self-defense and skills potentially applicable in *vale-tudo* or in a real-life situation.

Still, the Gracie fighting system wasn't exactly judo and the Gracies made sure that everyone knew that.[52] Even if Kano's system had been its bedrock, they were adamant about distancing themselves from the judo matrix in every way, not just in name. A notion which in turn, judo could not have cared less about, essentially ignoring what the Gracies insisted in calling "real jiu-jitsu" as well as ignoring their claims that

---

[51] That is, until the global expansion and dominance of jiu-jitsu in *vale-tudo* in the mid 90s met with an old judo rival, western-wrestling. An old adversary (then and now) best represented by its American branch, and in which the rapid expansion of the, up to then, apparently unbeatable jiu-jitsu would clash and recede in face of the high and seemingly impenetrable wall, a basic wrestling technique called *sprawling*. Interestingly, one of the UFC founders, Art Davie, claimed that Rorion, in UFC 1, specifically requested that there be no wrestlers in the 8-man bracket. See: *"Let There be Fight: Pioneers Emerge"* https://www.sherdog.com/news/articles/2/Let-There-Be-Fight-59271

[52] In the 1930s, when their practice began to take a unique shape away from the judo ruleset, they were essentially still typical judokas. As exemplified by the confrontation between Takeo Yano and George in 1935 (where Yano took George down a total of 26 times); and the two matches between Helio and Yassuiti Ono in 1935 and 1936; and against Takeo Yano also in 1936 (where Ono took Helio down a total of 32 and 27 times respectively and Yano took Helio down a total of 6 times). The dominance of these two Japanese players on their feet over the two Gracie brothers, suggests not only that the Japanese held clear technical superiority over Brazilians in terms of takedowns. It also suggests that the Gracies at that point, were not "pulling-guard" and were trying to keep the fight standing instead, *"Against this background, Hélio and Ono Naochi [sic] finally had a showdown. Ono slammed Gracie to the ground twenty-seven times and even more surprisingly, the latter avoided ground combat, narrowly escaping defeat. By declaring a draw, the referee ignored the new jiu-jitsu rules recently adopted by the Brazilian Boxing Federation. The new rules aimed to introduce a scoring system of points similar to those used in boxing matches. Under these regulations, Ono was the winner, but the invisible hand of the establishment saved the Gracies"* (Cairus 2012a, pg. 100). For George vs. Yano, see: Cairus 2012a, pg. 89; Pedreira 2015a, pg. 313. For Ono vs. Helio, see: Pedreira 2015a, pg. 321 and 333; and for Helio's second match against Yano, see: Pedreira 2015a, pg. 331.

the Japanese were hiding something from the public with their limited judo.[53]

To be fair, a claim that was partially true, judo had become limited in its Olympic format. The part that wasn't true was that judo was purposely "hiding" something while the Gracies were the ones teaching true pre-Meiji *jū-jutsu*. A widely repeated yet erroneous notion, since these were styles in which neither Maeda or Omori had any experience training under.[54] As the Gracies saw it, what they were practicing and teaching was simply a more complete form of fighting. Which was true because their recipe for fighting assimilated more than judo did, all while keeping it more grounded in reality.[55]

The Gracie system had for all intents and purposes two systems. The first one that was practiced privately with live-sparring among their family and instructors (and that would later evolve into the group classes through Carlson). And the second one that was formatted to attend a wealthier clientele who were taught in private and without the focus on live-sparring. The first was judo with an inclination for *vale-tudo* and what would actually work in a real-fight; the second, where it didn't overlap with the former, was harder to test in real life and was generally speaking more hypothetical in nature with less live-action (or *randori)* than the first.

---

[53] Considering that judo had support from both the government and the private sector and that the Gracie Academy sustained itself for much of its history with the help of its prime benefactor Oscar Santa Maria (keeping in mind the number of children they had to feed), it is a fair assumption that the pressure of being absorbed by judo would have been immense. Yet, no matter how hard I try, I simply can't imagine either of them submitting to judo's hierarchy. It wasn't akin to either of their personalities or ambition.

[54] The term *"real jiu-jitsu"* and the claim that the Japanese were hiding it from Westerners, both came from the *Guanabara Federation* 1967 manual explaining the history of jiu-jitsu in Brazil. The manual was likely to have been written by Hélcio Leal Binda and was approved by Helio, the federation's president. According to Reila, the manual was modeled after the local Basketball federation's manual (Gracie 2008, pg. 407). For further discussion on their disagreements with judo, see: Pedreira 2015b, pg. 103. For a list of the federation's full board, see: Pedreira 2015c, 139.

[55] As Carlson remarked in an interview in 1987, *"...judo and jiu-jitsu are the same thing. Only that jiu-jitsu is a more complete art* [that includes strikes]. *"* Source: "Entrevista com Carlson Gracie – 1987" https://youtu.be/m-b6A8fX34o.

Additionally, these private classes targeted the wealthier echelons of *Carioca* society and had as their primary purpose to sustain them financially. However, due to the nature of these private lessons (being free of intense and competitive rounds) students often skipped the empirical trials that something like *vale-tudo* demanded for example. Which had the negative effect of allowing untried techniques to make their way into their curriculum. Hence, this model was in many ways a *hypothetical* system designed to teach students to defend themselves in case of an attack on the streets and against a clueless opponent. The problem is that even if this model is better than no training at all, the absence of empirical trials makes this system less efficient than a system forged by the trials of reality.

Another issue with the private classes model was that it had its limitations in terms of appeal and didn't give its practitioners the thrill of live action that a younger and more competitive crowd would be craving. As we all know, young males are naturally competitive toward each other. They compete for turf and for symbols of social status in order to gain social prestige and impress the ladies.

Learning in the format of private classes simply wasn't a vehicle for this competitive drive to find full expression. A younger generation of practitioners simply needed more. Naturally, those responsible for leading jiu-jitsu at the time saw not only a need, but also an opportunity in copying what had been working so well for judo. They codified this attempt at finding a mien for a competitive youth (while simultaneously creating a new business model) in 1967 with the foundation of the *Guanabara Federation.*

The federation, the ranks, the competitions and the rules might have been heavily influenced by judo, but they certainly weren't judo ranks or rules. Truth be told, it wasn't the first time that BJJ would borrow from judo and neither would it be the last. Still, judo wasn't alone in influencing BJJ's ruleset as it was taking shape. The Gracie recipe for success had many ingredients.

As noted earlier, the Gracie fighting system was influenced to a considerable degree by the *vale-tudo* fight scene. An influence that can be noticed in what I call the *progression-paradigm* created in 1975.[56] Which is essentially the accumulation of an ascending number of points as the contestant progresses, controlling the position and moving toward the submission throughout the match.

A progression that much like in a *vale-tudo* fight, aimed at rewarding dominant control where one could potentially strike down on the opponent with punches, elbows or knees for example. Yet the *progression-paradigm* from *vale-tudo* was not the only addition that made their way into the overall body of *what jiu-jitsu was* in those days. There were values they held close to heart that certainly weren't from judo.[57] Their unique *patrician-turned-warrior-ethos* were the building blocks of the jiu-jitsu culture they were nourishing, as it drifted from judo in both technical and cultural terms and shaped itself anew and according to their own worldviews and technical preferences.[58]

The Gracie brothers (now Carlos and Helio) had essentially framed their reality and that of those around them to adhere to a specific outlook of combat that went well beyond fighting. To them, jiu-jitsu was a way of life and a way of framing the world surrounding them. As they saw it, they were missionaries of sorts, out to prove the supremacy of their style by any means necessary.

But to carve out a whole new brand of judo during its peak in popularity, the Gracies needed more than just a new belief system. Above all, they needed new converts, but not just any converts, they needed

---

[56] For further discussion on the *"progression paradigm,"* see: Drysdale 2022c. For the inclusion of this paradigm into the jiu-jitsu ruleset, see chapter 8.

[57] In terms of these values, it is worth reminding ourselves here that Carlos was an immigrant from the northern city of Belém do Pará in the middle of the Brazilian Amazon. A region known in Brazil (to this day in fact) for its lawlessness and masculine values, and where disputes are settled then and there. These values are just as descriptive of Carlos' and Helio's youth as anything could be. As they saw it, jiu-jitsu wasn't a medium to raise healthy citizens as judo claimed it was (even if the Gracie clan claimed so, their actions often spoke otherwise), but rather to assert the turf dominance of their style and academy over other styles to prove that their jiu-jitsu (the real one) was indeed the best fighting system on the planet.

[58] For a discussion on some of these changes, see: Pedreira 2015a, pg. 494.

committed missionaries to reinforce the cohesion around the new faith. Not an easy task when we consider that they were up against martial arts that were far more popular and fueled by Hollywood movies, the Olympics, television series, pro-wrestling, comic books and pop culture in general.

The solution to expand their brand was two-fold. First, they raised an army of children who lived and breathed jiu-jitsu and could pass on and perpetuate to future generations the cultural legacy and beliefs that they were crafting around their practice.[59] Second, they sought to challenge and defeat the opposition at every opportunity and by any means necessary...

As the Brazilian saying goes, *"no amor e na guerra, vale-tudo"* (in love and in war, anything goes).

---

[59] For this glue to stick, even a distinct diet played a role in shaping their collective belief in the vision they were cultivating. Carlos, beyond being the leader of the clan during the early years of BJJ, was also obsessed with a specific diet which was prescribed to all family members. Despite not having invented that particular diet nor being a nutritionist, the diet became a staple of their group cohesion. The diet actually belonged to an Argentinian nutricionist named Juan Estève Dulin and was published in 1949 in a book titled *"Alimentación Racional Humana."* For Carlos Gracie's interest in diets, see Cairus 2012a, pg. 113 and Pedreira 2015c, pg. 212.

Chapter 4

Anything Goes

**Introducing the Gracie fighting system:
Carlos, Helio, Carlson and Robson.
Photocred: Brazilian National Library.**

"It is not hard for firmly united, clever, and courageous men to do great things in the world. Ten such men affect 100,000, because the great mass of people have only acquisition, enjoyment, vanity, and the like in their heads, while those ten men always work together."
Jakob Burkhardt, Judgments on History and Historians, chp. 71.

During the *silent years* between the Kimura vs. Helio fight and the rebirth of jiu-jitsu at the hands of Rorion and Royce Gracie (1951-1993), jiu-jitsu was immensely outshined by traditional martial arts.[60] The Gracie family essentially inhabited (in terms financial, political and social) a hostile landscape for growth that was increasingly dominated by martial arts fueled by Bruce Lee movies that weren't, in their view (if not in our own), realistic enough. Or at least certainly not as real as *vale-tudo* could get.[61]

This was even more truthful in case the fight hit the ground, which they knew or hoped it would. Yet despite this isolation, their *patrician-turned-warrior-ethos* (to the benefit of us all) did not allow them to remove that one foot from the reality of combat they had witnessed as protagonists and/or bystanders of the *vale-tudo* scene in Brazil.

Throughout the *silent years*, the Gracies and their students needed to remain relevant somehow. Lacking the reach in media that other styles of fighting possessed to various degrees, or the influence at the government level that judo possessed, the Gracies struggled to keep their heads above water. Being severely outmatched in terms of reach and credibility, the Gracies and their students would continue a long history of harassing the competition, dating back to the days of them jointly attacking Donato Pires dos Reis, Oswaldo Baldi and Manuel Rufino dos Santos.[62]

---

[60]   To be clear, by "silent," I don't mean insignificant or irrelevant since I am writing a whole book largely centered around the events that took place during this time period. What I mean by "silent" is that after the highly publicized fight between Helio and Kimura in 1951, jiu-jitsu essentially went into a hibernation phase where there wasn't much happening for them in terms of publicity (at least in comparison to Helio's fight against Kimura in the giant Maracanã Stadium and later with the UFC in 1993) and where jiu-jitsu was for the most part an unknown and idiosyncratic style that was practically an exclusivity of the Carioca south-zone. It was also during this period that the jiu-jitsu we practice today began to take a new shape away from judo. Cleary, it isn't an insignificant period.

[61]   Although to be fair, others have reached similar conclusions about the reality of combat. Styles such as the Soviet martial art combat-sambo, Japanese shooto and pancrase, were not too far off the mark in terms of their approach to reality. Ultimately the reason why they did not grow into something like the UFC is because they simply lacked the marketing.

[62]   A quick note on Manuel Rufino dos Santos: The episode consisted on a number of exchanges and insults in the press between Rufino dos Santos and Carlos Gracie. Eventually they fought in a grappling match and Santos was declared the winner. The insults and exchanges however, continued nonetheless. Eventually, the Gracie brothers would join forces to attack Santos just outside the *Tijuca Tenis Clube* (incidentally the same arena where the first jiu-jitsu World Championships were held) where Santos taught *luta-livre*. The brothers were eventually condemned to two years in prison and later pardoned by the dictator at the time, Getúlio Vargas, with who they had connections with through one of their students. For details of the Carlos Gracie vs. Manuel Rufino dos Santos fight and other confrontations, see: Pedreira 2015a, chp. 12

In order to assert themselves, if not vent their frustrations at their stagnation in terms of territorial expansion, they sought to be a thorn in the side of their competitors and impose themselves in any way they could. Years later, the territorialism made the practice of dojo-storming rival gyms and challenging rivals a reality and (as they saw it) even a strategical necessity. They were warriors after all, and warriors do what warriors do. It's just that, *to be a warrior*, one can and should stick to fighting in a ring in a professional manner and within agreed upon rules. Over the years, some of the Gracies did this, others didn't.

Which in essence meant that their actions didn't always fit the public's expectation for how a martial artist ought to behave. To put it differently, the Gracie Academy might be the academy where the well-off of the south-zone of Rio trained, but that didn't necessarily mean that it was the academy of the *nice guys*.

To be sure, they could be nice guys when needed, depending on the circumstances, but they could also be the tough-guys (also depending on the circumstances). With this in mind, when it came down to the competition, their territorialism stood out like a sore thumb. The record here is straight and uncontroversial in terms of how they dealt with the competition they didn't like. In this regard, at least some members of the Gracie Academy weren't anti-bullying (even if much of their focus went into self-defense), they *were* the bullies and those who stood in their way would quickly learn why they shouldn't.[63]

Clearly this was all very removed from Kano's original educational goals which are perhaps best embodied in judo's slogan of *jita-kyoei*

---

[63] For accounts on the Gracie brother's history of street-brawling see: Pedreira 2015a, pg. 193; 233 and 235. For dojo-storming, see: *"Problemas com a Família Gracie"* https:// youtu.be/b8IPOuxatyM ; and *"Ruas e Eugênio dão suas versões do dia em que Rickson desafiou a Luta-Livre."* https://www.youtube.com/watch?v=4i0Xnpq9DyM ; See also interview with Armando Wriedt (Drysdale 2020, pg. 253).

(mutual benefit).[64] Unless "mutual" was exclusively restricted to the members of the Gracie family and academy. In this sense, jiu-jitsu under Gracie interpretation, was the embodiment of tribal loyalty coupled with fighting skills and an eagerness to display them anywhere: in the ring, in private, or in the streets if the occasion called for it. And it didn't take much for that to happen. It was all fair play, as long as the dominance was established and the competition either conceded or was defeated in order to reassert the dominance of their jiu-jitsu. For the Gracie Academy then, there were two kinds of people in this world: *friends and foes.*

Of course this doesn't mean that they didn't have formal relationships with rivals such as Fadda and his academy, or with others such as Roberto Leitão from luta-livre, who spoke highly of his relationship with Helio when we interviewed him for *Opening Closed Guard.* It is just that Oswaldo Fadda did not pose a threat to the Gracie Academy in terms of demographics given the distance between the two academies and the different social classes they attended (as distant from one another as their academies were).[65] Additionally, the Gracie instructors needed someone to compete against and Fadda was one of the few to present them with competition, *"without Fada's academy, the Gracies would have had few credible opponents."*[66]

Despite all this, their tough-guy approach didn't quite work then. Even given their superiority in skills when compared to the competition and in terms of their understanding of the reality of combat, people

---

[64] *"As long as we coexist, each member of society and the groups organised within must function in harmony and cooperation with the others. Nothing is more important than living prosperously together. If everyone acts with the spirit of mutual cooperation, each person's work benefits not only himself, but also others, and attaining this together will bring mutual happiness. Activities should not engaged [sic] in simply for self-interest. Once started, it is only a matter of course that a person will find goodness in harmony and cooperation upon realising that his efforts will increase the prosperity of all. This great principle of harmony and cooperation is, in other words, the concept of Jita-Kyoei, or mutual prosperity for self and others."* See: http://kodokanjudoinstitute.org/en

[65] The Carioca neighborhood of Bento Ribeiro is located in the north-zone of Rio, on the opposite side of the Gracie Academy's home turf.

[66] Pedreira 2015b, pg. 34

simply weren't interested for the most part. Judo, karate, kung-fu and pro-wrestling were popular and credible; the Gracie brand of jiu-jitsu simply didn't have the same star power.

Interestingly, as the Gracie family split into various camps with Carlson, Rolls and others growing older and wanting their own place to shine, they carried with them this martial spirit of the supremacy of the "real." Unlike other martial arts that jiu-jitsu's representatives were so intent on overthrowing by any means necessary.[67]

Which is to say that, by and large and over the span of many decades, "reality" remained *the* key component of jiu-jitsu's DNA. Even when we consider *vale-tudo's* decline in terms of public acceptance over the years, the sportive practice of jiu-jitsu (from 1967 all the way to 1993) was still framed around the premise of "as real as it gets." All the way up to its democratization in fact.[68] Not in terms of its ruleset, but in terms of the cultural norms and other practices that kept a lid on any technique that wouldn't be applicable in a real fight (see chapters 21 and 22).

The birth of their first federation in 1967 was the beginning of a new era for jiu-jitsu. Led by younger blood with new ideas, methodologies and worldviews. Despite this, their adherence to reality would not only survive but continue to evolve. This time by the hands of the man who I will argue now, to be the most important character in this whole story. With "real" in mind we now turn to him and his underappreciated role in the history of jiu-jitsu in Brazil.

---

[67] On a side note, during the author's introduction to jiu-jitsu in Brazil in the late 90s, jiu-jitsu and *vale-tudo* (much like judo and jiu-jitsu decades earlier), were practically synonyms.

[68] Although the introduction of "guard-pulling" into jiu-jitsu was certainly a drift from reality. Guard-pulling, was an early marker of departure from traditional judo as well as a key feature of its democratization process. Taking someone down is hard, pulling guard isn't. See: Pedreira 2015a, pg. 280; and Cairus 2012a, pg. 102-103

PART 2

The Second-Wave and the Carlson Gracie Era 1967-1993

"Don't confuse Gracie jiu-jitsu with Carlson Gracie jiu-jitsu"[69]

Grandmaster Carlson Gracie

---

[69] *"Não confunda Gracie Jiu-Jitsu com Carlson Gracie Jiu-Jitsu"* Source: *"Carlson Gracie vs. Marco Ruas"* https://youtu.be/r3KnX-q194g

Chapter 5

Carlson... As Real As It Gets

**Carlson Gracie. Photocred:
Brazilian National Library.**

*"I know that many people consider me a bad guy. Those who know me,
however, know that is not the case. Some go as far as censuring me
because I often take it easy on my opponents when I find them helpless
before me. They say that, if the opponents could, they would kill me.
What can I do? Many times, I stepped into the ring with a preemptive
spirit to 'demolish' the opponent. But when I begin to take advantage
I cool down immediately. I begin to see before me a human being just
like myself. It is a conflict inside my 'being' so I try to win as quickly as
possible to avoid spilling any blood."[70]*

Grandmaster Carlson Gracie

---

[70] Source: Revista do Esporte, 1959, 1st ed.

Born Eduardo Gracie, later having his name changed to "Carlson," due to a spiritual revelation his father had, Carlson is the center piece for the history of both *vale-tudo* and jiu-jitsu in the 20th century. He is central not because he was perfectly positioned to continue a family tradition that had begun with his Uncle George, but that now belonged to him as the new enforcer of the supremacy the Gracie brothers were after. More than this, Carlson was a martial arts visionary and a conduit between the old *vale-tudo* tradition that began in the 1930s and the world of MMA today for reasons that will become clear ahead.

Carlson was practically born in a kimono and took his first steps on the mats under the auspices of his father Carlos and his Uncle Helio.[71] Over the years, he would fight extensively as he fit into the shoes of becoming the clan's new prodigy and champion. *"Garotão"* (big boy), as he was known, not only met his family's expectations for him, but went on to dominate Brazilian *vale-tudo* rings in the 50s and 60s.[72] Which doesn't mean that the road had been paved for him in advance. Quite the contrary in fact.

As any adult well knows, there are the theoretical lessons we learn in school, in church and from our parents. And then there are a whole new set of lessons that only trial and error can truly teach us. Learning how to fight successfully in a ring against a competent opponent who resists your every move is one of those lessons that can't really be taught theoretically or inside a gym. You need to live and feel these lessons in the heat of battle. The more you engage in these heated battles, the more the complexity of the technical, physical and psychological spheres of combat are unveiled to the fighter. An expertise Carlson would earn

---

[71] In Reila's biography of her father Carlos, her brother Carlson described his early days as a student: *"From there I developed many things. When I wanted to learn something new, I never forgot it. I have excellent memory and took advantage of it. I was very persistent, like my father. I would research positions and then invent a way to get out of it. I invented many moves this way"* (Gracie 2008, pg. 309).

[72] That is, until he met Ivan Gomes and Euclides Pereira, in a couple of those rings, later befriending the former and opening a gym with him in Rio. Both Ivan Gomes and Euclides Pereira are next to Carlson the greatest *vale-tudo* fighters of that era. Carlson fought Gomes to a draw and lost to Pereira, Carlson's only loss in his career. Both Gomes and Pereira retired undefeated and fought each other to a draw a total of 5 times.

through his own merits inside the rings and always against much heavier opponents.[73]

By engaging repeatedly in the ring against the very best fighters in Brazil at the time, Carlson would become the member of the family who most actively put the Gracie Academy's hybrid fighting method to the test. Beyond that, Carlson would play the leading role in opening up the practice of jiu-jitsu for all who wanted to train with a focus on high-performance. Simply put, Carlson managed simultaneously to improve on jiu-jitsu for *vale-tudo* and also take the first step in democratizing jiu-jitsu. All while nourishing a fierce meritocracy where performance (rather, than popularity, marketing or money) established the hierarchy on the mats.

More than this, he was known for his infinite levels of charisma as well as for a unique ability to forge champions in the competitive environment he would spend the second half of his life creating. For these reasons, it would be no exaggeration to think of him as a conduit of sorts, between the old *vale-tudo* days and the later version of it revived by his cousins Rorion and Royce through the UFC in 1993.

Deprived of a competitive jiu-jitsu scene sufficiently developed to challenge him, he sought to be challenged elsewhere, where he indeed did have tough competition in the not so glamorous, but tough *vale-tudo* scene in Brazil.[74] His experience there, helped him accumulate the kind of know-how that had few parallels in the entire country. Naturally, his views on fighting were shaped by this experience inside those rings.

When Carlson took over the family's baton, their view on fighting was well established in between judo and *vale-tudo*. For that *first-wave*

---

[73] With the exception of Jean Monier who was lighter (Pedreira 2015b, pg. 156). As an example, Carlson weighed in at 76kg against Gomes, who came in at 90kg (Pedreira 2015c, pg. 51).

[74] As far as the competition in jiu-jitsu goes, Carlson had little competition to dispute his throne, not Helio (who was too advanced in age and unlikely to match Carlson's youth), nor João Alberto Barreto, nor Pedro Hemetério. Despite Helio's claims that jiu-jitsu's hierarchy was himself first, then Carlson, João Alberto Barreto and Pedro Hemetério (Gracie, 2008 pg. 313). One of the few jiu-jitsu fights Carlson had took place in 1950, where Carlson fought Pedro Hemetério to a close fight won by points (Pedreira 2015b, pg. 23) and again that same year against José Maria de Melo (student of Carlos Pereira) where Carlson won with a straight foot-lock (Serrano 2014b, pg. 473). Carlson also drew in a jiu-jitsu match the first time he confronted Waldemar Santana in 1955, despite dominating his opponent the entire time.

of practitioners, jiu-jitsu had a clear definition that can be more or less summarized as follows: *"We may practice and teach in a quasi-sport like format, but we know how to fight and have plenty of family members and students who can prove it."* Fighting was the family business, it was also how they structured their own internal hierarchy. In short, fighting and winning were not only noble, but also the fastest way to prove yourself and advance within the fiercely competitive familial arena Carlos and Helio had created for their sons and nephews.[75]

Carlson took over this responsibility to raise the family's standing by accepting it not with words but rather with actions. More accurately, by quite literally stepping up to the mark with punches, kicks, clinches, takedowns and chokes. Accumulating over the years the sort of knowledge and experience that had few parallels in Brazil at the time. Which later on, also gave him the edge over other coaches when it came time to pass on this experience to anyone who wanted to join his army of *casca-grossas*.[76]

In all fairness, there were other names worthy of note in the history of *vale-tudo*. Figures such as Ivan Gomes, Euclides Pereira, Waldemar Santana, George Gracie, Geo Omori, Roberto Ruhmann, Passarito and others. Men who dedicated their lives to perfect the craft that we now celebrate as "MMA." They, as well as a plethora of other names buried in time. Since they were more concerned with the process of trial and error inside the gym and ring, than they were busying themselves with flattering celebrities and politicians, marketing, or concerned with creating a personality cult around themselves.

Not that these men wouldn't have liked to indulge in these things too, but that they chose instead the harder route of getting hit in the face

---

[75] Whether Carlos thought of these consequences or not when he decided to have so many children and urged his younger brother to do the same, the creation of this competitive ecosystem inside the family was the inevitable consequence of having so many male children bred in a world where dominance meant being able to defeat people with submission holds. Certainly, a hard reality to digest by the many members of the Gracie family who perhaps had other passions and qualities that were of no use whatsoever in a ring.

[76] On a side note, he accomplished all this without having a single street-fight on his record, always choosing instead the harder route of fighting in a ring and against skilled opponents.

for a living. To the detriment of their teeth and health and to the benefit of MMA fans today. Keeping in mind that to elevate these men alongside Carlson, is not to attack Carlos and Helio (or anyone else for that matter) or their methods. They have their place in history and it has been acknowledged by the martial arts world *ad nauseum*. What hasn't been acknowledged (or at least, sufficiently acknowledged) is the sweat, blood and lives of the men who crafted the world of *vale-tudo* by fighting in it repeatedly.

Sticking to the Gracie Academy, Carlson was the person most responsible for turning their fighting system into the empirically tried and tested one that it would become over the years. A process that culminated in his students being the best jiu-jitsu representatives in the late 60s, 70s, 80s and early 90s in Brazil. As if this were not enough, the best *vale-tudo* representatives jiu-jitsu had in the 90s could also be found inside his gym on the Figueiredo de Magalhães Street.

Carlson's experience matters here because the fighting system that Carlos and Helio were teaching at the original Gracie Academy had not been sufficiently tried before him. And if there is one thing I know for certain and in which I can speak with authority, it is that in terms of fighting, theory and practice are very different things. Experience matters more than people realize in terms of crafting a practical and effective methodology to pass on to further generations.

Knowing *what works* and *what doesn't* is not a theoretical sort of class. These are lessons that can only be learned from the experience gained when someone is *actually trying to defeat you with all they have*.[77] This process of trial and error, of perfection and of selection *cannot* take place inside our heads and is difficult to create inside a gym without a large pool of competitive individuals. Only a highly competitive arena can achieve this degree of realism as well as the expertise that follows it. The more real, the better.

---

[77] Which isn't to say that only fighters can teach well. To the contrary, from my experience some of the most successful coaches were not great fighters. My point is that techniques must be tested in real situations extensively before they are taught. Good coaches, even if they aren't great fighters, understand this and nurture the environment in accordance with what has been empirically tried.

It was Carlson who tested them all repeatedly in the ring until he began to reach the same conclusions and strategies that contemporary MMA fighters and coaches have reached and make use of today. For example, the conclusion that moves that are so common to self-defense methods in various martial arts (such as wrist-twisting, reaching for punches to block them and arm manipulations of standing opponents) are fantasies that simply don't work when someone is fighting back.

The technical and tactical conclusions which are common knowledge today for fighters, coaches and fans alike, were reached by Carlson and the other *vale-tudo* fighters of his generation decades ago. Even if still in a crude way, the building blocks of the reality of a fight were all there, being developed and worked out in the skills and tactics of men such as Carlson, Ivan Gomes and Euclides Pereira. With this in mind, Carlson's approach to combat was molded after an impetus to fight efficiently and win among the best competition available, rather than to defeat clueless aggressors.

This while simultaneously defending the family name during a crucial period in the history of jiu-jitsu when not much was happening for the Gracie Academy and for jiu-jitsu in general. Not to mention a time when jiu-jitsu and *vale-tudo* were still embryos of what they would become one day. It was also a time where Oscar Santa Maria had lost all his faith in Carlos; where the Gracie Academy was alone responsible for feeding and housing a growing number of children and grandchildren in multiple families and at a time when the Guanabara Federation was nowhere near as big or as profitable as the IBJJF is today. No small responsibility for our *"Garotão"* who loved the beach, the ladies and the south-zone lifestyle.[78]

---

[78] Santa Maria would go onto sue Carlos in 1963 for all the properties he claimed he gave Carlos as requested by "Mago Lasvojilo" the Peruvian spiritual entity Carlos told Santa Maria he communicated with. See Cairus 2012a, pg.193; and Pedreira 2015c, pg. 57.

Moreover, Carlson was all too aware that the Gracie brand of jiu-jitsu was under serious threat after Helio's loss to Waldemar (more on this in forthcoming chapters) when he half-jokingly suggested that if it were not for him, the Gracie family would be making a living from selling bananas in Brazil.[79]

The responsibility and the understanding of the fight game crafted by experience, gave Carlson a very specific vision of fighting well beyond his own career. He would take on the job of being the evolutionary bridge between the original curriculum of the Gracie Academy and a more modern and sophisticated approach to combat. In fact, I would go as far as saying that the bridge was indeed a larger one. Carlson was, in a sense, the bridge between the proto-MMA scene that began to develop in Brazil in the 1930s and its contemporary practice inside the UFC and other major MMA events around the world.

If we pay close attention to Carlson's vision toward fighting, in structural terms at least, it is virtually the same one held by contemporary MMA fighters and coaches today and followed a certain recipe:

a) *Sem-kimono* (no-gi) is more realistic than training and fighting wearing one.[80]

b) That fighters should be complete and master all spheres of combat: striking, takedowns and the ground-game.

c) Learning how to take someone down is just as important as being able to keep them down.

d) Ground-and-pound is a fundamental aspect of this control process and a highly useful path to victory (unlike the view that only the submission mattered).

---

[79] *"Se não fosse eu, os Gracie estariam vendendo banana no Largo do Machado."* (If it weren't for me, the Gracies would be selling bananas at the Largo do Machado."). Pedreira 2015c, chp. 33 ft. 5.

[80] Which doesn't discount its usage for reasons I explain here: Drysdale 2022a. To illustrate the gi vs. no-gi issue, during his fight with Passarito in 1953, Carlson broke with his Uncle Helio's tradition and attempted to take off his gi jacket mid-fight. See: Pedreira 2015b, pg. 101.

e)   Holding the high ground was much better than fighting from the bottom.[81]

f)   Being athletic/strong is important and in no way is in conflict with being a skilled technician.

g)   Lastly, Carlson established what was possibly his most import-ant contribution as a coach—so crucial in fact, that today we take it entirely for granted, his insistence that, *for purposes of high-performance, lessons shouldn't be taught individually in the form of private classes, but rather in groups of indi-viduals who sparred live and attempt to defeat each other in real-time*, as in the *randori* practice in judo.

Throughout his life on the mats, Carlson kept an open-ended approach to fighting. As he saw it, as long as it worked in the ring, it should be assimilated into the curriculum. Even if for that he had to break with tradition. Not being closed minded or constrained by pride, he was able to keep his eyes on performance above all other measures.[82]

As for the group classes that Carlson preferred, it is worth reminding ourselves here that the original Gracie Academy paid its bills primarily with private lessons, which, as everyone who trains knows, isn't the speediest way toward evolution or high-performance. As the saying goes, *iron sharp-ens iron*. Carlson understood this and accordingly, he created his own meth-odology. One that had evolved out of the original Gracie fighting system but that had high-performance, rather than profit, as its primary objective.

He accomplished this by changing the practice to a whole new adap-tive zone for jiu-jitsu to evolve in, away from its matrix (not unlike the

---

[81]   When Carlson fought Waldemar the second-time in a *vale-tudo* match (the first had been a jiu-jitsu match and ended in a draw, despite Carlson having dominated), Waldemar would take Carlson down early in the fight. Interestingly, Carlson would not follow his Uncle's strategy of playing-guard and stood back to his feet as soon as the opportuni-ty presented itself. Source: *"Carlson Gracie Documentary"* https://www.youtube.com/watch?v=Sc634-syYcs.

[82]   To be fair, the Gracie fighting system was originally built on that same premise, but it was Carlson who would continue to assimilate and adapt as *vale-tudo* evolved from its birth-roots of the 1930s.

Gracie brothers had done to judo). Giving jiu-jitsu the time and space it needed for it to be completely redifined. One that was redesigned for the purpose of giving jiu-jitsu an empirical and final frame for what "as real as it gets" really meant.[83] From this main initial framework onward, there were only minor evolutionary increments as attested by how contemporary coaches and fighters still prepare for MMA today. The incremental evolution we have been seeing in MMA, since Royce's victories beginning in 1993, is nothing but a continuation of a process that began long ago and which Carlson is the stand-out figure.

This becomes more obvious when we compare the evolutionary jump that took place between the methods of the original Gracie Academy and how Carlson would be teaching in Copacabana to men such as: Murilo Bustamante, Amaury Bitetti, Ricardo DelaRiva, Paulão Filho, Sergio Bolão, Zé Mario, Vitor Belfort, Cássio Cardoso, Marcelo Saporito, Carlão Barreto, Rodrigo Medeiros, Alan Goes, Wallid Ismail, Fernando Pinduka, Parrumpinha, Otavio Peixotinho, Ignácio Aragão, Ricardo Libório, Antonio Rosado, Ricardo Arona, the Nogueira brothers, André Pederneiras and a plethora of other very competent fighters that any MMA fan will immediately recognize.[84]

There is no exaggeration here; take a close look into the overall skillset and fighting ability of Carlson's direct students as well as how they fought. Then look at how MMA fighters are trained today. What changed? The only thing that has changed is the improvement of the training methodologies, the quality of the techniques and, consequently, the overall quality of the fighters. Which we should notice in passing, is exactly what an open evolutionary canon would call for when free to evolve through competition within an arena that tests their limits against

---

[83] Due to *vale-tudo* being mostly banned in Brazil during the 70s and 80s, Carlson had fewer opportunities than he would have liked to prove himself as coach to that style, immersing instead as a competitive jiu-jitsu coach. Which doesn't mean that he had ever abandoned his views on fighting "as real as it gets." When *vale-tudo* came back in the 90s, the transition for his troops from competitive jiu-jitsu to MMA was fairly quick.

[84] Many of these fighters would help give birth to the now legendary "Brazilian Top Team," whose offshoot is now the most successful MMA team in the world: "American Top Team," founded by Ricardo Libório another one of Carslon Gracie's many black-belts.

rivals of close or equivalent caliber.[85] But in terms of scope, approach and open-source mindset as outlined in the recipe above, very little has changed. People just got better... As they should.

Over the years, fighters adapted and evolved, all the while never managing to quite break free from the paradigm of fighting that was best represented by Carlson's approach to fighting. In other words, Carlson's vision ensured that *vale-tudo* went on with and without him, but not without the paradigm he had played the leading role in shaping.[86]

As for striking, Carlson saw the importance of incorporating striking into training fighters and all his students learned some striking before transitioning to *vale-tudo*. It is important to remember here that at the end of the day, the fighters that represented him had come from the practice of competitive jiu-jitsu and none of them relied on striking more than their jiu-jitsu to win (with the notable exceptions of Vitor Belfort and Rogério "Minotouro" Nogueira). For the most part, they just knew they should know how to strike and that being a skilled ground-fighter or even takedown artist, simply wasn't enough, or better, normally wasn't.[87]

---

[85] Speaking of "equivalent caliber," within the flourishing American martial arts landscape of the 90s (of what was briefly referred to as "No Holds Barred" or simply *"NHB"* and later, in the Dana White era would be rebranded "MMA"), Carlson's students would only find rivals within the elite circles of American wrestling, an art that had had far more time for trial and error and that were the natural rivals of jiu-jitsu/judo going back to Ad Santel and Henry Webber's and their matches against Kodokan graduates.

[86] On a side note, I am not suggesting here that *no one* before Carlson had ever thought about being a well-rounded fighter and of forging their skills through the fires of tough competition. Clearly the idea is not a new one and we can go as far back as ancient Greece in order to find examples of this. But contemporary MMA does not descend from ancient Greece or from Japanese shooto. It descends from Rorion's export of an old recipe for pitching style vs. style Brazilians called *vale-tudo*, and in terms of *vale-tudo* no one in the 20th century (the century in which it actually evolved) was better positioned to speak of it with authority than Carlson was.

[87] On another curious note, it is worth remembering here that when Royce fought in UFC 3, his camp flew Carlson from Rio do California, to help Royce prepare for the fight and corner him. Considering the size of the family, it would have made no sense to bring Carlson to the USA just to corner Royce unless they knew that Carlson was the most experienced and knowledgeable of them all in terms of fighting and coaching. Especially considering how disaffected Royce's father Helio and his cousin Carlson had become over the years. Although Una Proença, in her interview in Part 3 of this book, gives another reason why Carlson was in Royce's corner in that UFC.

Furthermore, it is also important to remember that Carlson, while he was inside the Gracie Academy, was the most experienced and dominant *vale-tudo* fighter among all of them. Something which his record clearly demonstrates with a total of 19 fights and 1 loss. Considering the length of time in he had trained with all the instructors at the Gracie Academy, his dominance over all of them, it is highly unlikely he did not leave a considerable mark in their whole fighting system, strategies and overall canon of techniques. Not to mention how much they all respected and looked up to him.

What I am arguing for here, is that Carlson had gradually and significantly improved on jiu-jitsu for *vale-tudo*, making sure it was in sync with *vale-tudo's* own evolution. This at a time where Rickson was a toddler and Royce hadn't even been born yet. In this sense, Carlson's methods, were a clear marker of evolutionary diversification from the original Gracie Academy and their approach to real-fighting. A notion that his rivalry with his Uncle Helio would only further highlight.

Helio and Carlson's differences most likely stemmed from several disagreements, including Helio's desire to hold onto power and control; Carlson's increasing reputation and independence; and Helio's bias toward his own children. Perhaps not surprisingly, their views on fighting and training also differed. Time would not only help sever their personal relationship, but also make clear their different stratagems toward fighting in general (more on this in chapter 7). The division would only widen when Carlson decided to finally leave the Gracie Academy in 1964 to begin his own program and teach as he saw fit. Teaching anyone who wanted to train hard, regardless of surname or finances.

In fact, Carlson's most lasting legacy would begin when he decided to open his own gym and put his methodology to the test. His contributions as a coach are the subject of our next chapter.

Chapter 6

The Beginning of a New Era for Jiu-Jitsu

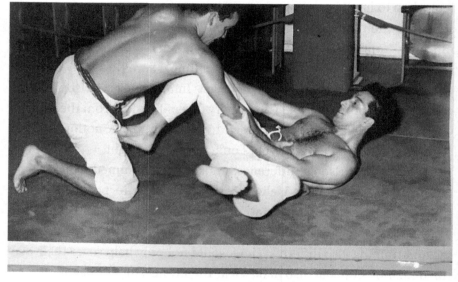

Carlson Gracie and Georges Mehdi in the open-guard position. Photocred: Mehdi Academy.

"Carlson's jiu-jitsu was an extension of his personality. Carlson was a totally different type of human being from Carlos and Helio. His jiu-jitsu reflected the difference."[88]

Roberto Pedreira

Despite all his craft inside the ring, Carlson's true fighting-genius was best displayed in his role as a visionary, passionate and committed

---

[88] Pedreira, 2015b pg. 150

coach. It was in those shoes that he would make his biggest contribution to the gentle-art and its evolution. After all, fighting well is one thing, but being able to pass on this information and know-how to others is an entirely different matter altogether.[89]

Carlson could do both and the biggest push to create the competitive training environment that jiu-jitsu needed in order to place its evolution on the fast track, was his. Accordingly, his academy dominated the jiu-jitsu landscape during the late 60s, 70s, 80s and all the way up to the early 90s. From that point onward, the professionalization of academies, business minded expansion and unprecedented (and unexpected) growth of jiu-jitsu after the post-Royce era were simply too much for our good old *garotão*, now in his early 60s.[90]

His success as a coach is not difficult to explain. Unlike the Gracie Academy who opted for a private-oriented business model that prioritizes the comfort of the student (nothing wrong with that view, but it isn't an approach to forge the champions that Carlson was after), Carlson was interested in *casca-grossa* fighters. To him, it didn't matter who the student was or their overall social-standing, finances or their last name. He wanted to train champions and that was the only valid criteria and measuring stick for Carlson. That is what he wanted and where he placed his life-efforts after retirement from the rings.

---

[89]   José Tufy Cairus, besides being an early researcher of jiu-jitsu history, also happened to have frequented Carlson's gym to train. He describes the atmosphere: *"One day, I went to Carlson Gracie's gym located in Copacabana. A relaxed, mature individual whose persona contrasted starkly with his aura as a tough fighter warmly welcomed me. The gym was fully booked and a question puzzled me back then, why did Brazilian jiu-jitsu only become popular among the middle class in the 1980s? According to my father, the Gracies had been around for decades. Nonetheless, they rarely practiced Brazilian jiu-jitsu outside their upper class circles. The atmosphere at Carlson Gracie's gym was quite different from that at my father's dojo* [Cairus' father taught Kodokan judo], *where the routine resembled military drills. At the same time, there was no question that every aspect of that peculiar world involved hypermasculinity* (Cairus 2012a, pg. 1).

[90]   These tournament results are abundant and can be found in Pedreira 2015c. They are also confirmed by our interviewees.

All this clearly at odds with how jiu-jitsu was taught and practiced by the original Gracie Academy. Carlinhos Gracie comments on this:

"(...) the Gracie Academy only had private students, and there were no groups or classes. Carlson was [sic] a team of competitors. Carlson created competition Jiu-Jitsu, Jiu-Jitsu in groups, which never existed, just private classes. Carlson was the first guy who taught in groups in the Gracie family."[91]

These differences are further highlighted by his students Fernando Pinduka, Ricardo Libório and Paulo Filho below:[92]

"In the family, he was the only one who taught everything and to anyone, while the rest of the family was more reserved. He had great respect for the student and didn't deny teaching them. We had great human material to work with and our training was geared toward competition, unlike the others, who praised self-defense and a lighter version of jiu-jitsu."

"You can see out there the legacy Carlson left. To me, he was the most important figure in the history of MMA. Look at Dedé [André Pederneiras, founder of Nova União and coach to former UFC champion José Aldo among many others] doing great with Nova União, Brazilian Top Team, American Top Team, Vitor Befort, Minotauro and Minotouro, that came from DelaRiva, and who came from Carlson's roots. He trained so many fighters and teachers... People can't forget him. If it weren't for him, we would not be here today."

---

[91] Drysdale 2020, pg. 69

[92] Respectively, Pinduka, one of Carlson's oldest students alive; Ricardo Libório, the founder of the biggest MMA team in the world today; and Paulo Filho, one of the most dominant fighters of his era.

"He had practical know-how, he knew what worked and what was fraudulent. That was the secret to having trained as many champions as he did."[93]

Carlson's views began to take shape inside the original Gracie Academy where he took an initial framework and methodology to meet the standard of "as real as it gets." Yet, what Carlson did with this initial framework was to improve it by doing the most urgent task a coach has- open up the practice so that evolution can take place and *ensure that the room stays hot with high-level competition for long periods of time.*

In his view, a competitive practice full of *casca-grossas* was the fast-track for mutual improvement. This recipe may seem obvious to us now, but even though it already existed then, it had not yet been explored to its full potential and was at risk of dying off as an embryo had Carlson not made it a top priority for the growth of jiu-jitsu. Without it, it is unlikely that jiu-jitsu's rapid technical growth spurt would have taken place after the founding of the CBJJ/IBJJF in 1994 (assuming competitive jiu-jitsu could even have survived without Carlson during the 60s, 70s and 80s in Rio).

What is more likely is that jiu-jitsu would have remained a niche practice of the Gracie family centered largely around private lessons for business men, politicians and celebrities. Furthermore, and as anyone who knows anything about fighting understands perfectly well, evolution and techniques are *not* the product of individual geniuses thinking about moves from the comfort of their home or on the edge of the mats watching others train. *Evolution and innovation are necessarily a byproduct of competition, accidents and improvisations.* The more of it, and the harsher the lessons the trials teach, the stronger the pressures for this evolution to take place.

By creating that space in the Figueiredo de Magalhães Academy in Copacabana with the ideal brother-partner-rival Rolls (more on this in chapter 12), Carlson was essentially giving birth to our contemporary understanding of *what jiu-jitsu is.* In terms of how it is almost unanimously

---

[93] Source: *"A Quinze Anos o Mundo Perdia Carlson Gracie"* https://carlsongracieteam. org/15-anos-sem-carlson-gracie/

practiced today in academies the world over. Not that hard and competitive training didn't exist in the original Gracie Academy—it certainly did. But the problem was that it was limited to the family members and a few instructors who were die-hards. In short, it wasn't open enough in a way that could accelerate evolution nor could it create the framework of training that would finally find a wider outlet to express itself after the jiu-jitsu boom of the mid-90s.

A move that was, for all practical purposes, a crucial moment for the history of jiu-jitsu. Because it came to be the fork in the road that would set apart the original version of jiu-jitsu coming out of the Gracie Academy from the one that the rest of the world would come to practice after Royce and the UFC popularized it. Naturally, his academy had an appeal to many who previously had no access to jiu-jitsu. Due to this, and perhaps unsurprisingly, *"against a background of democratization (...) Carlson's dojo became the Mecca of jiu-jitsu practice in Rio de Janeiro."*[94]

Of course, Carlson wasn't the only person to teach in groups and open up to all social classes either. As early as 1955 George Gracie claimed to have developed a teaching methodology capable of teaching up to 50 students at a time. Oswaldo Fadda had also done so well before Carlson even opened his own academy.[95] But the reality of this discussion, is that despite George being a successful fighter, he did not achieve Carlson's prominence as a coach/teacher, while Fadda had neither the practical know-how that Carlson had, nor did he train as many champions as Carlson did, not even close in fact.[96]

---

[94] Cairus 2012a, pg. 203

[95] Pedreira 2015b, pg. 145

[96] It is worth noticing that when Rorion told the world a story that had a Helio-centric spin to it, initially no one questioned it. Over the years, many other martial artists and disaffects in general (mainly within the *jiu-jitsusphere* itself), began to raise the question of whether the Fadda lineage was a non-Gracie lineage and whether Oswaldo Fadda's name could not counter balance Rorion's Helio-centric approach to history. Although we now know that the Fadda lineage is in fact, according to the evidence available, also a Gracie lineage (Drysdale 2020, pg. 193). What never occurred to most of these critiques, skeptics and disaffects, is that, despite their skepticism being sensible, it was Carlson's crucial role in reshaping jiu-jitsu that had been the most neglected one all along. Although perhaps it was his surname that made him a non-candidate to this role.

As for the original Gracie Academy, it lacked any group classes. Even if family members and a few selected students got together in a small group to train at the end of the day, in evolutionary terms at least, this is a very impovireshed approach. Sporadic encounters of small groups competing against one another creates little to no evolutionary pressures. Large groups, in small geographical locations, cohabiting in an environment of consistent and high intensity conflict on the other hand, create the sort of pressures necessary for rapid evolution to take place. The Figueiredo Academy was exactly that sort of environment.

It is in this sense that I am insisting here that Carlson was, for all practical purposes, an evolutionary split in this history, from judo and toward what we now call "BJJ." Separating the *first-wave* of practitioners from the *second* one that would, for all practical purposes, give shape to the brand of jiu-jitsu that took over the world after 1993.

Keeping in mind that the sort of evolution Carlson had his eyes on, was one still grounded in the reality of combat above all else. For Carlson, any drift from this supremacy of the real (the excessive usage of lapels for example) would have encountered difficulty surviving inside his academy. The practice of *"confere"* (more on this in chapters 21 and 22), coupled with the unanimous understanding of jiu-jitsu as being an art meant to teach one how to fight realistically (not necessarily win medals), achieved this effect of binding evolution to reality. In other words, the cultural and technical practices inside the Figueiredo Academy maintained evolutionary pressures on a very specific course.

Perhaps the main differences between Carlson's vision and today's competitive jiu-jitsu scene can be explained by how Jean Jeacques Machado referred to Carlson's approach to jiu-jitsu as a "short" one. By this, he meant a practice that was centered around the kind of jiu-jitsu that was geared for real-fighting, even if less sophisticated and with less *"firula"* (fluff). Carlson's understanding of jiu-jitsu was one centered around precision and meant to work everywhere. It was, as his student Pinduka referred to it, a "total jiu-jitsu."[97]

---

[97] Source: *"Entrevista com Fernando Pinduka"* https://youtu.be/URqCAPV6uAw

Regardless of what we may think of Carlson's "short" jiu-jitsu, the truth is that it did work everywhere, as the performance and results of his many students can attest to throughout their complete dominance of the jiu-jitsu competitive landscape. The same cannot be said about more contemporary approaches to jiu-jitsu with their sport specificity or for the self-defense approach to jiu-jitsu taught inside the original Gracie Academy, with its dependence on the opponent being mostly unskilled.

For Carlson, jiu-jitsu had to work everywhere and against anyone. Otherwise, *what was the point?* Of course, some might argue that practitioners in general are just fine practicing a version of jiu-jitsu that is suitable only under a specific competitive ruleset with or without the kimono. Or in the case of self-defense, perfectly fine only being prepared to defend themselves against an attack by an untrained (if not also unathletic) aggressor.

Carlson, however, would have seen these views as limited and even impoverished for purposes of the practicality of real-combat (despite their technical sophistication in the case of modern competitive jiu-jitsu) because they were limited only to very specific environments. For him, the lion should know how hunt *everywhere* and under *any circumstances* for his training to be worthwhile. It is in this sense that Carlson's views on jiu-jitsu were more grounded in the reality of combat than what was practiced inside the original Gracie Academy and also what is currently being practiced in competitive jiu-jitsu.

Good jiu-jitsu for Carlson meant efficiency in combat against skilled opponents, not the coolness of fads and excessive *firula*, or undertried self-defense systems. Ultimately, what Carlson had, was a *"highly eclectic and comprehensive view of jiu-jitsu. For him, it really did include everything, as long as it could be used in a ring."*[98] And here perhaps, lies his true brilliance. Not only did he understand the need to cultivate a Spartan-like environment of survival of the fittest, he also had the wisdom to place efficiency in terms of combat as the guiding principle of their daily practice.

---

[98] Pedreira, 2015c, pg. 163-164

Nevertheless, the question remains, *why has Carlson's importance for the history of jiu-jitsu been so neglected and underappreciated?* Why don't more members of his own family, as well as their many followers, acknowledge his importance? Is it because he wasn't that relevant for the history of jiu-jitsu? Or is it because we are witnessing here the jiu-jitsu version of a *Game of Thrones*? Or perhaps this neglect was the inevitable side-effect of only having one male son (and not a professional marketer at that) to highlight his father's accomplishments? These questions are important ones as they teach us exactly what we need to know about our past in order to comprehend our present and they may even, if we grant them the time and the thought they deserve, help us enlighten the path to a better future.

Yet before we can answer any of these questions adequately, we need to first understand a conflict taking place inside the family between its two leading generals. A little insight into this war and how it spread into the *jiu-jitsusphere* of Rio, can perhaps help us understand its vital role in shaping jiu-jitsu's evolution and future landscape.

Chapter 7

Two Generals in a Civil War

A rare moment with the two generals standing next
to each other to take a picture with a child.
The child is symbolic of the future of jiu-jitsu.
Photocred: Mestre Guedes via Marcial Serrano personal archives.

"[Carlson leaving the Gracie Academy] *created a certain rivalry in the family [...] It was as if two generals were in a civil war. My whole life I fought against Carlson's students, looking at him as a rival, even though we were brothers.*"[99]

Master Carlos Gracie Jr.

During jiu-jitsu's *silent years* (1951-1993), Carlos Gracie, perhaps tired of the academy (if not the whole fighting world altogether) was gradually replaced by his younger brother and political heir Helio. Over

---

[99] Source: *"Carlson Gracie Documentary"* https://www.youtube.com/watch?v=Sc634-syYcs

time, Carlos became increasingly involved in mysticism and in tutoring his financial patron Oscar Santa Maria (arguably BJJ's first major sponsor) into the occult and other practices in which Carlos posed as a guru to the gullible Santa Maria.[100]

As Helio took over the helm, his advancing age coupled with a highly domineering personality, led him to become increasingly estranged from his nephew Carlson, the new and upcoming *fighting-alpha* of the family. A distancing that would eventually be described as a civil war inside the family ranks.[101]

While it would be difficult to single out any particular event that would mark the beginning of their disaffection for one another, Helio's loss to Waldemar and Carlson later avenging this loss, seems to be a good place to start.[102] This estrangement between the Gracie family's two leading figures (now that Carlos was slowly moving into retirement from jiu-jitsu) would have long term consequences, not only for the family itself but also for the evolution of jiu-jitsu away from their private oriented model and toward a more open, competitive and democratic teaching methodology. Consequences that are ultimately still echoed in contemporary debates of *what jiu-jitsu is*.

Carlson posed a problem to the strong and territorial personality of Helio. On one hand they were all related and with the same family mission in sight, to dominate the martial arts scene in Brazil and assert

---

[100] Carlos held a lifelong fascination with the supernatural and the alleged powers it granted him. He was known for giving guidance and instruction to those around him based on the alleged supernatural powers he claimed to possess. For Carlos Gracie's relationship to mysticism, see: Gracie 2008, chp. 12 and 36; Pedreira 2015a, pg. 322-323; Pedreira 2015b, chp. 3; and Cairus 2012a, pg. 112-113

[101] Considering the political context of the times, it is not unreasonable to suppose that their different personalities, were colored by the political context of the time. Specifically, in regards to Helio's penchant for authoritarian worldviews. Tufy Cairus comments: *"In assessing Hélio's affiliation to radical ideologies one is tempted to affirm that he was simply swept up in a strong political trend, but in some ways his support for this Brazilian version of fascism was predictable. In addition, the party placed a premium on youth, virility and aggressive manliness. Hélio's bellicose persona and past transgressions made his affiliation with the 'green shirts' unsurprising."* Cairus 2012a, pg. 108.

[102] Clips of the fight between Carlson and Waldemar can be seen here: *"Carlson Gracie Documentary"* https://www.youtube.com/watch?v=Sc634-syYcs

jiu-jitsu's domination over other styles. On the other, as Carlos and Helio aged, it was clear that Carlson was perfectly placed to replace them both. He was perfectly placed because he was younger, more charismatic (in accordance with the aspirations of a younger generation) and had the privilege of building on the previous experience his Uncle and father had accumulated in life.

More importantly, Carlson was quickly becoming a better fighter than his father and Uncle ever were. Add this to the fact that Carlson, as Carlos' eldest son, had an equal if not stronger claim as the heir apparent to the Gracie Academy than his Uncle Helio did (they were 19 years apart). Luckily for Helio, Carlson wasn't interested in politics and never disputed Helio's political leadership during that era. Carlson was into *fighting* and, much like his Uncle George before him, was willing to fight anyone, anytime, anywhere and under any rulesets. And fight he did. He possessed the kind of courage that is seldom celebrated, particularly when we think that courage coupled with victory are so fundamental for distinguishing rank in the fight world.

Unfairly, much of the celebration of courage and performance during that era was entirely allocated to Helio. Especially after the jiu-jitsu boom of the mid-90s, when Rorion told the world a Helio-centric narrative where the highest-seat in the history of jiu-jitsu in Brazil was (conveniently) enjoyed by his father. Something that we now know to be a very incomplete narrative.

Helio, undoubtedly had his merits in his career on the mats and they are all well-known and celebrated, but, as history would have it, the role of marketing has always proven to be a stronger force than that of merit. And truth be told, Carlson not only fought more than Helio did, but his opponents were far more qualified ones as well. Of course, Helio fought Kimura, but he lost to Kimura, and it wasn't close. The only thing that could be said about that fight is that Kimura was heavier (albeit certainly not 100kg as was claimed years later, Kimura weighted 90 kg for that fight), more experienced and didn't finish Helio as quickly as he claimed he could have.[103]

Considering the time lapsed and how selective the telling of this history has been over the years, the blow to the credibility of the Gracie Academy caused by Helio's loss to Waldemar has been severely underestimated by those holding the pen of historical remembrance. Conversely, the restoration of their reputation by the hands of a young Carlson certainly had the opposing redeeming effect on the academy's morale.

Helio was certainly valiant in taking on his much younger and heavier former student. For this act of bravery, he should be commended. However, even the disparity in weight and age did little to lessen the blow in Helio's reputation that the loss to Waldemar meant. Because truth be told, most people don't understand (nor do they care to understand) the impact of age, weight, and short-notice in the outcome of a fight. Most people (fans in particular) are simple-minded in this regard and care only to learn "who the best" truly is. They are almost completely oblivious to all the nuances of a fight and the preparation leading up to one.

Besides, we need to remember that Helio had been relentlessly marketed in the press as the Brazilian national champion (even though no such thing existed then) by his brother Carlos and himself. Which had the desired effect of creating a certain aura around Helio inside and outside the Gracie Academy. Something that not even his loss to Kimura did anything to diminish.

Yet this time it was different, in the fight with Kimura, he has fighting a great and well-known Japanese champion when his brother Carlos interrupted the match once Helio was caught in a judo technique called *ude-garami* (later renamed "kimura," in BJJ circles after the man himself). In the case of the fight with Waldemar however, Helio was fighting a former student and janitor and was carried out of the ring after being

---

[103] According to sources, Helio's weight was 60kg. that day. Others contested this. They claimed instead that Helio weighed more. For details of the Kimura fight with Helio, see: Pedreira 2015b, chp. 2; and Cairus 2012a, pg. 122

knocked out by a soccer kick to the head, showing a severely bruised and swollen face.[104]

The perks from the reputation they built over the years are clear and were certainly leveraged well by the Gracie brothers. Nonetheless and as the world of show business would have it, this sort of celebrity also brings with it the pressure to maintain itself in the face of new challenges. Naturally, losing to the academy's former janitor and student Waldemar did enormous harm to the academy's standing and to Helio's specifically.[105]

When Carlson avenged his Uncle's defeat the following year, it wasn't only a victory, it was a vindication of the family's repute in the Brazilian fight scene in which Carlson was lauded as the family's champion and hero. How Helio felt about all this we will never know, what we do know is that those who knew them both don't like to talk about it.[106] But it is easy to imagine that if on one hand it pleased Helio to watch Waldemar lose, then on the other I am certain he would have been much happier if it were himself, rather than his nephew Carlson, the one being celebrated on the shoulders of the members of the Gracie Academy.[107]

Any fighter can understand the feeling of watching younger generations take over from where he has left off. It is a bitter pill that every fighter has to swallow as he ages; the prouder the fighter, the more bitter the pill. And if there is one thing we know about Helio and that everyone agrees on, it is that he was a proud individual. With that said, I can't

---

[104] Pedreira 2015b, pg. 138; See also: Cairus 2012a, pg. 152.

[105] It is worthy of notice here that this fight was also emblematic of social and racial disputes in Brazil at the time. Waldemar's black skin was representative of the lower classes and slums of Rio and had his fan base reflected in that same demographic. Conversely, Helio, who inhabited the upper echelons of Carioca society, had that audience as the core of his support base. The comments in the press make vivid the social and racial disputes intrinsic to the fabric of a conflict that was representative of much more than a grudge match between student and master. For more on this, see: Pedreira 2015b, chp. 6.

[106] Throughout the interviews, people would discuss "off the record" the relationship between Helio and Carlson. It is a taboo of sorts in jiu-jitsu circles. Perhaps because those who don't like to discuss it are worried that opening the books would damage jiu-jitsu as a whole. Few of our interviewees would speak about it openly.

[107] The celebration of the victory of Carlson over Waldemar is the cover for this book.

imagine it sitting well with him watching his own students celebrating Carlson after he defeated Waldemar. Was he genuinely happy for his nephew being lifted as the family's new champion?

There is much regarding the relationship between Helio and Carlson that we simply don't know anything about because people do not talk about it or do it hesitantly. Even Reila's biography of her father, a book that is remarkably frank in its description of the family dynamics, does not tell us much about what led to this family feud. Considering that a single event (however traumatic) is unlikely to have been the only cause for their civil war, other reasons must be considered to help explain this crucial, yet largely neglected, piece of jiu-jitsu history. With this in mind, perhaps the civil war can also be explained by acknowledging their obvious differences in terms of personality and methodology.

In professional terms, these differences were in regards to their methods, something that became clear to me when I began to interview Carlson's students from that era. Carlson's insistence on group competitive-classes set him apart from the rest of his family. His vision (now gaining momentum thanks to the Guanabara Federation) would over time continually distance itself from the self-defense-oriented model taught at the original Gracie Academy ran by Helio.[108]

This different approach in terms of methodology is perhaps the greatest technical marker between the original methods of the Gracie Academy and Carlson's. A distancing that became clearer and wider as Carlson eventually created an entirely new environment for a competitive view of jiu-jitsu to flourish in and diversify itself from the methods of the original academy.

Besides, the two academies targeted very different demographics. Carlson didn't even charge many of his students whereas the original Gracie Academy centered is focus on a private lesson format aimed at wealthier classes who could afford them. In terms of approach, Carlson had a more realistic and hands-on approach to practice, methodology

---

[108] Worthy of note here, is that the federation is likely to have further severed Helio's relationship with his nephew Carlson. As the federation and its tournaments gave Carlson a mean to outdo his Uncle in competition.

and overall goals (breeding champions rather than making money). They also differed significantly in terms of personality and in this regard, Helio had proven to be somewhat territorial and set in his ways, a personality trait that certainly had its upsides.

Had it not been for Helio's stubbornness, it is unlikely that their version of jiu-jitsu would have survived the spread of judo in the 1940s and 1950s. What is more probable is that they would have been incorporated back into judo instead or even disappearing completely. Particularly at a time where few people in Brazil were interested in training what they insisted on calling "jiu-jitsu." For that, Helio's obstinacy and pride were a huge contribution to BJJ. His efforts in keeping the small army compact and believing in a common mission, ultimately gave time and space for jiu-jitsu to survive long enough to set it on its own evolutionary course after the creation of the Guanabara Federation (founded and presided over by Helio himself).

On the other hand, this same domineering personality and rigidity are not necessarily the right qualities for growth and the creation of an evolutionary competitive arena to develop and advance the art technically and demographically. In some ways, Helio, by being so controlling and hesitant to open up the practice of jiu-jitsu, worked as an evolutionary restrictor of sorts.

This was particularly true given that Helio was so intent on making his own children the main protagonists in this story. A paternalistic trait that had the downside of limiting the size of the competitive arena for jiu-jitsu to evolve in. Something Carlson was set on correcting as he wanted a more open arena for all *casca-grossas* of the world to join, regardless of their last names.

Tufy Cairus comments:

"Carlson was in many ways the antithesis of his Uncle Hélio, which reflected on his jiu-jitsu teaching philosophy and consequently, in what type of clientele he targeted. Furthermore, unlike his father Carlos, Carlson had no patriarchal ambitions concerning the expansion of the clan [...] Carlson was once an outstanding professional

fighter, but over the time, he became a colorful individual who cultivated traits based on the beach culture of the typical Copacabana resident of his generation [...] Regardless of the existence of a social and spatial hierarchy, the inhabitants of Copacabana shared a strong ethos of beach culture. Carlson recruited his students from the sizable middle class of Copacabana beach goers. The relaxed atmosphere and reasonable prices contrasted starkly with the rigidity and high prices of the Gracies dojo in downtown. Conversely, Carlson's classes were relatively free of ritualistic drills, despite the harshness of the training routine. Carlson engineered a system based on his peculiar personality and winning charisma. Although cockfighting was declared illegal in 1961, he remained a cockfighting aficionado his entire life. Carlson sought inspiration to create a fighting system from his experience in Rio de Janeiro's underground cockfighting arenas. He revered potential Brazilian jiu-jitsu champions for their aggression and their capacity to endure limitless punishment without surrendering - like a pure-breed fighting gamecock [...] Despite his nearly anarchic method, Carlson was a skilled fighter who increased his chances of producing champions by making Brazilian jiu-jitsu affordable to middle class students. Finally, he was a highly competitive individual who sought every opportunity to beat his rivals, particularly his Uncle Hélio Gracie. As a result of his peculiar coaching, Carlson's students had the upper hand whenever competing against his Uncle's pupils."[109]

Carlson's sister and their father's biographer, Reila Gracie, also comments:

"With the opposite posture to that of Reylson [presumably the same posture from the original Gracie Academy as well], *where the gym oriented itself to the children of higher classes, great part of Carlson's students had discounts and some, unable to pay, learned for free. In*

---

[109] Cairus 2012a, pg. 201

exchange for discount or membership, Carlson demanded that they give their best, which made it possible for him to train an elite squad.[110]

Simply put, Carlson's perseverance in creating an arena filled with competitive and driven young men, was a key factor in setting him apart from his Uncle. In fact, I would go as far as saying that, if it were not for Carlson, jiu-jitsu would have remained (in technical terms at least), aimed primarily at self-defense. *Was the self-defense model enough to grant cohesive expansion for jiu-jitsu after Royce's revolution?* I seriously doubt it, just take a close look at how jiu-jitsu is practiced almost exclusively today around the world and you will see Carlson Gracie's jiu-jitsu there.

Methodological differences aside, what is clear to me is that the war between Carlson and Helio was a divisive moment in the history of jiu-jitsu. It is equally clear that during that same period there were other relevant factors in the shaping of what we now refer to as "BJJ." Namely the inception of the Guanabara Federation and its importance in giving a competitive outlet for Carlson's vision to flourish.

It is to the birth of this new sportive vision for jiu-jitsu, its ancestor rulesets and their role in reshaping the Gracies original interpretation of judo that is the subject of our next chapter. After we learn a little more about our history from the testimonies of those who lived these events first hand.

---

[110] Gracie 2008, pg. 388

"The Golden Age of Jiu-Jitsu"
Grandmaster Fernando Pinduka

Interview with members from the second-wave:

Antonio Carlos Rosado (1ˢᵗ half)
Fernando Pinkuka
Arthur Virgilio
Orlando Saraiva
Otávio Peixotinho
Romero Cavalcanti

Grandmaster Antonio Carlos Rosado

Rosado is the only person Carlson ever
promoted to red-belt. Photocred: Rosado
personal archives.

"This is my opinion, Helio wasn't too happy about Carlson teaching jiu-jitsu to everyone. Carlson was the one who opened jiu-jitsu for all who wanted to learn it, everyone knows this. I think Helio was more focused on his guys only, which I can understand, he wanted to keep his secrets for his own children. Very different from Carlson who had no restrictions, Carlson saw all his students as his children."

Grandmaster Antonio Carlos Rosado

Rosado, as he is known in jiu-jitsu circles, is the only man Carlson Gracie has ever promoted to the rank of red-belt. He became known in Brazil as one of Carlson's best students and gained notoriety in Rio after his sparring sessions with Rickson Gracie before his fight against Zulu. Rosado still teaches classes daily in Rio, he was born on January the 4th, 1949 and I interviewed him over the phone on the 8th of June 2022.

1- How and where did you begin training jiu-jitsu?

I first began training judo under Augusto Cordeiro around 1959, but to be honest, I didn't really identify with judo, but I knew Carlson from his fights. I saw him fight "King Kong" *in the America Clube at Tijuca* [1964]. *My brother in law was called Toninho and he was a friend and student of Carlson and took me to train with him still at the Avenida Rio Branco Gracie Academy. Later I signed up Carlson's school. I still have a receipt signed by Carlson when I signed up to train with him in 1967 at the time he was still partnered with Carley* [Gracie]. *I also trained with Pedro Hemetério whenever I went to São Paulo for work and with Barreto Manguetti here in Rio for a while too. Later I reenrolled at Carlson's Figueiredo de Magalhães Academy as a blue-belt. I am the oldest student alive from the days of the Figueiredo Academy.*

2- What was Carlson like?

Even luta-livre guys liked Carlson. Everyone loved him. At Carlson's gym, everyone who stayed got good because those who didn't have the heart to stay the course would quit. There were no baby-sitters there, no one took care of you. Who had to take care of you was you. In other words, you either survived among the other lions or you would succumb and get your little bag and leave. That was Carlson, what he really wanted was to train champions, that's all he cared about. We built a family of warriors there. Carlson didn't care about the money part, he didn't have any business sense, as long as he made enough to get by he was happy, not really worried about tomorrow. And if he had any money left he'd shared it with those who needed it. There is no other like him, he'd come from the US with a new pair of shoes and someone would say "hey Carlson, nice shoes" *and he'd take them off and go* "here, they are yours." *And he'd grab some old flip-flops and go home wearing them instead, he didn't even ask for the guys shoes in return. He's done this for me before, to take off his own shoes and gift them to me. Watches too, where he'd have a brand-new watch and some-one would comment on it and he'd take it off and give it away, he'd do things like that all the time, he had no attachment to any-thing material.*

3- What about his grading system? How did it work?

It was all merit based. It depended entirely on the student's per-formances and potential. Which didn't mean anyone got promoted too fast. When I was a purple-belt I did well against all black-belts I trained with. Carlson took a lot of pride in that.

4- What was Carlson's training methodology and vision for jiu-jitsu like?

I trained under Carlson for decades and can speak with author-ity on this. I never saw Carlson teach a class around positions. He was more about correcting what you were doing wrong in the moment, if you were smart and paying attention, you'd listen and correct yourself. Under Carlson, everyone had their own style. If you go to most gyms, the students all more or less follow the instructor's game, but not Carlson, he had a style of teaching that was tailor made for the student, he did this by exploring your own attributes, he never imposed and told you what to do, instead he added to your game and always worked around correcting and fixing your own natural progression. He would just scream at you and tell you what to do mid-practice with that big voice of his was unforgettable. We could hear him coming up the stairs and the whole energy in the room would change. I remember when we would be training in case he wasn't in the room, as soon as we heard him coming up the stairs you could feel the energy and the pace in the room would change. When we heard his voice... it was like an injection of adrenaline to everyone on the mats. Another thing about his teaching, I never saw him teaching a self-defense class [at this point, I can hear Rosado's wife from a different room: "except to women!" which made Rosado laugh and agree with her before he continued]. *But to men, never. I never had a self-defense class under Carlson. I know self-defense because it came naturally to us through our training.*

5-   What about *taparia*?

More often than taparia, Carlson would put boxing gloves on one person to strike the other who had to clinch and take the other one down. This was a lot of fun and we had to stay sharp. It also had the effect of putting a lot of pressure on us to get the job done, because in case you couldn't take your training partner down, the whole room would be watching and teasing you for taking a beating and not being able to finish the job. Carlson did this a lot. On Saturdays we would often train in swimming trunks and use slaps to keep it real, as a reminder of what a real fight would look like when we grappled. But the slaps weren't that hard, it was more of a reminder.

6-   I like the idea of a reminder to keep the practice of jiu-jitsu with a foot in reality.

Look, I'm not one to criticize technical evolution. In my day we also ended up in a lot of these positions like 50/50 for example, but the difference was that by keeping it real people didn't want to stay in those positions. The gloves and slaps had exactly that function of keeping it real. Jiu-jitsu is a real-fight, not a sportive practice, it was created for practical reality. Of course, some of these new moves are beautiful to look at, but I wonder, "have you actually beaten anyone with them?"

7- How do you think technical evolution takes place?

I always tell my students, I don't want to have a huge arsenal I can't use. I had my sequences and they were trained enough to outdo my opponent's defenses because I practiced them daily. No matter how many times they practiced the defense, I had so much more experience in attacking because I did it to everyone. It was just that my offense was always better, because I did it 10 times a day to 10 different people while you only defended it against me. I had an antidote and answer to all of your defenses, if you wanted to keep up with my offense you had to improve on your defense just in order to survive. That is what raises the bar for our training, trying to outdo one another competitively. Of course, some are better than others, but we all need to be challenged to grow. Sometimes you win, sometimes you lose, that's normal to me, no big deal. The world won't end because you lost. Some people preach invincibility, that is a tremendous slip in my opinion. Even if I beat you today, I don't believe that I will always beat you. I may lose tomorrow! It's an illusion to repeat these stories of invincibility. I'm a grounded person and I know of people's limitations because I have them too, you are a man just like me. Then there are those who create these images. I don't believe in any superman. To me we are all the same. If I had to fight you, I don't even know how old you are but you would have to defeat me in combat, not by intimidating me. I'm 73 now, and you are a young and healthy fighter so you would probably win, but you would have to beat me with fists, not by intimidation or yelling at me. I don't think you are a superman, I think you are a man just like me. But people keep building these pedestals for themselves and paint themselves into a corner because now they feel an obligation to be invincible and won't fight. I am aware of my limitations, but I was trained for war and my coach was Carlson, who believed in me even more than I believed in myself. My belief in myself came from him.

8-   What was the dynamic like between Carlson and Rolls' students?

The main difference between Carlson and Rolls, was that Carlson was like a big dad [paizão], and Rolls was more like an older brother to everyone. Even though the relationship was always good between all of us, on the mats it was very competitive whenever we trained against Rolls' guys. We went at it. It was friendly but also competitive. Whenever we did cross-train, it wasn't light training, it was like a fight. Like when Rickson came over to train with me. He didn't just want to train, he went there to get me. Training was with friends and training partners, but if someone from a different gym came over to humiliate you, it was a fight.[111] But as soon as the round was over we hugged each other and it was all good, the rivalry ended then and there.

9-   Was the culture in the Figueiredo Magalhães Academy different from the one in the original Gracie Academy?

Just by the way Carlson ran his business I would say that yes. My guess is that 90% of Carlson's students didn't even pay a membership. It is unexplainable, I would try to pay him and he wouldn't take my money, I could afford it but he wouldn't take it. I would try to pay for my son at least and Carlson would say "no way I'm charging your son!" He didn't have any business sense, he did things for you for the pleasure of having you in his gym.[112] That alone

---

[111] Rosado is very humble and does not like to talk about this. But when Rickson came over to prepare for his fight against Zulu, Rosado was still a purple-belt and was defeating Rickson (already a black-belt) in practice. Carlson Jr. who was present, confirms this in his interview for this book. The only time Rosado discussed this topic in public can be seen here: *"Rosado dá a sua versão sobre treinos com Rickson Gracie"* https://www.youtube.com/watch?v=zVaoMiI3l_o

[112] The practice of not charging competitor students became common in Rio after Carlson.

created a very different environment than the one inside the Gracie Academy. Just to give you an idea of what that academy was like, we had the mat area, then a two-meter walkway before the bench where Carlos Gracie would often sit to watch us train, and then there was the bathroom door. This happened twice where I'd get to the gym and there would be people grappling in the bathroom! You know how sometimes when we go out of bounds and we stop to reset, but in this reset, we never really begin in the same position? Those guys didn't want to stop, so they would start on the mats and keep going until they ended up all the way into the bathroom just so they didn't have to reset [laughs]. Normal occurrences in the academy. So yes, very different places.

10- Why did Carlson open a gym with Ivan Gomes but not Robson or Helio?

I'll tell you something. Carlson left Helio because Helio was too controlling and he [Carlson] wanted his own life. He had great respect for Helio, so much that when Helio got to the gym he would step off the mats, get it? Helio would take over the mats. So much so that in our rematch, when Rickson submitted me, Helio was coordinating everything. Imagine me fighting Rickson in the gym with Helio as referee, determining when we started, when we stopped, how long we fought, and Carlson would simply step off the mats. I can even understand the respect Carlson had for him, Helio imposed respect, he was the big boss.

11- What were the main differences between Helio and Carlson?

I don't like to talk much about it because I don't want anyone to misinterpret things, but I have the deepest respect for Helio. He fought Waldemar for 3 hours and 45 minutes [sic] in his forties and Waldemar in his twenties, much stronger than him, so you need to respect that.[113] If it weren't for him and Carlos we wouldn't be here now and jiu-jitsu would have disappeared in the air, they kept our history alive. But Helio was very territorial, his children had to be the best in the world and he taught jiu-jitsu only to his favorites, his own children and a few other students, João Alberto Barreto, Armando Wriedt, etc. But Carlson opened jiu-jitsu up for everyone, if you went to Carlson's gym, he'd teach you, he didn't differentiate and taught everyone who wanted to learn. This is my opinion, Helio wasn't too happy about Carlson teaching jiu-jitsu to everyone. Carlson was the one who opened jiu-jitsu for all who wanted to learn it, everyone knows this. I think Helio was more focused on his guys only, which I can understand, he wanted to keep his secrets for his own children. Very different from Carlson who had no restrictions, Carlson saw all his students as his children.

12- You were awarded your red-belt by Carlson, right?

I am the only red-belt awarded by Carlson. I received it from his hands when I was only 40. Most people are given the Grandmaster belt as an honorary achievement. Not me, I received mine for being a fighter. When [Alvaro] Mansur complained that I was too young, Carlson told him to line up his best guys to fight me and put the belt to the test. Carlson received no reply. That settled the matter.

13- Any memorable stories about Carlson?

I got one for you. There is a good friend of mine called Sergio Bufara that I met on this occasion through Carlson. Carlson once came

---

[113] Worthy of note here, is that when Carlson defeated Passarito in 1954, the fight was scheduled for 3 rounds of 30 minutes each. With no winner (and after much arguing), the fight was extended 2 more rounds of 30 minutes each. At which point the referee decided Passarito could not continue and Carlson was named the victor. In between the fighting and the arguing, the fight lasted just under 4 hours. Long story short, lenghty fights were common in those days. Sources: Pedreira 2015b, pg. 116-119; Serrano 2014, pg. 354; and Revista da Semana ed. 23.

to me and said, "Rosado, I am spending the weekend at a friend's ranch, it's a really nice place in Teresópolis, his name is Sergio, do you want to come with me?". *I said, sure, why not. So, Carlson gave me the address and on the day we agreed to meet there I showed up and rang the doorbell and introduced myself as Carlson's student, so Sergio invited me in but Carlson wasn't there. Can you believe that Carlson never showed up? I ended up spending the whole weekend at the house of a complete stranger because Carlson never showed up! We ended up telling stories about Carlson the whole time* [laughs] *that was Carlson for you.*

(continues in Part 3)

Grandmaster Fernando "Pinduka"

Carlson stands next to Fernando Pinduka shortly
before his fight against Marco Ruas in 1984.
Photocred: Pinduka personal archives.

*"Carlson gradually became aware that he needed to make a method-
ology and a training program of his own to be alone and follow his
path within jiu-jitsu outside of Hélio's control. Carlson's methodology
was very different, he advocated a high intensity training in relation to
the duration of the matches in competition. He would often say that "if
you want to be a lion, then you need to train with lions..." Training sessions were long and physical conditioning was acquired through hard
practice."*

Grandmaster Fernando Pinduka

"Pinduka" is one of the oldest members alive from the *second-wave*.
Chosen to represent jiu-jitsu in the 1984 *vale-tudo* challenge of jiu-jitsu
vs. various other arts, his confrontation with Marco Ruas has become
legendary. Pinduka was born in 1953 and was promoted to black-belt
by Carlson Gracie. Today he holds a 9th degree red-belt and still actively

teaches classes in Copacabana, Rio de Janeiro. This interview took place in writing on May 19, 2022.

1- Who are you and can you tell us a little about your story in jiu-jitsu?

My name is Fernando de Melo Guimarães, but in the fighting world I am known as Fernando Pinduka, I started in jiu-jitsu in 1966, at the age of 12 at the academy of Professor Hélio Vigio, who was from the first generation of students under Grandmaster Hélio Gracie. I spent two years at Hélio Vígio's academy, from 12 to 14 years old. In 1968 professor Vígio joined the civil police and was soon promoted to police chief and as a result his presence at the academy decreased a lot and he began giving to his assistants the responsibility for teaching classes. Seeing in me a promising student with an advanced technique for my age, he suggested to my father that he take me to Professor Carlson Gracie so that from now on I could have classes with him. Vígio referred me to Carlson, that's how I arrived at his gym. But it wasn't at Figueiredo Magalhães yet, it was at Av. Copacabana 583, on the third floor at the back, in a small room. In 1976 he invited me to be his assistant where I learned how to teach. In 1978 I was awarded a black-belt and continued as an assistant until 1982, the year of Rolls' death. In my opinion, that was the golden age of jiu-jitsu.

2- What was your relationship with Carlson like?

As I said before, I met Carlson in 1968, starting as his student when I was only 14. I trained under him for 20 years, from 1968 to 1988. In 1985 [the fight was in November 1984, so Pinduka is describing an event either late 1984 or early 1985] *right after the vale-tudo that I fought defending jiu-jitsu in the challenge against luta-livre, we went out for lunch and I asked Carlson permission to put some mats in my gym room, where I taught weight lifting classes daily.*

He gave me permission but with the condition that I would not stop going to his gym, so I had to keep my word. From 1992 onward, we talked again and I made him understand that I didn't have time to go to his gym as my daily commitments multiplied with gym classes, weight training, jiu-jitsu at my own gym plus the time allotted to my newborn son. So, I started to visit the gym and train sporadically until 1999, soon after he decided to go to the United States for good and we only saw each other a few times after that, whenever he came to Brazil. Carlson was a sensational person, devoid of any self-interest. When he liked someone, he really liked the person, but when he didn't, there was no one that could change his mind about it. I consider Carlson a second father.

3- At some point in jiu-jitsu history, Helio and Carlson became rivals. How did that happen?

With the sporting success of Carlson's academy in the jiu-jitsu competitive world forming countless champions. This stirred the spirits of Hélio and Rolls in the competitive sphere, as there was a very disputed eliminatory rounds between the students of those three in order to select the representatives for the Gracie academy in competitions. As Carlson's students became more successful, occupying more spots to represent the Gracie academy, a great rivalry began between the three, to the point that they all went their own way and began to compete against one another, each one having their own team. Thus began the sporting rivalry between Hélio and Carlson, where Hélio seemed convinced that Carlson taught his students just to beat his own family.

4- What was Carlson's methodology like?

Carlson gradually became aware that he needed to make a methodology and a training program of his own to be alone and follow his path within jiu-jitsu outside of Hélio's control. Carlson's meth-odology was very different, he advocated a high intensity training in relation to the duration of the matches in competition. He would often say that "if you want to be a lion, then you need to train with lions..." Training sessions were long and physical conditioning was acquired through hard practice. But we loved that place, you could stay at the gym all day if you wanted and there was a great exchange of positions between the students who helped each other a lot, the whole team was all very united. We were all very close.

5-   Did Carlson teach self-defense? And what was it like?

Self-defense has always been the basis of jiu-jitsu. Then with the creation of the [Guanabara] federation, came the medals, diplo-mas, the glamor of being champion and the vanity of the recogni-tion of victory made training for championships and tournaments overcome interest in self-defense. I recall that in jiu-jitsu, before the emergence of federations, the classes were directed toward self-de-fense with the aim of defending yourself on the street. I had many classes with Carlson, because I was prepared to be his assistant. And classes for beginner students at the white and blue-belt lev-els were about learning how to throw punches and kicks, ground fighting, traumatic blows, all within the self-defense program. The Gracie Academy's program was an original program with pre-de-termined techniques, while Carlson's program presented similar techniques to Hélio's program, but added many variations in rela-tion to possible attack and defense reactions during the confronta-tion, which generated a greater number of positions, differentiat-ing our program. His study and creation of new combinations of movements both in jiu-jitsu and in self-defense made him a differ-ent kind of teacher, with a closer look at each individual student in order to organize a specific game exploring the characteristics of each one of them.

6-   Which one was the most dominant team then?

The Carlson Gracie team was the most victorious team in the history of jiu-jitsu, without a doubt. In the overall point count placement of the academies, the first place was always Carlson's. In all belts and categories there was a Carlson student on the podium. Carlson formed an army of great fighters who shone in jiu-jitsu championships as well as in combats behind closed doors, when fighters from other academies visited the academy to test their knowledge. They were usually defeated and many would join the academy and become students, recognizing the superiority of the principles adopted by Carlson Gracie.

7-   Any memorable stories of Carlson?

I have great memories in life with Carlson Gracie. I will describe an episode that was unforgettable and had people talking about it for a long time, "the day Carlson expelled Fernando Pinduka." In addition to being a jiu-jitsu athlete, I was also a soccer player in parallel with my training. I played beach-soccer for many years and Carlson loved soccer, but he lacked the skill for the game, so he decided to become a soccer referee instead, so he took a refereeing course and became a professional soccer referee. To gain experience with the whistle, he joined the Carioca Beach Sports Federation, which organized beach-soccer championships. It was a very organized championship and with a lot of seriousness from its leaders who demanded to follow the same norms of professional federations. The games were held on the sands of the beaches of Copacabana, Ipanema and Leblon with more than twenty teams that had their own colored shirts and demarcated fields, all representing their neighborhoods and their streets of origin. One day, Carlson Gracie had been selected to referee an important semi-final match between Juventus Copacabana vs. Colúmbia do Leblon.

I was the Juventus defense player and this game was marked by a great rivalry between the two clubs and by rough plays by both sides. At some point in the game, I was unfairly hit and retaliated with an elbow and injured my opponent. Which I understood as a response to a previous aggression, but Carlson didn't call a fault against me and only considered my retaliation. I was kicked off the field alone and the guy from the other team stayed in the game. But we still won the game anyway. The day after, when I arrived at the gym to train, Carlson was overjoyed at having kicked me out of the game and told everyone about his great achievement. That day there was practically no training, just the review of the game and Carlson spent the whole week making fun of me over that episode... that was Carlson for you. A great human being. Miss you coach.

Grandmaster Arthur Virgilio

Arthur Virgilio, on the right, before a match.
Photocred: Arthur Virgilio personal archives.

"As for Rolls, you need to remember that at the Gracie Academy there wasn't much live-sparring, lots of private lessons. Whereas Carlson opened a gym with lots of live-sparring, and this made a big differ-ence. Over time, we understand that the larger the mass, the greater the quality of the result and Carlson did this for jiu-jitsu."

Grandmaster Arthur Virgílio

Arthur Virgilio is a former mayor of the capital of the Amazon state, Manaus. He served as a federal congressman for that state from 1995 to 2002 and senator from 2003 to 2010. Then again, as mayor of Manaus from 2013 to 2020 and also worked in the office of former President

Fernando Henrique Cardoso. He is a 9th degree red-belt and one of Carlson Gracie's oldest students alive. He was also in Carlson's corner next to Rolls for the last fight of Carlson's career against Waldemar Santana in December 1970. Our interview took place over the phone on November 8th, 2022.

1-   Can you tell us about your beginnings in jiu-jitsu?

I began around 1959 with Haroldo Brito who taught judo but had also been a student of Helio's so he also taught jiu-jitsu, even though I didn't know we were doing jiu-jitsu, they just called it ne-waza then. I trained with Oswaldo Alves there who was a student of Brito. By 1962, I was training with Reyson Gracie. After, around 1965 or 1966 I began training with Carlson.

2-   Despite being a student of Carlson's, you were also good friends with Rolls. How much do you think Carlson's views influenced him?

A lot. They were similar in some ways. Both were brave, both modest, humble by nature. But I think Carlson helped Rolls a lot and I'd say that Rolls over time was developing an even more refined technique than Carlson's. Because Carlson's jiu-jitsu didn't require much for you to win, it was to the point and simple, everything he taught you was meant to work. That and because when Carlson was in your corner he was very energizing, he'd say something like "get up!" and the person would hear Carlson's commanding voice and find a way to get up. It was truly something remarkable to watch. As for Rolls, you need to remember that at the Gracie Academy there wasn't much live-sparring, lots of private lessons. Whereas Carlson opened a gym with lots of live-sparring, and this made a big difference. Over time, we understand that the larger the mass, the greater the quality of the result and Carlson did this for jiu-jitsu.

3- How did practitioners see jiu-jitsu in those days?

To us, jiu-jitsu was like a cult [seita]. I didn't know this at the time, but I liked jiu-jitsu because it made me feel privileged, special in a way. Other people didn't get it, but to us, it really was like a cult.

Grandmaster Orlando Saraiva

Saraiva referees a match in a gi at a
tournament he organized, coached and
fought in. Photocred: Saraiva
personal archives.

*"Just to give you an idea, all of the Gracies who weren't Hélio's chil-
dren would go train with Carlson. Years later, Hélio's guys ended up
going to train under Rolls, who picked up this competitive approach
to jiu-jitsu from Carlson. It's impossible not to associate the history of
Rolls with Carlson's own history, but everyone tries to hide this because
many of the family members are resentful toward Carlson."*

Grandmaster Orlando Saraiva

Orlando Saraiva was an orphan who found jiu-jitsu inside the government institution where he spent much of his youth. It was there he
met one of Carlson's friends and student Master Osvaldo Paquetá.[114]

---

[114] The late Paquetá was one of Carlson's oldest black-belts and became known by a younger
generation of jiu-jitsu practitioners as the videographer who played the leading role in
recording jiu-jitsu events in the 80s, 90s and early 2000s in Brazil.

Later, Saraiva trained and taught under Carlson as well.[115] After moving to São Paulo, Saraiva alongside Otávio de Almeida and Oswaldo Carnivalle became one of the fathers of jiu-jitsu in that state. While jiu-jitsu was little known in Rio in the 70s and 80s, it was even less known in São Paulo during that same period. Despite this anonymity, Saraiva played a crucial role in staying the course, teaching, and organizing jiu-jitsu events in the countryside and by doing so helping supply the demand of jiu-jitsu instructors of the post-Royce era. His efforts in developing jiu-jitsu in São Paulo during the quieter years of jiu-jitsu helped set the foundation for its rapid worldwide growth from the mid-90s onward. Saraiva was born in 1951, he is a 9th degree red-belt and no longer teaches classes. The interview took place in writing via his son, Henrique, on August 17th 2022.

1- You began training at the FUNABEM as a child, how did you end up there and what was your routine like?[116] And how did jiu-jitsu help you get along with other young people there?

I lost my father when I was about 2 or 3 years old and my mother when I was 7. We used to live in the favela of Jacarézinho (Rio de Janeiro). But when my mother died, I went to live with my sister who was married and after a while she got divorced and had to put me in a government program, because she was very young and had no financial conditions to raise me and work at

---

[115] Saraiva is humble and does not like to talk about this, but Paquetá describes the time where Carlson took Saraiva to train at the original Gracie Academy: *"Carlson spoke so much about my students that Helio one day said:* 'bring over Paqueta's students,' *so I took them. So, they put* 'Rolliszinho' [Rolls] *against Orlando Saraiva and when he blinked, Orlando tapped him. Helio was livid and called Rolliszinho inside and ordered that the training continue. An hour later Helio came back with Rolliszinho and asked to put them against each other again, but Orlando was already tired, which doesn't take Rolliszinho's credit from him, who took a little longer to do it, but he beat Orlando, so they ended in a draw."* Source: Tatame Magazine December, 2009.

[116] FUNABEM stood for *"Fundação Nacional do Bem-Estar do Menor"* (National Foundation for the Wellbeing of Minors) and replaced SAM (Service for Assisting Minors) in 1964. They were both government programs to give shelter to homeless, abandoned and orphan children in Brazil.

the same time. I arrived at FUNABEM when I was 10 years old and knew nothing about any martial art. One day, I was walking by the room where Paquetá taught, and heard a noise and thought it was a fight, so I went there to see what was going on and ended up finding it interesting and asking to try out a class. In those days I was always getting into fights and I thought I was good at it and would beat everyone in class... but when I started training there under Master Paquetá, I discovered that I didn't know anything. Jiu-jitsu taught me to be calmer and after I began training I didn't get involved in fights anymore. Jiu-jitsu really changed my life.

2-   Master Osvaldo Paquetá is famous in the jiu-jitsu world for his footage, archives and historical videos on the edge of the mat. What about the Paquetá that you knew personally, what was he like when you met him at FUNABEM?

Paquetá had a father-son relationship with his students. I also lived with him whenever I ran away from the FUNABEM and spent weekends at his house, then I would come back and he would arrange things and cool everyone down so I wouldn't be punished by anyone. Another funny story was that FUNABEM was divided into wings, and had a part of juvenile offenders, who were caught on the street committing crimes and lied about their age as they did not have any papers or documents, so they ended up there in FUNABEM with other real minors. Paquetá liked to take us there and some big guys would arrive who had just been arrested and he would say: "Hey champ, I'll give you a choice, choose one of the boys here, if you win, I'll let you go..." and they'd always chose me because I was the smallest one but these guys would always take the biggest beatings... and Paquetá and Waltinho Guimarães would just laugh at them.

3-   In the early 60s, you and Rolls trained under Carlson. What were those sessions like?

Those training sessions were like championships. Paquetá told us to play hard. The first time I trained at the Gracie Academy I was a green-belt and trained with Rolls but I didn't know who he was. I ended up doing well against him and Carlson invited me to go train in Copacabana under him. I trained with Carlson from approximately 1967 to 1976 when I moved to São Paulo. But me and Rolls only really started training together as black-belts, when he also started training under Carlson. He was a very nice guy and at the time he was already being prepared to be the new champion of the Gracie family, as Carlson had already retired. But he wasn't yet the legend that he would later become. What I always see in interviews nowadays is that people try to take the shine off Carlson and place it on Rolls. But all of us from the old days know that Rolls went over to train under Carlson after losing to Cícero Sobrinho (Barradas student) and Carlson called him over and said: "If you spend your whole day training self-defense with Uncle Hélio, you will never be good at jiu-jitsu!" And Rolls started to visit Carlson more often, and eventually he ended up becoming a direct student of Carlson. Later they became partners and he became a legend in his own right. But when he got there he noticed the level of the students there: Serginho de Niterói, Carley Gracie, Rocian Gracie, Walter Guimarães, Reyson Gracie, Arthur Virgilio, among others... There were a lot of good people on those mats training under Carlson... it was a climate of great competition and a brotherhood at the same time.

4-   How important do you think Carlson was for the development of competitive jiu-jitsu?

Just to give you an idea, all of the Gracies who weren't Hélio's children would go train with Carlson. Years later, Hélio's guys ended up going to train under Rolls, who picked up this competitive approach to jiu-jitsu from Carlson. It's impossible not to associate the history of Rolls with Carlson's own history, but everyone tries to hide this because many of the family members are resentful toward Carlson. Carlson was certainly the greatest and the facts are there for those who want to see them, both Carlinhos and Jacaré's [Romero Cavalcanti] students and most competition teams in jiu-jitsu history are associated with Carlson in one way or another, even Hélio's sons learned indirectly from Carlson's jiu-jitsu.

5- What was it like to arrive in São Paulo at a time when jiu-jitsu was only breaking new ground there? Being the most experienced fighter in the region must be good, but practicing an unknown art must also bring its problems. How was that phase of your life helping the spread of jiu-jitsu in São Paulo?

When I left the Air Force, Paquetá had me replace him at FUNABEM as a jiu-jitsu teacher as he had risen in position. But in 1976 I was transferred to São Paulo, the capital and then to Mogi Mirim in the country-side. When I arrived in São Paulo, Carlson had referred me to Master Pedro Hemetério who I trained under for a while and then I met Mestre Otávio de Almeida who was starting to organize events in São Paulo and we became very good friends. I taught at his Academy and we worked hard to make jiu-jitsu grow in the state with events that didn't have any support from anyone. I remember that the first Campeonato Paulista in 1976 was held with 34 athletes. We had no physical structure, financial support and no qualified people. I organized, fought, refereed, coached my students... doing all those things in the same day. And I remember that in 1978 or 1979 I brought Carlson over for an event. I started this exchange between São Paulo and Rio, taking my students to fight in Rio and inviting people to come over and train with us. In

1979, Rolls brought people from Rio to fight at an event in Novo Horizonte, which Nahum [Rabay] organized. I remember when Master Moisés Muradi who, was my student, fought against Royler Gracie in one of these events.[117] Many members of the Gracie family came over to compete, Rolls was there too. In 1981 I started to do an event called "Copa do Sol" (Sun Cup) and people from Oriente [team from Niterói in Rio] came to participate. People from the Gracie family and even Carlinhos in an interview mentioned these events we were organizing at a time when jiu-jitsu had almost no events at all.[118] Only some in Minas Gerais, São Paulo and one or two in Rio.

When Mestre Otavio passed away, I continued organizing them in São Paulo's countryside and Moisés Muradi started organizing them in 1989 in the capital. In 1994 I organized a Circuito Paulista here in São Paulo where Royler came to fight, Saulo Ribeiro was a purple-belt, Fabio Gurgel too. And we had 600 athletes, which was a lot at the time. Then I set up a league in 1996 and did it until 2005 or 2006, where we had several elite athletes that emerged from these events. Many of whom became big names in jiu-jitsu today.[119] I organized referee courses and many events, because my vision was always similar to Carlson's in that the athletes had to compete in a lot of events to get their competition rhythm going, so I'd organized them and put people to fight as much as possible. I

---

[117] Master Moisés Muradi is the current President of the Confederação Brasileira de Jiu-jitsu Esportivo (CBJJE) in Brazil.

[118] The interview where Carlos Gracie Jr. talks about traveling to compete in a tournament organized by Orlando Saraiva can be read here: https://www.graciemag.com/pt-br/carlos-gracie-jr-faz-o-balanco-de-18-anos-de-mundiais-de-jiu-jitsu/

[119] The author himself has competed in many of the tournaments organized by Saraiva in the interior of São Paulo as well as in tournaments organized by his many black-belts in the region. A short list of known competitors that competed regularly in Saraiva's tournaments were: André Galvão, Bruno Frazzato, Demian Maia, Gilbert "Durinho" Burns, Givanildo Santana, Gustavo Falcirolli, Leandro Lo, Luis Theodoro "Big Mac," Marcelo Garcia, Marcus Buchecha, Michelle Nicolini, Mendes and Miyao Brothers, Paulo Streckert, Reinaldo Ribeiro, Thiago Stefanutti and many others.

held events until 2018 and today due to health reasons I am retired, but my students continue to do so. Today I am very happy to see the level that jiu-jitsu in São Paulo has reached, both in terms of its athletes and the organizations here. Happy to have played a part in this growth.

6-   What makes jiu-jitsu so universal, to the point of changing the lives of so many people?

I believe that the cultural factor influences its popularity a lot. The happy and spontaneous way of Brazilians, together with the most efficient art in the world, created this superpower that is Brazilian jiu-jitsu today. Jiu-jitsu has great value and with this profession-alization of events and improved teaching methodologies, I'm sure it will be the most practiced martial art in the world soon, if it isn't already.

7-   What is the one lesson from Carlson that you never forgot?

Carlson taught us to be humble and at the same time aggressive and fearless and this I always passed on to my students, who must take this lesson for life. We shook hands and the fight started. We had to do our best, even if you lost, you had to show heart. He argued a lot with opponents at tournaments, always fighting for his students, but always ended up shaking hands and respecting all his opponents at the end, regardless of results. Carlson's jiu-jitsu was the most efficient because we trained to compete and win, gi or no-gi, with time limits or without them, jiu-jitsu or vale-tudo and we were always training hard and ready for competi-tion. Not to mention giving opportunities to people like me who didn't have the money to pay for a gym membership. He also stim-ulated competition, which today is the flagship of jiu-jitsu's growth worldwide.

8-   What are your overall thoughts on jiu-jitsu today?

I learned jiu-jitsu as a fighting style, even though the rules have been improved a lot, it turned into a sport and became more accessible to everyone, we can't let the fighting side die, the competition... otherwise we'll become little more than Yoga in a gi. This view of jiu-jitsu as a business, and everyone thinking only of making money and making jiu-jitsu for everyone really changed jiu-jitsu a lot. In some ways for the better, in others not so much.

Master Otávio Peixotinho

Carlson awards a belated black-belt certificate to
Peixotinho in 1995 that was arranged by Rosado. Peixotinho
was originally awarded his black-belt in 1983.
Photocred: Otávio Peixotinho personal archives.

*"Carlson never cared about contracts or money, all he wanted was for
people to represent him, that's it. He just wanted people to say* "coach, I
don't care about anything, I just want to represent you and for you to be
proud of me." *That's all he wanted, he was* 'raiz' *to the fullest."*

Master Otávio Peixotinho

Originally a student of Rolls and later Carlson, Peixotinho is one of the
most iconic and known practitioners belonging to the *second-wave*. He
was also one of the most active competitors during the 80s and fought
against Rickson, Royler, Rilion, Mauricio Gomes and many others.
He is still actively training in Rio and holds an 8th degree coral-belt.
Peixotinho was born on June the 4th, 1959 and our interview took place
over the phone.

1- Tell us a little bit about your beginning in jiu-jitsu and what was it like training in those days.

I started jiu-jitsu because I didn't want to get beat up on the streets. That is all I can tell you [laughs]. I wanted to learn how to fight and kick-ass. Once at the beach, some kids took my swim trunks off me and ran away with them. I had to go home naked... I was so angry I told myself I would get them all back. That led me to jiu-jitsu. I first started with Rolls Gracie in 1974. My Uncle was man-ager to Ivan Gomes who was partners with Carlson in a gym. Even though he trained with Ivan and Carlson, he recommended I start my training with Rolls. There was a lot of self-defense training then, but it wasn't for sports, it was for "porrada," there were no rules there, get it? Sometimes, the older and more experienced guys would train "taparia" style. Later I started training with Carlson's students. Because in those days, they were in the same academy... There was some rivalry of course, but it was of the healthy kind. In 1976 I went to Carlson, because overall, I thought Carlson's game was more efficient. Carlson had more experience as a master and in training casca-grossas.

2- What were Carlson's classes like?

In my days, he didn't show too many moves or any specific meth-odology. He would sometimes have others show the move and then come over later to correct them, but it was all in the moment. He paid a lot of attention to the white-belts. He would look at the stu-dent and place the emphasis on his potential strengths. What is the use of teaching a triangle choke to a guy with short legs like me? Carlson really had a vision for a true jiu-jitsu, a jiu-jitsu that would work everywhere, not just in the gym. It was a style very oriented toward porrada. He taught us the guard to prevent us from getting hit in case we got taken down. Sometimes, he'd have one of us wear boxing gloves and the other had to clinch and take the first one down. Other times, we would try to hit each other in the face from inside the guard.

3- What was Carlson like as a person?

He was after building champions, he wanted tough-guys, cas-ca-grossas, he wasn't so interested in the money issue. Maybe at the end he regretted this when he got into a fight with the guys from BTT because, truth be told, he never cared about money. Carlson never cared about contracts or money, all he wanted was for people to represent him, that's it. He just wanted people to say "coach, I don't care about anything, I just want to represent you and for you to be proud of me." *That's all he wanted, he was "raiz"* [literally "roots," but meant to describe someone truthful and real in an old-school way] *to the fullest. He was all about the truth and being real. After a while, he didn't even charge me to train anymore. He wanted to train champions... That and wanting his guys to beat the students from the Gracie Academy* [laughs]. *He was such a human person though, he treated everyone equally man, always helping out, paying for people's food all the time, such a big heart.*

4- What about the kimono in *vale-tudo*? How did Carlson feel about it?

Carlson didn't want people fighting [vale-tudo] *in the kimono because he didn't want them to give the opponent any advantage. Look at Royce, he gave his opponents an advantage* [by wearing a kimono] *and look at what happened once he started fighting tougher guys? Carlson had a total of 19 vale-tudo's. He had experience in fighting and he taught mostly with the kimono. But for the pros, he told us to take off our jackets. But some of us didn't want to take our jackets off for fear of getting some skin disease, those mats were always so filthy, it was old-school there* [laughs].

5- What was the vision they had of jiu-jitsu in those days? Carlson's students turned out to be great *vale-tudo* fighters. Why is that? Did he look at jiu-jitsu differently?

Look, in 1993 and 1994 there was that boom, right? Carlson's students took advantage that they were next to a legend in terms of "porrada." But vale-tudo was persecuted and mostly banned, so they all went back to competitive jiu-jitsu. In 1991, there was that challenge with luta-livre and Carlson prepared them for porrada, and they won everything, even Fabio Gurgel went there to learn and prepare [Fabio was a student of Romero "Jacaré" Cavalcanti, not Carlson]*, because everyone knew Carlson was a bad-ass in* "porrada."[120]

6- What was the competition scene like in those days?

I'll tell you a story. Up to 1981, I represented the Gracie Academy. I actually trained at the academy at the Figueiredo de Magalhães Academy that in competition represented the Gracie Academy alongside the other Gracie Academies. In 1981, the rivalry was at its height. In those days, there was an eliminatory tournament we did from 1975 till 1981. I had to fight many of Rolls and Helio's students to find out who would represent the Gracie Academy against the other non-Gracie gyms. In the 74, 75, 76 the tournaments were at the Mello Tenis Club in the suburbs. Later we had Copa Company in the south-zone which is much nicer. We were basically moving jiu-jitsu up socially I'd say.

---

[120] The *"Desafio Jiu-Jitsu contra Luta-Livre"* that took place in 1991 was a challenge between the representatives of these two rival arts as they both fought for the prize of being the most dominant style in Rio.

7- When did Carlson begin representing his own team the "Clube Carlson Gracie de Jiu-Jitsu"?

In 1981, I remember well because I have a diploma from that year where you can read "Clube Carlson Gracie de Jiu-jitsu" on it. That was when we were competing for the first time against the Gracie Academy. From that point onward, we didn't compete against each other in the in-house trials anymore, only officially at the tournaments.

8- What were the rivalries like between Carlson and Rolls? Helio and Carlson weren't close. It was clear that they had a rivalry between them. Where did it come from?

Carlson and Rolls were very competitive during their student's matches, each wanted their students to win, but it wasn't too serious. They would just make fun and tease the other one in case their guy won. As for Helio and Carlson, well, that was a bit more serious, more aggressive. It's hard to say, but I think that whole story with Waldemar Santana messed with egos. Because that whole thing about who is the family's "number one" has a very important value to them, get it? I think Helio might have changed after he had his own kids. For a long time Helio was like the super dad to everyone because his brother [Carlos] was going around having babies with so many women. Helio came in and gave emotional support to them so that Carlos' children didn't suffer, but I don't think it was enough. Helio went as far as saying that the only real black-belts out there were his own kids! Are you going to tell me that Bustamante, Zé Mario, Libório and so many others out there don't deserve a black-belt? Is that it? That these guys don't know jiu-jitsu? Only his kids knew real Gracie jiu-jitsu? C'mon. The truth of the matter is that Helio never had any love for Carlson. Helio never even said hello to me [laughs] except one time where I beat everyone as a purple-belt and he looked over to me and said, "this kid is going to be good." Never spoke to me afterwards. Floresta said it best once, "Peixotinho, Carlson guys have no value to Helio." And I'm a cool guy, I talk to everyone. It was a big rivalry between Carlson and Helio, it was all emblematic of who was the "number one" in the family.[121]

9- How did Carlson feel when Royce Gracie lost to his student Wallid Ismail in 1998?

Everyone saw Carlson's reaction. First thing he did was to check on Royce after the fight to make sure he was ok. Afterwards he kept saying "it all stays home" [ta tudo em casa]. But at the same time, he loved it when his students won. Carlson didn't want war with everyone, but with Helio he had a personal war. It normally didn't affect the students, but sometimes it did. But between them, there was a strong rivalry.

10- Were Carlos and Helio hard on Carlson when he was fighting?

Hard? Once Carlson told me that they had a guy follow him around all day so he couldn't masturbate before the fight [laughs]. They had a guy guarding him all day to stop him from jerking off! [laughs].[122]

---

[121] On a side note, the responsibility for being the family's "number one," had the upside of framing the entire narrative around this new "alpha." I have no doubt that such a support network boosted the alpha's confidence in himself. More than that, I can also imagine the intimidation factor of having to square up against the baton holder of the tradition being equally real. An intimidation that must have been shared by referee. Particularly in the days where refereeing was not only more biased than it is today, but also where being biased was acceptable. And perhaps even expected in some cases.
A competitive environment such as this one, we should note in passing, had its pros and cons as we will see ahead.

[122] Despite being unfounded, it is a widely held belief in the fight world that withholding ejaculation before a fight increases the fighter's natural aggression and grants him extra strength in the fight.

11- You have been a critic of jiu-jitsu losing its martial side over the years and becoming increasingly sport oriented. When do you think that began?

When CBJJ was founded and then later when it went to the US. Others tried to organize other rules but CBJJ had so much credibility. The rules got in the way because they forbade too many things like foot-locks and heel-hooks. In my days you could body-slam. A fighter needs to know how to defend these things, jiu-jitsu is about self-defense and fighting porra! The whole thing became too soft in my opinion. And these guys want to get into the Olympics? What Olympics man? Forget that. Every fighting style has its own essence, Kano wanted "the way," the polite, the Olympic, you see... But that's not us.

12- For many years, *vale-tudo* was frowned upon and banned in Brazil, especially in the 80s where you couldn't even organize an event. But in the 90s it made a comeback. How did Carlson prepare his guys then? He seemed to have a very top oriented approach to jiu-jitsu.

Man, try to pass DelaRiva's guard in those days, or Murilo Bustamante's, Cassio Cardoso, or Allan Goes. Go try my friend. Have you seen Bustamante's guard? It was geared toward "porrada." But yes, he prioritized staying on top. But remember, in those days, you could up kick your opponent from the bottom, from guard. Today you can't do that if the opponent is on his knees and that changes everything you know... So many good guys there. Carlson knew a lot in kimono and without it. Carlson's style was perfectly adaptable for a fight. His jiu-jitsu was very fight oriented, get it?

In other words, Carlson's jiu-jitsu worked well with a kimono, without one or in a vale-tudo. Watch Paulo Filho, that's a great way to understand Carlson's game.

13- We have to admit that the CBJJ/IBJJF are doing an incredible job organizing and giving structure to jiu-jitsu around the world. In my opinion, their bigger tournaments look like the Olympics. What are your thoughts on this?

They give the fighters so much prestige. A guy wins a big CBJJ tournament and goes around the world teaching seminars. The World Championships are so big today, truly, Carlinhos needs to be congratulated, such a good businessman and visionary. But at the same time, I'm just not that interested anymore. I miss vale-tudo and the confere.

14- Why do you think jiu-jitsu is not as well represented in MMA as it used to be?

Easy, people don't teach self-defense like we used to train it, they don't teach the student how to fight anymore. They only train in the kimono and then want to fight? That way they can only lose. Although today it would be impossible to teach jiu-jitsu in the US like in the old-days, they'd deport me straight away [laughs].

15- Because both the students of Carlinhos and "Jacaré" became excellent competitors and very competition oriented, I wondered if because they had Rolls in common as a teacher that this was due to Rolls having a more specific competition-oriented view than Carlson for example.

Rolls dojo-stormed man. He liked to fight. Rolls would never let any of this happen, I'm telling you. He would not let this happen, he was like a pitbull, I'm telling you.

16- How much did Carlson influence Rolls?

Carlson helped him a lot. I think Carlson made Rolls more aggressive. Man, have you seen that picture of them training taparia?

Imagine, Carlson and Rolls exchanging blows! Carlson had 19 vale-tudo fights, Rolls had one against a karate guy in 74 or 75, I was actually there, I had just started training. And you are going to tell me that Carlson didn't teach him anything? Come on... But it's hard to say how much he actually influenced him, I started training in 1974. By 1970 Carlson was already retired. So, I saw only Rolls compete and it was something truly incredible to watch, good at everything, judo, wrestling. So talented. He tapped everyone with everything, wrist-lock, foot-lock, chokes, everything. Such a tragedy that his time was up so soon...

17- You knew Rolls well, what are your thoughts on him?

Rolls was the link that united them all, get it? Both sides of the family drank from the fountain of his knowledge. He was so respected, that when he showed moves, even Carlos and Helio were quiet in the room. Rolls was the only person with the power to unite the family, because he was the only person everyone both loved and respected. He is the lost link.

Master Romero Cavalcanti

**Romero "Jacaré" Cavalcanti at the original "Master"
gym in Ipanema. Later rebranded as "Alliance."
Photocred: Romero Cavalcanti personal archives.**

*"Each one had his own way of teaching, three very different ways. Rolls
preferred us starting on our feet more often, while Carlson was more
ground-oriented with emphasis on takedowns when they got closer to
competitions. As for Master Hélio in downtown, he was more about
private classes and self-defense with little focus on competition."*

Master Romero Cavalcanti

Romero Cavalcanti or *"Jacaré"* (alligator) as he is more commonly
known in the jiu-jitsu world was a direct student of Rolls, one of the
few to actually receive a black-belt from his hands and is one of jiu-jitsu's most influential leaders. After Rolls' death, he would open his own
gym in Ipanema and call it "Master Jiu-jitsu." Eventually rebranding it
"Alliance." The team he founded would become one of the most successful jiu-jitsu teams in history. He was born on October 22nd 1952 and lives
in Jurerê, Brazil and still actively teaches seminars. "Jacaré" is an 8th
degree coral-belt and our interview took place over multiple audio files.

1- Master, tell us a little about your first steps in jiu-jitsu?

I started when I was 12 years old or so with Jaildo Gomes, brother of Ivan Gomes, famous fighter from Paraíba, who taught classes in Copacabana. Eventually I made it to yellow-belt under him. The classes were already very busy and there was always atemi [strikes] at the end, which were basically a simulation of a real-fight but with no punches, just open hand slaps.

2- We know that there wasn't that much going on in Brazil in terms of jiu-jitsu in the 70s and 80s, at least compared to what would go on later in the 90s. In other words, there weren't many practitioners in those days but the ones who trained were die-hards. What was jiu-jitsu like in those days? Tell us a little bit more about it.

I disagree with you a little. It is true that in the 90s we had our first national tournament, but in the 70s we had jiu-jitsu tournaments we competed in as far as São Paulo. The tournaments were good, but the black-belts there had the level of our blue-belts in Rio. Once we had a big group organized by Robson Gracie and we stayed at Pedro Hemetério's gym and practically invaded their local tournament. And we forced them at the time to organize some super-fights between Rio and São Paulo on the spot.[123] We won most of the fights but at the end a big brawl broke out and we got into the bus and drove back to Rio.

But in the 70s in Rio, there were other tournaments in the suburbs too, but I agree that the 90s had many more competitors and events. I just don't think that the 70s were that quiet. We had tournaments at the Mello Tenis Clube, at Tijuca, Montanha, in the Olímpico and Monte Líbano. The tournaments were warming up after the Guanabara Federation started. Just to give you an idea, the south-zone had: Carlson, Rolls, Álvaro Barreto, João Alberto

---

[123] Marcial Serrano confirmed being present at this event. See: Drysdale 2020, pg. 100-101; and Serrano 2019, pg. 353 and 363

Barreto, Oswaldo Alves, Tarciso. In the suburbs we had Mansur, there was the Oriente academy in Niterói, we had Munir, Fadda and other gyms in the suburbs. In the 80s things took a bit of a dive after Rolls' death. But in the 90s it blew up. But in general, things were still small in Rio. We had about 2 tournaments per year. Maybe 3. It was a great time for jiu-jitsu though.

3- *Vale-tudo* was mostly banned in those years for being too brutal. It was very hard to get a license to organize an event. Rolls was born during that era. He never had a chance to shine in *vale-tudo*. Maybe things would have been different had he been alive or in his prime in the 90s. Do you think he would have gone the *vale-tudo* route had he had the chance?

I remember that as a child in the 60s there were crowds of people trying to enter the Tupy TV station to watch the vale-tudo fights. It was madness. In those days you could still watch these fights on TV. Later it was banned and seen by society as savagery. But I am certain Rolls would have been interested, he was very open-minded and very competitive. So much so that when Rickson fought Zulu, Rolls had asked Helio to let him fight Zulu instead, but Helio wanted to test Rickson. Had he survived to live the vale-tudo era of the 90s, I have no doubt he would have been involved and had his students fight in it too.

4- Although he was a student of Grandmaster Helio during his child-hood, when Rolls became older, he began to train with Carlson. What is the level of Carlson's influence over Rolls and his jiu-jitsu?

Yes, Rolls had his father-Uncle Hélio as his teacher, but then he started to attend harder training sessions under Carlson, his older brother, who really shaped him and shaped his competitiveness. But mostly he developed by himself, because he was beyond tal-ented, very studious and intelligent, and always open to learn and absorb other styles like wrestling, judo, sambo, boxing and a lot of competition-based jiu-jitsu of course.

5- Were there major differences in terms of methodology between Carlson and Rolls? And between them and Grandmaster Helio Gracie?

Each one had its own way of teaching, three very different ways. Rolls preferred us starting on our feet more often, while Carlson was more ground-oriented with emphasis on takedowns when they got closer to competitions. As for Master Hélio downtown, he was more about private classes and self-defense with little focus on competition.

6- What percentage of Rolls' focus was on self-defense, *vale-tudo* and competitive jiu-jitsu?

The focus was well balanced, the competitions were sporadic, not like nowadays. When it came close to competition, the focus was on hard training and always starting from our feet. Self-defense classes were for executives and then there was another kind of training that wasn't really a self-defense class. For example, Carlson and Rolls would have one student wear boxing gloves and try to knock the head off the other one while the second one had to block and clinch. Or we'd take our jackets off and train taparia to prepare us for a real-fight.

7- Were Rolls' training sessions competitive and tough? What were Rolls' classes like and his overall vision of jiu-jitsu?

When Rolls first started teaching, he taught at the Gracie Academy on the Rio Branco Street and pretty much taught their self-defense system. Helio in those days taught very little so he had Rorion and Rolls teach instead. But Rolls began to seek out Carlson in order

THE RISE AND EVOLUTION OF BRAZILIAN JIU-JITSU

to improve his game and started teaching small groups, which is pretty much when I started training under them. Actually, Toninho was the one who taught classes, he was a brown-belt under Carlson. In those days, Rolls would eventually teach a little self-defense here and there and teach us how to escape a head-lock for example, but the training was almost all in group classes and aimed at competition, passing-guard, starting on our knees and we'd go to war. That is pretty much when competition jiu-jitsu really started.

8- Carlson had most of his ring experience in *vale-tudo*, perhaps not surprisingly, his best students became very successful *vale-tudo* fighters in the 90s. While two of Rolls' main students went on to become very successful competition team leaders, yourself and Carlinhos. Is this just a matter of correlation or did they differ in how they saw and trained jiu-jitsu?

Yes, I agree. You see, when Carlson left the Gracie Academy, he already had a different view of things, he taught very few self-defense privates. Carlson's academy was all about competition, same as Rolls. So much so that the in-house tournaments to decide who would represent the Gracie team in competition, it always turned out to be pretty much a dispute between Carlson and Rolls' students. That in-house tournament was harder than the actual event it was selecting us for. This is why I think it is fair to say that Carlson and Rolls were the fathers of competitive jiu-jitsu.

9- At some point in the 80s or 90s, competitive jiu-jitsu became the dominant brand of jiu-jitsu, whereas up to then it was largely split between competition and self-defense. How do you think Rolls would have seen the takeover by competitive jiu-jitsu?

Well, competitive jiu-jitsu really began with the Guanabara Federation. But in the Gracie Academy, the classes were privates targeting self-defense, with a little rolling session at the end and only with the instructor. They basically had no group classes. While Carlson in Copacabana was always teaching group classes. In his smaller room, you could fit in maybe two pairs, but Carlson would throw in four pairs taking turns in there and make it all work in the tight space, when the class in fact had 20-30 people in there, watching the others go at it. Carlson rented the small mats when he wasn't using them, and Toninho and Rolls would teach small groups. The class format was a lot of self-defense, but sort of shifting toward bigger groups of students of three to five or more who would eventually start training among themselves. Over time and as Carlson and Rolls shared the now famed Figueiredo de Magalhães academy, the classes became all group classes. In those days, I didn't see Carlson teaching much self-defense anymore. Rolls in his turn, when he had the smaller mats downstairs, he taught self-defense and trained with the students at the end. But when he had the bigger mats, he taught a group class and it was competition oriented. Carlson on Tuesday, Thursday and Saturday did the same. Sometimes Rolls would teach self-defense too, but over time it was taught less and less.

10- You became one of the founders of one of the biggest teams in the history of jiu-jitsu. How much of Rolls' methodology and vision have you transposed into your Alliance's vision and methodology? In other words, how much did Rolls influence Alliance?

Well, Rolls influenced me a lot and in a very positive way, as I stayed with him from the beginning in late 1974 until his death in 1982. So, I was able to absorb a lot and of course, later with Rickson, I was also able to mix both styles and teach my students in the same way I learned more from both of them. With my students and then teachers Fábio Gurgel and Gigi [Alexandre Paiva] we were able to create our own methodology, but Rolls was the basis of everything.

11- What is your take on what some people are now calling American jiu-jitsu?

What they are talking about is a more no-gi oriented version of jiu-jitsu. These are guys who don't throw themselves in the fire and compete in the gi, get it? To be frank, it is not clear to me what they mean by AJJ... it's all the same thing. Gi, no-gi, it is all the same thing, it's all jiu-jitsu. Take the ADCC for example, it should be called Abu-Dhabi jiu-jitsu championship, it's all the same thing! It's a lot of sensationalism in my opinion, they are trying to create a new identity as if they hadn't had their roots elsewhere. Speaking frankly, it is quite ridiculous. In truth, when we started training, it was all jiu-jitsu. No one called it Brazilian jiu-jitsu or Gracie jiu-jitsu. And had it not been for Rorion trying to have a monopoly over the name maybe none of this would have happened.

12- But in cultural terms do you think it changed? In some ways the commercialization of jiu-jitsu removes some of the authority from the coach and places it in the hands of the student, or customer. Which is typical business practice I suppose. When I started training in Brazil at least, it wasn't so commercialized, probably because there was no money to be made to begin with.

The student always has to be well taken care of. Rolls treated them like students and clients. Carlson was more like a father figure and had that sort of relationship with his guys. At the Gracie Academy, the students were all treated as customers, they even had their own towel, soap, shaving cream, tooth-paste, shampoo, etc. That process began then. Later Carlson started that creonte thing for students who weren't loyal. But the student should always be treated like a customer. Today we have a broader business vision that started with Gracie Barra and now we at Alliance are also using. The relationship should always be one of customer and business. I treat my student well because he is my client. Before, if a student left the gym, he was treated as a creonte. But over the years my view on things changed and became more commercial. Of course, it isn't only commercial, but it is a business vision that we need to have in order to survive.

Ricardo Azoury

**Rickson Gracie discusses the instructional they were
about to film with Ricardo Azoury (on the right).
Photocred: Luca Atalla personal archives.**

*"The crowd Rolls and Carlson taught was much younger, they had
less money too. Naturally it was a more competitive crowd who
got more rounds in. Man, do you have any idea what it is like to
get beat up by Maurição [Maurício Gomes] and Marcio "Macarrão"
Stambowsky? They crushed me! And I trained with them every day
[laughs], imagine putting one of those guys against those who only
did private classes?"*

Ricardo Azoury

Ricardo Azoury was not only a jiu-jitsu practitioner and close friend of
Rolls, but was also the photographer who registered through his photography many of jiu-jitsu's highlights during the *second-wave*. Most
of the pictures of Rolls that survive today (the good ones at least) were
taken by Azoury. He passed away on the 3rd of July of 2022 in a car
accident near Itaipava in Rio. I was discussing this book with him on
the phone the day before. The picture of Rolls that heads chapter 10 is
his and used here with his permission. Being a jiu-jitsu practitioner,

but also a journalist, his interview offered a very different perspective of the *second-wave*. His interview took place over the phone on the 31st of May, 2022.

1- The Figueiredo de Magalhães Academy is a fascinating piece of this history to me. Can you talk a little bit more about it?

Look, before the Figueiredo de Magalhães Academy, what did we have? We had the downtown Gracie Academy, it was far, there were no subways then... it was hard to get to. The downtown Gracie Academy had a different kind of clientele too, they were targeting the upper class of Rio and training wasn't so cheap, so that was one crowd. And then there was a different crowd, a rougher and fiercer one, less refined. When Carlson opened his school in Copacabana, there were two small mats and the demographic was completely different from the downtown academy, it was a much younger crowd, very much into surfing.

What happened was that sometimes we would all show up there at the Gracie Academy downtown to train, it wasn't a big group, but sometimes we would go there to train, very informal, no real methodology or anything. When they opened the Figueiredo de Magalhães Academy, it was huge and having all that space really changed things for us. What happened was that that building drew a lot of young people. Remember, we are talking about the 70s here, so we are talking about surf, rock n' roll, youth liberation... and this young crowd rallied in that gym and embraced all that. Also keep in mind that we were living under a military dictatorship at the time and these kids were opposed to all that, against what we saw as old and inadequate, against the oppression of women, against all that the military represented. It was also a crowd that liked combat and we brought that energy of a hopeful youth to the mats with us.

We didn't care who tapped who, it was all about having a good time, the overall atmosphere was very relaxed. And I think Rolls had a lot to do with that, he stimulated us to learn from all, challenge ourselves and an overall methodology that was creative and competitive in a healthy way. The Figueiredo de Magalhães Academy had that, it was that sort of environment where we could be free to express ourselves, not only in terms of training, but in every way. So much that when we looked over to our coach, he was one of us too. Rolls was a friend of mine since I was a child, but he was also my coach.

2- I also know you have some insight into how jiu-jitsu popularized the super-fruit açaí. Can you share it with us?

Our group of friends all followed the diet [the diet that Carlos Gracie popularized], so we were obsessed with fruit. It was common for us to go to SEASA to buy fruit together. And açaí has an interesting connection to jiu-jitsu. There was this store called Arataca that sold fruit and products brought over from Pará, in the Amazon, it is still there actually. It was right next to the Figueiredo de Magalhães Academy too. Sometimes, that store would have açaí but the fruit rotted quickly so you had to be quick about it. Somehow, we found out that there was actually a pilot from Varig Airlines who would sometimes fly the açaí over and sell it to the owner of the store in a small container. So, when we found that out, we knew when to go and we'd buy the whole supply of açaí from the guy [laughs]. We'd go to someone's home, mine or Rolls' and be making açaí all day, it was like an açaí party. Years later, one of Carlinhos' students opened a small açaí shop at the Barra neighborhood and most of his clientele were jiu-jitsu guys, due to this connection I am telling you about. Barra also had a lot of surfers who trained too. They help popularize it in Rio and then to the world. In other words, the jiu-jitsu brotherhood we created at the Figueiredo de Magalhães

Academy is responsible for spreading açaí to the world [laughs].
*So Figueiredo de Magalhães had that characteristic, there weren't
many of us, but we were friends who shared a similar and very
specific cultural outlook on life.*

3-   Carlson and Rolls were business partners, but their students competed against one another. Off the mats, they were brothers who
got along. Why did they teach separately instead of combining
the group?

*Good question... Well, first of all, they were brothers but Carlson
was the big name of that era. Because Helio was a lot older than
us, Carlson was the fighter everyone looked up to. The problem
was that he wasn't a good business manager. So, I think this helps
explain why they decided to do things separately and have their
students pay them separately too. They only split the rent.*

4-   Would you consider them separate teams? Did they teach differently?

*Initially we were all one team, and we represented the Gracie
Academy. Carlson being the older one, established a sort of hierarchy there. Not Rolls though, he was our age and we did everything together, he was one of us. What I am trying to say is that
they were different. I wouldn't say their teaching styles were rad-
ically different, but they were definitely different. Look, why does
Rolls have the reputation of being the father of modern jiu-jitsu?
A reputation he deserves in my opinion. Because he introduced
other styles into jiu-jitsu, when jiu-jitsu had been more of a ground
game. Carlson in my view, was an exceptional representative of
old jiu-jitsu. As for Rolls, from early on he identified with other
martial arts. While Carlson didn't teach much stand-up, he taught
a baiana* (double-leg takedown) *and that was it. In vale-tudo he
taught stand-up, but in the kimono not so much. Carlson was*

rougher around the edges, Rolls was more refined in a sense. So, they both have these subtleties in terms of style that certainly influenced things. If there was any division, it wasn't at all clear to me. I was friends with guys who trained with Carlson and sometimes we trained together. Peixotinho and Pinduka trained only with us for a while. Some trained with both. In other words, there were no clear lines drawn in the Figueiredo Academy.

5- Do you believe Carlson had a more *vale-tudo* oriented approach to jiu-jitsu?

Probably, yes. You can take a look at his students and they all did exceptionally well in vale-tudo. Where they were identical is that we all trained to submit our opponents, we didn't train for points, we trained to submit but also thinking about fights. We'd say, "why would you do that move? It won't work in a fight, it's a waste of your time." We didn't train for sport, we trained to fight.

6- What were the tournaments in the 70s like?

They were very small, we fought half a dozen guys over and over again. Most of them we knew personally and some we even trained with daily.

7- Why did Carlson and Rolls prefer to teach group classes over private ones?

I'd say that group classes, regardless of people's preferences, made it possible for a different demographic to train, who otherwise could not afford privates lessons. Also, a class with a bigger number of students has the potential for more money too. The crowd Rolls and Carlson taught was much younger, they had less money too. Naturally it was a more competitive crowd who got more rounds in. Man, do you have any idea what it is like to get beat up by Maurição [Maurício Gomes] *and Marcio "Macarrão" Stambowsky? They crushed me! And I trained with them every day* [laughs], *imagine putting one of those guys against those who only did private classes?*

8- Did Helio and Carlson get along? In what ways were they different?

I'm not sure if they were at odds, it wasn't clear to me if there was anything rift other than the rivalry on the mats. But they were certainly different, Helio was very radical in his ways. Carlson was the exact opposite. But as far as rivalry, Carlson always celebrated a lot when his guys won. It didn't matter if they were from the Gracie Academy or one of Rolls' guys. And when he was refereeing he was absolutely emotional and biased toward his guys [laughs].

Bob Anderson

Bob Anderson was an early bridge between
the jiu-jitsu practiced in Rio and other
arts such as wrestling and sambo.
Photocred: Bob Anderson personal archives.

"About 95% of what I showed them were takedowns, but eventually something would come up on the ground. For instance, turtle position, Rolls would ask "what would you do from here?" *I'd show him some wrestling techniques and he'd say* "that really works for us," *or he'd say* "I don't really know about that one..." the whole process was a lot of fun and resulted in a lot of collaborative work and brain-storming."

Bob Anderson

Bob Anderson is a grappling standout in his own right. He originally come from a traditional wrestling background but fell in love with the game of submissions. Over time, he also gravitated toward sambo and judo. His acquaintance with the Gracie family, and Rolls in particular, is legendary and humorously told here. Bob was born on November 6th, 1943 and I interviewed him over the phone on the 25th of May, 2022.

1- Can you tell me a little about your beginnings in wrestling?

It all started from playing football actually. I was told by my football coach, Bob Bonheim, to go out there to wrestle. That and I used to watch pro-wrestling with my Portuguese grand-mother, she used to watch pro-wrestling with Gorgeous George and be screaming and yelling at the TV the whole time [laughs]. *One day the wrestling coach approached me and asked me if I wanted to join the wrestling team. I told him* "no way I am jumping off the top of any ropes!" *He explained that amateur wrestling, the kind in the Olympics and in college,* "wasn't like that", *and kept insisting that I'd try it, until I finally agreed and got hooked.*

2- Did you have any experience in any other grappling style other than wrestling?

A little judo in my senior year of college because the judo coach told me it would help with my wrestling. I ended up doing well and winning a few championships. But judo was after wrestling season. I trained judo in college at Adams State in Alamosa, Colorado. A month training and I was beating black-belts because of my wrestling background. And then I trained some sambo too. In the 80s Russia said that sambo was up for a vote to be a part of the Russian Olympics [1980] *and I wanted to make the Olympic team. So, I ended up being a sambo coach, competing and raising funds.*

3- You are well known in Brazil for having taught wrestling there and to Rolls Gracie specifically. Can you tell us a little bit about that experience?

In 1977 I was requested by FILA [Federation Internationale Des Luttes Associees] and the AAU ["American Athlete Union"] to develop wrestling in Brazil, to bring their standards up and to teach them. I went down there and I'm at the airport for two and a half hours wondering and asking everyone around me, where the people responsible for the wrestling division were. All of a sudden Rolls and Carlson Gracie show up. Rolls spoke a little English, not great but enough to communicate and was apologizing for being so late. After taking me out for a nice dinner, Rolls gave me a room in his house to stay in. Being a wrestler, I was used to not having 5-star treatment and all that, so I did not mind that at all. We got to hang out a bunch, train a lot and do fun stuff together and became good friends.

He was quite the jokester and fun to spend time with. He'd always been playing jokes on me. One time, Rolls and I were at a bazaar and we had a whole crowd of people around me, pointing their fingers at me and talking to each other about me. I'm wondering, "what the hell did I do wrong?" So I started calling out Rolls for help but he just ignored me. So all of a sudden the crowd started screaming at me in broken English "Hulky! Hulky!" He had told the woman who was helping me shop for my purchases that I was Lou Ferrigno who played "The Incredible Hulk" in the popular TV series and they believed him [laughs].

I remember also that he'd take me out for these fruit drinks and would throw a bunch of that caffeinated Guaraná stuff in my drink before our training, I'd drink it all and then be teaching and talking at 100 miles an hour afterwards [laughs]. We got along

*very well, had fun together, did a bunch of dumb things together.
Pretty down to earth guy.*

4-   What was the training like?

*When Rolls took me to his gym I was wondering why everyone
was wearing judo jackets, I thought I'd be teaching wrestling there.
I was informed by Rolls that they were developing wrestling and
that these were the better athletes that they were trying to develop
to get into the Pan American games. So, when I got there I was a
bit confused but after some talking, I told them to take their jackets
off so we could wrestle.*

*About 95% of what I showed them were takedowns, but even-
tually something would come up on the ground. For instance, turtle
position, Rolls would ask* "what would you do from here?" *I'd show
him some wrestling techniques and he'd say* "that really works for
us," *or he'd say* "I don't really know about that one..." *the whole
process was a lot of fun and resulted in a lot of collaborative work
and brain-storming.*

*At some point however, I began to realize they weren't really
doing judo because their standing position was really weak. At the
time I had no idea of what jiu-jitsu was so I asked,* "what is this
stuff that you are doing?" *I remember Rolls showing me a black and
white video, Super 8 I think, where a 6 feet tall, 215 pound karate
guy was talking about how great karate was. Rolls was going to
be challenging this guy and told me that he wanted to pitch his
students against the karate guy's students, a 5 vs 5 sort of thing.
Basically, Rolls' guys absolutely destroyed the karate students, followed by Rolls going against their coach. Rolls was maybe 170 lbs.
at the most, while the guy was easily 215. Well, he got karate guy to
the ground and began to beat the day-light out of him until he got
the submission. Rolls then explained to me that what he had done
was jiu-jitsu and this was why it was superior.*

5- What was Rolls like?

Well to start – at the time I was completely unaware, but Rolls was a big hero in Rio, and it's to my understanding that he was also a policeman. There was this one story I remember, I believe that it was a Brazil vs Argentina soccer match and because of the game, traffic was absolutely insane. Rolls had run late in his training, and had become so frustrated with the traffic that at some point he just pulled his car onto the walk-way. So, there he is just driving on the sidewalk going 25-35 mph honking his horn, getting people to move out of his way. When we finally got to an off-ramp, we quickly saw below us that there was absolutely no parking there. Rolls then just parks his car on the off-ramp [laughs]. When we finally got down to the stadium, Rolls spoke to some guys and then I think he might have flashed his badge? Can't remember, but we got in! The stadium was so packed – you could not even walk in it so we just sat on the stairs and watched an amazing game.

6- Do you think he believed that jiu-jitsu had a problem in terms of takedowns and he wanted to solve that problem?

The passing of Rolls was a huge loss to jiu-jitsu. I truly believe that had Rolls continued developing the sport, jiu-jitsu would have been a lot stronger on the feet [takedowns] and had he kept practicing some of the things I taught him, their take-downs would have a much better form, because frankly once on the mats, Brazilians absolutely destroy.

7- Did you ever train with him?

I often joked with Rolls, you know, athletes always joke with one another about how "you are too weak for this" or "you can't do that..." and I'd tease him. His wife, however, Angela, she couldn't believe I would talk to him like that and would just go off the Richter scale when she heard me. The day before I was leaving, and I bring this up because I think Angela, his wife sort of put him up to it. We had just finished working out when Rolls said "come over here and let's try some jiu-jitsu" and I agreed by saying "ok, stand-up and let's go" and he wouldn't stand-up, he would not go with me on his feet at all.[124] So, he laid down, opened his legs and said, "here, get in here." And I said, "you want me on top? I'm bigger than you, I'm 200 lbs." And he'd fire back, "don't worry about it, I'll be ok." So, we fought for at least half an hour, in the gi first. The whole time I was trying to keep his legs off from choking my brains out and keeping him from getting an armbar or something similar. Prior to this, I had done sambo and judo, so I had some background on how to defend myself there. This match went on for at least half an hour – by the way Brazil is an incredibly warm and humid climate, so during this toe to toe we were just roasting in those jackets. Eventually I stood up and said, "wait a minute, lets fight like real men". So, we cast off our gis and we went toe to toe for another 40 minutes at least. Unfortunately, I wasn't smart enough to take off my wrestling shoes so finally he caught me with a heel-hook because I couldn't slip away. That's my excuse for losing that day [laughs].

8- Were Rolls questions exclusive to wrestling or did he have other questions for you?

When it comes to sambo, Rolls would ask about a position approach and see if he wanted to add it, this was part of our brain storming sessions. I'd tell Rolls it was so much like jiu-jitsu, except there are a lot more points awarded for takedowns. I told him that he would be good at sambo and that during the Pan American games sambo would be featured – I then invited him to stay with

---

[124] Reila confirms this episode in her biography of her father Carlos.

us at my house. From there I helped him sign up even with no paperwork and not technically being a Brazilian national champion but I managed to get him to compete. Rolls ended up going against one of my USA guys in the finals who took Rolls down right away, but once down Rolls was able to get a submission. My USA guy is still probably peeved about how I brought a Brazilian guy up here to beat him – and he probably thinks he would have won if Rolls weren't here. By the way, Rolls was the first true Pan American champion recognized by a world organization like FILA.

9- It is often said in Brazil that you taught Rolls some armbars and shoulder locks, is this true?

He knew the moves, but sometimes I'd show him a move he knew from a different angle or different position. But the "Americana" armbar [key-lock] I taught him. The Gracies in general don't like to give credit to anyone other than themselves for any moves, it's just the way they are. But Rolls was different, he made sure to call the move "Americana" after me.

10- Where did you learn the Americana from? Judo or sambo?

In training for the 1968 Olympic trials, I traveled up to the Los Angeles YMCA, where there were guys around the age of 70. One of them asked me to roll with them, so out of courtesy, I did. All of a sudden one of them caught me in this kind of armlock. I found later, that just until the 50s, the USA had submission-wrestling in its history and in some of its colleges. This submission style was taken out as a means to help grow and develop the sport at a high school and college level, but it was there that I learned the Americana armbar. Unfortunately, I do not remember his name.

11- Back to Brazil, Carlson shared the gym building with Rolls. Were his guys there too? Could you tell the difference between Carlson's and Rolls' students or were they all a bunch of jiu-jitsu guys to you?

To me they were all just a bunch of jiu-jitsu teenagers who wanted to learn wrestling from me and I was there to teach. Carlson's guys would have been there too, But I really didn't know who was who.

12- What was the good-bye to Rolls like? Any contact after that sambo tournament? What was your final episode with him like?

I was saddened to learn of his passing, especially in that type of accident. He was supposed to come back and he had some seminars set up. But once he went back to Brazil I just completely lost contact with him.

Chapter 8

The Evolution of Jiu-Jitsu Rules and its Departure from Judo (1936 to 1975).[125]

Helio, always at war with judo.
The caption reads: "Judo is a Joke!."
Photocred: Brazilian National Library.

"Well, Brazilian Jiu-Jitsu developed into a different martial art in a Darwinian style, let's say, in the sense that isolation makes it different from traditional Kodokan Judo."[126]

Luis Otavio Laydner

---

[125] Copies of the 1936, 1967 and 1975 rules were provided to the author by Master Guedes via Marcial Serrano who owns the originals in Brazil. The 1954 ruleset made its way here thanks to Pedro Valente who had a copy of an old newspaper explaining them. Serrano also provided me with a copy of the CBJJ 1994 ruleset, but considering it is very close to the current IBJJF ruleset (in structural terms at least), I found their discussion here to be unnecessary.

[126] Drysdale 2020, pg. 122

When the Gracie brothers made their first moves to depart from judo, these moves were neither sudden nor were they a fully developed plan of action. Finding themselves split in between the professional competitive scene that was in the hands of the boxing commission, judo itself and still bolstering their *patrician-turned-warrior-ethos*, had the side-effect of creating the fissure from where BJJ would eventually be born out of,

"The Gracies adamant refusal to abide by Kodokan rules and to resist the ones enforced by the Boxing Commission is key to understand how they survived the early confrontations with Japanese martial artists while creating a local jiu-jitsu style. [...] If the Gracies accepted Japanese rules, they would stand no chance of victory against skilled Japanese throwers. Similarly, adopting the new rules that determine victory by points established by the military that controlled the Boxing Commission would turn draws into defeats. This became clear by analyzing fights in which the Japanese martial artists thrown [sic] and dominated the Gracies. One should bear in mind that inconclusive draws allowed the Gracies to keep their aura of invincibility intact."[127]

It was an old strategy that had worked remarkably well for Carlos and Helio over time. First, insist on your preferred ruleset, time limits and uniform. Then claim this ruleset to be "real jiu-jitsu." In case you win, herald it as the most significant fight event in history. In case you draw, claim you really won, because you didn't lose. And lastly, just in case you lose, call it a "moral victory" and *"after enough time, people would tend to forget that the victory was merely 'moral.'"*[128]

Carlos and Helio's eccentric ways had the expected side effect of ostracizing them from the fight scene in Rio. Their careers had no shortage of rivals and critics to give testimony to this self-imposed isolation. On the other hand, had it not been for their stubbornness in doing things

[127] Cairus 2012a, pg. 97

[128] Pedreira 2015b, pg. 201

their own way, I have serious doubts there would have been any possibility for a Brazilian style of judo/jiu-jitsu to flourish out of their academy.

With that said, the self-inflicted isolation had the downside of putting them into a situation where if they wanted to expand, they needed to keep their students engaged with more than private lessons. What they needed was something that got and kept students excited about being ranked, preparing for a tournament and winning the prestige awarded by medals... In short, the Gracies needed what judo had. Their first moves for this began early in 1951, when they tried to organize a nationwide league.[129] A move they followed by organizing an in-house tournament in 1954, using their own modified ruleset and later still, by organizing their first federation in 1967 around the 1954 ruleset (with minor modifications to be discussed below).[130]

The problem was that by treading in judo's path they would inevitably (and as could have been foreseen) bump into the same problems that judo had as it expanded away from a martial practice and into becoming excessively sportive. Without a doubt, treading in judo's path so closely had its benefits, but the downsides were there just as well.

Their new federation was meant to give jiu-jitsu a new organizational shape to follow in judo's footsteps. However, it had the effect of laying the seeds for two apparently contradictory but non-mutually exclusive consequences. If on one hand competition creates the necessity for better athletes, technical improvisation, adaptation and hence evolution.

---

[129] In 1951 the brothers were attempting to organize a *"Confederação Brasileira de Jiu-Jitsu"* in order to "nationalize jiu-jitsu," since, as they understood it, the Japanese were preventing or hiding "real jiu-jitsu" with judo rules. Helio's attempt at appealing to nationalism to achieve this is made obvious here, *"The simple fact that there is a foreign influence in the national sport already is antipathetic. Beyond this, the Japanese who live among us do not have technical conditions to supplant us. I even believe that the Japanese champion coming to Brazil* [presumably Kimura] *is the admittance of the Japanese colony here that not being able to defeat us by their own hands, they appeal to the greater assets from their homeland."* Whereas in 1953, the Gracie brothers set on the less ambitious goal of organizing a new jiu-jitsu ruleset under the patronage of the boxing federation. See: Serrano 2016b, pg. 262; and Serrano 2021, pg. 322.

[130] It is indeed an irony of destiny that Helio, the man who was the leader of the Guanabara Federation and who, presumably, made all the ultimate calls in the creation of its rules, would later be such a disgruntled enemy of the competitive jiu-jitsu ruleset he had created. Perhaps never imagining that it would take a life of its own and away from the Gracie Academy and its original teaching methods.

Then on the other, this does not mean that this evolution is necessarily being steered toward the reality of combat that their jiu-jitsu was meant to embody in its original vision.

Unguided evolution may well lead the art away from the reality of combat even while clearly evolving. Sportive jiu-jitsu as we know it today, created the environment for strong selection pressures. But this was done by athletes positively selecting the techniques for victory under that particular ruleset, not necessarily techniques tried for and by the reality of combat. Which is in fact, an old problem that any combative practice has to deal with at some point during the course of its life. Particularly as it undergoes democratization.

What this meant for jiu-jitsu was that for all practical purposes, the 1967 federation created the possibility for the cornerstone that had upheld jiu-jitsu up to then (the reality of combat), to be fractured by competition rules. Regardless of this being completely unpredictable (or completely predictable) for anyone at the time. At any rate, the federation had both the desired effect of creating an outlet for a competitive youth, while simultaneously creating the potential for internal division among their ranks. At least in terms of their definition of *what jiu-jitsu was*.

Nevertheless, competitive jiu-jitsu in Brazil did not begin in 1954 with their in-house tournament or in 1967 with the foundation of the Guanabara Federation. It had a much older history while it was still part of judo in technical terms and, believe it or not, under the auspices of boxing rules and their federation. A brief recap of these rules, and how they evolved from judo to today, can help us understand how the Gracies were changing their understanding of grappling and redefining it as they saw fit and as time went by.

Chapter 8.1

Jiu-Jitsu under ther Boxing Commission

REGULAMENTO DE JIU-JITSU ENTRE PROFISSIONAES

PRIMEIRO

Os luctadores subirão ao ring com kimonos apropriados e resistentes, japonezes, com mangas até metade do ante-braço.

SEGUNDO

Os luctadores subirão ao ring de pés descalços, sem gordura de especie alguma no corpo, unhas dos dedos das mãos e dos pés devidamente cortadas.

TERCEIRO

O ring de combate deverá medir, pelo menos, cinco metros por cinco metros, ou seja vinte e cinco metros quadrados. Sobre o assoalho do ring deverá haver um acolchoado ou artefacto similar, com a espessura maxima de uma pollegada, e sobre o mesmo uma lona com a necessaria resistencia.

Jiu-jitsu under the Boxing Federation.
Photocred: Master Guedes via Marcial Serrano.

In 1936, jiu-jitsu matches in Brazil were organized and judged by the *Federação Brasileira de Pugilismo* ("Brazilian Boxing Federation") in

Rio de Janeiro, the Brazilian capital at the time. Unsurprisingly, the rules followed a very similar format to boxing. The rules of the *"Regulamento oficial de Jiu-jitsu para profissionaes"* were released in August, 1936 and used a point system that wasn't quite the one used in boxing and neither was it the one used judo/jiu-jitsu either.[131] It was idiosyncratic to the environment in which jiu-jitsu was evolving into. The rules were:

a)   Superior defense – one point
b)   Superior technique – one point
c)   Superior offense – one point
d)   Superior efficiency – one point
e)   Superior takedowns – As when opponent lands flat on his back – one point

The rules most resembled boxing in the sense that:

a)   The fight took place inside a ring
b)   The fight had a ring-referee
c)   The fight was judged by 3 table-judges
d)   The fight had a fixed number of rounds with breaks in between
e)   The victor was determined based on a point system

In case there was a draw in any of the rounds, each fighter would be awarded 5 points. Like boxing, at the end of the fight, the judges would add up their points and give the victory to the fighter with the greatest number of points or call it a draw in case they had an equal amount of points. That was what the professional circuit of judo/jiu-jitsu looked like in Rio in 1936 when BJJ was beginning to take shape.

---

[131]   Pedreira 2015a, pg. 338-339

Chapter 8.2

The Gracie In-House Tournament and the 1954 Ruleset

**Waldemar tries to pass Carlson's open-guard
in their first jiu-jitsu match in 1955.
Photocred: Brazilian National Library.**

The problem was that Carlos and Helio weren't really on board with either the official judo ruleset that was accepted by all judo/jiu-jitsu practitioners worldwide, nor were they on board with the boxing federation overseeing these events. They wanted to do things their own way. As a result, the history of the Gracie brothers in the 1930s and 1940s is marked by an infinite amount of arguing over rules, time limits, uniforms and other disagreements Carlos had over what was the norm in competitive judo.[132]

It wasn't until their in-house tournament at the Gracie Academy in 1954 that Carlos and Helio would be able to implement a vision they saw fit for what they understood judo/jiu-jitsu to be.[133] Since they couldn't defeat judokas in a traditional judo ruleset (and considering their ambition), the next natural step for the Gracie brothers was to create their own sphere of influence. Despite the 1954 ruleset being remarkably influenced by judo, it becomes clear that there is a division in terms of how they perceived the practice of judo/jiu-jitsu at the time. Namely that there was an emphasis on ground-fighting, something that would over time become a defining staple of their fighting system. In 1954 the rules were:

a)   Holding opponent down for longer than 30 seconds – 1 point
b)   Imperfect takedown – half a point
c)   Classic takedown [presumably an *ippon* or perfect throw] – 1 point
d)   Initiating offense – 1 point
e)   Mount – 1 point
f)   Back-control – 1 point
g)   Fleeing ring – 1 negative point

Notice how in terms of rewards this ruleset bears similarities with judo in that it placed takedowns at equal hierarchical standing with controlling positions on the ground (1 point). Also notice that while the 30 seconds of uninterrupted control is the equivalent of an *ippon* in judo (ending the fight), in the Gracie brother's ruleset, this is acknowledged with "1 point." Keeping in mind that since the ruleset says nothing about "guard-pulling," we can safely assume that it was permitted. The "guard"

---

[132] For examples of different rules and the arguments surrounding them. See: Pedreira 2015a, chp. 12

[133] For contrast, it is worth noting here that at the same time, judo rules did not reward anything on the ground other than a choke or straight armbar (which ended the fight), or for "holding technique" for 30 seconds (considered an *Ippon* which also ended the fight) and the *osaekomi-waza* (half-point) for "holding" opponent for 25 seconds on the ground. Also worthy of note is that guard pulling and "to grab's opponent leg from a standing position" (presumably a single or double-leg) were both prohibited. Source: Kobayashi, Kiyoshi and Sharp, Harold E., The Sport of Judo. 1956 (2nd ed.), pp. 99-102. Rutland, Vermont: Charles E. Tuttle.

as those who train jiu-jitsu well know, would become the defining feature of BJJ over the years, though obviously not indigenous to the Gracie Academy or Brazil.

What is curious to me and to the point of this chapter, was their insistence in *doing as judo was doing* in terms of organizing themselves into a tournament format while simultaneously maintaining themselves close enough to their judo roots in technical terms. Despite still not admitting that they had simply been doing judo all along. Which is to say, the process of diversification from judo was in motion, but far from complete in 1954, as these rules clearly demonstrate.

During this period, judo and jiu-jitsu were certainly becoming more distinct from one another, but the level of compatibility was still significantly high. They began this process of separation without ever admitting or acknowledging that they were simply modifying judo to their personal preferences (although the emphasis on ground-fighting could also have been a side-effect of the tighter physical spaces their training was confined to, giving birth to the necessity of beginning their practice on the ground or on their knees). To them, it had been "jiu-jitsu" all along. Their own rules however, tell a different tale.[134]

134 Pedreira 2015a, pg. 494-495

Chapter 8.3

The Guanabara Federation and the 1967 and 1975 rulesets

 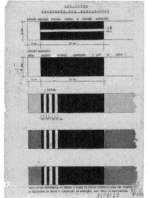 

On the left, notice how a national "Confederação" was already envisioned, but didn't become reality until 1994. In the center, the Guanabara Federation rulebook with its ranks. To the right, the 1975 ruleset. Photocred: Academia Oriente via Master Marcial Serrano and Master Guedes.

The move to begin their own federation in 1967 was a decisive moment in the history of jiu-jitsu. Because in essence, the move laid the foundation for what later would become the CBJJ/IBJJF system. On another note, despite being largely modeled after judo in terms of belt ranks and tournaments, the following rules (particularly the one from 1975) show clearly that there was a conscious and organized attempt to move away from judo. The 1967 rules were:

a)   Full takedown – 1 point
b)   Mount – 1 point

c)   Back-Control – 1 point
d)   Overall superiority – 1 point
e)   Fleeing the ring or taking kimono off – 1 negative point

Notice that the only difference between the 1954 and 1967 rulesets is that the 1967 deemphasizes takedowns (by not awarding the "half-point" for an imperfect takedown) and abandons the "1 point" after 30 seconds of control on the ground. These differences may seem small and despite not yet emphasizing rewards for ground-control above takedowns, they are not irrelevant. These changes clearly demonstrate that their interpretation of jiu-jitsu was going through a gradual shift.

Moving forward, the most obvious identifiable difference between judo and jiu-jitsu in the 1975 ruleset is their emphasis on scoring more points for controlling positions on the ground. In the 1975 ruleset, the changes were both large and relevant:[135]

a)   Choke - 2 points
b)   Armbar - 2 points
c)   Foot-lock- 2 points
d)   Guillotine - 2 points
e)   Mount - 4 points
f)   Back-take - 4 points
g)   Knee-on-belly - 3 points
h)   Takedown - 2 points
i)   Guard-pass - 2 points
j)   Sweep - 2 points
k)   Holding opponent for longer than 30 seconds - 2 negative points
l)   Defective mount - 4 advantages
m)   Defective back-take - 4 advantages
n)   Defective Knee-on-belly - 3 advantages

---

[135] The points awarded for submissions here are presumably for almost achieving the submission; or the equivalent of an "advantage" under IBJJF's ruleset.

o)   Defective takedown - 2 advantages

p)   Aggression ("combatividade") standing - 1 "combatividade point"

q)   Aggression on the ground - 3 "combatividades points"

What is fascinating about the 1975 ruleset is how much of an evolutionary leap it was when compared to its 1967 counterpart. If somewhere between 1954 and 1967 the shift in their interpretation of jiu-jitsu were minimal, the same can't be said only eight years later in 1975.

Notice how in 1975 there was an enormous emphasis on the ground as exemplified by so many more points being awarded for ground-control, failed attempts to control the opponent on the ground and points for submissions attempts. All while takedowns suffered a loss in terms of importance as exemplified by the much smaller rewards in 1975. Keep in mind that in both 1954 and 1967 takedowns were held at equal standing in relation to ground-control and that an imperfect takedown in 1954 was rewarded half a point.

Fast-forward to 1975 and you see the opposite approach, with ground-positions receiving not only a much higher place in terms of points awarded, but also in how an imperfect ground position (mount for example) grants the competitor "4 advantages" where in previous rules, they awarded nothing. Also take note that while 30 seconds of control granted you "1 point" in 1954, in 1975, anything beyond 30 seconds got you penalized for stalling (- 2 points). Yet another example of the shift their views were undergoing.

As anyone could have predicted, granting higher rewards for efforts on the ground was bound to push evolution in precisely that direction. *What happened in terms of their thinking between 1967 and 1975?* It is clear that there was a shift in their thinking away from judo toward an even more ground-oriented approach to jiu-jitsu than the one they previously held, *but why?*

A number of possibilities come to mind:

a) Personal preferences of instructors who increasingly became deficient in terms of takedowns
b) Continued limited mat-space which hindered the practice of takedowns
c) A strategic move to increase the incompatibility between judo and jiu-jitsu
d) A belief that, for self-defense purposes, takedowns were less important than a more developed ground-game
e) The belief that a "baiana" (a.k.a. "morete-gari" in judo and "double-leg" in wrestling) takedown was enough to take the opponent down in a fight and developing other throws was unnecessary
f) A strong belief (however inaccurate) that "jiu-jitsu" was originally a more ground-oriented art in the days before judo

Or, what is even more likely, a combination of all these non-mutually exclusive factors set BJJ on a completely different evolutionary track. Still, while it would be impossible to clearly identify a definitive departure point from judo, if pressed to do so, the 1975 ruleset seems to be the strongest candidate to signal this departure.[136] For what it's worth, what is clear from all these various rulesets is that jiu-jitsu has never stopped undergoing change.

---

[136] In Opening Closed Guard, I identify 3 key moments for this departure: 1) the disagreements in terms of rules in the matches between Helio Gracie and Yassuiti Ono; 2) The 1967 Guanabara Federation; and 3) the founding of CBJJ/IBJJF in 1994. What I had missed was that the biggest leap toward a ground-oriented interpretation of jiu-jitsu had taken place in 1975, not 1967. This was due to me not having a copy of the 1975 ruleset at the time. See: Drysdale 2020, pg. 345.

Chapter 9

What is Jiu-Jitsu After All?

Saraiva observes a child applying a heel-hook in the gi.
Photocred: Orlando and Henrique Saraiva personal archives.

"Unlike Kodokan judo, jiu-jitsu does not have a 'philosophy.' Jiu-jitsu can be whatever anyone wants it to be, which is the good news, and also the bad news."[137]

Roberto Pedreira

The term "jiu-jitsu" has been used and abused by the most various characters since it was first introduced in the West shortly after the Russo-Japanese War of 1904-1905. Curiously, the only consistency in

---

[137] Pedreira 2013, pg. 53

the word is that it has been *consistently inconsistent*. For their part, the Gracies not only appropriated the term, but began to modify it according to their understanding of what "real jiu-jitsu" meant to them during specific eras. In fact, during most of the 20ᵗʰ century, jiu-jitsu might have been firmly in the hands of the Gracie family, but that didn't mean that it was ever completely clear what they meant by the words "jiu" and "jitsu." The term has always been, and still remains, an adaptable one.

Contrasting other martial arts cultural practices that had a more rigid technical and cultural matrix in the East, the Brazilian version of jiu-jitsu has always had a more flexible set of guiding principles to frame its practice (possibly as a side-effect of Brazilian culture itself). In essence, what this absence of a fixed-curriculum and cultural matrix meant (as the ones judo possesses for example) was that the teaching methodology and evolution were an open source model.

Which, on one hand facilitated innovation (because it isn't fixed) while on the other, this model suffers from the potential down-side effect of excessive technical diversification (including diversification beyond the practical and realistic) as well as cultural and political division. Especially if it is not constrained by very specifically set boundaries in terms of hierarchy, culture and ruleset. Something BJJ never quite managed to accomplish in a definitive manner.

Throughout the history of jiu-jitsu in Brazil, the solution to this lack of a rigid curriculum and set culture was case by case. Under this flexible system, the art adapted according to the cultural norms and the economic opportunities that encircled its practice. Which meant that over time, the Gracie version of jiu-jitsu became a highly adaptable hybrid between judo and whatever culture and leadership happened to be shaping and governing jiu-jitsu during these eras.

In all fairness, the original Gracie Academy had attempted to solve this problem early on with their own self-defense curriculum. However, as discussed in chapter 3, this program simply wasn't fulfiling enough for a competitive youth hungry for a challenge. Neither was it a model for growth. Beyond this, if a competitive league had worked so well for judo (not to mention other sports), why wouldn't it work for jiu-jitsu?

The arts were not so different after all. Their solution? To redefine their practice and attempt to frame it under a competitive ruleset. Which, like any attempt at a definition, will solve some problems, but not without first creating new ones.

As discussed in the previous chapter, the issue the Gracie brothers had on their hands had less to do with the enormous effort of getting the Guanabara Federation off the ground and more to do with something else. Namely, that by creating a sportive tournament format they were in reality creating exactly the sort of environment that would eventually steer their practice away from the martial end of the spectrum and toward the sportive end. As Pedreira notes: *"When a martial art exists in two forms, the original self-defense form and a sport/competition form with rules determining* 'winners,' *the boundaries tend to blur, and effectiveness in self-defense can be sacrificed to effectiveness in scoring points in a rule governed contest."*[138]

Which is exactly the conundrum any and all martial arts have always found themselves in. Where should these limits be set? Where does the *martial* end and where does *safety* begin? Should the impetus to *sell*, *popularize* and *entertain* be checked in case it compromises the *integrity* of the art? If so, where are these boundaries? Can tournaments incite *evolution* without first permanently severing the art's fighting *roots*?

A tournament format carries a fundamental problem in its DNA, competitors don't care about idealism; they care about winning. Once the limits of the competitive practice are defined, competitors naturally become masters at treading the borders of what the rules allow in order to minimize effort while maximizing outcome. Worse still, from a competitor's perspective, it makes perfect tactical sense to do so. *By masterfully treading the line of what the rules allow for, winning competitors are doing nothing but following economic logic.*

In their defense, the Gracie brothers did their best to maintain a more martially oriented practice throughout the years. They did this by constantly reinforcing strong cultural and technical buffers to maintain

---

[138] Pedreira 2013, pg. 32

reality as the guiding principle of their practice (more on this on chapters 21 and 22). But as economic logic would have it, and despite the efforts and pressure from its leadership, it was only a matter of time before jiu-jitsu began to drift from its fighting roots in favor of strategies to win medals.

Could the federation's leadership have done things differently? Maybe. But no one could have had the foresight to prevent the novelties and intricacies that competitors are capable of. Particularly when given a competitive space and a specific ruleset to practice and exploit freely. Neither Kano, Carlos, Helio nor Carlson could have foreseen the full extent of the possibilities that a kimono could grant competitors when they decided decades later to use lapels and sleeves to control and off-balance opponents.

At any rate, what is clear is that jiu-jitsu has always struggled with defining itself. Which, as Pedreira notes, is the good and the bad news. Flexibility is both beneficial and desirable, but should it exist free of any boundaries and principles? Personally, I find that certain guidelines are necessary in both cultural and technical terms. I wouldn't frame them in any definitive way, but hold and fixate them to very specific directing principles.[139]

To conclude, regarding their original self-defense curriculum, despite it having survived the trials of time by making its way into the 21st century, it did so only with a minor presence after the events of 1993. At least when compared to the competitive framework they had fashioned in the 1975 ruleset. The one that was most exploited by Carlos' eldest son,

---

[139] All martial-arts suffer from a tug of war of sorts that bears resemblance to what happens to species in the wild. The tension is in between the maintenance of genetic information and its openness to evolvability. A system that is immutable (but manages to survive and reproduce nonetheless), lacks evolutionary outlets because it is closed off (like a curriculum for example). Conversely, excessive volatility makes a system unstable and organized patterns that carry potential can quickly disappear (like fads on the internet for example). As an evolutionary theorist suggests, evolution takes place on the edge of chaos, sufficiently mutable to adapt while being sufficiently stable for efficient organized patterns to remain and reproduce. Back to martial arts, a possible solution is to empirically discover which of these organized patterns are useful for the reality of combat while artificially getting rid of any pattern that isn't. However appealing the latter may be.

Carlson, and that was destined to go onto colonize the globe a couple decades later.

However, Carlson needed competition. His dominance in the competition sphere needed to be challenged if jiu-jitsu was to evolve beyond a niche practice of the Carioca south-zone. He would be rivaled by a man who was treading in Carlson's footsteps with the ambition of outdoing not only him, but everyone that came before him as well. He would attempt this by raising the bar in terms of instruction and insight. Much like Carlson, his impact on the *second-wave* of jiu-jitsu practitioners was both crucial and unforgettable.

Chapter 10

Rolls, The Lost Link

The Gracie Prodigy.
Photocred: Ricardo Azoury personal archives.

"Rolls was the only person with the power to unite the family, because he was the only person everyone both loved and respected. He is the lost link."

Master Otavio Peixotinho

On June 6, 1982, Romero Cavalcanti had the worst day of his life. On that day, the founder and leader of what would become one of the most successful competition teams in the history of jiu-jitsu lost his now legendary mentor in a hang-gliding accident in Mauá, Rio de Janeiro.[140]

Romero wasn't a Gracie, but he was one of the many Brazilians who would come to mourn the death of one of the most influential characters in the history of the gentle-art in Brazil. Rolls Gracie (or "Hollis" as Brazilians pronounce it), died at the young age of 31, but not without leaving a mark on the family and on that generation of jiu-jitsu practitioners as a whole. Like many notorious men who die young, his career is perhaps most notorious not because of what he did but rather because of his underdeveloped potential.

The mark Rolls would leave on the jiu-jitsu community as a whole and on the *second-wave* of practitioners in particular, was not in terms of fighting results in either jiu-jitsu or *vale-tudo*. Having died so young and having fought during an era in which jiu-jitsu competitions were less developed, Rolls had fewer opportunities to prove himself competitively.[141] Still, when he did fight, he normally won. Where he did leave an enormous mark was in terms of the impact he had on his students and people who were directly influenced by him.

Rolls' story is instructive of the internal dynamics within the Gracie family as Reila's biography of her father Carlos gives ample testimony to. Despite being a son to one of Carlos' many mistresses, Rolls wasn't raised by his mother or father, but instead by his Uncle Helio and his wife Margarida, whom Carlos entrusted with raising him. Long story short, Rolls had two fathers and two mothers, his biological ones who didn't raise him and the non-biological ones who did. The story of his upbringing is fascinating and told in some detail by his sister Reila.[142]

Throughout the Gracie's history with jiu-jitsu, there had been a tradition in the family to determine the "number one" and who would

---

[140] Pedreira 2015c, pg. 215

[141] *Vale-tudo* was mostly banned by the authorities during Rolls' heyday. He did however have one recorded *vale-tudo* victory against a karate representative. The fight can be viewed here: *"Mestre Rolls Gracie vs. Karate"* https://www.youtube.com/watch?v=bC-BJ03RqLGA

[142] Gracie 2008, pg. 410 and 452

become the new poster-boy for the advancement of the family name in newspapers and fights. The Gracies had always had an alpha-champion to represent them, a tradition that traces back from George, to Helio and to Carlson.

Unlike the first generation of Carlos' male children which consisted of Carlson and Robson and where Carlson reigned supreme in the family ranks, Rolls had plenty of competition within the family growing up. But after Carlson's retirement, that position was up for grabs and with no shortage of young men to fight for the spot.[143]

As is well known, young boys tend to solve their disputes the only way they know how to... by fighting with one another. Add to this that fighting is literally the family business and you have the perfect recipe for a fierce eco-system of aspiring alphas. One may even wonder if Carlos and Helio had done this intentionally or if it was a side-effect of having so many males in the family. Either way, the result of having so many young boys growing up with *vale-tudo* and jiu-jitsu as the dominant background to their upbringing had a predictable outcome. Rolls was one of the candidates who aspired for that spot, but there were other candidates such as Helio's oldest sons Rorion and Relson, as well as Rolls' own brothers Carley and Crólin.[144]

Before we can put into perspective the influence that Rolls left on jiu-jitsu, we need to first understand his overall standing in his family. Not being raised by his father and being somewhat ostracized by Helio, Rolls was not only a gifted athlete but had also been raised in the ideal environment for his gift to flourish. Moreover, he was driven, and adventurous. These qualities make themselves plain not only due to his passion for jiu-jitsu and combat in general, but also his passion for surf and hand-gliding, the hobby that would ultimately claim his life.

Despite Helio having raised Rolls, it was obvious that he wasn't prepared to treat Rolls as the one to replace Carlson as the new family

---

[143] A competitive environment such as this one, we should note in passing, had its pros and cons as we will see ahead.

[144] Gracie 2008, pg. 412

champion, choosing to prepare his biological and eldest son Rorion for that spot instead (as it turns out, kin-selection is a real thing after all...[145]). The problem was that Rorion simply wasn't the right guy for the job.

Parents *can't* choose who their children will be or what they will be good at. Children tend to have a mind of their own, to have their own talents and to aspire to go their own way, regardless of the pressure their parents put on them. The best we can do is to steer them with good values and education and reinforce good behavior while punishing bad behavior. What happens next is entirely up to them... A bitter pill for Helio to swallow since he so eagerly wanted one of his own to achieve the prominent rank of replacing Carlson as the new family champion.

As life would have it, Rorion did not fit into the shoes and become the new family champion as his father Helio wanted. Nonetheless, years later, Rorion would make his father proud by helping create the UFC and opening the doors for hundreds of thousands of Brazilians immigrants to live and teach jiu-jitsu abroad. But in the days where Carlos and Helio were in charge, it wasn't about who was the best marketer with an eye for business who held the high seat of prestige. On the mats, as anyone who trains well knows, those skills are useless.

With that said, in the competitive environment that Carlos and Helio had created for their many children, Rolls simply stood out as the next in line. Accordingly, because he wanted it the most, he became the best in that generation. His Uncle, however, wasn't prepared to concede on any of this with the sort of bias that is perhaps best exemplified by two

---

[145] Kin-selection is the theory in evolutionary biology that posits that parents are biologically inclined to make sacrifices for their own offspring. Reila, in her biography of her father Carlos, makes clear the preference that Helio had for his biological children, Rorion and Rickson, over his many nephews such as Crólin, Carley, and Rolls, even if they all grew up together as one big family. Such an insight may also help explain the distancing between Carlson and his Uncle Helio over the years, if not also help explain Rolls' departure from the Gracie Academy to train under Carlson. Reila also describes a conversation shortly after Rolls' death in between Helio and Crólin, where Helio sensing what he felt was everyone's excessive mourning and respect toward Rolls, allegedly made disqualifying remarks about Rolls. The remarks were in regards to his supposed irrelevance in terms of his deeds in jiu-jitsu. See: Gracie 2008, pg. 410-411; 455; and 489.

stories Reila and Robson tell us about Helio's favoritism for his biological children:

Rolls: *Daddy, you are always saying that Rorion will beat me, and that he is better than me, but during our whole lives, I always beat him.*
Helio: *What I say is that if Rorion trained as much as you do, he would beat you, because he is more focused on details.*
Rolls: *But daddy, "if" doesn't exist.*[146]

And:

Robson: *Uncle Helio, would set things up to screw over Rolls. Once, Rolls was driving from Manaus* [Amazon] *through Bahia* [north of Rio] *and went to his ranch in Petrópolis where there was a tournament being held. Helio called him out to train, Rolls said:* "Train? I've been driving for 2 days, train?" *but Helio insisted. So, Rolls said:* "Ok. But only if it's against Rickson." *Which is what Uncle Helio wanted anyway, Rickson and Rorion. What did he do? Crushed them both. No preparation, he had been driving for two days. Uncle Helio had to concede that* "yeah, this one doesn't give into exhaustion" *(este ai não se rende ao cansaço não). Get it?*[147]

From all accounts, Rolls was an absolute monster on the mats. Still, and at least according to a couple of our interviewees who knew and trained with him, it wasn't always like that. Rolls was hungry for knowledge and for furthering his skillset. In time, he would eventually seek Carlson out as a new reference. This, likely due to reasons given in the two conversations above, as well as Helio being unable to be either the father or coach to grant the technical and emotional support the ambitious and competitive Rolls was craving.

---

[146] Gracie 2008, pg. 455

[147] This segment took place during Robson Gracie's interview for the Closed Guard project and did not make it into the book that tells this story.

Here we should keep in mind that the competition scene in Rio in those days, despite being very small in comparison to today, was slowly picking up momentum. This was in large part thanks to the Guanabara Federation as well as the satellite gyms that were beginning to pop-up all over Rio: João Alberto Barreto's gym; Oriente; Munir; Kioto; Armando Wriedt; Augusto Cordeiro; Alvaro Barreto; Jacê; Koma; Fadda; UEG; among others.

It was a competition scene that was dominated by Carlson and his students (to his delight). And there was nothing Carlson wanted more than to prove the efficiency of his teaching methods to the rest of his family, something those who knew him best give ample testimony to. It is in this climate of family feuds that Rolls decided to begin training with his more charismatic and experienced older brother Carlson and the jiu-jitsu crew he was assembling at the Figueiredo Academy in Copacabana.

When Rolls left the Gracie Academy and began training under his older brother, Carlson claimed that Rolls was like a *"galinha morta"* (dead-chicken).[148] Although this is possibly an exaggeration made by Carlson, less intended to insult Rolls than it was to throw a jab at his Uncle Helio, who is credited with having trained Rolls up to then. Regardless of where Rolls stood technically when he began training with Carlson, it was obvious that Carlson and the students that he was training offered Rolls the sort of challenge he was hungry for.[149]

Carlson's decision to prioritize group classes allowed for a more competitive atmosphere. Unlike the original Gracie Academy's system, Carlson's criteria for selecting students was not based on whether they could afford it or not, but whether or not they were hungry for a challenge, an approach that was custom fit for Rolls' appetite.

---

[148] According to Reila, after Rolls lost in a sparring session to Sergio Iris (one of Carlson's best students who also defeated Rorion in competition) Carlson told him that *"With Helio's method you will never win kid!"* (Gracie 2008, pg. 415; and 458.). See also interviews with Paquetá (footnote for Saraiva's interview), Saraiva's interview and Carlson Gracie Jr.'s interview.

[149] Carlos Gracie Jr. mentions another reason for Rolls departure: Rolls was fed up with Rorion bossing him around at the Gracie Academy where they both taught. See Carlinhos' interview in Part 3 of this book.

Over the years, Rolls' curiosity led him to train and compete in other grappling arts such as judo, sambo, and wrestling, where he incidentally fared quite well considering his total lack of experience in any of them. In reality, Rolls was giving continuation to an open-minded mentality that had started with the original Gracie Academy in the 1930s that led them to borrow from other styles anything that would augment and improve on their skillset. An effort later expanded on by his brother Carlson.[150] The criteria being, not whether it is *cool, old, new,* or *sophisticated,* but instead: *"does it work or not?"*

If Rolls' story were limited to his reputation on the mats among those who knew him, that would be enough to warrant his mention here, but Rolls doesn't have his place in this book because of his skills. Rolls played a more significant role in helping shape the brand of jiu-jitsu practiced by the *second-wave* of practitioners. The generation that would set in motion the Cambrian explosion of techniques of the mid-90s in Brazil.

The subject of our next chapter is his role in helping lay next to his brother Carlson the foundation for this explosion to take place.

---

[150] Although this initial openness was not a steady staple of jiu-jitsu during its middle-history in Brazil. Tufy Cairus comments: *"Brazilian Jiu-jitsu's relative isolation also took a toll on its technical development. The creation of a local jiu-jitsu style occurred throughout the 1930s, 1940s and 1950s was also a product of a combative exchange between it and other martial arts styles, notably the Kodokan judo. From the 1960s onward, the social seclusion of Brazilian jiu-jitsu within its upper class quarters kept it in relative isolation severed previous technical interactions."* Cairus 2012a, pg. 204.

Chapter 11

The Figueiredo Academy: Surf, Porrada, Taparia, Açaí Parties and a Brotherhood from the South-Zone

From left to right, Caíque, Buchaú, Otavio Peixotinho, Cássio Cardoso, Carlson and Rosado celebrate another title for the team. Photocred: Otavio Peixotinho.

Carlinhos at the Figueiredo Academy in the early 70s. From left to right: Chicão, Rolls, unknown, Ronaldão, Carlinhos Gracie Jr. and unknown. Photocred: Carlos Gracie Jr. personal archives.

"What happened was that that building drew a lot of young people. Remember, we are talking about the 70s here, so we are talking about surf, rock n' roll, youth liberation... and this young crowd rallied in that gym and embraced all that. Also keep in mind that we were living under a military dictatorship at the time and these kids were opposed to all that, against what we saw as old and inadequate, against the oppression of women, against all that the military represented. It was also a crowd that liked combat and we brought that energy of a hopeful youth to the mats with us (...) The Figueiredo de Magalhães Academy had that, it was that sort of environment where

we could be free to express ourselves, not only in terms of training, but everything, culture, music, all that."

Ricardo Azoury

From 1964-1985, Brazil was under a military dictatorship that ruled the country with a semi-iron fist ("semi" only in comparison to what its neighboring countries experienced). Repression, violence, torture and persecution were how the military dealt with any deviation from their political doctrines or anything that wasn't deemed sufficiently patriotic by its generals. Fearing a public uprising or a civil war they felt their coup had avoided, the military and its agents were in a state of constant high-alert against anything deemed subversive or that questioned their authority.

The military rule could not have been more at odds with the feelings and aspirations of the Brazilian youth of that era. Much like the American and European youths of the 60s and 70s, they were seeking freedom from authority and from a world they increasingly came to see as overly conservative. To these aspirations, not even the *casca-grossa* jiu-jitsu youth of the south-zone was immune.

Not unlike the youth in the rest of the Western world, they let their hair grow long, liked to smoke weed, listened to rock n' roll and couldn't stand their parents reproaches. In the south-zone of Rio specifically, they also liked surf and açaí, which were welcome additions to their local culture of samba, *futebol*, beautiful women and... jiu-jitsu.[151] What wasn't new at all, was their descent from a long tradition of street-brawling and the domineering warrior-ethos that had been a staple of the Brazilian version of jiu-jitsu since it began its war of separation from judo.

When I first had the idea of writing this book, I originally envisioned a chapter on the evolution of *vale-tudo* and how it impacted

---

[151] While it is undeniable that Brazilian surf is heavily influenced by its Californian equivalent, it would be inaccurate to equate the two beach cultures. Rio has its own distinct beach culture that in no way resembles anything in California.

the Gracie brothers views on fighting, a chapter on Carlson, one on Rolls and one about the birth of the CBJJ/IBJJF. These chapters were to be followed by the era of expansion of jiu-jitsu in the mid 90s and 2000s all the way up to my current views on the new jiu-jitsu that was taking shape in the USA during what I refer to as the *fourth-wave*. I planned to supplement the literature available with the testimonies from those who lived that era and could speak as eye-witnesses to the various changes jiu-jitsu had undergone in recent decades.

What I didn't expect is that by interviewing the members of the *second-wave* of jiu-jitsu, they would make me aware of something I had completely missed in my previous readings and in *Opening Closed Guard* as well as in my first thoughts regarding the organization of this book, the importance of the Figueiredo de Magalhães Academy and how it became a new temple for jiu-jitsu. One that would help give jiu-jitsu its current form, both in technical and cultural terms.[152]

Despite having trained under Carlson, Rolls would eventually become a partner with his brother in the now legendary Figueiredo Academy, located in the historic neighborhood of Copacabana in 1972. The three-story building had its first and second floors occupied by the brothers as they alternated their practice. The larger mats on the second floor were used by Carlson and his students on Tuesdays, Thursdays and Saturdays, while Rolls used the two smaller ones downstairs. Then, on Mondays, Wednesdays and Fridays, Rolls had the bigger mats upstairs and Carlson, the two smaller ones.

Speaking frankly, I have my doubts if Carlson and Rolls fully understood what that new environment truly meant for jiu-jitsu and its future. One way or another, the new space had the inevitable consequence of setting them on a whole new evolutionary pathway beyond what the

---

[152] Reila has similar remarks about this. She calls the Figueiredo de Magalhães academy an "informal rupture in the family." The departure of Carlson, Rolls and later Carlinhos from the original Gracie Academy were all signs of this rupture. See: Gracie 2008, pg. 458.

original Gracie Academy had previously sanctified. A parting that was made concrete over time, especially since Carlson's academy was not only physically distant from the original Gracie Academy but just as distant in terms of their clientele and the culture that governed the dynamics between its members.

This exposure to a completely different set of environmental elements (in our case here different demographics, social-norms and training methods) coupled with physical isolation had the added benefit of accelerating its evolutionary diversification away from the original Gracie Academy. Not unlike the original Gracie fighting system had done to judo throughout the 30s, 40s and 50s in Rio when Carlos and Helio had taught to the *first-wave* of practitioners. This vision however, was now giving way to an entirely new generation of practitioners led by Carlson and Rolls and with the beach culture of the south-zone as its background.

I argued in *Opening Closed Guard* that one of the key ingredients for the growth and spread of jiu-jitsu from Brazil to the world was the overall relaxed manners that are as representative of jiu-jitsu as they are of the Carioca culture in the south-zone with its very specific, unique and energetic lifestyle. In between this beach lifestyle, culture, music, food and energy, the south-zone of Rio has the sort of atmosphere that is difficult not to fall in love with.[153]

Tufy Cairus comments,

"The dissemination of Brazilian jiu-jitsu among middle class practitioners became associated with the trendy lifestyle of the new Gracie generation. The appealing Brazilian jiu-jitsu's way of life in the 1980s combined naturalist dietary habits, beach culture and martial practice without the rigidness of Asian disciplines and provided the practitioners with a great instrument to enhance their masculine performances in the public sphere."[154]

---

[153] Drysdale 2020, pg. 331

[154] Cairus 2012a, pg. 209-210

All these elements became increasingly visible to me as I reread Choque, Jiu-Jitsu in the South-Zone, Tufy Cairus' Phd. dissertation and Reila's biography of her father. But mostly this became clear to me when speaking to members of that *second-wave* of practitioners such as Otavio Peixotinho, Antonio Rosado, Ricardo Azoury, Pinduka, etc. There was a certain nostalgia in their voices when they described their practice in that academy. I could almost feel the energy in the room inside the Figueiredo Academy and it was the kind of energy I was all too familiar with.

It was the fist-bump, the hugging, the flip-flops, the açaí after practice, the joking manners on and off the mats, etc. These were all key ingredients for the popularization of Brazilian jiu-jitsu all over the world, well beyond its technical canon. All in all, it would be difficult to ignore the role and impact of these easy-going manners in the global acceptance of BJJ. As I have come to see these events, there is no question that aspects of the south-zone culture made its way through BJJ into places as far away as Australia, Chechnya, Europe and all the way back from Japan after a very unusual and unexpected makeover in Rio.

To strengthen my point, notice how the vast majority of instructors, leading representatives and teams that would supply the demand created by Royce can trace their roots directly back to the Figueiredo de Magalhães Academy. Indeed, it is no exaggeration to claim that, in more than a few ways, the Figueiredo Academy is the cultural and technical birth-place of the BJJ practice that would become a world craze from the mid-90s onward.[155]

Perhaps this claim I am making may be better understood when we take a look at how the Gracie Torrance Academy has been run since its founding or how the Valente brothers teach in Miami today. Both of these academies are largely modeled after the original Gracie Academy's

---

[155] While I am not suggesting that the original Gracie Academy did not play a role in helping give birth to what we now refer to as BJJ, in reality, the culture and methods of the Gracie Academy are not the ones that represent what the vast majority of practitioners understand jiu-jitsu to be today. The most widely disseminated interpretation of jiu-jitsu today had a very specific birthplace on the Figueiredo de Magalhães Street, number 414.

curriculum and approach to jiu-jitsu and remain the most faithful representations of that system (particularly the Valente brothers academy), largely centered around self-defense oriented private lessons that target wealthier members of society while fulfiling their demands and expectations.

Despite all practitioners today referring to all these different schools as simply teaching "jiu-jitsu," it is quite obvious that (in cultural, technical and methodological terms) the vast majority of the *jiu-jitsusphere* is at odds with the original definition of jiu-jitsu taught inside the original Gracie Academy. What is practiced today by the remaining offshoots of that academy (whose jiu-jitsu did not undergo the process of transformation that the rest of jiu-jitsu underwent inside the Figueiredo Academy), is something entirely different. All in all, these differences were nothing but the materialization of an identity issue that began with the founding of the Guanabara Federation and the methodological differences between Helio and Carlson.

In short, the Figueiredo Academy came to embody a division of sorts in jiu-jitsu between the Gracie Academy's version of jiu-jitsu and the one being promoted by Carlson and Rolls, more hierarchical vs. less hierarchical; more self-defense oriented vs. more competition and performance oriented; social-elites vs. for all; older vs. younger. A division that becomes increasingly obvious the less dependant we become of the official Helio-centric version of events.

Unquestionably, the differences between the Figueiredo practice led by Carlson and Rolls and the one led by the Helio at the original Gracie academy weren't small. But who was responsible for this? *The civil war between Helio and Carlson? The youth of the south-zone with their surf-culture, revulsion for authoritarianism and preference for a more relaxed approach to jiu-jitsu? The physical distance and price difference between the two? Or the Guanabara Federation with its sportive vision for jiu-jitsu?* All of the above? Regardless of the reason(s), the reality is that there was a rift in jiu-jitsu and it began well before Royce and the UFC brought jiu-jitsu to the world stage.

Some of these transformations may have been inevitable, some were inevitable. Other transformations were in terms of where the practice of jiu-jitsu ought to sit along the spectrum between sport and martial art, while others were in terms of difference in personalities by the protagonists most actively responsible for shaping jiu-jitsu at the time.

At the end of the day, in the midst of the revolution led by Rorion and Royce, the definition of *what jiu-jitsu is,* still remains unclear. Today, whether we like or accept this or not, we don't have *one single jiu-jitsu,* instead, we have multiple *jiu-jitsus.* While identifying these evolutionary markers is a privilege granted only by hindsight.

With that said, it is clear that Carlson and Rolls' academy on the Figueiredo de Magalhães Street is a fork in the history of jiu-jitsu. Between the youthful, energetic and the fiercely competitive environment Carlson and Rolls had created for their students, the most widely accepted understanding of *what jiu-jitsu is,* was born out of that building and I just can't see anyway around that.

Lastly, despite having copied Carlson's more democratic and open approach to competitive jiu-jitsu, it would not be accurate to say that Rolls did not have his own ideas of what jiu-jitsu should look like. Having died so young and not reaching his full potential as either a fighter or as a coach, it may be difficult to identify any major stylistic differences between Carlson and Rolls. Still, given what we know and the interviewes in this book, I think it is fair to say that their differences, even if small and barely perceptible, weren't irrelevant.

Chapter 12

Brotherly-Rivalry

Carlson and Rolls: The partnership that would forever change jiu-jitsu and set the stage for its evolution. Photocred: Marco Imperial personal archives.

"Competition is necessary in my view. We see this in many places. Where there are two good coaches with two strong teams, jiu-jitsu takes off."

Marcelo Siriema

When Rolls began to teach separately from Carlson, a very important change for the evolution of BJJ took place.[156] Carlson's students dominated the in-house trials that determined the official representatives

---

[156] According to Reila, Carlson was too messy and unorganized for Rolls' taste. See: Gracie 2008, pg. 460 and 484. Carlos Gracie Jr. makes similar remarks on this. See: Drysdale 2020, pg. 77.

for the Gracie Academy during the late 60s, and early 70s in Rio.[157] He achieved his goal of proving to his Uncle Helio that his teaching methods were indeed superior (at least in terms of competitive performance). Nevertheless, complete dominance without the real threat of competent rivals has the negative effect of slowing down technical progress. After all, *why train hard if there is no threat of ever losing?*

Even his brother-rival Carlinhos concedes that Carlson's efforts in turning jiu-jitsu into a more competitive jungle were enormously beneficial to jiu-jitsu. *"It was a great help to have my brother Carlson as a rival. I think this is what helped Gracie Barra become as big as it did."*[158]

Opponents are a mandatory ingredient for evolution to take place. Excellence comes knocking on the door when the threat of losing is real. With that said, the absence of tough competition would have had the negative effect of pitching team members against themselves (in a political and social way) in case they didn't have an opposing team to wage war against. Or at least that is what my experience inside gyms has taught me.

This is why Rolls is so relevant to this discussion. It was Rolls and his students who stepped up to the mark and posed a challenge to Carlson's domination. Tournament results of this era show this with crystal clarity. In this sense, the rivalry between Carlson and Rolls was a crucial component in helping jiu-jitsu advance toward a more sophisticated and evolved approach.[159] An evolutionary process that would have been significantly impaired without them (if not impossible) and that, following

---

[157] According to Peixotinho up to 1981, in-house trials were held to determine the two representatives for the Gracie Academy in competition. The trials included all Gracie affiliated gyms, including Carlson's. It was only from 1981 onward that Carlson's students began representing their own academy. Later, Rolls would do the same and have his own team also represented independently from the original Gracie Academy. As for 1981 being the year they split, the information comes from the interview with Peixotinho who is confident of that being the year because he has a certificate stating that that is indeed the year. Although the split could have potentially taken place before 1981. More on this in the following chapter.

[158] *"Carlson Gracie – Reportagem – Sensei SporTV – 2009"* https://www.youtube.com/watch?v=JOWeCDAoi7Q

[159] Reila notes that as Helio aged and no longer taught classes, Royler and Royce began to train under Rolls at the Figueiredo Academy (Gracie 2008, pg. 468).

the recipe Carlson had created, would accelerate jiu-jitsu's evolution exponentially in the post-Royce Gracie era.[160]

From all accounts, the rivalry between the brothers Carlson and Rolls was of the friendly and healthy kind. Jean Jacques, one of our interviewees, recalls with no small degree of nostalgia how before classes began, both Carlson and Rolls would stand by the entrance of the academy trying to co-opt the other brother's students to switch over allegiances in a friendly and jesting manner. There was even spying going on in hopes of catching a glimpse of the "enemy's" techniques in preparation for war.

Curiously, even though they competed against each other in the in-house selection process that took place at the Gracie Academy in order to determine who the two official representatives of the team would be, the two groups co-existed in peace, harmony, and even mutual friendship. All this in an environment that tolerated occasional cross-training while respecting the boundaries of loyalty and business practice. Far from an easy balance to strike as any gym owner well knows.

This is exactly why I find this dynamic so intriguing. To me it is almost unbelievable that their friendship and mutual respect prevented them from being at each other's throats over the business they were both running as brothers, partners and rivals. This is especially true when we remind ourselves of the competitive environment in which the Gracie cousins and brothers were raised in. Competitive as their upbringing was, their tolerance and respect toward one another is quite endearing and rare.

Brothers, as anyone who has them well knows, can be incredibly competitive and even violent toward one another. But all it takes is a common enemy or a common cause for them to quickly forgive and forget whatever grievances they may have and unite in their shared cause. Carlson and Rolls may not have had a common enemy, but they did have a common cause in their aspirations toward a more sophisticated and democratic approach to jiu-jitsu.

---

[160] More on this in Part 3

What was important in their rivalry was how it cemented a model that would be further explored by the *third* and *fourth-wave* of practitioners. Even if in some ways, this model carried in its DNA the potential (now an actuality) of jiu-jitsu distancing itself from the reality of combat that Carlson prized so much. In Carlson's view, it had to work in a real-fight, that was the whole purpose of jiu-jitsu. Not necessarily medals (although he certainly loved watching his students win them).[161]

It would be helpful to remind ourselves that Carlson's interpretation of jiu-jitsu was a very specific one fit for the environment in which he had been bred. For Carlson, jiu-jitsu was a vehicle to win in a ring and on the mats. Did Rolls see it the same way? Or was there a subtle and hardly perceptible evolutionary drift from Carlson's views? An even more subtle one than Carlson's own drift from the training methods of the original Gracie Academy? Did Carlson with his "dry," "short" and to-the-point methods stant in contrast to Rolls' broader vision for a more encompassing jiu-jitsu and all its untapped potential? Something Rolls had an eye for as exemplified by his inquisitiveness toward other styles such as sambo, judo and wrestling.

Rolls understood and learned from Carlson that jiu-jitsu was far from reaching its full potential and that in order to further its technical development, the creation of a more competitive environment was imperative. What isn't clear to me is if his vision of jiu-jitsu was in total accordance with Carlson's.

Despite imitating Carlson's more *casca-grossa* oriented views on jiu-jitsu and creating a competitive environment of his own, Rolls' inquisitive and open-minded nature was steering him toward the creation of his own methodology. One whom all, including Carlson's own students saw as more sophisticated (which doesn't necessarily mean more realistic or combat-ready, only more sophisticated for the specific practice framed

---

[161] This may seem ambiguous to a reader accustomed to a narrative where competitive jiu-jitsu isn't fit for self-defense while a self-defense methodology isn't fit for competition. In my view, as well as in Carlson's (if I understand him correctly), they aren't necessarily mutually exclusive. Only that circumstances and rules have made it seem that way. In part 4, I expand on this and argue that a competitive format grounded in the reality of combat is not only possible, but necessary for jiu-jitsu to maintain its credibility.

by the Guanabara Federation). Furthermore, by lacking the *vale-tudo* know-how Carlson had, Rolls couldn't have gained such experience and kept his practice and focus orbiting around the only available competitive outlet for him at the time, jiu-jitsu competitions for himself and his students.

If this is the case, then the two brothers differed from one another in more than just business sense, even if some of these differences were imperceptible at the time they were taking place. Especially when we consider that diversification markers aren't always perceptible as they are occurring. Over time however, the results of these markers become increasingly visible as they drifted apart, while identifying this distancing and their point of origin becomes an easier task.

Of course, differences are only natural and all practitioners have their own preferences. What makes whatever differences Rolls may have had with Carlson unique to us here, is that they were both the lead protagonists of a crucial moment in jiu-jitsu's history that was giving shape to the *second-wave*. The wave that would be responsible for both spreading jiu-jitsu around the world and training the next wave who would play an even larger role in this expansion.

My overall impressions, based on the testimonies available, seem to point to Rolls being more concerned with jiu-jitsu for jiu-jitsu's sake than he was with jiu-jitsu as it befits a *vale-tudo* fight. In this sense, while *vale-tudo* played a fundamental role in shaping Carlson's interpretation of jiu-jitsu, its ban coupled with the growth of competitive jiu-jitsu circuit during the era in which Rolls was active, helped shape Rolls' fighting preferences to be less oriented toward *vale-tudo*. And, consequently, closer to the jiu-jitsu competition scene of that era.

Furthermore, if Carlson's students are a good indication of how Carlson saw and taught jiu-jitsu, then perhaps the same can be said about Rolls and his views. After all, it was from Rolls' classes that the two most successful teams of the post-Royce era would grow out of-Carlinhos Gracie with Gracie Barra and Romero Cavalcanti with Alliance.[162]

---

[162] Although in the flourishing landscape of the 90s, the growth of teams had as much to do with political craft as it did with coaching skills.

Admittedly, this is all very speculative and impossible to determine in any satisfactory way. What we do know however, is that Rolls would give continuation to Carlson's vision of competitive group classes focusing on a younger crowd from various social-demographics instead of the private classes model that was the bread-and-butter of the original Gracie Academy.

The young Gracie prodigy might have followed in his older brother's footsteps when he left the original Gracie Academy to develop in his own space. But Rolls wasn't Carlson any more than Carlson was Carlos or Helio. What both Carlson and Rolls had in common was their understanding that jiu-jitsu needed to move on toward a more competitive format open to all. Toward a jiu-jitsu that was more in sync with the aspirations of its *second-wave* members. Lastly (and if I am correct in that he had a more sportive outlook on jiu-jitsu), Rolls' interpretation was perfectly tuned for the new phase jiu-jitsu was about to undergo in the post-Royce era, when it became exposed to a much wider audience than ever before.

Chapter 13

Political Division and Beginning of the End of the Carlson Gracie Era

Cock-fighting: Carlson's inspiration for a
more competitive approach to jiu-jitsu.
Photocred: Master Fernando Pinduka.

"[Carlinhos] *I would leave in shock those early meetings, where we were all trying to organize jiu-jitsu. And I'd think to myself* 'why are we arguing over nonsense?' *They'd be in a room arguing, pointing the finger at each other and nothing got done (...)* [Siriema] *I think this is the definition of faith. Because you couldn't look at us then and reason* 'this right here will grow someday.' *It was all so small and chaotic.* 'Grow? How?' *Logic wasn't enough to make sense of that mess and get jiu-jitsu organized.*"

Master Carlos Gracie Jr. and Marcelo Siriema

Until 1981, all the Gracie affiliated academies competed under one umbrella, leaving the other non-affiliated Gracie gyms in Rio far behind in terms of tournament results. However, the overall (slow but steady) growth of jiu-jitsu in Rio during the 70s, led to the end of the in-house trials. Which was inevitable since the model for hosting trials could not have lasted forever, because the trials were quickly becoming as big (if not bigger), than the tournaments themselves. This excess of competitors would eventually lead Carlson to go his own way in 1981. An event that signaled a definitive departure that had been long in the making given the animosity between Helio and Carlson.

In short, this division basically meant that the Gracie clan went from being a single academy to multiple and from one competition team, to two (further splintering in forthcoming years). Even if these students were all still under the Gracie family in one way or another, a whole new generation of Gracies and their students had matured and were ready to open their own academies and continue the missionary efforts.

Between this growth of academies across Rio, the Guanabara Federation, Carlson's conflict with Helio, and the new culture arising in the Figueiredo Academy—all the elements were in place for the beginning of a whole new era for jiu-jitsu. With that in mind, it is worth reminding ourselves here that up to the founding of the Guanabara Federation, while under the direction of Carlos and Helio's interpretation of judo/jiu-jitsu, they all had a more or less clear definition of *what jiu-jitsu was*. This ensured the cohesiveness which in turn strengthened the Helio-centric monopoly of jiu-jitsu under his interpretation of it.

This dynamic was seemingly unbreakable and may have been, if it weren't for the fact that time takes its toll on us all. Inevitably, Helio's turn would come to slowly make way for a whole new generation of teachers with the methodologies that evolved out of the original Gracie fighting system with the Guanabara Federation as jiu-jitsu's testing arena. In some sense, this was a tribute to Helio; after all, shouldn't a master always teach his students to surpass him and be proud when they do?

The problem was that as this younger generation left to pursue their own paths, it was clear that their vision of what they were teaching was no longer in line with the one that the original Gracie Academy was so intent on enforcing. Something had changed alongside the growth of so many children into adulthood. They had grown up, and now they had their own aspirations and opinions.

Which was all for the better. Younger generations ought to always lead technical innovation because they are simply more imaginative and less restricted. It should fall on older generations to lead the shaping of the rules and the culture toward whatever direction the purpose of the art happens to be aimed at. Long story short, *political and cultural shapes shouldn't fall into the hands of the youth any more than technical innovation should be in the hands of seniors.*

The issue here however, wasn't only one of different generations asserting different viewpoints. As we have seen earlier, they also differed in terms of the purpose of their practice- should jiu-jitsu be centered around a self-defense curriculum as Helio insisted or *vale-tudo* and a more practical approach to combat as Carlson wanted? Or was jiu-jitsu a universe of its own and should assimilate as much as possible from other arts for the purpose of competition? *What is jiu-jitsu after all?* These protagonists may not have been asking this question yet, but time would expose these differences. And although they might have been small at this stage, they were far from being insignificant.

Unlike Kodokan judo, the Brazilian version of judo/jiu-jitsu led by the Gracie brothers never fully managed to establish an official hierarchy, curriculum (or at least one they could all agree on) and set of fixed cultural-values. This was partly due to Brazilian culture itself which, in general, is less hierarchical and organized than Japanese culture for example; partly due to internal family disputes; and also partly to the two different versions of jiu-jitsu that the founding of the Guanabara Federation exposed, *self-defense and competition.*

In this divisive landscape, it would be useful to understand Rolls as a centerpiece in the war of attrition between Carlson and Helio. If their civil war were a World War One battlefield, Rolls made his residency in no-mans-land. By maturing into his best years during the conflict between his Uncle and brother, Rolls served as a sort of buffer in the family. Preventing any further fragmentation and, by doing so, becoming one of the few people in the *jiu-jitsusphere* that could freely navigate both camps of the civil war.

I don't want to venture into this more than I already have. But at this point it becomes clear what an enormous loss Rolls death was. Not only as a widely loved human being, but also because Rolls was uniquely placed in all these disputes. He could have been the leader jiu-jitsu needed (not to mention the Gracie family itself) to unify its different interpretations and organize it under one single curriculum and definitive hierarchy, much like judo had done almost a century before. Perhaps this is far too ambitious of a goal. Nonetheless, if anyone was positioned to do it, that person was Rolls.

To remain concise and growing, jiu-jitsu needed someone with more than fighting skills, to replace Helio as jiu-jitsu's political leader as the patriarch aged. It needed someone with a mind geared toward structure and organization, someone respected enough on the mats to lead the army while still open to evolution. Or at least someone who was wise and respected enough to be willing and capable of delegating power in order to structure growth. Something Helio's territorial and biologically biased ways were unlikely to ever achieve.

With Carlson's retirement, Rolls was perfectly positioned, willing and able to become the next Gracie champion. But he had more than that going for him, he was also a strong candidate to be a political leader for jiu-jitsu. Of course, there were others with business acumen and initiative. Reylson was a savvy and hungry businessman who owned multiple academies in Rio and even a jiu-jitsu clothing brand at a time where no one even thought about doing so. He was also the first Gracie to open an academy in the US.[163] But Reylson did not have the kind of respect on the mats that Helio, Carlson and Rolls enjoyed. Which, in those days at least, had been the only way to rise through the ranks in the family.

---

[163] Pedreira 2015c, pg. 213

THE RISE AND EVOLUTION OF BRAZILIAN JIU-JITSU

Carley had all the potential to be a replacement to Carlson as he was also the heaviest of them all and was, according to those who knew him, very skilled. But Carley's early antagonizing with Helio's bossy ways probably left a bad taste in his mouth. Not to mention the lawsuit with Rorion he would have to fight years later in order to use his own name to teach jiu-jitsu.[164] As for Helio's eldest children, Rorion and Relson, they lacked the charisma and the same fighting credentials Carlson and Rolls enjoyed.

Rickson also became a leader in his own way and after Rolls' passing became the family's "number one," to Helio's pride and joy and fulfiling an old expectation. But Rickson was not a businessman, neither was he a coach of the caliber of Carlson or Rolls. Based on various testimonies of those who knew him in his prime and trained with him, he was also very skilled on the mats and was likely to have been the most dominant grappler in Brazil from the time of Rolls' death in 1982 all the way to the birth of the CBJJ/IBJJF in 94. Still, being the best on the mats, simply isn't enough, because effective leadership requires more than that.

Robson, the president of the old Guanabara Federation (now FJJRio), was perhaps the most well positioned person to become jiu-jitsu's political leader. The problem was that the federation never grew beyond Rio's borders, especially at a time when it was becoming clear in the early 90s that jiu-jitsu needed more structure and order (more on this in chapter 17) if it was to capilize on the possibilities unleashed by Royce's victories in the UFC.

As for Carlson, he was... well... *Carlson was Carlson.* Brilliant and brave in the ring, a visionary coach and perhaps the most charismatic of them all. Everyone loved Carlson (well almost everyone did). But Carlson wasn't the man to organize jiu-jitsu in political terms. His strengths lay in his passion for training Spartan like warriors. Moreover, Carlson's borderline anarchic, divisive and bellicose ways were the opposite of what jiu-jitsu needed if it was to become a truly global practice.

---

[164] The litigious battle was won by Carley Gracie and he was able to continue to use his own name to teach jiu-jitsu. For the court case between Rorion and Carley, see *"Gracie vs. Gracie"* here: https://caselaw.findlaw.com/us-9th-circuit/1471487.html

It is both ironic and unfortunate to acknowledge that Carlson's relaxed, unorganized and unthrifty ways were simultaneously what made him so loveable and also what prevented him from becoming more than a legendary fighter and coach (as if those were not enough). The man simply wasn't fit for politics or business, it's as simple as that.

He might have been the king in the ring and as a coach, but when it came time to scale jiu-jitsu in the post-Royce era, he was completely unequipped. His combative personality was more likely to disrupt jiu-jitsu's organization than it was to help it at a time when it had become clear that BJJ needed to scale in size. What jiu-jitsu needed was effective leadership able to perceive and adapt to the changes in time. What jiu-jitsu needed was fresh political leadership with a vision for the future.

By the time Carlinhos Gracie Jr.'s affiliation system began to cement itself in the jiu-jitsu political landscape during the 90s, it was starting to become obvious that the days for Carlson and his team to completely dominate competitive jiu-jitsu were numbered. It is equally ironic that the same process of democratization that he had played a leading role in kick-starting (by opening jiu-jitsu to all who wanted to train competitively), would be the same one to displace his team from the top of jiu-jitsu podiums.

Further democratization after all, also meant the end of the dominance of the *casca-grossa* approach to jiu-jitsu, the sort of jiu-jitsu Carlson Gracie's methods had been custom fit for. This time around, it meant a jiu-jitsu open to all who could afford it, *casca-grossa* or not.[165] For all practical purposes, what this new phase of "democratization" came to symbolize, was *the beginning of the end of the Carlson Gracie Era*.

***

It is impossible to estimate the depth of the loss that Rolls would be to jiu-jitsu and any attempt to do so is merely food for the imagination.

---

[165] Which we should add in passing, is a much broader audience than the one prized by the original Gracie academy that could afford costly private lessons. Group classes after all, beyond their competitiveness, have the added benefit of lowering costs significantly and making it more accessible to the economically less fortunate.

However, he did leave an heir of sorts. Many of his students would be divided among Rickson who was teaching at the original Gracie Academy, Carlson who remained at the Figueiredo Academy and Romero who was on his way to opening his own gym in Ipanema.

Yet Rolls' legacy would be given continuation mostly by the efforts of his younger brother. Carlos Gracie Jr. (or "Carlinhos" as he is best known in Brazil) would not only continue Rolls' teachings, but also build around jiu-jitsu the political and organizational fortifications it had long needed if it was to move forward and beyond an idiosyncratic practice of the Carioca south-zone.

Moreover, Carlinhos had the sense to understand the changing times and that, if jiu-jitsu was going to be further democratized, it needed to abandon some of its former tough-guy and hooligan like cultural traits it had inherited from a bygone era. Fortunately, he was able to achieve this without renouncing the jiu-jitsu that was nurtured inside the Figueiredo Academy.

Over time, Carlinhos would not disappoint and would achieve prominence as one of jiu-jitsu's most successful coaches of all time. More importantly, he would also achieve the much-needed position of successful political leader. He had credibility, the name, the charisma and an acute social intelligence. But above all, he understood well the dynamics of politics as well as how to manage power by delegating and sharing it. A rare skill in the history of jiu-jitsu.

Regardless of how his Uncle, brothers and cousins felt about it, the reality was that Carlinhos was the only one savvy enough to fully understand what the revolution set in motion by Royce and the UFC truly meant to jiu-jitsu. Accordingly, he began to make his moves just in the nick of time. Not in order to take the throne, because there wasn't really one to begin with. But rather to craft one from the ranks and files in what seemed more like an ungovernable land of small feudal lords fighting among themselves for power than it resembled an army poised to conquer the martial arts world.

Could Carlinhos be the one to finally create a unifying and comprehensive defintion of *what jiu-jitsu is?* Or is it already too late for any of that? At any rate, he was the one to create a much needed and reliable blue-print to give jiu-jitsu the longevity its history begged for and the direction it was lacking.

The jiu-jitsu warriors from the south-zone had finally reached the prominence, credibility and stardom they had been fighting for all along. A status that from the beginning of their war they believed was theirs by birth-right. Their revolution won a major victory by the hands and efforts of Rorion, Royce and the UFC in 1993, but it was far from complete. In fact, according to Carlinhos himself, it was only getting started...

Even though they were all united for the common cause of jiu-jitsu, the members of the *second-wave* in charge of organizing jiu-jitsu, still lacked a true sense of order and direction their victory was desperately in need of. Jiu-jitsu had won a major marketing victory for itself and now the world was watching and eager to join in on the fight. Naturally, as it befits every great victory in a war, its troops (old and new) wondered in unison, *where to next?*

"These were guys who were out to prove themselves no matter what."
Master Sergio Malibu

Interviews with members from the second-wave:

Sergio Malibu
Ignácio Aragão
Murilo Bustamante (1st half)
Jean Jacques Machado
Marcelo Alonso (1st half)
Royler Gracie
Luis Carlos Valois
Wallid Ismail (1st half)
Richard Bresler
André Pederneiras (1st half)

Master Sergio Malibu

Malibu having his hand raised.
Photocred: Sergio Malibu personal archives.

"In those days we had to prove it because no one believed that our style could defeat a Mike Tyson or a Bruce Lee for example."

Master Sergio Malibu

Sergio Malibu trained as a blue-belt under Rolls and is a well-known figure in the jiu-jitsu community in Rio. After the death of Rolls, Malibu became a student of Rickson and later taught at Master Jiu-Jitsu [later rebranded "Alliance"]. He was born on Feb/10/1958 and holds an 8th degree coral-belt. Our interview took place on July 3rd, 2022 in writing.

1- You were a student of Rolls, what was he like?

The family was beginning to see him as a leader, their new number one. Just to give you an idea of this, Helio himself would often bring Rickson over to train with Rolls at the Figueiredo Magalhães Academy in Copacabana where we trained. In those days, everyone considered Rolls to be a mentor of sorts. We all saw him as a source of knowledge. In some ways, he was ahead of the family, he was sort of the person that united them in all their differences.

2- What was Rolls' teaching methodology like?

Rolls was a very technical coach. In my opinion he was the most technical one. Carlson was also a great instructor. But Rolls' methodology, from what I heard, because I never trained with Helio, was that Helio focused more on self-defense than actual fighting. Rolls taught fighting, real-fighting as it would take place in the streets, because in those days that was normal. And I remember that after Friday's training he would tell us that we were ready for the weekend. That's when we trained porrada (brawling) and taparia (slap-fest), that sort of training was on Friday. So, he taught it all, real-fighting, competition training and a lot of self-defense, everything I learned in self-defense was in the beginning as a white-belt. Rolls had that trait that he picked up from Helio but he trained it in a competitive style. I remember that in order to get your blue-belt from Rolls you had to escape a front head-lock from one of his students who was on a rowing-team. His name was Bion, I think, strong guy. This guy would hold people in the head-lock and you had to get out if you wanted a blue-belt. Good times those were.

3- Carlson and Rolls were business partners, brothers and rivals, what was that like?

The rivalry between Carlson and Rolls was entirely sportive. The only students who would put up a fight against Carlson's guys were the students of Rolls. But those two had nothing but respect for each other. The whole thing was very respectful when Rolls was alive. Carlson had different policies, but we are talking about Rolls. In those days it was Helio, Carlson, Rolls and Relson's academies competing against one another in an in-house tournament to see who would represent the team in the regional tournaments. So, the rivalry was only on the mats, off the mats it was respectful. But Carlson had other ideas... Rolls' crowd, Rickson's and Relson's were closer to Helio. Carlson was mainly on his own, doing his own thing.

4- What were the differences in terms of teaching methodology between the Helio's Academy and Rolls'?

Helio taught mostly privates and the wealthier classes. Carlson and Rolls were in Copacabana and recruited just about anyone who wanted to train. Surfers, soccer players, anyone really. That's how it all started.

5- Rolls seemed to want to constantly be learning from other styles. Why was that?

Definitely, he would train judo, wrestling, boxing and absorbed everything he could into jiu-jitsu. Boxing was for fighting and if he won a fight, it wasn't for boxing, it was for jiu-jitsu, if he threw someone, it wasn't for judo, it was for jiu-jitsu. Everything he did was to help shape and improve and defend jiu-jitsu. Because jiu-jitsu simply didn't have the respect it has now and that it won after Royce and the UFC. In those days we had to prove it because no one believed that our style could defeat a Mike Tyson or a Bruce Lee for example. But I remember people back in the gym plotting to pick a fight with Mike Tyson to draw some attention. Or fantasizing about fighting Bruce Lee.[166] And those guys were fully confident that they would maul them both. The family wanted to put themselves and

---

[166] Malibu is referring here to conversations that must have taken place after 1985 when Tyson made his pro-debut. In other words, Rolls who died in 1982 could not have been part of these discussions. Also worthy of note here is that Bruce Lee died in 1973.

their methods to the test all the time. When Joe Louis visited Brazil, Helio challenged him too.[167] These were guys who were out to prove themselves no matter what. Until Rorion finally created the UFC and we shocked the world. Now everyone wanted to train our style because they all respected jiu-jitsu. And after that, Carlinhos took the World Championships to the USA and then it turned into the fever that we are witnessing today. And now it is normal for us to see other champions from other countries. So many people training, the whole thing just blew up.

6-   Was Rolls' jiu-jitsu creative?

You know what? The first time I saw an omoplata was Rolls applying one in 1980 and I never saw him train that technique in the gym.[168] These mobility type trainings that everyone does today, Rolls was already emphasizing that then, mobility, agility...

7-   Were Carlson and Rolls' vision of jiu-jitsu the same?

The vision wasn't the same, but the purpose for both was competition. Rolls trained a variety of techniques, Carlson was much older would find solutions to problems and Rolls would look for problems by throwing himself in the fire. Carlson was more of a coach, no longer a fighter. Rolls was more creative I think. Rolls' had his head in the future and with creative possibilities in sight.

---

[167] Although this challenge was widely propagated in the post-Rorion era, it is worth mentioning that when Helio first challenged Joe Louis in 1947 he was ignored and when he did it again in 1950 he was ridiculed by the press who called him a *"campeão do ridículo"* due to their different statuses in the fight world. Joe Louis did respond however to the second challenge with a counter-offer to fight Helio in boxing instead, which Helio refused. For details, see: Pedreira 2015b, chp. 1.

[168] Malibu might have seen the "omoplata" for the first time being applied by Rolls, but it wasn't the first time it was being used in jiu-jitsu circles. See appendix.

8- What was the overall impact Rolls had in competitive jiu-jitsu as a whole?

He died so young. I still think that overall Carlson's guys were still the most dominant, but we were getting close to them. There was simply no time. That's when Carlson took off in terms of tournament results and the guys from Gracie Barra and Alliance [off-shoots from Rolls' original students] began to catch up only 5-6 years later [1987-1988]. I actually helped Jacaré [Romero Cavalcanti] teach classes to Fabio Gurgel, Alexandre Paiva and Rodrigo Comprido and others. In those years Carlson took off as the dominant force in Rio until Carlinhos could rebuild the team. Because some people after Rolls' death went over to Rickson, like myself and others. Others stayed with Carlinhos, like Renzo the Machados brothers and Rilion. In other words, it took a while for Carlinhos to rebuild the team. Sadly, there wasn't enough time for Rolls' team to become the number one in Rio, he died too young.

Master Ignácio Aragão

Ignácio Aragão.
Photocred: Ignácio Aragão personal archives.

"Popular? People didn't even know what it was. I'd go to school full of scratches and bruises and people would ask me "what happened" *and I'd tell them, I was training jiu-jitsu and they'd say* "jiu-what?" *People didn't even know what it was."*

Master Ignácio Aragão

Aragão is one of Carlson's old time black-belts and in his prime was an active competitor and member of the jiu-jitsu community in Rio where he still trains. He was born on the 29th of September of 1963 and holds a 7th degree coral-belt. Our interview took place over the phone on May 25th 2022.

1-   What was your beginning in jiu-jitsu like?

I used to fight a lot in school so my mom decided to take me to Alvaro Barreto's gym [João Alberto Barreto's brother]. In those days you couldn't go cry to adults if someone picked on you. This was in 1977 and I was 14 years old. My coach, Alvaro Barreto, was an outstanding teacher but after a while there weren't too many guys to train with so I went over to Carlson's school.

2- What was the competition scene like?

Back in the day we had only one tournament per year. I was a 3x State Champion, ages 16, 17 and 18. Jiu-jitsu then was a practice for the middle-class and upper-middle class. You had to have money to train jiu-jitsu in the south-zone. There weren't a lot of black kids training for example.

3- When you started training, was jiu-jitsu popular in Rio de Janeiro?

Popular? People didn't even know what it was. I'd go to school full of scratches and bruises and people would ask me "what happened" and I'd tell them, I was training jiu-jitsu and they'd say "jiu-what?" People didn't even know what it was.

4- In 1967 there was a split in terms of what jiu-jitsu was. Was it self-defense? or was it a competitive ruleset? In 1994 this split became even more obvious. Can you comment?

There was a shift from the original view of jiu-jitsu geared toward porrada and self-defense and toward competition, this was due to economic reasons, get it? Everyone wanted to compete. In the 80s and 90s in Rio, sports were in vogue. The girls would workout, the guys all had a sport they specialized in. More so than today. Sports were more prestigious then. I saw a guy the other day holding hands with this beautiful girl, too pretty for him [laughs]. He looked so frail that if someone pushed him in front of his girlfriend he'd probably fall over and cry. It's a different world now.

5- I agree. I get the impression children are more obese, frightened and uncoordinated than they were during my childhood.

Of course. In those days if you wanted to be popular with the girls, you had to be good at some sport. Anything. So, you had to work out, train hard. Girls all worked out too. Especially in the south-zone, Copacabana, Ipanema... I chose jiu-jitsu for myself, because it gave us respect.

6- How do you think Rolls would feel about competition jiu-jitsu today and this division in general?

In my view, Rolls would have drifted toward a more competition-oriented view of jiu-jitsu, no way of knowing if I am right or wrong. He liked vale-tudo too and he would have helped Carlson's guys train for the luta-livre challenge at the Grajaú in 1991 and I'm sure he would have helped Royce in the UFC as well. He was such a well-versed teacher. But in general terms, I think he would have gone toward a more competition-oriented view of jiu-jitsu.

7- Jiu-jitsu exploded in such a way in the 90s that no one could have predicted, but the problem was that it wasn't clear who was in charge. There was so much division around. So many chiefs, but who was the head-chief? Also, the definition of jiu-jitsu wasn't really clear after Royce and the UFC either. It grew in so many different directions and it has so many different interpretations today: gi, no-gi, self-defense, jiu-jitsu for MMA, etc. Can you comment?

I totally agree with you. The Gracie family always had control of jiu-jitsu but they lost it today. This seems certain to me, the family no longer controls the growth of jiu-jitsu.

8- What are some of the main differences between training with a kimono or without one?

The kimono should be the foundation in my view and then think of training without one as your master's degree of sorts. In the kimono you can't make a mistake without paying for it. Learning how to get someone off balance is hard with the kimono, when you learn to do that, adapting to training without a kimono is easy. I believe this is the main reason why the luta-livre guys always had a hard time defeating jiu-jitsu guys, even when we took our kimono jackets off.

9- What was Carlson like as a coach?

Carlson was an outstanding teacher, but he wasn't much of the kind of coach that would show a lot of moves, his jiu-jitsu was very "dry." While Rolls jiu-jitsu was more generalized. Carlson taught a foundation and later the students would discover a game of their own. He would show a move and let people figure things out on their own. He was a believer in practice and lots of rounds and focused on the high percentage moves. Personally, I don't see it that way anymore, but Carlson did. What he was a specialist at was figuring out who didn't like who, and then making them fight each other in front of the whole class [laughs]. The result was that you would either quit the gym or would turn into a champion, and that's the sort of student Carlson wanted. He had a very competition-oriented mindset.

10- What was Rolls like as a person?

Just to give you an idea of this, one time I needed to make weight for a tournament when I bumped into Rolls who asked me how I was doing. I was going to compete against one of his students but

THE RISE AND EVOLUTION OF BRAZILIAN JIU-JITSU

that didn't stop him from giving me advice on how to cut weight. He was a very generous person... I'll tell you a story. The Gracies from the outside are very united, but among themselves they are always arguing. Once I saw an argument between Carlinhos, Rolls and Crólin. And Rolls said "You guys have to train even more, because I will teach my students everything. My idea for jiu-jitsu is to teach it to anyone who wants to learn it." *That was Rolls in a nutshell. I'll never forget that day.*[169]

11-   What about some of the differences between Carlson and Rolls?

When I got to Carlson, I was very skinny and kept getting caught in kimuras and Carlson would show me one way out. And I would ask him, "but Carlson, what if..." and he'd interrupt me and say, "that's it, other than that, don't get caught." Only one day later I was watching Rolls teach and a student asked Rolls the exact same question. He had four different answers to the question! He was more about teaching in detail.

12-   Carlson's experience was almost entirely in *vale-tudo*. Do you believe that his vision was a *vale-tudo* oriented one? Where jiu-jitsu had to work in a fight above all.

I'd say so. Listen, I trained with Carlson but not as long as some of the other ones did, guys like Pinduka, Peixotinho and Rosado. But speaking for myself, I agree with you. Vale-tudo helped shape Carlson's vision of jiu-jitsu in terms of how to teach it as well as what worked and didn't work in a fight. In that regard he had his own view of things.

---

[169] This event is later confirmed in the Carlinhos interview of Part 3, almost in the exact same words.

13- In general terms what would Rolls have to say about jiu-jitsu in the world today?

I think he would say that jiu-jitsu regressed in some ways and progressed in others. For example, one time I was training with Rilion and I was having problems with something and he said, "Ignácio, you need to have many guards, many types of guards to deal with different types of problems and to adapt to the opponent..." There are many new techniques that are very useful, others not so much. I don't like the 50/50 guard that the Miyao brothers use for example. Of course, they have their merit, but I just don't like that guard. I see a lot of things being taught on the internet that wouldn't work in competition, to me that is lack of good instruction. The instructors are teaching all the wrong things that wouldn't work even in competition. Even less so in a vale-tudo. In a real-fight there is a certain way of thinking you need to follow. There are non-negotiables in this type of thinking, you need to position yourself not to get hit first, so then you can advance your position and do damage. In my opinion jiu-jitsu is evolving in the wrong direction. Today jiu-jitsu evolves almost exclusively in terms of guards that wouldn't work in a fight. All this and most people don't even know how to take someone down! There are things we can borrow from modern-guards. For example, we can improve on the classic-guard [closed-guard], insert the butterfly-guard for example, which is highly efficient in my opinion.

14- Younger generations don't seem to see things this way though.

New generations have the privilege of having a jiu-jitsu that is built on the back of previous generations and it is good that they are improving on it, these guards are examples of this. This is all natural. In 100 years, anyone around the world will have access to more knowledge than all of us do now. This is generally speaking good.

There are many good things that have evolved from older things, things are more sophisticated in terms of offense and defense, but again, you have to clean things up a bit. People will come up with 50,000 different moves and maybe 5,000 of those will actually work. One time, Rickson was at a tournament and pretty much finished everyone the exact same way. In all his fights, he did the same thing, he would pass guard the same way and either submit from mount or submit after getting to the opponent's back. Then there was a guy right next to me who said, "is that all he knows how to do?" For some reason he looked over to me and asked me what I thought, I told him I thought he was wrong. "Why?" he asked. I told him it is because Rickson reduced moves to the most efficient ones. It's not that he doesn't know other moves, it is that he reduced what was most efficient to that particular situation and stuck to what was working.

15-   A minute ago, you described Carlson's jiu-jitsu as *"dry."* I suppose you meant this as something that had been reduced to what was most consistently efficient. I always believed that too. I don't care if a move is cool or not, old or not, complicated or not. The only relevant question is, *"does it work?"*

Yes, but you need to understand that even this is something that is dependent on the opponent you have. Not all opponents are equal, get it? The more resources the opponent has the more problems you will have. For example, Renzo was a fighter with a lot more technical knowledge and resources than Wallid Ismail. But Wallid posed a problem to Renzo because of Carlson's school of thinking. Now, personally, I'd rather be Renzo because he had more resources than Wallid. And after 45 years of training, I believe this is a better vision for jiu-jitsu. But again, Carlson, besides being an outstanding fighter and coach, his school trained many champions, how can you tell him that he was wrong?

Master Murilo Bustamante

Former UFC light-heavyweight and IBJJF World Champion Murilo Bustamante. Photocred: Murilo Bustamante personal archives.

"Carlson placed a lot of emphasis on moves that had a high degree of practicality to them like the kimura, guillotine, mata-leão [RNC], kata-gatame [head-and-arm-choke], etc. He had solid jiu-jitsu grounded in the fundamental aspects of grappling."

Master Murilo Bustamante

One of the most iconic figures from the 90s and 2000s in both *vale-tudo* and jiu-jitsu, Bustamante is a central figure in the history of jiu-jitsu. He began his *vale-tudo* career representing jiu-jitsu in the 1991 challenge against luta-livre at the Grajaú, became an IBJJF World Champion in 1999, and the UFC title in 2002. Murilo was born on July 30th, 1966, and is one of the head founders of Brazilian Top Team (BTT). He is a black-belt under Carlson Gracie and currently holds a 7th degree coral-belt. Our interview took place over the phone on June 13th, 2022.

1- Tell us about your beginnings in jiu-jitsu.

I began training in 1977 when I was 10-11 years old. My older brothers took me to train with Carlson at the Figueiredo de Magalhães academy. I trained in the kids class with Carlos Alberto. I recall that the kids trained a lot of self-defense, but as I got older, maybe when I was 13-14 I began to train with Carlson and the other adults where the focus was on live-sparring.

2- What was Carlson's methodology like?

It was a position a day but mostly training. As I got older, things changed a bit and became a little more practical. There was a lot of open-mat style training with a lot of heavy-sparring. Carlson, at the right moments, would stop training and give you corrections when he saw something worth correcting. He'd tell you to do it right a few times and then get back to training. This sort of training did me well, from that point onward the move would stick with me. I also recall discussing moves with him, you know, solutions to problems and sometimes he didn't quite know the answer and he'd think about it for a second and come back with a possible solution for us to try.

3- Carlson incentivized his students to train in other styles. What styles did you train in other than jiu-jitsu and who did you train under?

In boxing, I trained under Claudio Coelho, still train under him in fact. In the US I trained for a brief moment under a coach called Steve Petramale. But my boxing coach who's been training me since I was 18 years old was Coelho. When I was 25, around the time of the jiu-jitsu vs. luta-livre challenge of 1991 I began to box with him more consistently. I also trained judo with some of

*Rio's biggest names, first with Vigilio, then with George Mehdi
while I was a brown-belt and then at the Flamengo Club in the
80s under Mauricio Sabatini who gave me my judo black-belt
and is the judo coach I trained the most under. He was actually a student of Mehdi. I trained a little muay-thai as well but
not much.*

4- What was life in the Figueiredo de Magalhães academy like?

*There was a front-desk downstairs and two smaller rooms where
Carlson and Rolls alternated private lessons. Those small rooms
also had people training in them on the days that either Carlson or
Rolls had those mats, especially the guys who wanted to train every-
day like me. Upstairs there would be an open-mat session going
on. Normally with more people because the mats upstairs were a
lot bigger. We had a group of other guys who helped Carlson there
too like Saporito and Bolão, Marcelo Alonso and [Carlson] Junior.*

5- Did you have much contact with Rolls?

*Very little. Epecially because I was so young. But I remem-
ber that the shower was upstairs so we had to go upstairs if
we wanted to shower and the door would normally be closed
because they didn't want anyone watching them train. So, I'd
knock so someone could let me in and someone would open the
door. Normally Rolls, and I'd see that guy standing there with
that big mustache of his and he'd let me in and lock the door
again as soon as I left the room. As a kid it was always a bit
intimidating.*

6- I am under the impression that Carlson had a view of jiu-jitsu that
was heavily influenced by his experience in *vale-tudo*. Can you
comment on this?

Yes, very likely. I pursued a similar path as Carlson's in vale-tudo and would agree with that approach. He had a jiu-jitsu that was very grounded and that had a quick application to them. He wasn't too interested in moves that were too complicated or that required too much movement and time to apply. Later when I began fighting vale-tudo, I got it. In real life you need to put things into action quickly, you just don't have a lot of time to work moves. In a fight it is like you are always in a hurry. Carlson placed a lot of emphasis on moves that had a high degree of practicality to them like the kimura, guillotine, mata-leão [RNC], kata-gatame [head-and-arm-choke], etc. He had solid jiu-jitsu grounded in the fundamental aspects of grappling.

7-   In those days, you guys trained a lot of *taparia* and with boxing-gloves. I don't think a lot of the modern-guards we see today could have evolved in an environment where slaps and punches were part of the practice. In some ways the *confere* [to check] served as a reminder to students of what worked and what didn't in a fight. Do you agree?

Definitely. I'm just not sure other gyms trained taparia like we did. We did it most of the time on Saturday's at Carlson Gracie's school. We'd be in swimming trunks and go at it. At the end, everyone would go to the beach after and be covered with slap marks all over our bodies... Look, jiu-jitsu has grown a lot. Today the guy wins a tournament and becomes a sponsored athlete, teaches seminars and privates, etc. Many doors will open for those who win jiu-jitsu competitions today. As a result, guys want to win, not really caring if how they are winning would help them in a real situation. They are sport-jiu-jitsu professionals. On the other hand, I think that a lot of competitors out there today would have no idea of what to do in a real-fight. Some are winning events and don't even know how to take someone down. They fight to be on bottom with berimbolos, or they put you in a deep-half-guard or 50/50. These are moves that if you try them in a real-fight you would expose yourself a lot.

8-   Did *taparia* training hurt?

Not really, it would leave marks on us, that's all. In my beginnings
in vale-tudo I trained with slaps a lot. But we stopped because some-
times there would be a finger to the eye of the students or you'd hit
them too hard in the ear and that could cause them problems. But
over time we moved away from that. We also trained a lot with box-
ing-gloves on. One striking and the other trying to takedown the one
wearing gloves. This gave the student's jiu-jitsu skills a reality check.

9-   What are the main differences between jiu-jitsu in the 70s and 80s
      and today?

Today, what evolved was the customer service. In those days we
didn't plan the classes much. The student had to figure it out rolling
around. In that environment only the strong survived, there was
a process of natural selection going on. Today the services have
improved, the student doesn't train until he is prepared to train.
There are systems in place.

10-   Carlinhos described the relationship between Carlson and Helio as a
      civil war between two generals. What was the cause of their rivalry?

Hard to say. I don't really know when it started. But I definitely
saw some disagreement between them. Sometimes when one of
Carlson's students would fight one of Helio's things got really heated
in between them. They say that things got a lot worse when Sergio
Íris, one of Carlson's guys, defeated Rorion in a fight. I think it was
the first time someone defeated one of Helio's sons in competition.
I can't say for sure because I wasn't there to see, but it was what I
heard at the academy from the older Carlson students. This was a
big deal and sometimes I saw Helio arguing with Carlson over it.
Carlson, by the way, never talked back to Helio, he had the most

utter respect for his Uncle. But Helio would go crazy over these things. They were definitely very competitive toward one another.

11- Can you tell us a little about the preparation for the 91 *vale-tudo* against the luta-livre representatives? In a sense, this event was a prelude to the UFC because it was a coordinated effort by many people to bring back the *vale-tudo* tradition that had practically disappeared during the 70s and 80s in Brazil. That event also united all these different jiu-jitsu representatives from different academies to train together and fight under one banner: jiu-jitsu. Can you talk a little bit about that event?

Of course. The preparation was daily and led by Carlson. Some days we trained blocking punches and clinches, others we trained exclusively on the ground, etc. The event kept getting postponed because there was a lot of resistance to vale-tudo in Brazil at the time. At some point we were considering doing the event behind closed doors just to be able to fight after so much training. But the delays gave us all more time to train and understand the game of vale-tudo. We basically trained for 4 months straight for this event and we all matured. Marcelo Behring was a good friend of mine so I brought him over to train and he brought Fabio [Gurgel]. Others who were also Carlson's students would also come by to train like Zé Mario, Libório, Amaury [Bitetti]. Also, other fighters from different schools would also come help such as: Roberto Traven and Castelo Branco who were my opponents at jiu-jitsu events. Wallid even went to train with Carlinhos, Jorge Pereira, Ralph and Renzo Gracie and all those guys to prepare to fight Eugenio Tadeu. It was a unifying moment for jiu-jitsu.

(continues in Part 3)

Master Jean Jacques Machado

**Carlinhos Gracie and his student
Jean Jacques Machado circa 1987.
Photocred: Jean Jacques Machado
personal archives.**

*"It was pride. The honor of the family, to keep the legacy, it was 100% pride. That is what drove everybody to prove what we believed and we believed that jiu-jitsu is better, that is what kept everyone going. Because at the end of the day, what do we fight for? A medal? We fight for the pride to go back into the gym on Monday and look at your mas-*ter in the face and tell him 'I did it and next time I will do it even better.'"

Master Jean Jacques Machado

Jean-Jacques is not only one of the most known members from the second-wave, but he is also one of the pioneers of growth of jiu-jitsu in the US. On top of this, Jean-Jacques is a 2x ADCC champion. Our interview was originally meant as a promo for the *Closed-Guard* project and it took place in person in Los Angeles on November 14th, 2020. Jean Jacques was born on February 12th 1968 and is a 7th degree coral-belt.

1-   Jiu-jitsu seems to have gone through a quiet time in the 60, 70s and 80s but began to pick up momentum after the 90s. Can you talk about this?

It's true, jiu-jitsu went flat for some years. The rebirth of jiu-jitsu was interesting and started in the wealthier area of the south-zone of Rio de Janeiro and it grew slowly, mostly among people of that neighborhood. Back in those days you had maybe one event a year. Which meant that no one from that generation trained jiu-jitsu for a tournament. We trained purely for self-defense. To make sure that there wasn't any issues on the streets and you knew how to defend yourself in case something happened. Based on that, you would build such confidence that you felt like you were superman. You trained every single day to get ready for a fight. As time went by, we slowly had more tournaments happening. Then things started to take a bit of a different direction from the jiu-jitsu that I had learned, that one we had learned. In a sense this was incredible and allowed it to become such a huge sport around the world. But at the same time, we also want to make sure it did not lose its roots.

2-   What was living and training jiu-jitsu in Rio like in those days?

It was a very different atmosphere than the one most people know today. Evidently, a lot of situations happened in the 80s growing up, altercation on the streets, etc. There was nothing provoked by anybody, it just ended up happening such as a traffic situation in case someone almost ran you over and then you call them a bad name and the guy would stop to chase you, things like that. Then evidently, we had to defend ourselves. All these situations weren't about right or wrong, but I think they were situations that were needed for the growth of jiu-jitsu.

Which is why I think that a lot of people might misunderstand these fights. You see videos today of fights on the beach and stories you hear, but these events weren't provoked by any jiu-jitsu person. They were things that were necessary to create a story. To make sure that jiu-jitsu lived and proved everything that was taught to us and that will live forever. This is something that I believe, with this conversation we are having right now Robert, that the goal is for people to understand that there was never any altercation that I saw growing up that was provoked by any jiu-jitsu person. We learned jiu-jitsu to defend ourselves. We were never the aggressors in any of those situations and in all the fights I saw in the streets with Renzo, Rickson. All of them, we were all defending ourselves. Which says a lot.

3- It seems to me that among those almost 40 [including the Machado brothers] children there was a very specific internal culture they had to follow in terms of training, diet, rules, etc. Things would have to be strict, was it military like?

It was warm, but at the same time, everyone understood that you had to follow the rules. I mean, you had to, it was a big family. You had altercations, but man, no one ever lost respect for their elders. I would say that they created a habit for us to do things they felt were better for us. To this day, I use the Gracie Diet. It's something I still do. Because everyone did jiu-jitsu you wanted to train too. "I wanna be like them." Jiu-jitsu was the thing that since the first generation in our family, was there as a path. And there were no obligations, it was a natural passion to that lifestyle.

4- Can you talk about the relationship between Carlson and Rolls?

They used to share the same school. For years we used to go there and Carlson would be like, "hey, you should come train tomorrow with me" and Rolls would be like "leave the kid alone!" Man, it was like that for years. When you walked into that school, you would look right and it was Rolls' and look left and it was Carlson's school.

For years we had this. In a very positive way the rivalry inside the family against Carlson's students made everybody better. And there were no hard feelings. Today I beat you, tomorrow you beat me, no one got mad because competitive training helped everyone raise their level. And I am so grateful because if it weren't for that rivalry I might not have trained the way I did, or feel the need to win that match, it was all so important to find out which side of the family was doing better, Carlson or Rolls?

5-   Did they get along though?

Carlson and Rolls got along extremely well. They loved each other, respected each other. It was all just a funny situation. At the tour- naments, almost every single one of them, the finals were between a student of Rolls against one of Carlson's. And because we trained door to door, we used to keep the door a little closed so they couldn't see what we were doing in there [laughs] that's how we grew up. With our rivals right next door to us. But without Carlson, jiu-jitsu would be something else. The way he pushed his students, I think in a way, the rivalry he created inside the family... I take that as a very positive thing. It made everybody teach more, focus more. Because when it came to tournaments, they both wanted to be first. I think the benefit of all this was for jiu-jitsu as a whole. Everyone trained more, gave more instruction. It was an incredible time. There was no tournament if Carlson was not there.

6-   Carlson to me was the man who played the leading role in adapt- ing jiu-jitsu to a ring and *vale-tudo* fight because he was the one who fought the most. How influential do you think he really was in helping the adaptation of jiu-jitsu for *vale-tudo*/MMA in general?

I was talking to Carlson Jr. once and he mentioned something that made total sense. He said that we could see this in Carlson's fights.

He was trying to make the techniques shorter. He was good with his hands but he never wanted to make the techniques too long for vale-tudo purposes. And when you think about it 80% of the jiu-jitsu we learn in the gym we wouldn't use in MMA.

Which makes me think that Carlson did have a specific view on this, as if thinking, "I know I won't use all this, I have fought, I know what I need." And I think his ring experience led him to say "hey, short! Short! we are not going to use all that!" and looking at it all today, he was right. Especially his style of fighting and if you look at most of his students that fought MMA, they had a similar mentality. But again, jiu-jitsu is something so amazing that when we think about it, there could not have been a better person than Royce to show how incredible jiu-jitsu is. Having somebody physically, compared to other fighters, a skinny one and go there, get squashed by everyone and submit everyone after. I think that the shock to the world was watching someone who looked like they were losing but was in fact preparing to finish the opponent. But if a Carlson guy went there, a big guy who boxed the guy to be on top I don't think it would have had the same impact.

7- Jiu-jitsu in many ways followed in the footsteps of judo in terms of how it organized itself, but that doesn't mean things were easy for BJJ. Can you comment?

Yes, definitely, judo is such a well-organized sport, an Olympic sport. And I think it will be Olympic sport for another 100 years. You got to understand that judo has so many years being backed up by government. And if you think of jiu-jitsu it is almost as if we grew up in a backyard without any incentive. Everything in jiu-jitsu was one hundred times harder than it was for judo when you place them side to side. I think after so many years, the challenge that we have in organizing tournaments, to get sponsors, to become more organized evidently makes everyone go "what are these other people doing that is working and why can't we do the same?" *and I think it was an amazing turning point in jiu-jitsu to become popular, regardless of MMA, through the vision that Carlinhos* [Carlos Gracie Jr.] *had.*

Because I remember he used to come to teach seminars here in Los Angeles at our academies and once having dinner he looked up and said, "I want to make sure that you guys understand that we are going to conquer the world." *And I looked at him and thought* "what is he talking about?" *and he said* "I'll leave California for you guys, but we are going to take over the world." *We went with him, and not many people know this, but we actually opened for him the International Federation of Jiu-jitsu* [IBJJF] *to allow him to come to the USA to start the tournaments here. It was me and my brothers who did that for him in the beginning. And evidently, we did not have the same vision he had. I think the one thing that he does that is incredible, is to select the right people to work with him and be able to make these people see things the way he sees them. Later on, we all looked back into all this and he would say* "I told you, we were going to conquer the world." *This was in the 90s and there was no one doing jiu-jitsu and he was just starting to orga-nize the World Championships in Brazil. Which, by the way, in the beginning had few competitors. And then he organized the Pans in California, then it went to Hawaii, Miami and now we have tour-naments all over the world. He created something from nothing with a vision and was able to select people and make them see what he was seeing and here we are today.*

8- I argue in my first book that IBJJF became the Kodokan of jiu-jitsu, but our culture is still very Brazilian. But at the same time, I feel that sometimes BJJ culture is so relaxed it has no code to keep it together like judo has, it is very different.

I think we will get there, in a way it's better today than a few years ago. We need to teach younger generations of practitioners and make them understand things better and to act differently toward jiu-jitsu and their opponents. Because in my time there was no way a fighter would disrespect another fighter, no way. Impossible. Because we learned respect and I see today things that are overboard, publicity stunts that aren't how I see jiu-jitsu. Younger generations are losing their history. They need to understand how important all this is.

9- Perhaps the most interesting aspect of this story to me is that from the Kimura fight in 1951 all the way to 1993 there wasn't much happening for jiu-jitsu, but they stuck to it. The biggest contribution of that generation of Gracies to jiu-jitsu was that, despite no one caring, for four decades they remained faithful to their vision. They kept doing things their own way. This is astounding to me. Why?

It was pride. The honor of the family, to keep the legacy, it was 100% pride. That is what drove everybody to prove what we believed and we believed that jiu-jitsu is better. That is what kept everyone going. Because at the end of the day, what do we fight for? A medal? We fight for the pride to go back into the gym on Monday and look your master in the face and tell him "I did it and next time I will do it even better." That is basically why we trained, it wasn't for money or popularity. No social media, nothing. Just go out there and fight, no pictures taken. Nothing like that, we did not care about that. Back then you could not lie. You either do it or not. Today social media allows people to lie and that wasn't the case in our time. In our time, who was present saw what you did and you knew what you did and that is what matters the most. Today you take a picture or something and it looks like you did something you didn't do. Our pride drove us then and still does now.

10- Any memorable stories from that era? Anything, even if it is not jiu-jitsu related?

People sometimes make a vision of other people they look up to and expect that "he will never do anything wrong and always follow the rules," but we are all common people. We try to do the good things but we also have our moments when we realize "man, what did I do?" Ok, this is a good one and Rickson might get mad at me but I'll talk to him later [laughs]. In Brazil they had these firecrackers and this one was so powerful it sounded like someone was shooting a gun. One time, we were all driving slowly and we would see a crowd, light a firecracker and throw it in the middle of that crowd and watch people run around like crazy. It was just a way for us to have fun. It isn't something we are very proud of today, but we were young and at the time it was all very funny. But not today guys, don't do it! [laughs]. These are common things that people do and we are all common people like everyone. But it is all very funny because looking at all this today and how people see Rickson and imagining him doing such a thing seems unthinkable, but he did! And I was there with him doing such things.

11- What was it like growing up in an environment with your best friends immersed in jiu-jitsu at a time when no one knew what it was? What are your best memories of that era?

Thinking of all this, it's all like going back in time, like a movie, so many memories! Everything needed to happen as it did. The combination of everything made jiu-jitsu what it is now. Everything I do is based on jiu-jitsu, but I think my best memories were in that house, eating lunch with so many people in the house... man, what a privilege. Because in the big house in Teresópolis, we had 21 bedrooms in the house and I don't recall how big the dinner table was, but it was for more than 20 people for sure and I remember the kids stayed on the other side. All members of the family were there. You know that cartoon with the superhero house? That's how I think of it all today.

Marcelo Alonso

**Marcelo Alonso and Carlson in 1996. In the
picture, Carlson holds a CD of his musical
heroine, French singer, Édith Piaf.
Photocred: Marcelo Alonso personal archives.**

*"But what I saw Carlson pass on to others was confidence. That I saw
many times. He'd see Vitor* [Belfort] *a little tense before a fight and he'd
say 'What are you man? A chicken? You'll fuck this guy up!' He'd say and
do things with that hoarse way of his but he'd get his guys to believe him
and consequently believe in themselves."*

Marcelo Alonso

Alonso is arguably the most important MMA journalist in contemporary history. He began covering jiu-jitsu events before the UFC and remains actively reporting events and testimonies on his Youtube channel *"Portal do Vale-tudo."* Our interview took place on July 20th, 2022 over audio messages.

1- Marcelo, you are known as one of the most experienced and respected
    journalists in the history of jiu-jitsu and MMA. Tell us about your
    beginnings in all this?

*I began in judo like many Brazilians did. But eventually started
training under Claudio França who began teaching in the*

condominium I was living at the time. I majored as a biologist and was really into photography in those days so when França found this out he began to ask me to take pictures at the gym. And just like that I became the official photographer of the gym and for the tournament França organized with Joe Moreira and Marcus Vinicius de Lucia, the Copa Atlântico Sul. This was around 1991-92, before the UFC. Eventually I got hired by Kiai magazine and began photographing and writing for all sorts of different martial arts. Later on, I started to help three guys who got Tatame Magazine started (still as a newspaper). That's how I found out that my passion was journalism, so I quit my job as microbiologist and enrolled in my University to become a journalist instead. Later on, KIAI went out of business and I became the chief-editor of Tatame magazine and started to write for numerous other international publications.

2- How did you come to be so close to Carlson and his team?

Around this time, I met Oswaldo Paquetá, who became one of my best friends, and he introduced me to Carlson and his guys. When I first met Carlson, he was looking at all the pictures I had taken of some Gracie Barra guys and in that rough way of his, he jokingly called me a "fotógrafo creontão da pesada" (big-time traitor photographer). Keep in mind that that was Carlson Gracie I was speaking to when I was only 22. Naturally I was a bit intimidated. In moments like these, Carlson showed what a big heart he really had. He realized I became a little uncomfortable by how he approached me so abruptly so he wanted to fix things. He said, "ok, you may be a creonte, but you are an ok guy. Just show up sometimes at my academy to photograph my guys and you will no longer be a creonte." I did exactly that and eventually I became close to him and his guys. Me and Carlson became good friends over time and we spent a lot of time together. We became so close that he always made sure I stayed at his house whenever I traveled to Los Angeles for work. In fact, he'd be furious if I didn't stay at his house [laughs]. I had the opportunity to see all this up close, the early days of Carlson and Vitor [Belfort] *in the US.*

3- You saw Carlson teach many times, what were his classes like? Did he still teach competitive jiu-jitsu or was his focus on MMA already?

When I met Carlson, his focus was still jiu-jitsu. His students basically won everything in the early 90s. All divisions, first and second-place. It was crazy. But if you ask me if he was still teaching class? No. Students like to romanticize, but Carlson was a trainer of casca-grossas. He was the kind of guy that whenever he showed up at the gym people would try harder to show off and impress him. He was a legend, an idol to all those heavy-hitters. But classes? No, he'd be downstairs eating açaí with Paquetá and Amaury [Bitteti Senior]. *But classes in between 1992 and 2000 he didn't really teach anymore. Few guys from that generation ever saw Carlson wear a gi.*

4- What was Carlson's relationship to Helio? Did Carlson talk about him?

Their relationship was awful. People can romanticize all they want. Deep down, Carlson held respect for Helio, but he also resented him. He also held that same vision that Reila brought back [through her biography of Carlos Gracie] *that Carlos, his father had been cheated* [in terms of the role he played in the history of jiu-jitsu]. *Carlson never had a master-student sort of relationship with us, we interacted as friends so he always spoke frankly to those in his close circle. We'd be talking and I'd say, "... your dad? What about Helio?" And Carlson would go* "Tio Helio é o caralho! quem me ensinou foi meu pai" (Uncle Helio no way! My father was the one who taught me). *Their relationship was never great, Helio would say in interviews I did with him that Carlson was lazy. And I'd say* "well, Carlson might have been lazy, but he guarded the family's name ..." *and Helio would say* "no, it wasn't like that..." *They had their own internal rivalry. What Reila writes in her book really is true in this regard. And Carlson in his turn, instigated a rivalry with the Gracie Academy that was something very curious. Right before Vitor Belfort's debut in the UFC, I was staying with Carlson but told him,* "listen, I'll stay here with you but I have to go to other academies, I'm going to go see Rickson and you got to let me be!" *And he'd say,* "ok, ok." *You need to keep in mind that Rickson was the idol of that generation, and everyone would be asking* "what did Rickson say?" *wanting to know everything about my visit and Carlson would interrupt and say* "what is going on here? why are you guys kissing his ass?" *And his guys would be,* "no master, Rickson is the enemy... he's the enemy." *Get it? Carlson wouldn't let people idolize Rickson. He'd say* "Libório beats Rickson!" *He'd say these things, he wouldn't let any of his guys idolize Rickson. And regarding Helio, the only time I saw them next to each other in person was in Teresópolis and I saw Carlson approaching Helio, who was sitting on the table with the event's organizers, while Carlson was shaking everyone's hands. Instinctively I positioned myself to take a picture of that historic moment of Carlson and Helio together. And Carlson shook everyone's hands that day, but when it came to his Uncle, Helio did not extend his hand out to Carlson. João Alberto Barreto who was sitting right next to Helio extended his hand to shake Carlson's so he didn't lose face.*

5- In his prime, Carlson was one of the biggest *vale-tudo* names in Brazil. Did he pass on this experience to his students?

Honestly, I don't feel that I am the most qualified person to comment on this. But if you ask me what I saw, it was this. Like I said, I never saw him wear a gi or teach a class. But in 1991 [in preparation for the Jiu-jitsu vs. Luta-Livre challenge], *Fabio Gurgel said that he did get on the mats with them. Those guys did not know how to grapple without a gi so Carlson gave them many pointers.*

But what I saw Carlson pass on to others was confidence. That I saw many times. He'd see Vitor [Belfort] a little tense before a fight and he'd say "What are you man? A chicken? You'll fuck this guy up!" He'd say and do things with that hoarse way of his but he'd get his guys to believe him and consequently believe in themselves too.

6- What was Carlson's relationship with his students like?

It was crazy. Off the mats he never held a strict hierarchy of master-student. Of course, on the mats it was different and everyone would be whispering his name whenever he walked in. But on our trips it was a brotherhood like I'd never seen before. They'd be teasing Carlson and he never demanded to be treated differently because of his seniority, he was one of them, he wanted to be treated as an equal among them. He was a truly unique person. Speaking for myself, I recall times when I'd be arguing with Carlson over something and would suddenly stop and think to myself "shit man, this is nuts, I am arguing with Carlson Gracie! I am treating the old man like he is my friend, telling him to go fuck himself!" Truth is, he wanted to be treated that way. If you didn't treat him as a friend I think he'd be upset. He was such a simple person and didn't carry himself like so many of the Gracie's do in the sense that if he went out for dinner, he didn't make a point to sit next to other black-belts or rich-guys, he was the opposite of that. He wanted to be where the action and laughter were. Again, on the mats it was different, but those who broke through Carlson's intimate circle developed a very close and genuine relationship with him. So many stories... Many of our stories of him are on the record, but the best ones are off the record. If you sit at a table with guys like Allan Goes, Conan Silveira, Vitor Belfort, Wallid, Mario Sperry, Rinaldo Santos, Una Proença, Rodrigo Medeiros myself, people who lived with Carlson. Or even those who traveled a lot with him, recalling the good old days with him, I can guarantee you may spend 5-6 hours laughing nonstop like you never did in your life. Working for 3 decades in the martial arts industry there is no question to me that Carlson Gracie was the most charismatic and funny person I´ve ever met in my life.

(continues in Part 3)

Master Royler Gracie

Royler winning a match- the most successful Gracie competitor from his generation.
Photocred: Royler Gracie personal archives.

"He'd enter into endless fights to stand by his guys, and if he felt he was right about something, he would see it to the end. And sometimes this meant going against his own family. Ultimately, for jiu-jitsu to be where it is today, he played an enormous contribution. I'd go as far as saying that in regards to the changes from Helio to a younger generation, he was an instrumental figure in that process. We need to remember these things, Carlson was an enlightened person."

Master Royler Gracie

Helio Gracie's fifth son and a key member from the *second-wave,* Royler Gracie was born on December 6th 1965 and holds an 8th degree coral-belt. In addition to being a successful MMA fighter, Royler is also a 4x IBJJF and 3x ADCC world-champion, as well as a highly accomplished coach and team leader of Gracie Humaitá. Furthermore, he is one of the top 40 most successful BJJ competitors of all time.[170] He still actively teaches jiu-jitsu in San Diego, California.

---

[170] Drysdale 2022

1- I imagine that you were born wearing a gi. Who were your main instructors?

Look, when you are born into a family where everyone is a fighter, I think that everyone becomes your teacher in a way. I had my Uncle [Carlos], my father who was the main one, my brothers and cousins. But I always say this a lot, the ones who taught me the most were my students because they are always putting me against the wall asking tough questions. At first, I'd repeat back to them everything I had learned, like a parrot [laughs], later, you learn how to think about these questions in a deeper way. But I'd say my father was a very important teacher if I have to name a few. Rolls, with whom I trained with a lot when I was a kid, then I began training with Rickson. So, you can see there that I had 3 incredible people to learn from, on top of my other brothers, cousins and Uncle Carlos who, although I never took a class from him, I did see him wear a gi a few times. Although I should say I also trained with Carlson, but I wouldn't say he was ever my direct instructor, but he also taught me.

2- What were the classes at the original Gracie Academy like? Many people claim they were mostly self-defense oriented and that there were no competition classes.

When I began training at the Rio Branco academy [original Gracie Academy in downtown Rio], *I was very young. By the time I got there, the academy had shrunk a lot. Back in the day, they even had bleachers there for people to watch and there were three floors. By the time I got there, there were two smaller rooms left and classes were mostly private lessons. We had our own group sessions among ourselves, maybe 4, 5 or 6 of us. But there were no big classes of 30 or 40 students at a time for example. So, the academy in those days was more focused on private lessons. A few years later I began to train with Rolls, who was in Copacabana. There I had many group lessons with other kids under Carlson and Rolls. From there things evolved. When we left downtown and went over to Vasco's rowing gym at the Lagoa, that was when group classes really began, even though we still taught a lot of private lessons. So much so, that the only time we had group classes was at night, during the day we taught only privates, something we inherited from the original Gracie Academy downtown. In those days Rickson was the one who taught classes and our team wasn't called Humaitá yet, we still called ourselves the "Academia Gracie." Later we went to the Colégio Padre Antonio Vieira on the Humaitá Street where it still is today, over 30 years later.[171]*

3- The *confere* and *taparia* were part of jiu-jitsu during the 70s and 80s, but it lost strength during the 90s. Why did this happen? What was the purpose of these more realistic practices?

I think that when jiu-jitsu began in Brazil and began to grow, we had to prove that jiu-jitsu wasn't like any other martial art, that we were here to stay so we had to prove ourselves. This began with my father, my Uncle, my cousins, Carlson, those guys had to challenge half the world to gain the credibility and popularity that we enjoy today. I think that things were rougher then and that was necessary, because we had something to prove. Today it's different, we have already established that jiu-jitsu is one of the best, if not the best, martial art in the world. So today these things aren't necessary anymore, people respect us.

---

[171] Notice that the events Royler is describing here took place in the 1980's when competitive jiu-jitsu was largely dominated by Carlson's team. The adaptation away from the model of the original Gracie Academy toward a more competitive and collective approach to jiu-jitsu under Rickson and Royler are clearly influenced by Carlson's success as a coach as well as the recognition (acknowledged or not) of the efficiency of his methods for teaching a more competitive approach to jiu-jitsu.

4- Your father was the founder of jiu-jitsu's first federation in Brazil. Yet in a later moment, he becomes critical of competitive jiu-jitsu. Why do you think this happened?

My father started the federation with Helcio Leal Binda and others way back in the day. They did so because they wanted to get things organized. And my father in reality, was never against competition, he was against systems that were in place then and still are now, the point system, stalling. Toward the end of his life he'd say this a lot "we have nothing to prove in competition, what we wanted to prove we already did." *Because a point system ends up favoring someone who plays conservatively and he'd say that his jiu-jitsu wasn't developed to be defensive. He liked to watch tournaments and was very actively involved, but he just wanted something more dynamic. Today we see this a lot, people with their butts to the ground and stalling for 9 minutes and then sweeping with 10 seconds left on the clock. That's what he didn't like.*

5- Your father's relationship with your cousin Carlson was always very complex. How did you see this conflict?

Carlson was always a very competitive guy, he loved "rinhas." And I've never seen, to this day in fact, anyone so enthusiastic about tournaments... It was even something that bothered us, because he went out of his way to celebrate not only a good and aggressive jiu-jitsu, but also celebrating a lot when his students won, he was very combative in this sense. You'd look at him and ask yourself: "Is that guy his son? What is he to Carlson? What about his brothers and cousins?"

But at the end of the day, he'd do the same for us too. Many times, he'd walk up to me, tap me in the shoulder and say "you are a real rooster! You aren't easy, skinny the way you are and look at what you are doing to everyone! You earned that one!" *He liked a forward jiu-jitsu, Carlson was someone who always fired from the hip, he celebrated a lot for his students, as if they were all his children. I still haven't seen anything like it, I'm not even sure I can fight that much for my own guys. He'd enter into endless fights to stand by his guys, and if he felt he was right about something, he would see it to the end. And sometimes this meant going against his own family.*

Ultimately, for jiu-jitsu to be where it is today, he played an enormous contribution. I'd go as far as saying that in regards to the changes from Helio to a younger generation, he was an instrumental figure in that process. We need to remember these things, Carlson was an enlightened person.

6- When you were teaching, what was the proportion between self-defense and jiu-jitsu classes in those days? How did these two systems coexist?

It was reasonable. To give you an idea, our warmups consisted of us practicing self-defense for 10 minutes. Only after would we get into competition training. Our self-defense is something we have carried with us from the downtown academy, to Vasco to Humaitá, in other words, it was something natural to us and part of jiu-jitsu. I think today this has diminished but, in some ways, it is making a comeback. Few people enter a gym to become champions, most students want to learn how to defend themselves. But in those days, self-defense practice and competition were together, I'd say they were well balanced.

7- Many credit Carlson his emphasis on competitive jiu-jitsu, others Rolls. What do you think?

Both Rolls and Carlson played a huge role in the evolution of competitive jiu-jitsu. As I said, I trained mostly with Rolls and less with

Carlson. I trained with Carlson maybe once a week and I trained 4 or 5 days a week with Rolls when I was a kid. And Rolls was also a very competitive guy, if he heard that there was a karate tournament somewhere he'd try to get his guys to register to compete. As for Carlson I didn't watch him compete, that was before my time. I saw his students do well and him coaching them. But I can say that Rolls was one of the best competitors I saw and of course Rickson too. I never saw my father compete either, obviously that was also before my time. Everyone had their time, Carlson replaced Helio, then we had Rolls with lots of aggression and a new generation. So, these were all important events. It was fundamental that when Helio began to move into retirement, that he was replaced by Carlson, then Rolls, then my other brothers and cousins. It all seems like a smooth transition, but we need to acknowledge this link that was the Carlson and Rolls era. Let's just say that those two guys reinvigorated jiu-jitsu.

8- You made your name as a CBJJ competitor. How do you see competitive jiu-jitsu today? Many old-school guys complain that jiu-jitsu is losing touch with reality and became too sportive. Do you agree?

Since I was a child, I always loved competition, it was in my blood! One time I competed twice in the same weekend. It was something I loved. Wanting to be there is fundamental. But you can see that it changed a lot. I remember that back in the day, when I was a kid and I'd get to the Mello Tenis Clube to compete and the mats weren't even ready yet, they'd still be in the truck. And they'd be setting up the mats while I played soccer and when the mats were finally ready one of my brothers would come get me, "let's go kid, it's time!" and I'd leave the ball behind and go compete and go back to play ball afterwards. Today everything is far more professional, everything starts on time. We saw that at the last 2022 Masters Worlds they had 40 mat areas and almost 9000 competitors! That's a machine at work there. I think that the federation [IBJJF] needs to be congratulated for everything they are doing and for improving jiu-jitsu. But the rules, in my view, need to be rethought. It has become too tactical in my view, not aggressive enough. People just want to win because everyone knows that 20 years from now, no one will remember who took second place and how you beat them, people will only remember that you won, that is what will enter history, not whether or not you won by submission or advantage. Many matches have become monotonous in my view. I'm not sure what can be done, but making them more dynamic would be good. But maybe I'm wrong.

9- Clearly a lot has changed from the times you began training and today. What were the biggest differences between the 70s and 80s and today?

People often compare generations and that is silly, everything is always changing. We haven't stopped evolving. Jiu-jitsu like much else in life, is in eternal evolution. With that said, there are certain things that are eternal, they will never change, these things are the true foundation of jiu-jitsu, they are beyond time and space. What we need to understand is that we learned the best martial art in the world and we need to keep it that way, that's what I want to see moving forward.

Luis Carlos Valois

Carlson and Valois as a brown-belt.
Photocred: Luis Carlos Valois personal archives.

"He wouldn't move you to black-belt unless he had someone to fill in your spot as a brown-belt in that same weight class. This is why the blue-belt is the only actual belt where we had trials at the gym, because there were so many blue-belts. After that you would want the spot above you. And that had an effect on the team, because when Carlson moved you up to the next belt, you felt a certain sense of pride and responsibility in replacing a previous champion in that division. You felt the responsibility of carrying Carlson's winning name on your back."

Luis Carlos Valois

Valois is a 6th degree black-belt and long-time student and friend of Carlson. He also holds a doctorate in law and is a judge in the Amazon state. Our conversation took place on November 6th, 2022 over the phone. He was born on January 8th, 1967.

1-   Can you tell us about your beginning in jiu-jitsu?

I started in judo and was first introduced to jiu-jitsu through one of my father's friends from Rio, Arthur Virgílio, who would visit and kept showing me moves whenever he visited us and I remember liking it a lot. When I was 17 I moved to Rio to go to college and I asked him where should I train and he recommended I go train with Carlson so I asked him for an introductory letter so Carlson would welcome me. Because you need to understand, Carlson was an idol in those days so I was a bit nervous about just showing up, so I felt that a letter would make introductions easier. I also kept training judo at the AABB at Lagoa, with Shihan Oguino. Still looking for the place where Carlson taught because I had a letter from Arthur but not the address to his gym. One day I saw two children wearing a Carlson Gracie t-shirt so I asked their mom where the gym was and she told me where the Figueiredo de Magalhães academy was. When I got there, there were two mats upstairs where Carlson taught group classes and one downstairs where he taught private lessons but that he had turned into his private bedroom [laughs] he was already sleeping there on the mats downstairs.

2-   What was it like meeting Carlson?

This happened in 1985. I remember someone going upstairs to get him and the excitement waiting to meet my hero with my letter in hand. When I saw him coming down those stairs, you need to remember, I was only 17 and very intimidated, he was like a giant to me. A lot of people don't know this because Carlson has the reputation for being such a tough guy, but he was one of the warmest and most welcoming people you will ever meet. If I had to point to the most defining thing about Carlson, that would be it, how open-hearted he was toward everyone around him.

3-   What was the Figueiredo academy like?

I trained in the morning where all the actual paying students trained. Someone had to pay [laughs]. All the guys who didn't pay trained in the evening. Back in the day, it was part of the culture in jiu-jitsu for people to believe that not paying was a symbol of status. As if saying, "look, I'm so good I don't even have to pay." So, it was something those guys even bragged about. But I trained in the morning class where lots of other business men and other people who either worked at night or went to school also trained. I was one of those who went to school at night. But in those days, Carlson was teaching mostly in the morning so I am one of the few people from that generation that got to take classes regularly from Carlson and spend lots of time with him, listening to all that French music he loved [laughs]. After a while I learned to like it too. He had the habit of writing down the lyrics of those songs for us [laughs].

4-   What were Carlson's methods like?

I have a theory of what I think Carlson thought about jiu-jitsu. If you get two lay people with no previous experience and have them fight, what would happen? They would tackle each other and hit the ground, right? Jiu-jitsu, our jiu-jitsu, it is an extension of our nature. Grappling is as natural to us as walking, running and swimming are. If you had two guys on a deserted island, taught them only a few moves and gave them time to train, they would develop from that, right? In my opinion, Carlson knew all this already, so he would insist that we had lots of mat time. Let us roll for an hour straight sometimes. There was no clock! There was no such thing as "the time is up" with Carlson in the room. What he would often do, is mid rolls, he would stop everything and correct us. Tell us what we were doing wrong. What he did was to shorten our path to learning, so instead of us learning by trial and error, he shortened our path for discovering new things. He wasn't just a jiu-jitsu teacher, more than that, he was a jiu-jitsu coach.

5-   Anything else?

I remember that he wouldn't let you quit over being tired. You could tap out, but you could never stop mid round because you were tired. No. You had to tap and admit defeat in case you got tired. I also remember that we never started on our knees. We began in the closed-guard position but never on our knees.

6-   What was the criteria he used to promote people?

Carlson liked to win tournaments so he wouldn't move anyone up until he had someone to replace that person in that division. He wanted to win all divisions so he would make sure that all of them had someone with a really good chance of winning. There was no such thing as a specific amount of time to stay at a belt level. You stayed at a belt for as long as he saw fit. He had an elite selection of guys, always making sure that all categories were complete. He wouldn't move you to black-belt unless he had someone to fill in your spot as a brown-belt in that same weight class. This is why the blue-belt is the only actual belt where we had trials at the gym, because there were so many blue-belts. After that you would want the spot above you. And that had an effect on the team, because when Carlson moved you up to the next belt, you felt a certain sense of pride and responsibility in replacing a previous champion in that division. You felt the responsibility of carrying Carlson's winning name on your back.

7-   How did Carlson see the jiu-jitsu boom of the mid-90s?

He saw what was happening in the US, with his cousins Rorion, Royce the UFC, he saw all that and he knew that his guys were the best jiu-jitsu representatives in the world. He was certain of it. We all knew it. In fact, anyone who knew anything about jiu-jitsu then also knew that the best in the world could be found inside Carlson's gym. It had been that way for decades.

8- He had a rough relationship with his family over the years. Can you comment?

I remember those years. It was a period of his life where he was very angry. It was when his father [Carlos Gracie] died and his siblings kept all the inheritance [circa 1994]. He couldn't believe it. He even made a t-shirt about what happened, calling them on it and was wearing it at a tournament when one of his nephews [Valois could not specify which one] *attacked him over it and Carlson's guys went after him afterwards. I remember him saying things like "I am ashamed to be a Gracie." He said things like that when he was angry.*

9- Any final remarks on Carlson?

Carlson was the kind of person that always lifted people up. If you were down, he could sense that and he had a way to make you feel better. He had that gift. Always lifting people up, always smiling and making everyone around him smile too. But at the end, after that episode with the BTT guys, he lost that smile, lost his shine. It was clear that he was overtaken by a deep sorrow. For Carlson jiu-jitsu wasn't a business, it was a family. He made out of his students the family he felt he never had. When his team split, he felt betrayed. In fact, he felt betrayed twice, by his actual family then by the family he trained his entire life. To him, it was as if his own children had betrayed him. Then he got tired... I mean, his whole life was a fight, his relationship with his family was a fight in itself.

Master Wallid Ismail

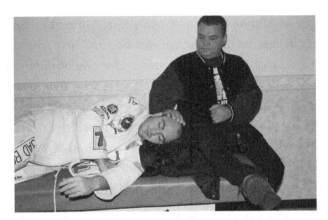

Carlson watches over Wallid before one of his fights in 1997. Photocred: Marcelo Alonso personal archives.

"Carlson trained his guys to beat everyone, including Helio's students. Can you imagine? If it weren't for Carlson those guys would probably dominate, then Carlson comes along and teaches jiu-jitsu to all these crazy guys with no money and who trained all day like maniacs to defeat everyone from the other side of the family. So yes, there was a great rivalry there and Carlson was highly competitive. Competition was in his blood..."

Master Wallid Ismail

Wallid is one of the most known figures from the *second-wave* and a long-time student of Carlson. He began to gain notoriety in Rio after he issued a public challenge to luta-livre members in 1990. What followed was the luta-livre guys attempting to storm a jiu-jitsu event and that was what led to the 1991 challenge where Wallid fought and defeated jiu-jitsu nemesis, Eugenio Tadeu. Wallid also went on to defeat Royce in a jiu-jitsu match in 1998. He is also the founder and owner of the MMA promotion Jungle-Fight, holds a rank of black-belt under Carlson and was born on the 23rd of February, 1968. The interview took place over the phone on October the 5th of 2022.

1-   How did your story with Carlson begin?

I came from Manaus where I train with Agui Almeida. I had heard of Gracies in the Amazon but had no idea who was who but I decided that I wanted to train under one of them, so I took a bus to Fortaleza and then another one to Rio. This was in 1983. Fortunately, I ended up in Copacabana and when I went around asking where the Gracies taught, I was pointed to Carlson's gym. When I got there, I looked for Carlson and told him that I came from the Amazon to train and that my father didn't want me in Rio and that I didn't have money to pay the gym, but I asked him if I could train there. Even his wife who was there asked him to let me train for free, she said "look at him, look how badly he wants to train." So, Carlson said, "ok, you can train twice a week here." So I stayed there and never left.

2-   What is Carlson's overall importance in history?

Carlson was larger than life. He was the man to popularize jiu-jitsu. Before him, jiu-jitsu was something for elites. The whole family only trained the "bacanas" [cool people] in those days. You had to have money to train and Carlson basically came along and opened a collective practice for anyone who wanted to train hard.

3-   What were the team results like?

Just to give you an idea, the amount of points Carlson's team had, if you added up all the other teams it would not amount to our team's total. We had practically a monopoly of jiu-jitsu events in those days.

4-   What about other teams like the [original] Gracie Academy, what
     sort of presence did they have at tournaments?

*Only a few family members. Not many others other than the fam-
ily members themselves. They were competitive of course, but you
couldn't compare it with our team.*

5-   How did the 1991 Desafio Jiu-jitsu vs. Luta-Livre come about?

*People were fighting in the streets all the time so I went to a local
newspaper and issued a challenge to them, this was in 1990. Later
that challenge basically served as a model for the UFC in 1993.
When those luta-livre guys came over to a jiu-jitsu event called
Copa Mameluque, that was because of my challenge to them in the
newspaper. They went there to tell us that they accepted our challenge. That was when Carlson went over to talk to them and calm
them down and to begin talks about the challenge.*

6-   What was the reception of Royce's victories in the UFC inside
     Carlson's academy?

*It was good, in general it was good. We only felt that we had much
better representatives for jiu-jitsu than Royce. But in general, our
perception was that it was good for jiu-jitsu.*

7-   How did the jiu-jitsu match between you and Royce take place?

*After he won in the UFC three times, me and Carlson went over to
Gracie Humaitá to issue a challenge to Royce for a future event.
Things got a little heated there. You have to understand that in our
head, we were the best and end of story and Carlson was always*

a strategist. He told me "when you get there, keep your head down and act scared." *Helio and Rorion were there too. Carlson told them that I wanted to fight Royce. Which wasn't a crazy challenge, I had already defeated Renzo and Ralph so there was a precedent. But things got heated and Royce wanted to fight me then and there, and I said* "ok, let's go then." *But people didn't let that happen, insisting that we should schedule the match for an event instead. Which is why we had gone there in the first place. You also need to understand that this was a time where there was a lot of rivalry between Carlson's gym and Gracie Humaitá. Eventually the fight ended up taking place in Rio.*

8- The relationship between Helio and Carlson was always troubled. Can you comment?

Carlson trained his guys to beat everyone, including Helio's students. Can you imagine? If it weren't for Carlson those guys would probably dominate, then Carlson comes along and teaches jiu-jitsu to all these crazy guys with no money and who trained all day like maniacs to defeat everyone from the other side of the family. So yes, there was a great rivalry there and Carlson was highly competitive. Competition was in his blood, I learned my competitiveness from him.

9- What was Carlson's jiu-jitsu like and what did others think about it?

It was simple, to the point and efficient. You know what the other side of the family would say about it? They called Carlson's jiu-jitsu "grosseiro" [unrefined or crude]. *I'll tell you one thing, nobody has*

better marketing than them, no one. You would see what was hap-
pening, they would say that it was something else happening and
everyone believes them. Even with the images right in front of them
showing otherwise, they still believed what they were told. It's the
best marketing in the world.

(continues in Part 3)

Richard Bresler

**Relson, Helio, Margarida (Helio's wife), Richard Bresler
and Rolls Gracie in Brazil in 1981.
Photocred: Richard Bresler personal archives.**

*"His confident manner was what I was attracted to and he said he came
from a family of jiu-jitsu champions and I was curious."*

Richard Bresler on Rorion Gracie

Richard Bresler is arguably the first American jiu-jitsu practitioner
and one of the few Americans belonging to the *second-wave*. His interview demonstrates clearly that the brand of jiu-jitsu that was brought
over to the USA by Rorion was the one taught inside the original
Gracie Academy, rather than the one the majority of *second-wave*
Brazilians were practicing during the 70s, 80s and 90s in Brazil. He is
the author of *"Worth Defending"* and still actively teaches self-defense in
Los Angeles. He was born on November 15th, 1951 and is a sixth degree
black-belt under Rorion. The interview took place over the phone and
over email.

1- You are one of the first jiu-jitsu students from the USA. When did you begin training jiu-jitsu?

> *I started training in July 1979 in Redondo Beach. I don't know when you started or what you were like or if you were the athletic type or not. But I was kind like the unathletic person, never really had any desire to fight but I definitely wanted to learn how to defend myself. Even though I competed back in the day in the garage, mid 80s, and only because I thought it was expected of me, but I never really enjoyed it.*

2- When you began your journey, what was it that attracted you to jiu-jitsu and Rorion?

> *His confident manner was what I was attracted to and he said he came from a family of jiu-jitsu champions and I was curious.*

3- The sport seems somewhat divided today in terms of how jiu-jitsu is taught. How did you learn it?

> *The jiu-jitsu that Rorion taught me was based on self-defense. How to protect myself in a real fight. When I started training jiu-jitsu, Rorion didn't talk to me about "sport" until later on.*

4- How would you define the jiu-jitsu that Rorion taught you?

> *The difference of what is being taught today is a sport except for what is being taught at Gracie University and a few others. Not enough focus on fundamentals for the average person.*

5- Did the name "Carlson" come up in conversation a lot during your years at the Gracie Torrance Academy.

> *There was not a lot said about him.*

Master André Pederneiras

André receives his coral-belt in 2019.
Photocred: Marcell Fagundes via Gustavo Dantas.

*"There were classes for the lower belts to learn the basics but when it
came to the higher belts and the competition team it was a war room.
You would get there and people would be sitting on the wall and you'd
walk up to them and go "wanna train?" and they'd say, "bora!" [let's
go!]. And we went to war [e saiamos na porrada]. Just going up those
stairs was enough to give you the butterflies [laughs]. It was a very
intense room."*

Master André Pederneiras

André Pederneiras (or simply Dedé as he is known among his friends) is
one of the most iconic figures from the *second-wave*. In 1993, he organized the first *"Brasileiro de jiu-jitsu"* (Brazilian National Championship)
and later became the president of the CBJJO. He is also the co-founder of
Nova União (alongside Wendel Alexander) but is perhaps best known for
being the coach of many UFC fighters. Among them, the former champion José Aldo. He was born on the 22nd of March, 1967. André received

his black-belt by the hands of Carlson Gracie in December 1988 and holds a 7th degree coral-belt. Our interview took place on January 12th, 2023 in person and in Las Vegas.

1- Tell us a little about your beginnings in jiu-jitsu.

In 1984 when I began training I had never even heard of jiu-jitsu before. When I was 17 years old I wanted to start lifting weights so I went to a local gym near my house. After they presented the membership program to me they told me that I could pick a fighting style, any of them, and that style would be added to my membership for free. I told the front desk girl I didn't want anything to do with any martial art but she insisted and said that she had to put a martial art down on my sign-up sheet. So I said, "ok, what martial arts do you offer?" *She read them all to me and I couldn't remember any of the names, except for jiu-jitsu which was the last one she read to me so I chose jiu-jitsu* [laughs]. *And that's how I began my journey.*

The coach was Rodrigo Vieira who had previously trained under Rolls. After Rolls passed, Rodrigo went over to train with Rickson. That was around the time I began training with Rodrigo in 1984 and we all competed under Gracie Humaitá where Rickson was teaching at the time. But then he was fired from the gym he was teaching at and asked Carlson if he could rent from him one of his rooms at the Figueiredo Academy so he could continue to teach his students. Similar deal to what Carlson had with Rolls. This was around 1985 or 1986. But it didn't work out there for whatever reason so Rodrigo went over to teach at the ICJG [Iate Clube Jardim Guanabara]. *But it was so far from my house that I couldn't make it there so Rodrigo asked Carlson if I could continue training under him. Carlson said* "ok, you don't have to pay, as long as you help Sergio Bolão teach the teen class." *And I said yes. I was a brown-belt then. Later I left to open my own place. I was in that academy from 1986 to 1989 more or less.*

2-   What were the classes at the Figueiredo Academy like?

There were classes for the lower belts to learn the basics but when it came to the higher belts and the competition team it was a war room. You would get there and people would be sitting on the wall and you'd walk up to them and go "wanna train?" and they'd say, "bora!" [let's go!]. And we went to war [e saiamos na porrada]. Just going up those stairs was enough to give you the butterflies [laughs]. It was a very intense room.

3-   Were there any self-defense classes being taught?

When I got to that gym in 1986 no one knew any self-defense.

4-   Valois was telling me that Carlson didn't move anyone up in rank until a spot opened up for that belt. Sounds like an interesting system. Can you comment?

Yes, it was like a ladder. Someone moved up to blue-belt because the blue-belt in that division got moved to purple-belt and so on. I even copied this model. To give you an idea, when B.J. Penn won the World Championships as a black-belt in 2000, he was originally going to compete as a brown-belt. But there were two other very competitive and more experienced guys in that division already. I made a bold decision to move B.J. up to black-belt in the weeks leading up to the tournament. I did this because I knew he had the potential to be the dark horse in that division since no one knew him! Turned out that he won the whole thing and that surprised a lot of people. It was a shot in the dark but it worked. So yes, I even took that mentality with me of moving people up to better complete the competition team.

5- When Carlson wasn't in the room, who was the authority there?

There really wasn't one to be honest. It was all very competitive but it all ended on the mats. To be honest, I think this is one of the reasons why we were so dominant in competitions. We were used to competing with each other every single day.

(continues in Part 3)

PART 3

The Third-Wave and the Democratic Era (1993-2007)

"All Streams Flow into the Sea"

Master Carlos Gracie Jr.

Chapter 14

From the Carioca
South-Zone to the World.

Left Picture: Richard Bresler, Steve Maxwell, Royce and Rorion in the
early 90s. Photocred: Richard Bresler personal archives. Right Picture:
The first "Mundial" (World Championship) in 1996 at the Tijuca Tenis
Clube. From left to right: Carlson Gracie, "Zé Beleza" Leão Teixeira,
Carlinhos Gracie Jr., Oswaldo Alves, Romero "Jacaré" Cavalcanti
and Royler Gracie. Photocred: Marcelo Alonso personal archives.

*"I want to make sure that you guys understand that we are going to
conquer the world."* And I looked at him and thought *"what is he talking
about?"* and he said *"I'll leave California for you guys, but we are going
to take over the world."*

Master Carlos Gracie Jr. to Master Jean Jacques Machado

In jiu-jitsu much like with life itself, most things are not under our
control. Some events give shape to circumstances that are to our favor,
others not so much. We call them *good* and *bad* luck respectively. Not
that we don't have agency, but that even this agency isn't entirely ours to
begin with. Instead, this agency is hostage to circumstances derived from
the actions of other agents that are well beyond our control. Long story
short, no agent is completely free.

Occasionally however, these agents find themselves in conflict with one another in the most unexpected ways. More impressive still, is when these conflicts themselves are precisely what thrusts a unique alignment to begin with. From these exchanges are born what we call "good stories." Some are so good, that they escape and even surpass the most creative works of fiction. The history of jiu-jitsu in Brazil is a bit like that. Fascinating, complicated, biased, political, familial, contentious and... aligned. It all works out in the end.

A Japanese martial art, transformed culturally in Brazil by absorbing aspects of Brazilian easy-manners, *machismo*, Californian surf-culture, blending it with a unique diet from an Argentinian nutritionist, later borrowed by a man of Scottish descent from the Brazilian Amazon (who claimed to be in communication with a Peruvian spiritual entity) and who taught a modified version of judo to his brothers and their many children, who in turn exported (alongside the açaí fruit) what they called jiu-jitsu to the rest of the world as Brazil's number one cultural export ever. And of course, creating the UFC in this process... I mean... you can't even make this up.

Yet, regardless of how rich and unusual this history may be, it would never have made a dent in the martial arts world had it not been advertised and sold by Helio's eldest son, Rorion Gracie, throughout the 1970s, 80s and 90s in the USA. For his part, Rorion wasn't really doing anything new. He was simply giving continuation to a long tradition of advancing the Gracie name in association with jiu-jitsu. The only difference is that under Rorion's direction jiu-jitsu would gain aspirations that were truly global.

For this star to align, jiu-jitsu would have to immigrate from the smaller skies of the south-zone in Rio to skies with greater visibility and more promise, Southern California. The place that perhaps next to Miami, most resembled Rorion's home in Rio. The move would inaugurate two whole new chapters in jiu-jitsu's long and winding history in order to make itself known to the world, the birth of the UFC with its meteoric rise as a cultural phenomenon, and the exportation of BJJ to the world following this rise.

Rorion was savvy enough to understand that if he wanted to sell his family's brand of jiu-jitsu to the world, there was no shinier shelf than Southern California, more specifically, Hollywood. Even though, to be completely accurate, the introduction between the Brazilian version of jiu-jitsu (or judo) and Uncle Sam began well before Rorion came to the USA in the early 70s.[172] Still, no one had been as successful in selling jiu-jitsu here, at least when compared to what Rorion was about to do.[173]

To begin with, the martial arts landscape during the 70s in USA was a very distant reality from its post-Royce era. Before Rorion introduced jiu-jitsu to the world in the 1987 Lethal Weapon movie, the understanding of martial arts to the general public in the USA was mostly limited to Bruce Lee, Chuck Norris, Jean-Claude Van Damme, boxing, pro-wrestling, comic books and other Hollywood-like and unrealistic (however cool) approaches to combat.[174] But Rorion had a better idea of what a real-fight would look like in case it was allowed to take place uninterrupted by film-cuts or boxing referees.

The problem was convincing an entire generation of martial arts fanatics that were raised on Hollywood films and comic books that what they knew, or thought they knew, didn't scratch the surface when it came to the complexity of a fight where "anything goes." Rorion knew, but how could he go about selling this, especially to people who

---

[172] Other than Yamashita who taught Roosevelt in 1905 (Pedreira 2019, pg. 14); John Obrien and Irving Hancock with books also in 1905 (Pedreira 2019, pg. 5); and Len Lenius with his own version of what he called *"American Jiu-Jitsu"* in 1922, (Pedreira 2021, pg. 159-160). What we now refer to as BJJ was first introduced by João Alberto Barreto and Flávio Behring in 1963 (Cairus 2012a, pg.185; and Drysdale 2020, pg. 130). And again, years later, by Reylson in 1982 in Miami, officially the first BJJ gym in the US (Pedreira 2015c, pg. 213).

[173] It is worth noting here that what these practitioners were referring to as "jiu-jitsu" had nothing to do with what we now refer to as BJJ. Jiu-jitsu then, was an eclectic term with even less fixed meaning than it has today. The techniques shown by Hancock and Lenius were much closer to a standard approach to self-defense than they are to the ground grappling we associate jiu-jitsu with today. It is also worth noting that none of these characters left a lasting legacy through students and schools. Until Rorion that is.

[174] Rorion worked as a technical advisor to Mel Gibson in that movie and wins the final fight against the big boss with a triangle-choke.

already seemed convinced that they knew exactly what a real fight looked like.

His solution for convincing Hollywood-educated Americans in the early 80s to give his family's version of jiu-jitsu a shot? Convince them to walk into a complete stranger's garage to roll around on the ground with Latino men who would teach them a style of Japanese martial arts only practiced by his family and a few others in Brazil and no one else. And if this all seems absurd to us now, it only goes to show the importance that Rorion had in helping disseminate jiu-jitsu around the world. Say what you want about Rorion, but what he did was something truly remarkable and it changed martial arts forever.

Nevertheless, the initial efforts of handing out flyers in parking lots were not alone. They were made in parallel with an old family formula of challenging rivals and beating them up (preferably in front of their students), to prove the supremacy of their camp.

Their strategy, much like the dojo-storming days and the *pit-boy* movement (see chapter 18) in Brazil later in the 90s, had mixed results. On the one hand, it did *prove* that they were overall better fighters; on the other, it also had the negative effect of closing doors and giving jiu-jitsu, or at least its practitioners, the reputation for being a gang of bullies. Which wasn't too far from the truth. Did the strategy work? Yes, without a doubt. Did the Gracie in Action tapes promote Rorion's brand of jiu-jitsu? Absolutely. *What was the problem then?*[175]

The bigger issue was that however appealing and fascinating it may have been to watch Rorion's family absolutely dominate other martial artists, it was far from a classy move. One may even call it a form of bullying to challenge instructors in front of their students to a fight in order to humiliate them in order to poach their students. Additionally, from a technical perspective, I personally don't find it impressive to put a choke on someone when they have never even seen one before.

---

[175] Gracie in Action were a set of VHS tapes sold by Rorion in order to promote the Gracie Challenge to other martial arts enthusiasts. It consisted of training sessions, street-fights and behind closed doors challenges where members of the Gracie family demonstrated the supremacy of jiu-jitsu over other styles.

At the same time, I don't know how else Rorion could have done it. In essence, his problem was the exact same one the Gracie Academy had during the *silent years* in Brazil (1951-1993), *how do we promote ourselves when we know we have a superior product but no one will believe us?* Beating people up in their gyms, in the streets or in garages worked to prove a point then and there, but proving it to a mass-audience? That is a very different story.

Rorion had originally been primed to become a replacement to Carlson as the new family's champion. An achievement that would certainly have made his father Helio very proud. But, as destiny would have it, the most important role he would ever play in his life wasn't inside a ring, but just outside of one. More precisely, just outside a cage in the shape of an octagon. That and giving rise to a wave of mass immigration to sell the style his next creation was designed to promote.

Helio's eldest son had spent over a decade in California trying to promote jiu-jitsu in any way he could to make his father proud. All with mixed results. He was certain that he had a quality product, something Americans wanted, they just needed a strong statement to be convinced of its quality. Therefore, he needed something big, something that would get things moving at a faster rate than the challenges ever could. Something that would grant jiu-jitsu credibility in everyone's eyes. He needed to prove the efficiency of his style to a mass audience. But considering that the challenges weren't working fast enough, the only solution was to create a bigger arena to display jiu-jitsu to a wider audience. What Rorion needed was to bring *vale-tudo* back somehow.

Rorion set himself on the task of creating a new arena for his family's brand of jiu-jitsu to shine. One where even if the fighters were all cherry picked, at least they were professionals who had the proper time to prepare for what they thought they would be encountering inside that cage. But the truth was that they had no clue, they had no idea how to swim, and they had no idea how deep the waters were either. Rorion's younger brother Royce on the other hand, had descended from a long tradition of knowing how to swim among sharks in deep waters. Royce and his family knew exactly what was about to happen inside that cage in 1993. That was a given, the real challenge now was getting the UFC off the ground.

With much effort and determination, Rorion succeeded alongside his younger brother Royce, Art Davie and John Milius.[176] Together, they gave birth to the second greatest martial arts revolution ever, second only to Kano's founding of judo.

These events are told in great detail elsewhere, so I won't retell them here.[177] It suffices to remember and acknowledge that had it not been for Rorion and Royce lifting jiu-jitsu out of obscurity in Brazil, none of us would have ever heard of either *vale-tudo* (MMA) or BJJ. Rorion's plot had worked so well that it gave birth to a goldrush of sorts as the jiu-jitsu missionaries attempted to supply the sudden and unexpected demand in the world market of martial arts. A shortage to be supplied in haste.

---

[176] Unbeknownst to most UFC fans today, the idea for the UFC was devised with the help of John Milius, who was the screenwriter for Coppola's classic "Apocalypse Now" and the film "Conan The Barbarian." Source: https://www.boxinginsider.com/mma/the-octagon-a-man-named-milius-and-his-imprint-on-the-ufc/

[177] The story of Rorion's early hustles to sell jiu-jitsu in the US and create the UFC is told in some detail by his first American student Richard Bresler. See: Worth Defending by Richard Bresler and Scott Burr. See also Pedreira 2015c.

Chapter 15

Jiu-Jitsu Mania in Gringolandia

From left to right, Rickson, Bob Wall, Chuck Norris,
Relson, Rorion, Richard, Renzo, (kneeling) Royler,
Carlos, Rilion, Rolker and Royce.
Photocred: Richard Bresler personal archives.

"I think the one thing that [Carlinhos] *does that is incredible, is to select the right people to work with him and be able to make these people see things the way he sees them. Later on, we all looked back into all this and he would say* 'I told you, we are going to conquer the world.'"

Master Jean Jeacques Machado talking
about Master Carlinhos Gracie Jr.

The worldwide interest in jiu-jitsu that immediately followed Royce and the UFC sparked a second craze for the art. This time, a more specific version of it from out of all places, Brazil rather than Japan. Jiu-jitsu had undergone a makeover of sorts as it absorbed aspects of Brazilian culture that made it more appealing to a world audience. In some ways, this Brazilian version of jiu-jitsu was simply another manifestation of the world's adherence to globalization and the new cultural expressions it was giving rise to.

This boom created a void that needed to be filled quickly before opportunists seized the moment.[178] Naturally, the initial torrent of Brazilian instructors that preceded and followed the birth of the UFC was from within the Gracie family itself. Rorion, as his project grew from a garage to bigger spaces, began bringing his family over. First his little brother Royce, still only a blue-belt, and later bringing others.

They had the name and it was quickly becoming a valuable asset. Indeed, the name "Gracie" was becoming so valuable, that Rorion thought it a wise idea to sue his cousin Carley for using his own name to teach jiu-jitsu. It was during this moment of litigious battles among cousins over the name "Gracie Jiu-Jitsu" that the now more popular term "Brazilian Jiu-Jitsu" took over as a replacement due to fear of any new potential lawsuits.[179]

But in some ways, Rorion's plot to popularize jiu-jitsu in the US had worked almost too well. Undoubtedly a good problem to have. Still, the worldwide feverish craving for everything *vale-tudo*, UFC, jiu-jitsu and Gracie related, had overwhelmed their ability to supply the demand with competent and trained instructors.

This same boom also offered the challenge of maintaining a logistical structure for the continuous growth and spread of jiu-jitsu. The Gracies,

---

[178] In the late 90s, the joke was that Brazilians would enter a plane wearing a purple-belt, be promoted to brown during the flight and already be black-belts by the time they landed in the USA. A joke that, unfortunately, wasn't too far from the truth. Frauds proliferated in the USA during this early boom. All it took was for the instructor to have a Brazilian accent for a naïve American audience to grant him immediate credibility.

[179] It is worth noting here, that neither the terms "Gracie Jiu-Jitsu" or "Brazilian Jiu-Jitsu" were ever used in Brazil prior to the UFC. It was all simply referred to as "jiu-jitsu." Just like no one living in Mexico refers to "food" as "Mexican food."

who had been working toward this moment for generations, knew that big things were set in motion by Rorion in California and they had no intention of missing out on the many promising opportunities that the moment had to offer. The problem was that it wasn't clear who was meant to do what. Which had the consequence of highlighting, if not further damaging, old family feuds and rivalries.

The one thing they all agreed on was that they wanted to keep the momentum going. *But how?* When jiu-jitsu exploded around the world in the mid 90s, its definition and political structure was very far from clear. People knew it was about taking people down and defeating them there and that the Gracies were at the forefront of these early moves, but that was about it. In essence what jiu-jitsu lacked was what the Kodokan represented for judo, an organizing body to grant it respect, credibility and to give the explosion in interest a purposeful direction.

It was a critical problem to be tackled, because whoever was in charge of organizing jiu-jitsu was going to wield the power to shape it as it moved into a very promising future. Which was in fact a necessity if the explosion in interest was to survive at all. Because, without clear leadership, organized ranks, courses, systems and rules, jiu-jitsu was indeed at risk of being kidnapped by phonies and marketing hustlers in general. Consequently, it ran the risk of (further?) fragmenting itself even before it had begun to take the larger shape its history was begging for.

In order to secure the revolution's first major victory in the world stage, jiu-jitsu needed order. Fortunately for everyone in this story, the blue-print for fortifying jiu-jitsu was being drawn in Brazil almost simultaneously to the rise of Royce and the UFC. I am referring here to the formation of the CBJJ by the hands of Carlinhos Gracie Jr. in 1994 (the parent organization for the IBJJF) that immediately followed Royce and his initial success in 1993. And if Carlinhos didn't know exactly how to do it, he was intent on figuring it out on the fly.

I noted in *Opening Closed Guard* that the IBJJF showed up on the scene almost too late to give order and structure to an art that had the ambition to become the most practiced and popular martial art in the world.[180] And I emphasize "almost too late," because much of the division in jiu-jitsu today can be explained by the fact that the growth spurt phase that followed Royce and the UFC far outdid jiu-jitsu's capacity to supply its new audience with credible instruction and systems:

"It is important to take note here of a crucial difference between Judo and BJJ. Judo grew out of a small room in Tokyo, and largely out of the mind of a single man with a broad vision. Kano codified a curriculum, a canon, a moral philosophy, not to mention a competition rule and regulation set, long before his art arrived on the world stage. Judo, in other words, grew outwards from an original small cell. Its Brazilian variant, on the other hand, proliferated widely, rapidly, and organically, to arrive at a critical mass that was simply beyond the structural capacity of whatever de facto organizational tendencies had evolved with it. Simply put, BJJ needed to build (or assert) the sort of structure that Judo had from the outset after having already experienced worldwide growth… and that was no simple task. Even though the CBJJ came into being just one year after the first UFC, it would take over a decade before they could come near the level of consistency, organization, and professionalism so typical of other martial arts organizations. They were still playing catchup to the unprecedented growth the sport had experienced globally.

(It could be argued that all of this came too late, and that the lack of cohesion the sport still experiences today is a side effect of this tardiness. The present-day multiplicity of BJJ events, rulesets, and formats stands in stark contrast to Judo, which has managed to remain surprisingly cohesive and within a single hierarchy over the past century…)."[181]

Simply put, jiu-jitsu was very far from reaching the high standard of organization its practitioners so readily take for granted today. To make matters worse, in those days, the shortage of credible instructors led people from around the world to have to travel to Brazil (as many did), be

---

[180] Drysdale 2020, pg. 64

[181] Drysdale 2020, pg. 58

dependent on learning from VHS tapes and then practice in their own garages with their friends (as many also did). Or simply move or drive long distances to seek instruction (some did that too). While this may surprise some new comers, the truth is that this was a reality well past the 90s and well into the 2000s. In fact, and however surprising this may seem to these new students, it is a problem still in existence today in many distant corners of the world.[182]

To an extent, this was just as true in Brazil as well. Interestingly, this always seems to strike non-Brazilians as surprising, but in reality, prior to Royce Gracie and the UFC, few people in Brazil outside of the south-zone in Rio had ever heard of jiu-jitsu. It wasn't until much later that it became a household name all across the country. And this happened more or less around the same time it blew up in the USA. The main difference was that Brazil had instructors around, many of whom found themselves pursuing other professions during the *silent years*, when few people in Brazil wanted anything to do with jiu-jitsu. It wasn't until the boom in the 90s that many of these older black-belts came back and began the process of supplying the demand, some in their hometowns all across Brazil, others by traveling the world to teach the gospel.

Simultaneous to all this, the boom was beginning to reap the desired results by bringing in fresh missionaries who I refer to as the *third-wave*. As this wave matured, it would join ranks with the Gracie family now living all across the world as well as other members of the *second-wave* who, despite their more advanced age, were eager to travel abroad to start anew with jiu-jitsu as the catalyst for a new life abroad. What both

---

[182] To give the reader an idea of this, once, while teaching my first seminar in Poland in 2006, I recall a van full of students already in their kimonos that had driven a very long distance to attend my seminar. I'll never forget watching that van unload. To my shock, it was full of white-belts. Not a single colored-belt was in it. Sensing my confusion, one of them approached me and introduced himself as their coach, which did nothing to lessen my shock and confusion and everything to heighten it instead. Knowing perfectly well why I would find it odd that a blind person was leading the blind, he gently explained: *"I don't know much, but I know a little more than they do, so they call me coach."* This was 2006 in Poland, but scenes like this one played out across the rest of the world in the 90s and early 2000s

waves had in common was that they would both came in haste to supply a sudden and feverish craving for more BJJ.

However ambitious Rorion's initial project may have been, I seriously doubt he ever thought he would be the precursor for the now most prized of Brazil's cultural exports: the south-zone's version of jiu-jitsu with its distinct beach culture of fruit, music, fit individuals and unique energy. The plan came out better than expected. Between the Gracie Challenges, Royce's performances, a plethora of hungry for work brothers and cousins (and an even bigger plethora of *third-wave* practitioners who were growing into their kimonos simultaneously to the art's own expansion), jiu-jitsu seemed invincible and poised to conquer the world.

The world had caught the jiu-jitsu bug, and the demands of the 90s was being supplemented as best as it could have been by Brazilians from the *second* and *third-waves* and to a smaller extent, Americans belonging to the *third-wave*. Still, their problems weren't over. With expansion, new problems were quickly approaching the horizon. One of the most enduring questions for BJJ to answer, once again reared its head, *what is jiu-jitsu?* This was now coupled with an equally troubling but even more urgent question, *how to grant order and direction to the explosion?*

Chapter 16

Feudal Lords, a New Architect and an Empire Up for Grabs

The Hand of the King, Marcelo Siriema
and the King himself, Carlos Gracie Jr.
Behind them, the empire they built together.
Photocred: Author's personal archives.

*"I began trying to talk to people who were in charge of different orga-
nizations (...) I noticed that people didn't have a vision for that and they
weren't prepared. So, I started creating, doing things... If you want to
do something, do it yourself, don't wait around for others."*[183]

Master Carlos Gracie Jr.

From the foundation of the Guanabara Federation all the way to the
foundation of CBJJ/IBJJF (1967-1994) the jiu-jitsu landscape in Rio was

---

[183] Drysdale 2020, pg. 62

dominated by the civil war between Helio and Carlson that gave jiu-jitsu its political coloring. As discussed earlier, this civil war played out in the tournaments organized by the Guanabara Federation that granted jiu-jitsu an arena to test and improve itself; in the Figueiredo de Magalhães Academy (which was the new cultural center of this phenomena, shaping its practice); and by the lines drawn between Carlson and Rolls Gracie as the two leading forces in competitive jiu-jitsu. It was in this landscape that the *second-wave* of jiu-jitsu practitioners came into maturity and did their part in continuing a long-held tradition of reshaping the meaning of *"jiu-jitsu."*

The importance of the Guanabara Federation is strengthened even more when we remind ourselves that the old tradition of *vale-tudo*, was for most of this period, not a viable option for the *second-wave* to test themselves in combat. Fittingly, jiu-jitsu competitions and the occasional rivalry with other martial arts (in the 80s, this meant primarily luta-livre) became the essential means by which the troops busied themselves in those days. It was with all these events in the background that the *third-wave* would begin to take shape. But in order to understand the *third-wave* and its aspirations, we need to understand the role played by Carlinhos in all this.

If we come to think of Carlos and Helio as the central figures of the *first-wave* and Carlson and Rolls as the leading figures in the *second*, then Rorion, Royce and Carlinhos were the central figures of the *third-wave*. Having so many children had the upside of creating an enormous army of competitive males raised in a Darwinian environment where the strong were the most respected. Nevertheless, the jiu-jitsu life isn't limited to being a competent muscle-man able to out grapple anyone. Well beyond credibility on the mats, being a leader requires political tact, business-sense and above all, knowing how to manage people.

In other words, just because an individual may be a strong figure on the mats coaching and fighting, doesn't mean they will be the best at the job of structuring and organizing the growing community. Carlson is a prime example of that. Competent as he was as a fighter and coach, Carlson lacked the qualities that jiu-jitsu's *third-wave* needed in order to sustain itself in face of the challenges its growth would inevitably expose it to.

Being so respected, Rolls was perfectly positioned to slowly walk into the shoes of becoming the family's new leader. However, his sudden death put an end to any possibility of what Rolls could have been as a political leader. For this reason, in between his death, Carlson's inability to lead large numbers politically, FJJRio's inability to grow beyond Rio and Helio's retirement, a power vacuum had been created inside the jiu-jitsu political landscape. A power that was up for grabs.

Although more than just a few coaches in jiu-jitsu having fought for a position of leadership the best way they knew how to, that role required a very specific set of qualities that most of these beligerant feudal lords did not possess. This in order to help reshape the messy landscape jiu-jitsu had evolved out of. But for all the infighting to be solved, jiu-jitsu first needed a blue-print for where it ought to go moving forward. What jiu-jitsu needed was a new architect of sorts.

The role of jiu-jitsu's political front man and leading coach would come to be filled by Carlos Gracie Jr., the founder of Gracie Barra (the largest jiu-jitsu team in the world); owner of Gracie Magazine; and President of both the *Confederação Brasileira de Jiu-Jitsu* and the *International Brazilian Jiu-Jitsu Federation* (CBJJ and IBJJF respectively) the two largest jiu-jitsu federations on the planet. Simply put, to refer to Carlinhos as the godfather of Brazilian jiu-jitsu is to put it mildly.

In many ways, Carlinhos is Rolls' heir and alongside his other notorious heir, Romero Cavalcanti the leader of Alliance, I grossly estimate that in between 70% and 80% of the competition circuit today can trace their lineages back to either Carlinhos or Romero and, hence, to Rolls himself and the Figueiredo Academy (think, Gracie-Barra and its off-shoots as well as Alliance, Check-Mat, Atos, Zenith, Brasa, Machado Brothers and many others).

I made the claim in *Opening Closed Guard*, that Carlinhos will go down in history as being a more important character in jiu-jitsu than his own father Carlos Gracie. And after spending more time with him during our last two encounters, I double down on this claim. His importance and role should not be neglected or underestimated simply because he is still alive. His critics however, claim that he is ruining jiu-jitsu by making it excessively sportive.

A claim that isn't without its merits, *jiu-jitsu has become excessively sportive in the post-Royce era*. On the other hand, claiming that organizing the ogres and turning them into an army of 8,600 competitors in a single event, can hardly be described as "ruining" jiu-jitsu. In reality, Carlinhos only adapted to the times in which we are all living. He was astute enough to understand the changes the world was undergoing, as well as the moment that the UFC created for jiu-jitsu in terms of potential. All he did, was to act quickly and with precision.

While many in the community may have many differences with the IBJJF system and the direction they are taking in general, it is undeniable that Carlinhos has, over the past three decades, played the leading role in shaping jiu-jitsu as it is today. Better still, he knew jiu-jitsu inside out and more importantly, he was good at teaching it. But above all, he had the vision for the growth of jiu-jitsu, as well as the greatest quality a leader can possess: finding the right people for the right jobs and delegating accordingly.

In 1996, when Carlinhos made the move to organize the first *"Mundial"* (Worlds-Championships) in Rio, he was laughed at by his peers, *"how can a World-Championship be held at the Tijuca Tenis Clube among Brazilians, and even worse, almost exclusively among Cariocas?"* It all sounds absurd now, but this was the collective perception that most members from the *second-wave* had of Carlinhos and his bold moves. And to illustrate the division of the era and knowing what we know about their competitiveness, it is easy to imagine the other members of the Gracie family asking, *"who made you our leader anyway?"*

Which in hindsight, were perfectly valid questions considering jiu-jit-su's actual mass and political standing in those days.[184] They were good questions that demanded equally good answers. Something, as we shall see further ahead, Carlinhos was set on answering with actions rather than words. Reminding ourselves here that all great empires were once nothing but small villages and that leaders never ask for permission.

---

[184] The 90s in Brazil were marked by political division. It was clear that BJJ was about to undergo mass expansion worldwide. What wasn't clear was who would be the leader of this new chapter in our history. To illustrate the division, see: *"Mesa Redonda – Wallid, Royler, Robson, Belfort, Etc."* https://www.youtube.com/watch?v=gbOlaHizdSo

Chapter 17

Taming the Ogres: Interviews with Carlos Gracie Jr., Marcelo Siriema and André Pederneiras (2nd half)

The 2019 IBJJF World Championships in Long Beach California.
Photocred: IBJJF archives via Jon Medina

"Order is Progress"

My 5th grade teacher[185]

---

[185] The quote is a play of words with the slogan on the Brazilian national flag that reads *"Ordem e Progresso"* (Order *and* Progress). My teacher's version read, *"Ordem é Progresso"* (Order *is* Progress).

Unknowingly perhaps, and despite their obvious differences in approach toward spreading the gospel of jiu-jitsu, the truth of this matter is that Rorion and Carlinhos worked hand in hand and did their father's ambition justice. Rorion did so by helping ignite the movement in the USA with his relentless marketing and creating the UFC by adding the unique ingredient in this recipe. The one that neither John Milius nor Art Davie could have added: *vale-tudo*. While Carlinhos did his part in Brazil by shrewdly noticing not only what Royce's victories meant for jiu-jitsu's future, but also acknowledging the mess jiu-jitsu really found itself in during the early 90s. More importantly, rather than simply noticing the mess, he was determined to do something about it.

The first time I ever sat across from someone to interview them, I had jiu-jitsu's godfather Carlinhos Gracie Jr., across the room from me. Which I suppose isn't a bad start as far as interviewing goes. But that was for the *Closed Guard* project. This time, I'd interview him without a camera crew, which had the benefit of making it also more relaxed and less formal. Better still, we had even more time to talk than in our first encounter. It would also be the longest and most detailed one in this book.

When I reached out to Carlinhos and Siriema, as usual, they were very friendly and open to discuss anything regarding jiu-jitsu, its growth and the overall landscape the IBJJF was carving out for the future of the art. At first, I suggested the interview be over the phone like the others had been, mainly because I wanted to be respectful of their time. Carlinhos was unshakable though, insisting in the friendliest of manners that the interview be in person and that we could talk it over breakfast or lunch.

Liking the idea of being able to have a longer discussion about the past, present and future of jiu-jitsu with the minds that are responsible for shaping it, I conceded. But that was only one reason why; the other one is because Carlinhos can be quite charming and convincing... And his persuasiveness won the day. So, I flew to meet jiu-jitsu's godfather, Marcelo Siriema and André Fernandes at the IBJJF HQ in Irvine, California.

I sat down with the architect and his chief-builders in their HQ conference room. It was a different building from the last one I had visited for the *Closed Guard* project. It was bigger, nicer and was beginning to do justice to what jiu-jitsu was on its way to becoming if Carlinhos could finish his life's project: *"Make Jiu-Jitsu the Most Practiced Martial Art in the World."*

For those of you who haven't met Carlinhos, he is extremely charismatic and known for his openness and friendliness to all those who approach him. I had already noticed these traits in our first interview a few years ago. This time however, I noted something new, an observation of my own, something that I had completely missed the first time we sat down to talk: Carlinhos is one of the most socially aware individuals you will ever meet. Between his good listening skills and how observant of people he is, it started to become clear to me why he is jiu-jitsu's godfather and how he built his empire. And it wasn't his family's name or even work-ethic alone that got him this far.

Typically, I don't notice people's overall behavior, but when I do I can also be quite observant, and this time around I did take note that Carlinhos is a master at reading the room around him. There is no question that empires are a long-term project, but without the right social skills, as well as the right architect and builders, they remain only a farfetched dream. Carlinhos' real talent was understanding this all too well and putting it all carefully into practice.

Once they had shown me their new HQ and small-talk had died out, we finally sat down in their conference room to discuss the purpose of my visit. I began by explaining the purpose of this second project that focused on a different period for jiu-jitsu's evolution, where Carlson posed as the central figure.[186] Much like in the first interview, Carlinhos didn't seem shaken by anything regarding the history of jiu-jitsu that happened to be new to him or contradicting anything he had learned

---

[186] A consideration to which Carlinhos silently and reflectively confided to me privately that *"Carlson realmente não teve o reconhecimento que merecia, eu só fui entender isto muito tempo depois"* [Carlson really didn't receive the acknowledgement he deserved, I only understood this much later].

from his family's tradition. Instead, Carlinhos always listened carefully to whatever came up in conversation.

I wanted to learn about the culture and life of the Figueiredo Academy that I was coming to realize had been the birth place that gave jiu-jitsu the cultural shape that made it so appealing to the world. At the same time, I also wanted to learn about the beginnings of the CBJJ/IBJJF in Rio, since I suspected that there was more to this story than what its surface revealed.

The interview didn't disappoint, and I was thankful Carlinhos convinced me to meet him in person instead of simply talking it over the phone. Between the interview, the observations and all the advice, I learned a lot from listening and observing the godfather, just as he was listening and observing me. Below, is the transcript of the interview. It has been divided into two sections. One pertaining to the jiu-jitsu landscape of the 1970s and 1980s and the other regarding his role today as jiu-jitsu's master architect.[187]

---

[187] This interview in reality, consisted of two separate interviews. One on June 14th at the IBJJF HQ in Irvine (with Andre Fernandes and Marcelo Siriema present) and the other on the 1st of September at the Las Vegas Convention Center where the 2022 Masters Worlds were being held (with Carlinhos and Marcelo Siriema present). The second interview was requested because I wanted to clarify a few points with Carlinhos and enhance the quality of the text. The interview below, is the result from the combination of both these meetings.

Master Carlos Gracie Jr. and Marcelo Siriema

Rolls Gracie and a young Carlinhos Gracie Jr.
at the Figueiredo Academy in Copacabana in the early
70s. Photocred: Carlos Gracie Jr. personal archives.

"If you look at CBJJ's first Mundial [World-Championship] *in 1996, specially the results of brown and black-belts. The elite came out of Gracie Barra, Carlson's gym on Figueiredo or Alliance. With Gracie Humaitá under Royler being the exception* [...] *So most of the winners in those days did trace their legacy directly to the that building* [Figueiredo de Magalhães Academy].*"*

Master Carlos Gracie Jr.

1- Your brother Carlson was the most iconic figure in the family in the 1960s in Brazil. Why did he open a gym with Ivan Gomes, an opponent who he scarcely knew instead of with your brother Robson for example?

Carlinhos: *Robson was never into teaching jiu-jitsu. He didn't think he could ever make money from it. Plus, Robson and Carlson didn't really get along. They butted heads a lot.*

2- And why did Carlson and Rolls not work as partners but chose to work separately instead, even if in the same building?

Carlinhos: *Initially they did teach together, but the problem was that Carlson didn't want to do any work so Rolls would complain that he had to do most of the work and then split the money with Carlson at the end of the month. It was from that point onward that they began to share the mats but to have their own students.*

3- This was probably good for jiu-jitsu, people need rivals to grow and there wasn't much competition for the Gracie family at the time in Rio.

Carlinhos: *Exactly. It was overall good for jiu-jitsu that they went their own ways. Eventually they would end up having their students competing against one another. First in the in-house tournaments to see who would be the official representatives of the Gracie Academy. Later when Carlson left to compete under "Clube Carlson Gracie de Jiu-jitsu" the in-house tournaments stopped and from that point onward, Carlson became an enemy of sorts. Of course, we were brothers and he was always messing with me in a joking way, but I came to see his students as my competition. Eventually he even had his own logo, first a circle with his name in it, then a rooster, then two bull-dogs. While the Gracie Academy had an "A" and a "G" inside a triangle. Rolls, in turn, eventually founded his own club too, it was the "Gracie Jiu-Jitsu Clube" and his logo was the one that Rorion uses today with the two stick-figures inside the triangle. That was never Rorion's logo, that logo belonged to Rolls.*

4- How competitive and friendly were Carlson and Rolls toward each other?

Carlinhos: *Rolls and Carlson had a huge rivalry, it was friendly though, they'd tease each other a lot in case one of their students defeated the other's student. But it never got too heated between those two. On the mats, their guys would try to kill each other though. To me Carlson's students were enemies. But this was normal in the family, my father Carlos and Helio argued all the time too. This is normal I suppose.*

Siriema: *Competition is necessary in my view. We see this in many places. Where there are two good coaches with two strong teams, jiu-jitsu takes off.*

5- Why did Rolls leave the Gracie Academy to teach with Carlson? He had trained with Helio his whole youth.

Carlinhos: *Because Rorion was the one running the show as Uncle Helio began teaching less and less. Rolls once told me, "I'll work for Helio, but I'll never work for Rorion." So, he left to work with Carlson instead.*[188]

6- What happened to the Gracie Academy after Rorion left for the US?

Carlinhos: *Rickson replaced him. First at the Rio Branco location [original Gracie Academy] and then later the Vasco Clube and finally the Gracie on the Humaitá Street where Royler took over eventually.*

7- What impact do you think the Figueiredo de Magalhães Academy had on jiu-jitsu? I believe that building was far more influential than it has been given credit for.

Carlinhos: *If you look at CBJJ's first Mundial in 1996, especially the results of brown and black-belts. The elite came out of Gracie*

---

[188] The internal rivalry between Rorion and Rolls is clear here as well as in the other texts cited throughout this book. Rorion, being the eldest son of Helio (who was in charge of the Gracie Academy then), was not likely to share the role of "alpha" with Rolls who probably felt underappreciated.

Barra, Carlson's gym on Figueiredo or Alliance. With Gracie Humaitá under Royler being the exception. Even Dedé [André Pederneiras co-founder of Nova União, one of the top teams in Rio at the time] *was a Carlson student, even though he began with Rodrigo Vieira* [who had also previously trained at the Figueiredo Academy]. *So most of the winners in those days did trace their legacy directly to that building.*

8-   When did you first begin teaching at the original Gracie Academy and why did you leave?

Carlinhos: *I started being thrown around and being used as a dummy when Rolls and Rorion taught their private classes at the Gracie Academy. Later, I trained with Rolls but still taught privates out of the Gracie Academy. Myself and Rickson did this. Rolls was hungry and we could give him a hard time so he would always push us to train with him when the day was over. Me and Rickson were both brown-belts at the time and we trained every day in the Gracie Academy, 4 or 5 of us at the end of the day after all the privates. But Rickson got a little big headed and Rolls called me to offer me a job to teach under him at the Figueiredo Academy. In a nut-shell, it was basically the same thing that happened with Rorion and Rolls before us. I felt that I would never be able to develop there as an instructor while Rickson was in charge. So, I went over to help Rolls teach at the Figueiredo Academy.*

9-   How was the training between you and Rickson in those days?

Carlinhos: *We trained a lot and went back and forth with each other. No one really dominated anyone. There was no rivalry in the sense where we'd refuse to lose to one another. Of course, everyone was trying to win, but no one really made a big deal out of winning or losing. We all had our good and bad days.*

10- Do you recall how and when you received your black-belt?

Carlinhos: *I began training in Copacabana* [at the Figueiredo Academy] *to be near Rolls as a brown-belt and one day he suggested to Uncle Helio that it was time and that I was ready for my black-belt. So, Uncle Helio told me to put it on the next day. There were some belts that hung off the wall at the gym, so the next day, I just grabbed a black one and tied it on myself* [laughs]. *This was before 1976, because I remember I have a diploma I received much later in 1976, but I had been promoted a few years before that, maybe 74 or 75.*

11- Were there other tough teams and tough opponents in those days?

Carlinhos: *In Niterói we had two good schools, Oriente Academy where Arruda, a former student of Uncle Helio, taught; and Munir who was a coach to Julio César, the leader of Grappling Fight Team* [GFT]. *Oriente even had a student who beat Rolls once, tough kid called Cicero, they were green-belts at the time I think. We were all young so I don't remember details. But that loss was before Rolls became an athlete, before he had his ascent. Once a judo guy called Paulo Boca almost beat Rolls in competition too. Rolls pulls guard at the end and won by decision. Boca became my student later but was originally a student of Oswaldo Alves. There was also Sergio Iris, also from Niterói. I think he was the first one to beat one of Helio's sons, he beat Rorion. Sergio Penha from Oswaldo Alves was really good too. He almost had Rickson in that one fight. I had trained with Sergio* [Penha] *a lot while I was learning judo from Oswaldo Alves and the day of their match I told Rickson about his strongest positions.*

12- Can you tell us a little bit about your brother Reylson? He seems like he had a more business vision of things, maybe even ahead of his time.

Carlinhos: *For a minute he was the only one of us making any money from jiu-jitsu. He bought a room in a shopping mall at the Gávea.*

His mats had pics of James Bond, he loved James Bond. He talked the talk too and had a more bells and whistles view of jiu-jitsu, more artistic. He didn't want casca-grossas around him, he wanted people with money. Reylson learned his jiu-jitsu inside the Gracie Academy. When he opened his school, he wanted something with a more Hollywood like view of things. He never abandoned the 36 classes that were the basis to give someone a blue-belt in those days.[189]

13- What was Rolls like?

Carlinhos: *He could be stubborn at times, and proud. People were scared of telling him things straight. The only one who always did so was me, I'd always tell him straight. He'd get mad, we'd argue, but I'd tell him.*

14- How did you take the news of his death?

Carlinhos: *We had just come back from Buzios when someone called and Jacaré [Romero Cavalcanti] told me the call was for me. It was a Sunday night. It hit me hard. I went for a long walk after I received the news, thinking about all this. It was all so sudden, Rolls was the leader in the family. Everyone respected him, even Uncle Helio. Rolls and my father were about the only two people Helio respected. Rolls respected him a lot too. And suddenly he dies, an irreparable loss to jiu-jitsu.*

15- When Rolls passed, you took over his classes at the Figueiredo Academy. In some ways you continued his work with Gracie Barra wouldn't you say?

Carlinhos: *I took over the classes because Rolls' wife [Angela] asked me to. Robson asked me to as well. When Marcio Macarrão and*

---

[189] The original Gracie Academy's followed a program with 36 lessons. Upon completion of these lessons, the student would be awarded a blue-belt.

Mauricio Gomes got there, I was already a black-belt. These guys all respected and looked up to me. So, one day, the students got together and decided that they would remain under me, most of them at least [some would go over to Carlson or Rickson]. *In 1984, two years after Rolls' death, I went to Barra to teach and opened a school there.*[190] *But I was already branching off before that. About 6 months before his death, I told Rolls that I would begin teaching with Crólin at my father's house in Redentor, which was nice because I didn't have to pay rent and could charge a lot for my privates. In those days, life was good, ladies, beach, no rent, private classes, training, so it was all really good. Of course, Rolls wasn't too happy about this but I explained to him that this was necessary for my personal growth, that I wanted to get married and have kids one day so I wanted to do my own thing. I kept training with Rolls in the morning so we remained close. One day, Rolls told me he wanted to open a really big jiu-jitsu academy in Rio and that he wanted myself and Crólin to come teach and be partners with him, so I immediately agreed and just told him to let me know when. That was shortly before he passed.*

16- Any good stories of Rolls?

Carlinhos: *I remember one time, that I was beginning to have a hard time with his students so I asked,* "Rolls, don't you think you are teaching them a little too much?" *Helio would put that in our heads, because they could turn on us one day. He had that experience in his life with Waldemar* [Santana]. *So, Uncle Helio would say,* "be careful who you will teach!" *I had that mentality too, it was a common way of thinking then, so I told Rolls* "your kids will lose one day! Be careful!" *Rolls looked at me dead serious and said,* "you want to be good? better than others? Then train more than them.

---

[190] This is the school that would later become known worldwide as "Gracie Barra," the largest jiu-jitsu team in the world today.

The only way to be good is to train even more than they do, not by hiding jiu-jitsu from them." *That hit me hard. I said it as criticism to his ways, but that day my mentality to teach changed completely and I began to teach my students everything. And that helped me because my students got better faster and it all came back to repay me at the end. Rolls had a very open mind.*

17- Peixotinho described him as the lost-link in the family. Do you agree? I also wonder what your role would have been in all this had he not passed.

Carlinhos: *Yeah, you can say so. Had he not died I don't know what would have happened. He was my leader. I would never do anything had he not made a move first. I would never have created anything. I think I would have tried to convince him to do what I did, but he could be stubborn, I'm not sure he would have listened to me anyway. He had a business sense, but he never cared about getting involved or organizing tournaments. At the end of the day, he was an athlete, not an organizer.*

***

Pans organized by the CBJJ in California 1996.
Leading from the front and at the center
of the table is Carlinhos Gracie Jr.
Photocred: Marcelo Alonso personal archives.

"In those days, there were people faking ID's, trying to sneak in (...)
But slowly we began to gain their respect. We developed a policy of
not negotiating with "terrorists." People fought back, they didn't like
our rules so they'd boycott and we told them, "ok, go ahead..." but we
didn't budge."

Master Carlos Gracie Jr.

18- What about the açaí fruit? Azoury was telling me that it was the
    crew from the Figueiredo Academy that began to popularize it in
    Rio at a time when the fruit wasn't common anywhere.

This is the story of açaí. My father came from Belém, land of the
açaí, he was raised on it. On the Camões, in between the Figueredo

de Magalhães and Domimgues Ferreira Streets there was a store called Arataca who sold products from the north and northeast of Brazil, and it was owned by a man called "Seu Cici" [Mr. Cici]. *I think his store is still there in fact. It was nothing but a hole in the wall. And my father would go there and buy açaí from him. The fruit was all liquid, no one froze anything in those days and we'd blend the açaí with all sorts of different fruits, or we'd eat it with tapioca, or Minas cheese. Eventually, the whole crew from the Figueiredo Academy, both Rolls and Carlson's students, began to buy açaí as well. It became something we did as a group, so it became associated with jiu-jitsu in Rio.*

19- What was training jiu-jitsu like in the years immediately before and after Royce and CBJJ?

Siriema: *I started in 1990 or 1991. In those days everyone had to be ready for anything and all the time. For a professional or for a street fight. Even in the gym we had to be ready for the* "confere" [to be checked]. *Sometimes it was like a circus, Carlinhos would put two kids against one adult* [laughs]. *We had a pair of filthy and stinky boxing gloves to practice takedown with strikes, anything could happen.*

Carlinhos: *The classes were random too. No one ever knew what we would be training that day* [laughs].

Siriema: *We took it hard on people too, things were different then. I had friends that were scared of going up those stairs and they'd rather train with me in private. And I'd say,* "man, you can train with Carlinhos Gracie and you want to take classes from me?" *Many people wanted to train but they were scared.*

Carlinhos: *It was like becoming a member of a special forces team, they'll start with 200 and end up with 10 elite guys, for example.*

That's how it was in those days. The guy would have to be practically a masochist to get slapped in the head and keep training. So, most would quit.

Siriema: *Yes, out of 20 white-belts who entered, only 2 would stay. There were barely any white-belts. Listen, I loved the opportunity to train at Gracie Barra in the early 90s. But today, I wouldn't want to train in that environment, not with my herniated disk. I wouldn't be able to train jiu-jitsu there. It was a rougher crowd, more demanding. Just to give you an idea, if you won a tournament by fighting on the edge of the mats, you'd be scorned. It was an embarrassment not to throw yourself whole heartedly into the fight. Even if you won, if you did it in an ugly manner, you'd be scorned by your teammates and they'd say* "fighting on the edge of the mats is for cowards." *You just can't do that today. Times have changed.*

Carlinhos: *It wasn't just about winning, it was about winning well, winning with honor. Not by being flaky or running.*

20-   How did the *Federação de Jiu-Jitsu do Estado do Rio de Janeiro* ["FJJRio" and former Guanabara Federation] move from Helio's hands into Robson's?

When Robson took over the federation, Uncle Helio had taken a step back. I think he was tired of the lack of support from other gyms. Robson began to create a movement of the gyms that weren't satisfied with Uncle Helio's presidency. Lots of arguing in those days. So, they organized a meeting with the gym owners to find out what we were going to do next. That's what I heard, but I wasn't there. People tried to organize against Uncle Helio and wanted me involved but I wanted nothing to do with it. I won't go against Uncle Helio on anything. And some of those guys would say "but Helio isn't doing enough" *and I'd say* "not me, you guys do whatever you want." *The truth is, that there were a lot of people who were discontent with Uncle Helio. Because he would do things that would upset people. A fight would be over and he'd step in and make them fight again because he didn't feel that the fight counted. If anyone said anything he'd ask* "are you scared? No? Then fight again!" *and coerce them to go again. People respected him, they were also afraid of him. He was like a feudal lord who meddled in fights all the time and would referee the matches of his own children. And this upset a lot of people, even though no one had the courage to confront him on anything. So, when things came to a vote [Carlinhos could not specify the year in which this happened], the majority voted for a change, they voted for Robson to become the President.*

21- What about Copa Company, what happened there? It was perhaps the most important tournament in those days.

This was before the CBJJ and I brought what I believe is the first sponsor to jiu-jitsu, a clothing brand called "Company," *owned by one of my students called Mauro Taubman. The brand was known in Rio and was becoming associated with jiu-jitsu, all the best guys were being sponsored by them. I helped them organize two tournaments, helping in the background. But during the second event two of its competitors sued him. Buchaú and Mcdowell, who were my students. Can you believe this? They sued the guy who was sponsoring jiu-jitsu! So, I kicked them off the team,* "Are you idiots? Are you crazy? You are a bunch of nobody's!" *Mauro had used a picture of them while in motion for an uchimata to promote the event. So, I'd tell them,* "he is promoting you guys! And you repay him by suing him?" *Believe it or not, Carlson and I went to court to testify on opposite sides. I told Carlson,* "you are an idiot. They are promoting you! Your team is winning his tournament and you are testifying against him?" *I was so angry I told Mauro, "look, this will hurt me. But if I were you I'd end it all. Stop sponsoring everyone, including me." I told him to stop everything because those guys were idiots, jiu-jitsu didn't deserve his efforts. Everyone boycotted him. All jealous and mad at me, "Carlinhos this, Carlinhos that..." I could have kept it all for myself, but I opened the sponsorship for everyone in jiu-jitsu. Even Jacaré [Romero Cavalcanti] boycotted this event. So, I told him, if I were him, I'd tell them all to go eat soap. And that ended his involvement with jiu-jitsu. I was angry not just at the guys who sued him, I was angry at the jiu-jitsu community as a whole who never had an event like that and instead of supporting the guy, they went after him or were silent about it all.*

22-   Why did you create an organization outside of the Federação do Estado do Rio de Janeiro instead of working with your brother Robson?

Carlinhos: *I tried influencing Robson. But it was hard. As a former athlete, I felt frustrated because I'd see guys from judo and other modalities traveling the world to compete. When we competed, we traveled to the suburbs of Rio. We didn't have the prestige that other sports had. I had problems that I wanted addressed, me, André Pederneiras, Carlson, "Jacaré" [Romero Cavalcanti], etc. But Robson didn't have a school or any students, so he didn't feel that same pressure. So, I thought, "if we are the ones lifting jiu-jitsu and training people, we should be organizing it too, us the coaches." Robson was all about events and rules, but had no followers. He was purely a politician, if he worked solely for the schools he would have been useful to us, but he wasn't, he was clashing with us and just doing whatever he wanted to do. So, one day I told him to forget it.*

23- What did you do next?

Carlinhos: *One day I got all the schools from Barra da Tijuca together and asked them,* "what do we want? Leblon, Ipanema, Copacabana are there. Let's do something in our own neighborhood to help grow jiu-jitsu here." *That is when I started the Associagão da Barra da Tijuca to organize tournaments in the Barra neighborhood, me Jorge Pereira, Marco Vinicius, Claudio Franga, Zé Beleza. Our first event was in the Veiga Almeida, at the Americas Avenue, beautiful venue. Robson wanted to close the whole thing down because we weren't asking for his help or authorization. So, I told him,* "if you manage to stop this, I will abandon everything and come work for you. But first, I want to see you try to shut me down." *Robson shut down nothing. Carlson and others supported the effort.*

24- Was it hard to get this association off the ground?

I'll tell you a story to give you an idea. Albertinho, one of Carlson's students, the son of "Apaga-vela" [Candle-blower] *who used to take care of Carlson's roosters for cock-fighting. He lost a match and came yelling at me,* "fuck Barra guys!" *All mad and acting all tough. So, I went to talk to him,* "what's the matter man? You come from Copacabana to insult us here? Why are you angry at the event?" *and he told me to go to hell and told me that Barra guys could eat it. So, I brought all the instructors from the association together and said,* "see that? Is that what you want? Albertinho is a light-feather, but tomorrow someone bigger than him will smack you in the head, is that what you want? These younger guys talking to us like that? Are you going to fight them all? Isn't there any hierarchy here? Is this what you guys want for jiu-jitsu?" *They said no.* "Good then, are you with me?" *They said they were.* "Good, Albertinho will never again compete in his life, do you guys support me? If he enters any event, we will pull out all our students. And they will have to choose between 1 competitor or 200. Are you with me or not?" "Yes," *they all replied, ok good. So, I told Carlson, "I am going to retire Albertinho" and Carlson laughed at me, I remember this well.*

Three weeks later, Rio Sports Center hires Carlson to teach and they spend all this money to organize an event. They invited me to participate. I told them I'd support, but only one problem: Albertinho. "If he competes the Associação da Barra da Tijuca is out." *No one believed me. In those days no one believed in anything, it was every man for himself and no unity to be found anywhere. They said "ok, whatever." On the week of the tournament no one from Barra signed up and then they'd call all the gyms and the Barra gyms would tell them to come talk to me instead. By Wednesday the organizer was panicking and called me to change my mind.* "I told you so! That if Albertinho entered we wouldn't support!" *So right then and there, they stopped Albertinho from competing. They didn't let him in. Carlson couldn't believe it* [laughs]. *At night, the doorbell rang, it was Albertinho, who came over to beg,* "Are you trying to destroy me??" *I told him,* "Yes, I am. I organized a tournament, let you in and you come over here to disrespect us? I will give you one chance… if you ever do that again you will never enter another jiu-jitsu tournament in your life, do you understand me?" *And that was it, he became a friend and a fan after that. Everyone else got scared.*

Remember, in those days, every time someone tried to do an event in a nicer venue there would be a fight and we would go back to square one. With all those ogres, thousands of them in a tournament and I told them all, whoever brawls in here [quem sair na porrada aqui] *will be kicked out, and I'll retire you forever. You are out. I don't care how strong, big, good or tough you are. No one fought. And I told them,* "if you take your kimono jacket off after the match in celebration you will be punished by having to donate food to charities." *I did this so people didn't accuse us of* punishing them only to take their money. Once we gathered 10,000 kilos of food.

We did this until people stopped being disrespectful toward referees and the event. In the beginning, some big names in jiu-jitsu were put on trial because they didn't take us too seriously. They'd come with attorneys so we had to hire our own attorneys too. So, we'd say, "your punishment is 200kg of food if you don't contest it, but if you contest your punishment and lose the trial, it is 600kg instead, understand?" It got rough sometimes, and people wanted heads to roll when things got heated. Our attorney sometimes would have to intervene to calm people down. Our own attorney would end up having to calm everyone down and protect the accused [laughs].

There was one time where someone even tried to lock the accused in the bathroom so he'd stop intervening in the trial. One of them, a known guy in the community, challenged us and didn't show up to the trial and decided to go to the beach instead... I said, "ok, let's wait and see what happens." Shortly after, a mom of one of his students tried to sign her son up to compete in one of our tournaments, so we told her that he owed us from that infraction and his signature was no longer valid until he answered for the infraction. And then the mom would go complain to the guy... In those days, there were people faking ID's, trying to sneak in... it was absolute chaos. In the first trials we had to bring in some heavy weights to be part of the board, people everyone respected like Bustamante, Bebeo and Castelo-Branco. It wasn't easy, the penalties went up, at one point the fine went up and they had to pay us 1000kg of food to give to charities. But slowly we began to gain their respect. We developed a policy of not negotiating with "terrorists." People fought back, they didn't like our rules so they'd boycott and we told them, "ok, go ahead..." but we didn't budge.

On another occasion we had the Brazilian Nationals and it would be televised by Globo TV. For the first time ever, one of our events would be televised. They would go there to film all the *black-belt matches, it was a big deal. Luizinho* [business mind behind Nova União but not a fighter or coach] *found a problem somewhere, got everyone together and boycotted the tournament. A lot of people boycotted so we knew we'd have a lot of Gracie Barra guys in the finals, so I sat everyone down and told them, "you will have to fight, you will fight your friends and I don't want to hear it, you will have to fight for real." You know what happened? Globo came over and filmed, out of 10 divisions, 8 were won by Gracie Barra. And it turned out to be incredible marketing for our team. Those guys were all livid, and I thought to myself "you idiots, you missed out on the best opportunity of your life to get your students on TV..." After that, we just kept on doing things our own way.*

25- Why did you start the CBJJ and not your older brother Robson who was best positioned to become its president given his seniority and standing?

Carlinhos: *Around 1993, André Pederneiras organized a tournament and called it* "Copa Brasileira de Jiu-Jitsu" [Brazilian Jiu-Jitsu Cup]. *I was there, I think it was at the Clube Hebraica, it was actually a good tournament. That got me thinking. Pederneiras, in those days was a new jiu-jitsu coach, he didn't have the status he has today. But he was getting things in motion, so I saw a threat to control. So, I began to think* "pretty soon Pederneiras will be doing everything" *so I went to Robson* "see Robson? You only organize a state-championship and he is organizing a national event. You guys keep arguing over non-sense while others are taking over." *So I proposed to Robson,* "how about this, let's start a confederation and you be its president and let me organize and run the FJJRio." *He was ranked higher than me after all. And he went* "no way." *You know why he said no? Because in those days, the FJJRio was already on its feet and running. All that was required was to keep it running.*
 The CBJJ I was idealizing didn't exist, it was a utopia because jiu-jitsu barely existed anywhere outside of Rio and no one thought

that the rest of the country could have a strong jiu-jitsu presence like we had in Rio. The whole thing was a far more ambitious project, but it didn't exist and it would be a lot of work to get it off the ground, so Robson said no to my proposal. Robson thought I was being a smart ass by trying to take over something that was ready and functioning. So, I just moved on and founded the CBJJ and immediately organized an event at Akxe Academy, the first official "Campeonato Brasileiro de Jiu-Jitsu."

The difference between the two was that Pederneiras organized an event and called it the Brasileiro. I started an official legal entity that was meant to give jiu-jitsu credibility. How can you have a national title without a confederation to run and operate it? When Robson saw the Akxe tournament work, he came over to me and joked that people were talking about impeaching me [laughs]. What impeachment man? That was when he saw the potential. He hadn't seen it before, but he saw it after that tournament.

At first, he helped me with documentation, he had a lot more experience than me in that regard so Robson helped. But when he saw the tournament work and the potential that the CBJJ had, that was when he began to realize the mistake he had made, "now Carlinhos, the younger brother is the one who is on top of everyone..." That was what they were all thinking. After that Robson began to apply pressure so that his federation remained the leading organization in Brazil and I said no way... you are State Governor, but I am the President of the Republic, the Confederation ranks above State level federations. So, we began to butt heads after that and Robson would say, "I created a Frankenstein!" referring to me and the CBJJ [laughs]. But the vision was mine, so I had to keep doing things my way.

Things got so bad that eventually I had to disenfranchise the FJJRio from the CBJJ. They came after me, telling me that I was destroying something that began long before, in the days of the Guanabara Federation, etc. And I told them, "listen, on the mats, Robson is my senior because he outranks me. But in terms of our tournaments, I have to do what is best for the CBJJ and Robson needs to fall in line with everyone else. You can't be a federation that is constantly clashing with its senior organization." *And that was pretty much the end of that episode.*

26- Was the *Brasileiro* organized by Pederneiras the same event in which Carlson and Robson were about to get into a fist fight because of a match and you had to intervene?

Yes. André Pederneiras organized the Brasileiro at the Hebraica and I went there to watch. In that event there was a match between Rey Diogo and Daniel Simões and Daniel won but Carlson wouldn't accept the results. Carlson got all his students together, all these huge guys and had them sit on the mats and stop the whole tournament until the result of the match was reversed. And Robson was arguing with Carlson who was upstairs and yelling back and forth and insulting each other. Carlson said, "I'll kick your ass!" [vou te meter a porrada!] *and Robson goes, "I want to see you try, you wuss!"* [quero ver você tentar seu frouxo!] *And Carlson goes "what??" and was coming downstairs to fight his brother Robson* [laughs]. *At that age they were about to go at it, can you believe it? So, I intervened,* "are you crazy Carlson? Are you going to fight your own brother here in front of everyone? It will make jiu-jitsu look bad, look at what you are doing? You are going to ruin the tournament."

So that's what happened, who was going to challenge Carlson and his heavy-weights? The tournament was about to end. Andre was panicking and asked me to help him, so I spoke to Carlson, "look at what you are doing. Let's do this, let's cancel this fight. Monday they both grapple at my academy, bring them over and they can fight again, whoever wins gets the medal, deal?" *Carlson agreed and they did exactly that. Come Monday they went at it, Rey Diogo won and Carlson was happy. Those days were hard, people wanted to boycott us, to discredit our attempts at organizing jiu-jitsu, you see? Over time, we finally began to turn the tide and change that chaotic environment into a decent and civilized one.*[191]

27-   Did your father intervene in any of this?

No, he was far too old by then [Carlos died in 1995]. As he aged he became more removed and retreated into his own world. He liked to sit there and watch people compete. Sometimes he'd place a medal on the winner.

28-   Tell us a little bit more about the birth of CBJJ/IBJJF and the difficulties it faced.

Carlinhos: *The problem was that those ogres had no vision. They were all thinking about the now, not thinking ahead. And they would get jealous and say* "look Carlinhos is making all that money" *and I'd think to myself,* "of course, I work hard for it" *but I'll bring everyone with me, and everyone will be good with me. I am lifting the community, if everyone worked with me, we would all benefit together. And those guys were mad at me. Did they want to stay in those small venues in Rio forever? I was opening doors for them.*

Siriema: *What I saw, when I began working for CBJJ and had decided that I wanted to live my life for jiu-jitsu, was that jiu-jitsu had no direction. It was every man for himself. Today at least, jiu-jitsu is on a track, it is going somewhere.*

Carlinhos: *I would leave in shock those early meetings, where we were all trying to organize jiu-jitsu. And I'd think to myself* "why are we arguing over nonsense?" *They'd be in a room arguing, pointing the finger at each other and nothing got done.*

---

[191] This event is also retold here: https://carlsongracieteam.org/15-anos-sem-carlson-gracie/

Siriema: *Those meetings were a complete lack of practical action. Nothing got done.*

Carlinhos: *It was everyone trying to be more and better than the person next to them. They weren't thinking about what was best for jiu-jitsu.*

Siriema: *I think this is the definition of faith. Because you couldn't look at us then and reason* "this right here will grow someday." *It was all so small and chaotic.* "Grow? How?" *Logic wasn't enough to make sense of that mess and get jiu-jitsu organized.*

Carlinhos: *When we organized the first Pans in Los Angeles, people said* "who are you going to fight? There is no one there!" *and I'd say,* "you want to start big?" *I took 120 competitors with me. They were fighting one another. A few Americans only. It was small.*

29- Was that the Pan that Carlson won and his students lifted him in the air after?

Siriema: *That one is a bit controversial and people lifted Carlson up in the midst of an argument over which team won that day* [laughs].

Carlinhos: *Carlson didn't win shit* [everyone laughs]. *We won by one point. I never cared about points. I wanted the event. Whether my team won or not, I didn't care. But that day, Gordinho was paying attention and he came over and said,* "Carlinhos, these guys are fixing it..." [Carlinhos, os caras armaram...]. *Because Carlson was a point ahead, but the guy who scored that final point entered as Carlson Team* "B." *So technically the point didn't count. So, I brought the guy over, looked him in the eye and asked* "which team did you enter as: Carlson 'A' or Carlson 'B'?" *And he put his head down and said* "B". *And Gracie Barra guys went crazy over it* [laughs]. "You stole it you sons of bitches!" *and then Carlson's guys did the same and went crazy over it as well, celebrating as if they had won by lifting Carlson in the air. Huge confusion that day, good times* [laughs].

30-   Did Carlson meddle in the rules?

Carlinhos: *Carlson meddled, yes. He was respected, had a big team and was constantly giving his take on things.*

Siriema: *One time I saw Roleta stick his foot in* [Eduardo] *Jamelão's belt, sweep him and land in mount. And Carlson just walked on the mats and said:* "Stop everything now!" (parou tudo agora!) *and made them go back into position* [laughs].

31-   And he wasn't the referee?

Siriema: *No, he wasn't even Jamelão's coach* [laughs] *that was just Carlson being Carlson. Of course, he couldn't have done that, but who was going to challenge him in those days?*

Carlinhos: *He was like a feudal lord.*

32-   But the problems didn't end there, did they?

Of course not, later Luisinho founded CBJJO [Confederação Brasileira de Jiu-Jitsu Olímpico] *to compete with us* [CBJJ].[192] *And Nova União, who was on its way to become the best jiu-jitsu team*

---

[192] This was not the only organization attempting to compete with the CBJJ during the late 90s. There was also the *"Super Liga"* (see: *"Mesa Redonda – Wallid, Royler, Robson, Belfort, Etc."* https://www.youtube.com/watch?v=gbOlaHizdSo). Later the CBJJE (*Confederação Brasileira de Jiu-Jitsu Esportivo*) was founded in São Paulo by Master Moisés Muradi. The CBJJE today is the only nationwide league still in operation other than the CBJJ itself.

in the world, thought it wise to boycott us because of Luisinho.[193]
*That guy basically ended their competition team by preventing
them from competing in our tournaments. It got worse for them
when we moved the tournaments to the USA and they couldn't
afford to travel here. So, they slowly lost their position of being as
competitive as Gracie Barra and Alliance.*

33- How did Carlson feel about you taking the lead and running the
confederation [CBJJ]?

Carlinhos: *In the beginning, Carlson was the biggest beneficiary of
all this because his academy was winning everything. At the end of
the day, the team title was his. This is why I got so mad at him over
the Copa Company issue. It made no sense, he was positioned to
win all those tournaments, why would he testify against the guy?
Against the guy who is putting you way up there? He never had
a good answer to these questions. On the other hand, he loved all
events, he was addicted to competition.*

Siriema: *He loved cock-fighting, he liked to watch guys go to war
and was by nature an antagonist. Not that he was ever against our
work, but that by antagonizing, he was just being himself. It wasn't
necessarily anything bad.*

34- Was it hard to structure jiu-jitsu then? It all seems to me rather
chaotic.

Carlinhos: *When Robson was organizing the tournaments for the
FJJRio, there weren't even stripes being given to the Grandmasters.
It was all very informal, there were no actual rules in place. I*

---

[193] Luisinho was a businessman helping Nova União. Though not a founder, coach or even a
black-belt on that team.

noticed it was all very political even though they were trying to copy judo a bit.

They'd get together, Robson, Mansour, Munir, Amélio Arruda and a few others. And they would decide among themselves who would receive their stripes, only in jiu-jitsu! The problem was that there were no rules in place. They promoted people according to their personal preferences. This was around 1992 or 1993. And I'd say, "we need to change this, let's promote the black-belts according to systems." Because it went like this. The guy who was a master, didn't want anyone else to become a master, and they'd go, "for there to be a master, the previous one must die" *and I'd go* "are you guys crazy? Jiu-jitsu is going to grow to the world, we need rules and systems!" *It was all very provincial and short sighted.*

35-   I place Royce Gracie and the UFC in 1993 as a dividing moment in the history of jiu-jitsu and martial arts in general. But it is interesting to notice that things were beginning to move a bit faster in Rio even before Royce and the UFC. Perhaps because your generation reached maturity and began to think of jiu-jitsu differently.

Siriema: *After Royce, you no longer had to explain to people what jiu-jitsu was. People knew what you were talking about because they knew about Royce's victories. But 1991 was a very important year for jiu-jitsu in Rio, the Jiu-Jitsu versus Luta-Livre Challenge drew a lot of attention to jiu-jitsu in general.*

36-   Can you tell us a little bit about the origin of the CBJJ/IBJJF ruleset?

Siriema: *I was only a blue-belt at the time so I didn't have much say. Remember, if you were a blue-belt in those days you couldn't even open your mouth to speak, but a number of coaches would meet in a garage to discuss rules, Dedé* [Pederneiras], *Murilo* [Bustamante], *Carlson, etc. We didn't feel exactly like a new organization, we saw ourselves as a continuation of the Guanabara Federation [FJJRio] so our starting point was the ruleset they had created. The problem was that these rules were poorly written and organized, it was a lot of work to change all this. But I saw an intelligence behind them. The sort of thinking that I didn't see in those meetings. We aren't sure who created them but there was a lot of thought that went behind them. It had principles to it.*

Carlinhos: *All I can say is that everything in those days had to be approved by Helio. Nothing would be done without his approval.*

Siriema: *For example, in the Guanabara rules, competitors aren't rewarded for escaping a bad spot, because that would teach people to put themselves there and then get good at escaping them in order to win. That would be a backwards way of looking at things. Imagine letting someone mount just to escape and score points? What would happen if you did that in a fight? As we see it, jiu-jitsu is a martial art and the rules can't be ahead of its overall efficiency, but must be shaped by it while safe-guarding the practitioner's physical integrity. We always try to strike that balance.*

37- How was the move from Rio to California and the formation of IBJJF?

Siriema: *When we came to the US, it was clear that we had to rethink a lot of things. We had lived in a very small world where we would just call each other and meet in a garage and decide the future of things. All of a sudden, we found ourselves in a position to explain rules and systems to the whole world. The rules we had were poorly written in Portuguese and it was poorly translated into English.*

When we got here, kids were competing under the same rules as adults. We saw many parents that seemed somewhat frustrated they had not been fighters themselves and were putting their kids to fight as if they were roosters. Their matches and positions were full of rough plays [grosserias] and the press was photographing exactly that, and the image of jiu-jitsu that was being created wasn't a good one, it wasn't the one we wanted. We had to rethink a lot of our rules and it fell to me to rewrite them and make them more detailed and sensible.

38- Will jiu-jitsu continue to grow?

Carlinhos: *As we see it, in other styles, agility and speed are crucial. With jiu-jitsu you can stay active for many years. I still train today... Last week I trained 5 times. I can manage, I don't have to go too hard, I'm 66 years old and I can still do this. In which other sport can I do this? So older guys in other arts have to punch a bag or jump rope. In jiu-jitsu you can actually train every day and not get punched in the face, you see? There is longevity in jiu-jitsu. In my view there will be thousands of schools and every martial art school will teach jiu-jitsu in them. The competition will be fierce, we have 7 billion students in potential. There will be thousands of schools, thousands of shows. People love to workout, every person who works out is a potential practitioner, that is our vision for the future.*

39- Can we professionalize jiu-jitsu?

Carlinhos: *Yes. Look, this is what I think will happen. In MMA no one needs to understand it to enjoy watching it. Jiu-jitsu is different, it requires education. That is our job, we need to educate people so they can be entertained by it. If we can get enough people training, we can get them watching it and change things. This is why our focus is in making the schools grow. Professionalization will be a side-effect of these efforts. These professional shows will be successful but where will the athletes be coming from? Where are they going to get good in the first place? By competing in our tournaments.*

Siriema: *We made it this far because jiu-jitsu was efficient not because it is entertaining. We can't lose that. There is pressure from people who are coming into the sport to make it more entertaining, we need to strike a balance in these things. I don't believe we should recede in terms of rules and anything that make it less efficient. But there is a young generation out there that is efficient and entertaining, Mica [Galvão], Tainan [Dalpra] and the Ruotolo's [Tye and Kade]. They are entertaining, watching them is watching 10 minutes of uninterrupted action. Also, we don't know when exactly someone turns into a phenom, but we believe that in the short span in which he competes he won't accumulate enough wealth to live comfortably in retirement. This happens in other professional sports where they lose everything after retirement. In jiu-jitsu we want people to be able to have other sources of income after they retire. In time, they will depend on teaching seminars, opening gyms, and etc.*

Carlinhos: *People who learn how to make money outside of their professional careers will be fine. This is where we come in and help: by giving structure and credibility to jiu-jitsu tournaments we help the gyms grow alongside us.*

40- I think this efficiency vs. entertainment is a fundamental issue in jiu-jitsu.

Siriema: *Look, I never read the Wealth of Nations [Adam Smith] but I do believe that competing forces find their balance eventually. When 50/50 came along, people were acting like it was the end of the world because it was so unrealistic, but eventually things sort of worked out. Same thing with berimbolo's. Now the big debate is whether or not we should ban the use of lapel's in a 50/50 to trap the opponent's leg. From all accounts it is almost impossible to escape. We have many people say this to us. We normally give these things time to see if competitors can figure creative ways out of these situations, in general, we interfere as little as possible. But in this case, we might have to interfere and place some limitations.*

Carlinhos: *I have an opinion on this. We should let them use the lapel but only within a certain time frame. After a certain amount of time they have to let go.*

Siriema: *This past World-Championship [2022] I saw a guy wrap the other one leg with a lapel in the 50/50 and also hold the other free leg. He kept him there for 8 minutes and the referee gave the victory to the one who held the whole time.*

Carlinhos: *He trapped the guy the whole match and still won... Crazy.*

41- I'm in favor of allowing heel-hooks in the gi to solve the problem. What are your thoughts on this?

Siriema: *When I began training, there were stories of people blowing their knees because of the knee-reap. Back in those days the technology wasn't there to reconstruct someone's knee. But things have changed. We are open to discussing this with other coaches. Because if we allow this, this means people will be practicing them in the gym and the coaches and athletes need to be heard in regards to this added risk. When we spoke to the coaches about allowing heel-hooks in the no-gi divisions, many were in favor, but against legalizing them in the gi.*

42-　Today, IBJJF runs approximately 130 tournaments per year. We are here at the 2022 Masters Worlds and you tell me that there are 8,600 registered competitors. An all-time record. What is the future like?

Carlinhos: *Jiu-jitsu will continue to grow, next time, we will have 9,000, 10,000 competitors. Because we have a better product than our competition. We offer longevity to all demographics. Other sports can't offer this. We want to take over the world.*

Siriema: *We have a product that is much better than everyone else's. Jiu-jitsu has no competition, which is why we shouldn't fight among ourselves, because we really have no competition. There is plenty of room for growth for everyone.*

***

The interviews had gone well and lasted just under 5hrs between the two of them. My overall thoughts after speaking to IBJJF's leadership, was that they aren't going to stop growing anytime soon and neither is jiu-jitsu. Their recipe, according to Carlinhos, was rather simple: keep it oriented toward the efficiency of combat; and bring it to as many different demographics as possible by helping sustain and grow the thousands of academies around the world.[194]

"Most practiced" seemed to me like a good and realistic goal. Nonetheless, I began to question whether or not it was the best mark in the horizon. More than that however, at some point I also began to

---

[194] A side note is necessary here. It would be too simplistic to grant all the credit to the face or head of a company, business, federation or team. To do so, would not only be overly simplistic, but would also be unfair to others who do much of the heavy lifting behind any organization. At closer inspection, we find that the body is formed of various organs all equally necessary for the body to function toward its purpose. Despite Carlinhos being a visionary and outstanding leader with a keen eye for talent, it is my view that without men such as Marcelo Siriema and Andre Fernandes working next to him, the IBJJF would have remained nothing more than an architect's dream. The credit for the execution of Carlinhos' vision is largely theirs.

question whether or not "most practiced" and "efficiency for combat" are always compatible. It is not that they are mutually exclusive either, but in all sincerity, I wonder *who is in the driver-seat here, popularity or efficiency?*

I am not suggesting that only one or the other ought to be the metric in sight. Clearly, a balance must be struck. People make thousands of decisions every day. Some of these decisions lead to other decisions, which open new doors while closing others. The accumulation of these decisions makes the whole of who we are as individuals or institutions.

At least in technical terms, there was much that could be done and I kept thinking about whether or not "most practiced" should be replaced with "most efficient." Jiu-jitsu, even in its more sportive format, remains highly efficient for purposes of combat. Something Carlinhos was adamant about in our first interview for the *Closed Guard* project and repeated to me again this time around. The reality is that a mid-level competitor in jiu-jitsu, regardless of preferred technical style, can demolish 99% of the world's population in a fight...even if they pull guard...and I don't dispute that. The exceptions being elite MMA fighters and perhaps other elite martial artists. However, the same could be said about Taekwondo practitioners in the 80s.

In other words, jiu-jitsu for a long time held a primacy over other martial arts in terms of our adherence to the reality of combat. Do we still have that edge? After all, while I agree that most BJJ competitors today are perfectly capable of defending themselves if they had to, this does not mean that we are on the best evolutionary track to maximize this potential toward the efficiency of real-combat.

Additionally, I question whether efficiency and popularity are well balanced in all this and if we haven't drifted too far from the reality of combat in the name of an ambitious project of embracing all demographics. I follow this thought with another one, can jiu-jitsu be more efficiency oriented without reversing back to its more hooligan like days? If so, how so? Can we steer its evolution toward something that is practical and highly efficient? Free from *"firula"*? Would this view necessarily ostracize people *and* miss out on new practitioners? Hard to say. It could just as well be the opposite and that people prefer a more reality-oriented understanding of jiu-jitsu.

On the other hand, this same understanding of jiu-jitsu is likely to repel many demographics for the same reason that MMA gyms repeatedly fail all across the world while BJJ gyms thrive. One demographic can pay and takes less of your time, the other one can't, or refuses to pay and takes much of the coach's time while having high expectations for the coach in terms of the coach's involvement. We are speaking of basic economics here, simple as that... A notion Carlson had to learn the hard way.

Furthermore, it is my view that jiu-jitsu would benefit if we all made a greater effort at shaping jiu-jitsu culture much like judo does (not that that is easy to do). Because if we leave it up to trends and public opinion (particularly the internet), we will eventually be vulnerable to the irrationality of these trends. Judo after all, hasn't lasted 140 years without a cultural matrix for its practitioners to uphold. It is my understanding that jiu-jitsu today lacks some of the glue that kept its practice (however miniscule in those days) cohesive during the *first* and *second-waves*. In my view, jiu-jitsu today, lacks cultural cohesion and instead relies too heavily on how appealing it is in social terms.

Jiu-jitsu's popularity is desirable, it is overall good and we all benefit from it (I know I do). More students, means more tournaments, more ranks, more gear and more money. No one is denying that. My point is that to maintain the strong momentum, decision making needs to be placed with what is best for jiu-jitsu's integrity in sight, which may not always be in sync with what the majority wants.

People have proven in the past to be easily manipulated and to follow trends blindly. If the future of jiu-jitsu is in the hands of what the customer wants, expects or demands (and considering how manipulative something like social media has proven to be), then decision making is, for all practical purposes, placed in the hands of marketing hustlers. In accord with their ability to influence and manipulate, rather than being in the hands of seasoned leadership with longevity and credibility in sight.

To put it differently, popularity ought to be a side-effect of jiu-jitsu's integrity and credibility, not the metric for its success. What that metric ought to be, requires considerate thought and perhaps, this can be accomplished by asking ourselves a simple question, *what made jiu-jitsu special to us all to begin with?* And perhaps follow that question with another pertinent one, *have we learned anything from our past?*

Despite my views, it is undeniable that the boom of the post-Royce era was given order and direction by the organizational efforts of men such as Carlinhos, Siriema and Andre. Their work and effort have undeniably helped sustain BJJ's momentum as a global phenom more than the jiu-jitsu community realizes. Without it, it is my view that jiu-jitsu would have fragmented a long time ago. In case it does survive into the future as a cohesive body, then it will be thanks to their organizing and legitimizing efforts.

I have no doubts that Carlinhos didn't become BJJ's godfather by accident. He may not have been the most well positioned member of the Gracie family to lead or give shape to jiu-jitsu as it entered an entirely new phase with new meaning. Yet between his social and leadership skills, name and placement in time, at the end of the day, he was the one who did it.

For all practical purposes, what Carlinhos did for BJJ was to give it the most consistent logistical and organizational shape it has ever experienced throughout its long history from Japan, to Brazil and from there to the world. If his brother Carlson was the one to create the recipe for the brand of jiu-jitsu that would take the world by storm after Royce and the UFC, it was Carlinhos who created the oven for this recipe to grow beyond a niche practice or a short-lived fad. While he certainly isn't the inventor of jiu-jitsu either, his brainchild, the IBJJF, is the closest thing to a Kodokan equivalent that BJJ has ever had.

Moreover, whether his brothers and cousins (or anyone else for that matter) likes it or not, the reality is that if the future of jiu-jitsu is in anyone's hands, Carlinhos is that man. Correspondingly, and as one would expect, the perks derived from such efforts and responsibility are generous. Yet if the crown is as heavy as some say it is (and in case merit still means anything in this world), then the perks of victory should agree with the crown's weight.

Interview over, but never ceasing from voicing his stratagems for the future of jiu-jitsu, Carlinhos, toward the very end of our first conversation, had one last bit of wisdom to share with me. As if jiu-jitsu's godfather had not proven enough his worth as a leader as well as his savviness to become one, Carlinhos proceeded to explain to me his central thought process and philosophy from the beginnings, when he set himself the task of building a jiu-jitsu empire, "streams" Carlinhos observed "always flow into the sea."

Master André Pederneiras (continued from Part 2)

Dedé next to his student Gustavo Dantas after Gustavo
wins IBJJF Worlds at brown-belt in 1998.
Photocred: Gustavo Dantas personal archives.

"The Desafio Jiu-Jitsu versus Luta-Livre was televised nationally across Brazil, and this got everyone very excited about organizing other events. In those days I taught a lot, but I saw that the tournaments were terrible. One time at the Atlântico Sul event [South Atlantic] *I had to wait until 2am to compete* [laughs]. *This was the norm. People had no idea how to organize anything. I am also a judo black-belt so I have seen how they run things and I thought to myself "we can organize a nationwide event if we plan and organize it well."'*

Master André Pederneiras

1- No doubt there are many reasons why jiu-jitsu became a global
    fever. What are your thoughts on the reasons for this success?

Look, if you look at an art like judo for example, it is taught by hav-
ing the student drill a move millions of times. You basically repeat
the move so many times that eventually you get good at it. But this
has the negative effect of making the classes very boring. In jiu-
jitsu however, from the beginning, the student has a lot of freedom
to create and improvise. Every day you create something new. You
go "wow, I have never seen or even thought about this move before."
This happens all the time and all over the world. Which makes jiu-
jitsu exciting to a lot of people. This to me helps explain why jiu-
jitsu is so popular. Not to mention it being painful to keep getting
taken down over and over again, especially as you age. In jiu-jitsu
it is totally different, rolling on the ground delivers less impact to
your body while still going live. Which makes it more accessible to
all age groups. In what other combat art can you have this?

2- I worry that this same popularization will lead BJJ down the same
    path other martial arts have undergone as they lost credibility
    during this process. Back in the day, those guys trained jiu-jitsu
    with their eyes on the reality of combat. But all that is gone now.
    What are your thoughts on this?

Here's what I think. Jiu-jitsu also consists of atemi-waza (strikes),
which is exactly the taparia part you are talking about. What
people need to remember is that jiu-jitsu has this other side to it,
beyond the competition model. Those who want to train jiu-jitsu
with self-defense or a more realistic approach to fighting need to
request this from their instructors. Which of course will require
instructors to be prepared to teach this. Maybe some kind of course
that grants them some kind of badge that certifies that this instruc-
tor or his students have been trained under this more realistic

approach to jiu-jitsu. Like in the military where an officer can have various specializations.

3- Carlson was known for being disorderly and chaotic in his ways. Can you comment?

Not just disorderly, he was the most disorderly one out of all of us [laughs]. *When I organized that tournament in 1993 at the Hebraica* [the Brazilian Cup] *Carlson put a halt to the whole tournament when Rey Diogo lost* [laughs]. *We all had to intervene and beg him to ask his guys to leave the mats so we could continue. I was panicking...* "man, Carlson is going to ruin my tournament!"

4- There seems to have been a moment there in the early 90s where everyone agreed that jiu-jitsu needed to grow and become more organized. You took the lead and organized the first Brazilian nationals in 1993. How did everyone in the community perceive this bold move?

The Desafio Jiu-Jitsu contra Luta-Livre was televised nationally across Brazil, and this got everyone very excited about organizing other events. In those days I taught a lot, but I saw that the tournaments were terrible. One time at the Atlântico Sul event [South Atlantic] *I had to wait until 2am to compete* [laughs]. *This was the norm. People had no idea how to organize anything. I am also a judo black-belt so I have seen how they run things and I thought to myself* "we can organize a nationwide event if we plan and organize it well." *Now that I think about it, that tournament was supposed to have happened in 1991, but it took us two years of planning to get that event off the ground. And back in the day I had a partner who had a good financial situation, so I asked him to buy the mats and he bought brand new ones and he put the* "Mameluc" *logo on them. That was his clothing brand. But we still needed approval. So I asked Robson* [Gracie] *to give us his seal of approval so I could organize the event. And Robson asked for a percentage of the event's profits to give us his federation's* [FJJRio, former Guanabara Federation] *approval. Turns out that the event was a huge success and when Robson saw the potential and saw the fat percentage I had given him, I could see it in his eyes that something had changed. I can't confirm this, but I suspect him and Carlinhos got together and they must have had some kind of meeting to determine that they needed to move quickly. And the following year Carlinhos founded the CBJJ, an organization completely outside of the FJJRio. I think they were concerned that I would take the lead during that moment when jiu-jitsu was becoming known around the world. They knew I wasn't stupid, that I had a lot of people who liked and supported me and that I had a good reputation in Rio, so I definitely think they perceived me as being a threat of sorts. But that was never my intention, I never wanted anything to do with politics, I just wanted to see jiu-jitsu grow, to see it exactly where it is today. But the problem was that Carlinhos didn't even know how to organize tournament brackets* [laughs]. *I spend the next two years going to Carlinhos' house before every event to help him organize it. Throughout all this, I never asked for a dime, I wanted nothing. Of course he learned and did an outstanding job building the organization, but in those days, he needed help. I often joke that Carlinhos owes me twice. First, because my tournament in 1993 inspired him to start the CBJJ. And second because after Luisinho started the CBJJO* [Confederação Brasileira de Jiu-Jitsu Olímpico] *in 2002, that was when Carlinhos decided to move their whole operation to California.*

5- Can you tell us a little more about the founding of CBJJO? This was the organization that was promising to challenge CBJJ's leadership.

I wanted nothing to do with any of it to be honest. I remember asking those guys, "what do you think you are doing?" And they said, "we are going to start an organization to rival Carlinhos'!" And I'd say, "are you guys nuts?" *But Luisinho insisted that I needed to be the president because I had the credibility. So I agreed on one condition, I would help to lift it off the ground for one year then I was out and wanted nothing to do with it. Which is exactly what I did. So I asked Luisinho and Deo* [Wendel Alexander] "what is the purpose of this organization? To make money or to topple Carlinhos?" *And Luisinho said, "to topple Carlinhos!" So I said* "alright then, this is what we will do next, get the CBJJ calendar out, we will have all our events on the exact same days they organize theirs. Isn't that what you want? To divide? You want everyone to come over to CBJJO because you are paying the champions, right? Ok, let's see how it goes, let's do this." *And that really did split jiu-jitsu in two in Brazil because CBJJO was offering money and a lot of people chose to compete at our event instead.*[195] *Which hurt them financially. It was after all this that Carlinhos decided to make his move to the USA and things blew up after that. So that is why I always joke that Carlinhos owes me twice* [laughs].

6- But at the end of the day, CBJJO didn't take off. But today Nova União is back in the IBJJF sphere. Can you comment?

Around this time I was becoming more and more involved with MMA and a lot of our students were faring very well so that was where all my focus was going. One day, after CBJJO basically went out of business because Luisinho owed a lot of money to a lot of people, some of my students came to me and said "coach, we want to go back and compete at the CBJJ events, can we?" *That was when I went over to Carlinhos and asked what would it take to get our team competing for the CBJJ again. They welcomed us with open arms but Siriema explained to us that Luisinho had a debt with them. Something like R$ 6,000, can't remember. It was basically for registration fees*

---

[195] This is the event that led to Romero's team, Alliance, splitting in 2002. When names such as Leo Vieira, Fernando Terere, Eduardo Telles, Demian Maia, Eduardo Jameão and many others decided to compete for CBJJO instead.

from students that Luisinho never paid CBJJ for. So I paid the R$ 6,000 out of my own pocket and Nova União is still actively competing in the CBJJ and IBJJF tournaments.

7- Marcelo Siriema is a very underestimated character in all this in my opinion. Would you agree?

I've said this before and I'll say this again. CBJJ and IBJJF made it this far thanks to Siriema. I saw him grow up inside the CBJJ and everything he has done. I saw him stand up to all those guys, still as a purple-belt. Do you have any idea what it was like in those days to stand up against all those old-school black-belts as a purple-belt? Those guys would miss a deadline for signing up their students and then walk up to Carlinhos and Carlinhos would say, "talk to Siriema." *And then those guys would go to Siriema and demand that he register their students. And Siriema would say,* "no way, you are late, I can't help you." *I was there, I even saw people threaten him, and he'd say* "go ahead, beat me up, I still won't register your guys and you will be suspended afterwards." *I mean, don't get me wrong, Carlinhos is a visionary and I wasn't there for all the work they have done, but the guy who was there and stood up to all those guys was Siriema. I told him this once,* "if it weren't for you, the IBJJF would not be where it is today." *Carlinhos' might have been the idealist behind the whole thing, but in my opinion the guy who lifted it all up and did it, was Marcelo Siriema.*

Chapter 18

Pit-Boys and the (long due) End of Hooligan-Jitsu

"In the 1980s and the 1990s, Brazilian jiu-jitsu was also directly asso-ciated with upper class hooliganism. The media both celebrated and desecrated the booming martial art. The Gracies undeniably played an ambiguous role in this process."[196]

José Tufy Cairus

In the mid-90s, when jiu-jitsu became a household name, its lead-ership had to make a crucial choice in regard to the future of their art: remain a niche practice in Rio or adapt to the times and capitalize on the opportunities provided by their recently acquired clientele. Fighting and brawling in general were a feature of a specific kind of jiu-jitsu that died during this period as we all adapted to the changing times. This was because parents were unlikely to enroll their children into a pro-gram where they saw adults hitting each other in the head with filthy boxing-gloves or slapping each other around in speedos.

Commercialization brought with it the demands of political correct-ness and a softer approach to jiu-jitsu that was more appealing to a wider audience. The changing times, being less tolerant toward violence and alpha driven behavior in general, would leave their mark in jiu-jitsu in a way that would significantly modify its original warrior code. Which is perhaps an inevitable side-effect of democratization.

To give support to the potential growth that Royce and the UFC had unleashed, jiu-jitsu needed a serious and credible vehicle to help steer its

---

[196] Cairus 2012a, pg. 210

evolution into a new future. Even if for this to succeed, they had to offer some concessions to the customer's demands and toward what old-timers from the *second-wave* insisted in calling the "nutella generation."[197]

This context and need for change are perhaps best depicted by the CBJJ leadership as it is told in the interview with Carlinhos in the preceding chapter. Much like the ogres from the *second-wave*, their offspring, the *third-wave-ogres,* also needed taming if jiu-jitsu was to grow beyond the Carioca south-zone and into a truly democratized worldly practice. Since without taming its most vociferous representatives, jiu-jitsu was at risk of remaining merely an expression of "violence made in Brazil."[198]

Still, the tough-guy culture that was so defining of the "ogres" didn't die completely, not without a fight at least. Indeed, the tough-guy mentality found at least some expression in the *third-wave,* a swan song of sorts for a dying breed of young competitive men wanting to prove themselves to the world. A moment that was to a large extent a strong and underestimated force in the growth of jiu-jitsu in Brazil during the 90s, only behind Royce, the UFC and the CBJJ itself. I am speaking of the infamous boost in marketing to jiu-jitsu in Brazil by the hands of the so called *"pit-boys."*[199]

In the 90s, following the *Desafio de Jiu-Jitsu contra a Luta-Livre* in 1991 at the *Grajaú* and the birth of the UFC in 1993, jiu-jitsu and *vale-tudo* experienced a revival of sorts in Brazil. It was the end of the *silent years* and the birth of a new craze over everything jiu-jitsu related. For better or for worse, the awakening had considerable momentum added to it by some of its noisiest troops (because since time immemorial, bad news sells more than good news).

During this era in Brazil, teenagers and young adults all across the country were drawn to jiu-jitsu precisely because they saw in it a means

---

[197] Nutella as in the dessert: soft and sweet. Older Brazilians often contrast "Nutella" with "raiz" ("roots" in Portuguese).

[198] Cairus 2012a, pg. 215

[199] The so called *"pit-boys,"* as the jiu-jitsu youth of the mid and late 90s became known across Brazil, won their name thanks to their habit of taking their pitbull dogs with them everywhere they went.

for abusing the power jiu-jitsu gave them in order to impose their hooligan-like territorialism. For them, jiu-jitsu was interesting not because of its potential for health or because of its self-defense benefits. Jiu-jitsu was interesting to the *third-wave* in Brazil because its practice became associated with trouble-makers and bullies in general. In short, the *third-wave* was drawn to jiu-jitsu not because they wanted to learn how to defend themselves against bullies, but rather *because they wanted to be the bullies.*

Curiously, the *pit-boys* were an enormous draw for jiu-jitsu's *third-wave* in general. This was because boys in their youth strive for dominance and being a *pit-boy* was an appealing identity to many of them (or many of us I should say). In many ways however, the movement also threatened to further tarnish the reputation and standing of jiu-jitsu in Brazil. A reputation that, if truth be told, was never great to begin with and had always been associated with brawling, *vale-tudo* and violence in general.

In reality, the *pit-boys* were nothing but the most recent manifestation of a penchant for street-brawling that had started many decades before.[200] They were only original in that now they had a pitbull dog as a marker of this identity. It is to this piece of largely neglected jiu-jitsu history that we turn to next. I will illustrate it by telling it through the eyes of an aspiring *pit-boy* with no street-cred.

---

[200] Tufy Cairus comments: *"In the 1980s and the 1990s, Brazilian jiu-jitsu was also directly associated with upper class hooliganism. The media both celebrated and desecrated the booming martial art. The Gracies undeniably played an ambiguous role in this process. Although, while condemning violence through a standardized public discourse, they often were caught out by their acts and statements. Hélio Gracie, then one of the heads of the clan, defined for example homosexuality as a manifestation of* 'weakness and a disease.' *He said, however,* 'he could not condemn anybody for being weak or for their defects.' *Further, Hélio stated that* 'love is a manifestation of weakness and that he finds the ordinary man fragile as a child.' *Or Hélio's remarks on violence:* 'I am fully conscious of my capacity of being violent. I am the worst person I have ever seen. I put myself in the criminal's shoes and I know that I could do better than he could. Therefore, I know I am bad news; I am a wolf in sheep's clothes.'" Cairus 2012a, pg. 210

Chapter 19

A Short Tale of a Jiu-Jitsu Wannabe

"I don't recall exactly the first time I heard the term 'jiu-jitsu,' but it would have been in the mid 90s, and I remember well that it was a term associated with violence, cage-fighting, blood, hooliganism, cauliflower ears, and for some odd reason I couldn't quite understand, pit-bull dogs."

Although I was born in Provo, Utah (which may be as far from a Brazilian *pit-boy* as one can imagine), I was raised in the small colonial town of Itu in Brazil, where my parents decided to move to when I was still 5 years old. I was raised as a bi-cultural child, with one foot in the Mormon faith and the other in the Brazilian religion of soccer. An oddity that is perhaps best remarked by my secretive habit of taking a small radio to church on Sundays to keep up with the *Brasileirão* or the *Paulista de Futebol*, the two premier Brazilian soccer leagues.

With neither Portuguese nor soccer being my mother-tongues (Brazilian children, as you may already suspect, are quite skilled at the game by the time they are 5 years old), I struggled a bit to adapt. In school, I was relegated to the despised position of goalkeeper, where all the overweight, unskilled, and (apparently) gringo kids were forced to play. That is, if they wanted to play at all.

I did my best to acclimatize, and over time, I even became somewhat decent at the job, more out of stubbornness than actual skill. I even played for some small junior teams and managed to secure a bench position as goalkeeper for the best local junior team (Ituano F.C.). Which may sound more significant than it actually was. I never really got to play because, I suspect, my coach didn't quite trust me in the position. In retrospect, I can't blame him... I was far from a marvel in the field. So, no hard feelings.

Despite my most sincere efforts to blend in, these efforts did little to change everyone's perception that, at the end of the day, I was still the gringo kid. To make matters worse, I was born with a birth-defect called *pectus-excavatum,* which translates literally as "hole in chest" in Latin, which is pretty much an exact description of what it is.

In Brazil, soccer teams are typically divided among *com ou sem camisa* (with or without shirt). Needless to say on which team, all my friends made sure I was always playing for when they found out about my little secret. The "hole" over time, became increasingly asymmetrical and out of center in relation to the rest of my body as I matured into puberty and my heart grew in size. As it turned out, and as every evolutionary biologist well knows, nature isn't too kind, too asymmetry. Brazilians less so.[201]

Add to that the fact that the word "bullying" can't even be translated into Portuguese.[202] To them, being bullied was just a natural part of growing up. And if you have any Brazilian friends, you probably know that when it comes to nicknames they are unmatched in their creativity. Over the course of my years in Brazil, I accumulated several very creative ones. Some, I even learned to cherish over time.

Then there were the fights, which were quite common. Sometimes I'd stay in the principal's office and wait for one of my parents to pick me up, sometimes I'd fight, sometimes I would run home. One time I hid my backpack in the bushes to have an edge in the race that was signaled

---

[201] I am referring here to the theory in evolutionary biology that places symmetry in bilateral body plans as a prime fitness indicator when mating (judging) members of the opposite gender. Within this discussion, proportion is understood as a symbol of health and balance and, consequently, an indicator of quality in the courted partner. Naturally, animals tend to hide or disguise any asymmetry in order to increase their odds in the mating game. The infamous "duck-face" (the practice of looking sideways when posing for pictures) comes to mind here.

[202] Clearly bullying exists in Brazil. But especially in the days where I was growing up, it lacked the negative connotation it has in the English-speaking world. Complaining about it was the equivalent to an invitation to be made fun of once again for being so weak. The closest translation to the word I can think of is *"zoar"* which in English wouldn't be "to bully," but rather "to tease" or "to make fun of."

when the final school bell went off, sending us home. It got so bad that at one point my parents considered hiring a bodyguard to walk me home from school every day, and although initially I partially embraced the plan, I eventually decided it was a bad idea. And it still took me a while to convince my parents that having a security guard pick me up from school was only going to make my life more difficult. Eventually, we settled with moving me to different school in case things got too rough.

To say that I was frustrated is an understatement, I was angry. My parents, in hopes to teach me how to fight and gain some confidence, put me in Hapkido class. Which didn't help much and in fact, probably made it worse because once all the kids found out (and believe me, I tried to hide it from them), they *expected* me to know how to fight, and wanted to test me. So, in other words, the only outcome from my Hapkido experience was that I managed to give it a bad name on more than a few occasions.

I wish that this were all an exaggeration, but it is all too accurate. The above is an overall rough sketch of the disaster of a child that I was and the social climate of my childhood and teens. But things were about to change for this gringo kid. I don't recall exactly the first time I heard the term "jiu-jitsu," but it would have been in the mid 90s, and I remember well that it was a term associated with violence, cage-fighting, blood, hooliganism, cauliflower ears, and for some odd reason I couldn't quite understand, pitbull dogs.

These elements, when combined, created an aura of invincibility and dominance around those who trained jiu-jitsu (and around those who didn't but pretended to) followed by the respect, fear, and submissiveness of those who didn't train (and didn't pretend to either). They were collectively referred to as *"pit-boys,"* and the sub-culture they represented was a direct byproduct of the revolution in martial arts I had no idea had just taken place. But I was about to find out soon enough.

I later learned that they were called *pit-boys* because walking around with a pitbull dog was a welcome addition to the intimidation factor and became quickly part of their overall identity. *Pit-boys* and pitbulls were so commonly associated with "jiu-jitsu" that owning the dog in those days was practically synonymous with being an adept of the gentle-art. In other words, people simply assumed you knew how to fight.

Curious as to what the fuss was all about, I decided to rent some VHS tapes from the local video-store. My favorite tape had a skinny guy in a white kimono on the cover; he was squaring off against his opponent (who, by the way, looked as if Freddie Mercury and a pro-wrestler in speedos had merged into one), and the fight they were about to engage in, seemed to signal a battle between titans.[203] Although I had no way of knowing this in those early days, my first impression was not too far off the mark. What I was about to watch on those tapes (and that tape in particular) was nothing short of history in the making and the birth of a martial arts legend.

To say that Royce Gracie became an instant hero of mine would not do justice to the impact he had on me at the time. To this day, to think of what Royce was doing in those early UFC fights still gives me goose-bumps. There were groin-shots, teeth flying through the air, bloody-noses, knockouts, exhaustion, heart, perseverance, courage, discipline, and overcoming.

As if that was not enough, there were these strange choke-holds that Royce was using against his opponents who all seemed to have absolutely no immunity against any of them. They were fish out of the water, or more to the marketing of the time that went around promoting Royce's exploits, *the ground was his ocean, he was a shark, and most people had no idea how to swim.* It was as if a lion were suddenly introduced into an island filled with fat and juicy herbivores who had no idea that there were animals out there who ate other animals for a living.

Of course, in those early days, I had no clue of what was going on either. I was perfectly aware that I would have been like a baby llama thrown into the ocean against a starving great-white shark if ever pitched against someone who knew jiu-jitsu. I didn't even know what it was or

---

[203] I am referring here to the VHS cover for UFC 2.

how it worked, but it was obvious that it was elegant in a dominant way. Indeed, like a lion who owns the savannah and has no insecurities about ruling a kingdom that is his by birthright.

That was the image I had of Royce Gracie in my youth, he displayed the kind of courage and confidence that I thought only existed in the comic books I loved to read as a child. But this wasn't a comic book, this was not fake-wrestling. It was not a Bruce Lee or a Van-Damme movie either. This was different. This was brutal. *It was real-fighting. It was as real as it gets!*

Regardless of what I knew about jiu-jitsu then, I was sure that it was the solution to my problems in life. And not just some of them: Royce and jiu-jitsu, I was certain, were the solutions to *all of my problems.* From my first jiu-jitsu class onward, I had no more doubts about what my game plan was moving forward. My frustration found an outlet to vent itself and maybe even go somewhere. Yet it was not just anywhere, it was pointed toward a very specific destination. From the moment I rented those VHS tapes, I knew what I wanted to become and I knew exactly how to do it-follow in Royce's footsteps.

With no hesitation or afterthought, I wholeheartedly embraced my new identity and immediately began the makeover transformation. I shaved my head; bought as many jiu-jitsu t-shirts as I could find (preferably tight ones); started lifting weights and made a conscious effort to change my body language when talking to people. My favorite tactic was picked up from a magazine cover with Rickson Gracie on it and was known to jiu-jitsu adepts as *"pescocinho"* or "short-neck," as Brazilians sarcastically refer to it. Simply put, it refers to the habit of gazing down on people by lifting your chin up and exposing your neck. This can have the subconscious effect of establishing an air of superiority over those you speak to. Some still use it and, believe it or not, it still works on some people.

I even grew cauliflower ears on both sides of my head after only a few months of training (unlike some of my training partners, I swear mine were not mauled intentionally). The makeover into a *pit-boy* was now complete. Well, almost, because my mom didn't let me buy a pitbull. You see, this fearsome, arrogant, overconfident and aspiring bad boy still lived with his mom.

Walking around with a jiu-jitsu shirt in those days was like wearing a super cape of sorts: people avoided you, feared you, respected you, or were nice to you, depending on their strategy in dealing with the threat (or in my case, the perceived threat). The common denominator was that you were instantly awarded a high-status among everyone around you. All it took was a shaved head and some t-shirts. The cauliflower ears and the dog were just added bonuses to the intimidation factor, in case you had one, the other, or both. The more that went into the outfit, the more immediate street cred you were awarded.

Once, my friends from the gym and I agreed we would all go to a local club together all wearing our local jiu-jitsu team t-shirt for the obvious reason of intimidating the guys and impressing the ladies. The result was better than anything we could have anticipated. We ended up having 2-3 of their biggest bouncers follow us around the club all night, which had the effect of granting us credibility by leading people to believe we were actually dangerous.

Truth be told, we knew we couldn't handle any of those bouncers in a fight, but it didn't matter. We achieved our goal of showing off. Imagine being a club manager and feeling like you need to allocate 2-3 of your heaviest security guards to follow around a bunch of 16-year old teenagers with shaved heads because they were the biggest menace to peace that night? Pretty empowering from our perspective.

Of course it didn't matter that I had no idea how to fight. People believed I could, and in those days that's all that I really cared about. I was finally respected. But because I have always disliked fakes and phonies in general, I was not prepared to become one. Deep down, I knew that despite the instant respect my new identity granted me, the reality was that I wasn't as good as Royce and I would get murdered in that cage if I ever had to fight in one someday. So, I decided that the fancy label needed a quality product to match the pretension.

Over time, I would learn that Royce wasn't even the best of them, that there were these other guys in Rio who trained with Royce's chubby cousin Carlson, and they were even better than Royce! Later still, I would learn that Royce had a brother called Rickson that everyone told me was supposed to be better than all of them! But who was the best in all this? Where did they come from? Why are they so good? How come no one ever thought to take Van Damme down to the ground in one of those movies? Why are these Brazilians wearing a Japanese uniform? How many Gracies are there anyway? And the most troubling question of them all: Why do so many of their names begin with an "R"?

In an attempt to understand all this, I became a jiu-jitsu magazine addict and proceeded to buy anything, old or new I could find that had the word jiu-jitsu on it. Some of these magazines also reported on this other thing called "vale-tudo," which was the name of what was being practiced inside the cage I saw on those videos. Vale-tudo was basically where my beloved jiu-jitsu proved to everyone else that it was the best fighting system in the world. It was also in those magazines where I would find some hints as to what I needed to do next.

If only a few months prior I had any doubts about who the best jiu-jitsu fighters in the world were, now I knew. Clearly, the best fighters were those who are fighting and winning at the highest level, just like in any other sport, right? Fighting after all didn't take just skill, it also took courage, and courage is a big word. There seemed to be no one more courageous than those who were constantly pitching themselves in fearsome battles against the world's best. How could it be otherwise? The answer always seemed obvious to me.

I would learn names like Murilo Bustamante, Amaury Bitetti, Zé Mario Sperry, Rodrigo Comprido, Robson Moura, Vitor Shaolin, Nino Schembri, Leo Vieira and my personal favorite: Roberto Magalhães, a.k.a. "Roleta" (Roulette). He was my favorite not because I knew anything about him (I didn't) but because a blue-belt I respected told me I sort of looked like him and that we even had a similar body-type. That's pretty much all it took for me to decide to make Roleta's specialty sweep, the "helicopter-sweep" my specialty move as well. *Fake it, till you make it right?*

These guys weren't just the best in the world; they also all seemed like really nice people too. But more importantly, none of the guys who were actually winning looked like a *pit-boy* to me. *None.* Not one. It didn't take much longer for me to figure out that the *pit-boys* were all just a bunch of frustrated kids like myself and that none of them had anymore idea about how to fight than I did. What about these other guys? Roleta, Robson Moura, Nino Schembri and Leo Vieira? They all seemed like the sort of people I really wanted to be around anyway. Plus, flexing my neck upwards all the time was becoming exhausting, and I suspected I was beginning to damage my neck from the recently self-imposed bad posture. More importantly, I was just getting tired of flexing. I was ready for the challenge of trying to outdo my heroes.

I let my hair grow back and got rid of every jiu-jitsu t-shirt that wasn't from my own team. I relinquished entirely the idea of buying a pitbull, deciding once and for all that they were not for me. What I really wanted now, was not to be respected through pretentiousness. I wanted to pay the iron-price of hard-earned medals and win respect that way instead, by proving that I could do it. If not for respect, then for my own peace of mind and self-respect. I wanted to win respect instead of demanding it. I wanted to be tough rather than look tough. I wanted to be like my jiu-jitsu heroes rather than just pretending to be like them.

As for my friends, like most *pit-boys* of those days, they did not follow through with the jiu-jitsu lifestyle. Most either quit or became sporadic about training. And just like that, the *pit-boy* age saw its final days. But it mattered little to me, the episode became only a distant and embarrassing memory of a bygone era of transformation, albeit a necessary one. Now, I had a new collection of friends, a new family of sorts. One that was just as intent on living the jiu-jitsu lifestyle as I was by competing regularly while embracing a whole new set of values.

Jiu-jitsu had given me purpose and direction and I wanted to pay it back by representing the art well. A cycle of personal transformation was complete and a new one was about to initiate. From the moment I found jiu-jitsu, there was no more confusion. I knew exactly who I wanted to be and the values I wanted to represent in life.

Chapter 20

Malandragem and
Success in Jiu-Jitsu

"From my observations, Brazilians are naturally introduced to malandragem. It comes to them with less effort than it does to other peoples because it is so widely spread in Brazil. An observation always made all the clearer to me when I try to explain the concept to my American students who don't all instinctively grasp the concept and normally have to learn it by trial and error."

When I was a purple-belt, much like the rest of my friends and training partners, the thought of securing myself financially or developing a career outside of jiu-jitsu wasn't even considered. Naturally, we all struggled and took advantage of the Latino tradition of living with our parents for as long as we needed to in order to develop a career and/or get married. A privilege that the English-speaking world is rarely awarded, given our parents impatience with their children finding their way in life quickly.

Despite this advantage, the financial struggle was real, so I began to think of creative ways to make some extra cash through jiu-jitsu in order to pay for all my competitions and traveling. Since making money by teaching jiu-jitsu was out of the question (due to the low monthly fees and excessive competition in Brazil) I began to think of ways of capitalizing on the growth of jiu-jitsu around the world in the early 2000s. Which I did by writing a post in a fight forum in 2001 inviting foreigners to come live and train with me in Brazil for only 500 dollars a month (food, training, housing and transport included). Which at the time was a bargain for foreigners while simultaneously being a small fortune to pay for my efforts as an aspiring jiu-jitsu competitor.

Over the next few years, there was a busy influx of Swedes, Canadians, Americans and peoples from various other nationalities who visited me for weeks, months and sometimes coming back annualy or even staying permanently. Needless to say, it fell on me to train them as well as the more important and urgent task of helping them navigate the intricacies of Brazilian society and the many differences it had in relation to the rest of the Western world. Which to me, always felt like a fun and engaging exercise.

It was after coaching one of these visitors at a local tournament (more specifically during my explanation to him as to why he had lost), that I had realized the importance of simple day-to-day words as symbols of specific cultural practices. To my visiting friend, I couldn't explain why he had lost... The words were missing in my English vocabulary.

In Portuguese, the word "*malandro*" and its execution "*malandragem*," didn't make their way into my vocabulary forcefully. As a child, it was effortlessly absorbed, like every other Portuguese word I had also absorbed, and in parallel to the cultural context in which it was used almost daily by those around me (particularly males of lower economic strata). In fact, it wasn't until I began interacting with other Americans and Europeans visiting Brazil that it dawned on me that I couldn't translate the word to them or even explain the concept.

Words are not only a powerful tool for communication, they are much more than that. Through words we create symbols of not only our immediate physical environment but also our social one. Words are tools for interacting with others, who share these environments in exponentially complex ways. But words are also revealing as to what needs or doesn't need to be communicated in daily life. Which is to say, their specificity can teach us a thing or two about that environment as well as the lack of the need for this specificity in our own, because it is taken for granted.

The word *"malandro"* loosely translates as: cunning, deceitful, full of tricks and borderline thuggish in a street-smart way. It is also descriptive of someone who manipulates the rules to their advantage with mastery. As an example, think of a soccer player who upon a light contact with a member of the opposing team throws himself on the grass in an act of pain in order to impress the referee who will hopefully grant the opposing team member a yellow or red card. That is a classic display of *malandragem* and it can be seen everywhere in Brazilian society... Naturally jiu-jitsu doesn't escape its cultural reach.

In all fairness, the behavior isn't exclusive to Brazilians and can be seen just about anywhere one lives or visits. The difference is that the behavior is so ingrained in Brazilian society, that they have a word for it.[204] It is so ingrained in fact, that I had always taken it from granted that this behavior was nothing but a natural social occurrence. To illustrate this, consider that it wasn't until that tournament and my attempt at explaining the concept to my visiting friend that I had even given all this any thought.

Whenever I try to explain this to my American students by giving real examples, their understanding of it is often voiced back to me in the shape of the question, *"you mean lying?"* or *"being dishonest?"* or something equivalent. Yet the bigger issue here isn't the behavior itself (which is questionable), but rather that it isn't normally perceived as bad behavior or as behavior to be reprimanded by social peers, but that in fact, *malandragem* is often used in the context of a compliment given to someone who so cleverly manipulated the system to their advantage. The degree of the manipulation matters, but so does the execution and subsequent success in this endeavor, with the extent, complexity and level of success of the manipulation being determinant of its quality in a positive way.

---

[204] Once while having this conversation with an American friend, he observed that street basketball is exactly like that. Which is to say, *malandragem* isn't an exclusive Brazilian feature, it is only more widespread and worthier of commendation in Brazil. While in the USA the feelings may be somewhere between commendation and condemnation, depending on the environment.

Malandro is someone who can be a savvy business man who evades taxes, a womanizer with no boundaries or integrity, a car salesman who doesn't mention that the radiator is broken or even someone verging on a con-artist. Indeed, con-artistry can be understood as an extreme example of *malandro* behavior, but not quite a translation of the word. Since the line between a *malandro* and a criminal is drawn and is mostly clear. In other words, all con-artists are *malandros*, but not all *malandros* are con-artists.

A criminal who evades capture is a *malandro* because he wasn't caught, and in case he is, he loses the title because, had he been a true *malandro*, he would have managed to continue to evade the law. In this case, *"ele deu mole"* (he "dropped the ball" as in, he lost his *malandragem*). In sum, a malandro is someone who successfully manipulates the rules to his favor, with the lines between the ethical and legal being up to the individual himself.

In competitive jiu-jitsu, *malandragem* can be many things, but not all necessarily dishonest (which is why the word "dishonest" does not fare as an accurate translation), such as: purposely untying your belt to take a moment to breathe; circling the square matted area in order to avoid contact and buy time in case you are winning; stalling; wearing a lighter kimono and/or belt in order to make weight easier; use of tactics in order to win such as purposely not sweeping your opponent until the last few seconds of the match; going for a submission only to score an advantage and not actually finish it (perhaps knowing that the submission may not be actually possible for a variety of reasons); etc. Being a *malandro*, is essentially being an astute competitor and playing on the very edge of what is permitted by the rules, but not necessarily dishonestly breaking them or doing anything illegal per se.

Living in Brazil, requires not necessarily the assimilation of the behavior. But it certainly requires its acknowledgement, awareness as well as to grow a strong defensive system against it in order to not be taken advantage of by those who indulge in the behavior. From my observations, Brazilians are naturally introduced to *malandragem*. It comes to them with less effort than it does to other peoples because it is so widely spread in Brazil. Albeit its use and acceptance are largely contingent on upbringing, geography and social circles. Not to mention being far from being an unanimously accepted or tolerated behavior in Brazil.

An observation always made all the clearer to me when I try to explain the concept to my American students who don't all instinctively grasp the concept and normally have to learn it by trial and error. Which is to say, by competing extensively until they learn, unless of course, they don't learn. With the degree of their success in competition depending on their ability to quickly grasp this.

Conversely, I never had to explain any of this to my Brazilian students, who instinctively knew they had to manipulate the rules, the time, the score and the referee to their favor. It all came with little to no effort to them, possibly made easier to their collective exposure to soccer where the practice of *malandragem* is practically a necessity as well as the Brazilian penchant for womanizing where *malandragem* is equally useful.

Back to jiu-jitsu, I believe much of the resentment that the rest of the jiu-jitsu world feels toward Brazilians can be explained by this entrenched and often overlooked quality of Brazilians (quality here being used as a neutral word devoid of any positive or negative connotation). A resentment that is rarely spoken out loud due to political correctness, but that is real nonetheless. Something I am often reminded of when I am speaking to non-Brazilians who voice their disdain of Brazilians in a low tone and under their breaths.[205]

What foreigners need to understand is that however reprehensible some aspects of this behavior might be, in the haste to supply the demand created in the post-Royce era it wasn't always the most qualified or educated representatives of Brazilian society that were in a rush to make it to the promised land. More often than not, this group was

---

[205] On a side note, these feelings of resentment are likely to be nourishing dissident voices in the so called "AJJ" movement (see chapter 28 ahead).

composed by those who knew perfectly well that they were unlikely to have another chance in life other than the one Royce, the UFC and jiu-jitsu had just opened up for them. Simply put, the specific demographic that leaves Brazil to teach across the world *is not* your average Brazilian.

While this demographic is from various ethnic, social and economic backgrounds, what most of them have in common is that they are young, unexperienced, and few have ever held a job outside of jiu-jitsu. Some that I have met, didn't even have a bank account before they moved abroad (an observation that might help explain their success on the mats). Accordingly, they made sure not to waste the opportunity by maximizing it any way they could. Including making use of their street-smart skills to take advantage of any gringo naïve enough to take their black-belt rank for a badge of integrity.

Althogh I share with so many other foreigners a critical view on Brazilian *malandragem*, I notice that the same criticism of this aspect of Brazilian culture often misses the mark on the issue itself and takes the shape of unchallenged generalizations filled with borderline xenophobic remarks. As a Professor in college often remarked, *"toda generalização, é burra"* (all generalizations are dumb).[206]

None of this is a simple or objective discussion. It is full of nuances, prejudices, misinformation and ignorance, as well as cultural traits that are easily observable and present, despite our politically correct preference for not voicing them out loud. On a side note, *malandragem* is something fully acknowledged by Brazilians as a problem without any defensive posturing. In fact, when it is brought up it is often followed with either a sly smile in admittance or, in case more serious discussion ensues, remarked as an embarrassment and a major cultural problem in Brazil.

To this, I will add that *malandragem* and the *jeitinho brasileiro* (which I will translate as a tendency to improvise, cut corners and do

---

[206] The phrase is likely taken from Brazilian social critique and author, Nelson Rodrigues, who made the quote famous: *"Toda unanimidade é burra"* (All unanimity is dumb).

everything at the last minute), are single handedly the two biggest cultural obstacles Brazilians face and that directly hinder the country's economic, social and political development. Because *jeitinho brasileiro* is the opposite of forward planning while *malandragem* is, in essence, the normalization of corruption. Combined, they are a mockery of all *order and progress*.

On a personal note, at least in terms of jiu-jitsu, I have mixed feelings about *malandragem* and admittedly have often scored tactical advantages in order to win close matches while at other times, in total exhaustion, I rode that clock while eagerly counting the seconds in order to win. On one hand the astuteness necessary for high level competition is truthfully a display of a high level of intelligence and skill. On the other the manipulation of any situation to your favor does often come far too near the border of an unethical practice (that is, when we don't fully cross it) in what ought to always be an ethical one. Nonetheless, let us remind ourselves here that condemning from afar is cheap, ignorant and easy.

What is wrong is always wrong, by principle and under any circumstance. Still, competition coupled with ambition can, often blur these lines, while *malandragem*, only adds to the blur. As the popular adage goes, *nice guys finish last*... And competition, all competition, is in truthfulness a wild jungle filled with far more ambition and cunning than scruples. Furthermore, I have yet to see a successful fighter, in either BJJ or MMA, who has not indulged in *malandragem* in one way or another throughout the course of their careers.

Ambition, competition, *malandragem*... they all lay underneath what the 21st century commonly refers to as "success." These words are so determinant of our behavior that at some undetectable point we make them into critical values. They lead me to consider that language has as much power in it to expose the truth as well as to conceal it. And with this whole discussion of the merits and demerits of deception in mind, we would all do well to rethink what is it that is underneath these words to which we attach life purpose to.

If we do this, we may well reach the sobering conclusion that while some words are dubious, others aren't dubious at all. Some being seemingly unequivocal just do a better job at concealing from the surface all the *malandragem* that is implicit in their fabric. If we are willing to dig just below this surface, we may find that in fact, *malandragem* is nothing but the modest and poorly equipped cousin of what we assertively and commonly refer to in life, as "success...".

Chapter 21

Why did Jiu-Jitsu Evolve so Rapidly from the 90s Onward?

Carlson's student, DelaRiva, makes use of the guard
that is named after him to defeat Royler Gracie at the
"Copa Cantão" event. In the background, notice Helio,
Carlos and Robson Gracie.
Photocred: Ricardo DelaRiva
personal archives via Marcelo Alonso.

"In regards to jiu-jitsu's rapid evolution in the post-Royce era, the math is quite simple: more practitioners + more competitions + a high-level and organized league + technology = rapid evolution."

The *first-wave* of jiu-jitsu practitioners is somewhat of a puzzle to me. Their own children notwithstanding, how did Carlos and Helio manage to convince anyone to train under them? How did the Gracie Academy even survive? How did it endure almost complete isolation long enough to make its first move to organize itself into a league in 1967?

On paper, they did not have much going for them: They weren't Japanese, they weren't the most successful fighters, they did not even have black-belts. On top of all this, they were up against thousands of Japanese immigrants teaching judo, the most well-structured, prestigious and developed martial art in the world at the time. More than this, they were also up against the *luta nacional* of capoeira as well as the public perception in general, which wasn't always friendly toward them and their marketing methods. In short, there is no reason at all for them to have kept their doors open, let alone come one day to dominate the martial arts world.

Yet somehow, Carlos and Helio survived all this. They managed to create a fiercely loyal following of students that even if small became the bedrock of what we now refer to as BJJ. After interviewing men such as João Alberto Barreto and Armando Wriedt, it became clear to me that their devotion and zeal toward the Gracie Academy, and Helio in particular, was borderline religious.[207] How did the Gracies accomplish this? Strong personalities combined with an unwavering belief in what they were doing might help explain the enforced cohesion.

With that said, I find it hard to place Carlos and Helio as precursors of jiu-jitsu's technical (r)evolution. Adaptive evolution thrives under fierce competition, the more of it, the faster it takes place. The Gracie brothers, by isolating themselves inside a strong and cohesive cultural bubble (the one they themselves created), in a very significant way, slowed down their own technical progress. Nevertheless, they remained resolute in their beliefs and self-inflicted isolation. Unlike others, they refused to cave and allow themselves to be absorbed into Kodokan judo (like the Ono brothers did for example).

Both brothers were inception points in all this. They were pioneers and trailblazers because they stood their ground. *This, in my view, was Carlos and Helio's biggest contribution to jiu-jitsu; standing their ground against judo long enough for their children to come into maturity and for jiu-jitsu to flourish technically after them.* On the other hand, this made their role evolving jiu-jitsu very limited in technical terms.

---

[207] Drysdale 2020, pg. 161 and 253 respectively

Together, what they did do was something very important in the long run. They were the initial markers of a diversification process that would eventually lead to BJJ as we know it today. The initial split from the judo mothership was an enormous effort of resistance in both social and political terms, and no small achievement considering the circumstances and limited resources they had at their disposal at the time.

But in technical terms, BJJ's evolution had barely begun. Other than Helio's firm belief in the closed-guard position as a defensive tactic to tire out the opponent in a long match it is difficult to spot any evolutionary marker in their curriculum outside of what automatically came from the judo matrix and what they borrowed later from other styles in Brazil.[208]

To be clear, in terms of ground-grappling (or more accurately, ne-waza), the evolution would be in the hands of future waves of practitioners. The task of innovation and evolution would fall to the *second* and *third-waves* and their students. BJJ's technical evolutionary course would really begin inside the Guanabara Federation they founded in 1967. It was the move to found this federation that would begin to create the sort of competitive jiu-jitsu that eventually found its final technical evolutionary medium through the CBJJ/IBJJF tournaments from the mid 90s onward.[209]

---

[208] In his autobiography, Rickson claims that his father, Helio Gracie *"was to jiu-jitsu what Albert Einstein was to physics. He greatly improved the martial art by further developing a position called the guard..."* In reality, the guard wasn't improved in any significant way, at least not in comparison as to what the Japanese practitioners of kosen judo were already doing much earlier. As it was practiced during the era in Brazil where Helio was actively fighting, the guard was no more sophisticated than what was already well known all across judo and less so if we bring in the style of kosen into the discussion. Unless of course, by *"further developing"* Rickson meant that Helio was crafting caveats of his own. If this is the case, every practitioner, from blue-belt onward in fact, does the same daily.

[209] It is worth reminding ourselves here that evolution is by definition, a process of differentiation from previous forms and is normally slow and imperceptible when it occurs. It doesn't necessarily mean better or worse than before. It means strategic change and adaptation to new environments. And what is true in nature bears at least some similarities to jiu-jitsu's own evolution. Furthermore, in nature as in jiu-jitsu, evolution isn't linear or necessarily ascending toward the superior (assuming we can agree on what superior *is*) and does not necessarily mean progress toward the efficiency of combat (assuming that is the purpose of jiu-jitsu). "Evolution" only means adaptation. In this case, to the rules and the new cultural-environments its practitioners are exposed to.

It is not difficult to demonstrate that, at least in terms of the techniques available to Brazilians throughout most of the 20ᵗʰ century, the judokas from the kosen style were light-years ahead of Brazilians. In fact, this is true well into the 80s and 90s.[210] It was only then that the jiu-jitsu version of a Cambrian explosion would take place and set BJJ onto the rapid evolutionary course it finds itself on today.

The assertion that the techniques known to the Japanese were far more sophisticated than anything Brazilians knew during those decades is not an attack on anyone. It is simply a matter of fact (and not a controversial one at that) even if it rubs some die-hards the wrong way. The ground sophistication shown by the Japanese during these decades can easily be seen by observing techniques that were not part of the jiu-jitsu repertoire during most of its history in Brazil. Yet these same moves were already practiced in the judo style of kosen, moves such as: "x-guard," "butterfly-guard," "delariva-guard" and even "berimbolos."[211] These were techniques that were already known in the first half of the 20ᵗʰ century by the Japanese but that would only come into use in jiu-jitsu circles much later.[212]

It is important to note that this is not to say that jiu-jitsu practitioners of the *first* and *second-waves* were not skilled or that they could not defeat judokas on the ground. There is no doubt that they were skilled and could and did defeat judokas. What is important to understand here

---

[210] Drysdale 2020, pg. 323

[211] See *"Judo Berimbolo"* here: https://youtu.be/juy0VHecQ6c

[212] Which indicates, to me at least, that Japan in terms of *ne-waza* is likely to have had a strong competitive environment early in the 20ᵗʰ century. I say this because I don't believe it is possible to reach the conclusions of highly efficient techniques (for strictly sportive grappling purposes of course) described above by imagining them in your bedroom before you go to sleep. If Brazilians (who are generally speaking highly creative people) took decades to reach the conclusion of the practical efficiency of a "x-guard" or "berimbolo" (and in fact only did so in the late 90s and early 2000s after the inception of CBJJ/IBJJF with its highly qualified competition circuit) then it is not unreasonable to speculate that the Japanese must have had an equally competent competitive circuit early in the 20ᵗʰ century. If not in a league of sorts, then at the very least in dojos with many driven individuals looking to elevate grappling technically by pitching themselves against one another in a competitive manner and with the submission as the final goal.

is that the Brazilian practitioners from these first two initial waves were few and largely isolated and sheltered from high-level judo competitions.

In short, it was not that they could not have learned these things; it was that they were not exposed to them and had to gradually discover them on their own. In my view, this was done intentionally by the Gracie brothers so that their small army would not be discouraged in the face of judokas that most certainly would have defeated any of them in a high-level judo competition. What we do know for certain is that Carlos and Helio regularly challenged judokas but insisted instead that judokas compete in their own preferred ruleset.[213] While judokas could not have cared less about what the Gracies were doing. As far as they were concerned, an Olympic sport that was spread worldwide had nothing to prove to two eccentric brothers in Rio.

Due to the separation process between judo and jiu-jitsu being well underway by 1967, it is difficult to know how these Brazilians would have fared against elite judokas. Particularly the ones who were known to be *ne-waza* experts such as 1964 Olympic gold-medalist Isao Okano for example.

To clarify my stance here, members of the *second-wave* were undoubtedly skilled grapplers and I don't think they would have found themselves necessarily losing to elite judokas in a *"let's see who finishes who"* sort of format. In fact, I believe that only the very best judokas would have been able to put up a fight on the ground against Carlson's best students in the 80s. Which I admit may sound contradictory. So again, one can have access only to a simpler jiu-jitsu and yet be highly efficient in terms of performance. Conversely, one can have access to highly sophisticated techniques while simultaneously being highly inefficient in terms of performance.[214]

These *second-wave* practitioners, despite being very dominant grapplers, due to the constraints of competition and sheer numbers, had a limited technical arsenal from which to choose from. At least when

---

[213] See Pedreira 2015a, pg. 321 and 333 for examples of these disagreements.

[214] More on this in Part 4 of this book.

compared to what judokas had available to them during the same time period. Even if judo (which was on a rapid-evolutionary course of its own due to its prestige, number of competitors, tournaments and government subsidies), was content to relegate most of their *ne-waza* technical canon to books, memory of aging judo black-belts and kosen judo practitioners in a handful of universities across Japan. Either way, the reality of this discussion is that the information already existed in the judo universe. This was true even as judo's Olympic ruleset, with its takedown orientation, had effectively and for purposes of competition, made all these much older (yet sophisticated nonetheless) *ne-waza* techniques almost entirely obsolete for modern competitive judo.

This division can be summed up thusly: whereas Brazilians over time specialized on the ground, judokas specialized in getting people there, which had expected consequences. Over the years, the technical diversification of jiu-jitsu away from judo, increased to the point that over time they became virtually incompatible. Accordingly, in general terms, both camps would have prevailed in their domains of expertise even if judokas throughout most of the 20th century had a much larger *ne-waza* arsenal to choose from than their Brazilian counterparts had.

If we come to think about it, the tournaments and federation were there; the uniform was essentially the same as the one in use today and the one used by judo since 1907;[215] and the rules did not forbid any of the moves that only came about in the 80s and 90s in Brazil. Neither were these rules fundamentally different from the ones in use today by the IBJJF. *So why did it take so long for some of these moves to make their way into jiu-jitsu?*

You may ask what was it that set this Cambrian explosion of sorts in motion? A drastic shift in the environment is the answer: *High-level competition, larger competitive population, new technology and world cultural trends that opened up new technical possibilities for competitive jiu-jitsu.* In regards to jiu-jitsu's rapid evolution in the post-Royce

---

[215] In 1907, there was a redesign of the training uniform for longer sleeves. See: Pedreira 2018, footnote 91.

era, the math is quite simple: *more practitioners + more competitions + a high-level and organized league + technology = rapid evolution.* Long story short, it was only after the creation of a more demographically dense and highly competitive environment in Brazil during the mid-90s that Brazilians would come to (independently) reach the same technical conclusions that the Japanese had reached half a century earlier.[216]

With that said, the inverse is equally true: The Guanabara Federation had the opposite paradigm for many years because it had fewer competitors and sparse competitions. This meant it saw a much slower evolutionary rate than the one witnessed from the mid-90s onward. The math here is also quite simple: *fewer practitioners + fewer competitions + a less than fully developed league + poorly developed technology = slower evolutionary pressures.*[217]

As far as technology goes, the widespread availability of cheaper and superior recording devices tremendously accelerated the spread of new information about the sport, especially via VHS. A few years later, when the internet was added to this equation, the technical innovation was almost immediately transferred from one individual to potentially millions in a matter of seconds. Technology coupled with the CBJJ/IBJJF, combined with a burst of marketing led by the Royce Gracie revolution changed all that, and it changed it very quickly. *But was that it?*

Interestingly, it wasn't until recently that I realized there was another factor I had completely missed out on. One that was of equal relevance for jiu-jitsu's rapid evolution: cultural trends, particularly in the USA where BJJ would begin to take on a completely new shape away from what had been previously practiced in the south-zone of Rio. Perhaps it might seem strange and unlikely that a cultural trend aimed at safe-guarding people's feelings from reality, avoiding all pain and suffering at all costs

---

[216] Although we shouldn't discard the possibility of Brazilians having learned from books as well.

[217] The picture that heads this chapter is of a match that took place in 1987. Logically, competition has always led to evolution (all competition). I only use the mid 90s as a marker here because that was when tournaments became more organized and widespread, accelerating evolution tremendously. I could just as well have used 1967 as a marker, but I felt that using the mid 90s did a better job at illustrating my point because the pool of tournaments and competitors was much larger then.

and awarding trophies to those who didn't earn them would have any-thing to do with jiu-jitsu's evolution, but I strongly believe that it did.[218]

If the *pit-boy* movement in Brazil was a swan song for the ogres, then it was being played diametrically opposed to the new tunes the world market was interested in hearing. A world that had a whole new set of values in its sight and an entirely new understanding of what "good" was and how boys ought to be brought up. From the rise of political-correct-ness onward, boys cry and boys don't fight. Instead, they are more easily handed the rank and rewards that typically would have been reserved to the most deserving ones.

Some of these values may not belong in jiu-jitsu (or at least they shouldn't), but they belong to the world in general; permeating schools, television, work, institutions and political trends. Culture helps shape the thinking of all those exposed to it and jiu-jitsu practitioners (unfortunately) cannot escape this reach, even if the trends are weaken-ing and at odds with everything jiu-jitsu is meant to teach and embody.

Despite it being far from the point of this book to dive into the ori-gins or the take-over of a softer approach to life in the world, identifying the moment it made its way into jiu-jitsu and began to change its cul-ture is necessary as well as a much easier task. Additionally, it will help us understand jiu-jitsu's evolution toward the present moment. In both technical and cultural terms.

---

[218] I am not suggesting here that slaps were removed from jiu-jitsu only because of these cultural trends. Clearly their disappearance was also an inevitable side-effect of democra-tization since parents and most adults were unlikely to tolerate such practice. What I am suggesting is these factors, when combined, changed jiu-jitsu from a more warrior-orient-ed practice to a lighter version of it.

Chapter 22

The "Confere" and the Evolution Jiu-Jitsu Underwent During the Second-Wave.[219]

Rolls and Carlson square up for a *"taparia"*
session. Photocred: Marco Imperial
personal archives.

"The gloves and slaps had exactly that function of keeping it real. Jiu-jitsu is a real-fight, not a sportive practice, it was created for practical reality."

Grandmaster Antônio Carlos Rosado

---

[219] The word *"confere"* in Portuguese can be loosely translated as "check" or "to check." And was meant as slang to "check" the student's overall jiu-jitsu and make sure it was still grounded in the reality of combat. In this sense, *"taparia"* was only a form of *"confere"* but not the only one. Others included pitching one student with a pair of boxing gloves on while the other (without gloves) would be trying to take the first one down. The first in his turn, would try to hit the "grappler" on the way into the clinch. Others, included even throwing two teenagers against one adult… In other words, the preparation for reality intrinsic to the *confere* could be quite creative and even amusing.

Once, early in my jiu-jitsu journey, my coach Otávio de Almeida Jr. surprised us by requesting we take our gi jackets off. *"Tonight"*, he told us, *"we are going to train taparia." Taparia* (loosely translated as "slap-fest"), was basically jiu-jitsu with slaps. You could smack your training partner in the body, ear and head, just not the groin or face. Needless to say, that for a bunch of young and competitive guys to watch our friends get slapped around and engage in it ourselves was thrilling, funny, and nerve-wracking all at the same time.

It was as close as possible to *vale-tudo* (which is what we were all really interested in to begin with) as we could get, without severely hurting ourselves in the process. Well, at least that day no one got hurt. Of course, there were slap marks all over (and believe me, they hurt), but there was moderation when the strikes were to the head and other than the red marks across the body, it wasn't all that bad. For the most part, we had fun. But *fun* wasn't at all the point of *taparia*.[220] I don't know where the practice began, but the purpose seems obvious to me- *it was meant as an introduction to the reality of combat.*

If we are to be completely honest with ourselves, jiu-jitsu practitioners must admit that our current practice, in many aspects (but not completely) has drifted significantly from the reality of a fight. Which isn't to say that BJJ does not work in a real situation or even in a cage. To the contrary, I have used it myself efficiently before, inside and outside a cage. But the same technical explosion that led to jiu-jitsu's technical sophistication, in many ways also led it away from the reality of combat. *But how?*

The importance of the *confere* only became clear to me after interviewing members of the *second-wave* for this book. In essence, the *confere* bordered on a playful way of keeping jiu-jitsu grounded in reality in order to prevent students from developing unrealistic strategies to win

---

[220] It is worth noting here that the tournament termed "Combat Jiu-Jitsu" does bring back the *taparia* tradition. With one crucial distinction, *taparia*, was a weekly practice for students to learn how to fight efficiently for purposes of real-combat. While "Combat Jiu-Jitsu" is not a regular practice or class (at least not in any gym I am aware of), but rather a professional event offering entertainment, where individuals, not groups, train specifically for the occasion.

(by either point or submission). In popular vernacular, it was meant to *keep it real*. But in order to understand the acceptance of the *confere* then (and conversely why it would be difficult to bring it back today) we need to understand a bit of Brazilian *machismo* and also the environment in which jiu-jitsu was evolving in the Carioca south-zone.[221]

All in all, the development of a martial art is less influenced by the preferences or genius of its leaders and founders than it is by two other more potent factors: rules (as in its scoring system in competition) and environment (culture, norms, social-behavior, trends, hierarchies, etc.).[222] In order to understand the importance of the environment in this evolution, we need to remind ourselves of the moment Brazil found itself in during the years in which the *second-wave* (1967-1993) was active. Years where the military was in power (1964-1985) and upheld a very different set of values than the ones we live by today.[223]

Correspondingly, this era and the values of strength and hierarchy that came with it, fit hand-in-glove with Carlos and Helio's own worldviews. A notion that is reinforced by the military-like upbringing Carlos and Helio subjected their children to. In this sense, the *confere* was merely another manifestation of the specific moment Brazil, and

---

[221] Royler Gracie discusses an interaction with his father Helio when, being very motivated to win tournaments, he was beginning to train solely with them in mind. He tells us how he was reprimanded by his father for not being aware that in some more sportive positions he was using, he would get hit in a real-fight. *"Cuidado hein, você está se acostumando mau. Na rua (...) eles vão te dar é soco"* (Careful there, you are developing bad habits. In the streets (...) they will hit you). The exchange goes to show that despite these moves not being illegal, there was also a degree of coercive pressure from jiu-jitsu's leadership to prevent unrealistic sophistication in favor of moves grounded in the reality of combat. Source: *"Royler Gracie – Entrevista – Jiu-jitsu"* https://www.youtube.com/watch?v=kE_F6oOIAwY

[222] For example: it is not illegal to offend or be rude to someone, but this may cause social flak coming from the offended person and those who witness or hear about the offense. In other words, there is a cost to breaking the unwritten and unspoken rule. In jiu-jitsu terms, applying a rear-naked-choke to your opponent's face is not illegal per se, yet it is immediately frowned upon by everyone on the mats. These rules might be unspoken and unwritten, but they matter.

[223] It was an era in which *machismo* values were typically not only accepted, but even heralded as virtuous ones for men to uphold. These values of strength, honor and courage of the typical Latino brand tended to supersede values of pity, softness and political-correctness that have become the dominant forces in the 21st century.

consequently jiu-jitsu, were both undergoing. The primacy of the reality of combat above everything else and the values of hardship, merit, accountability and tough-love that came along with it, were qualities that made the journey from the original Gracie Academy into the Figueiredo academy and thus, into the *second-wave* of practitioners.

Jiu-jitsu evolved out of this warrior-like culture of the south-zone in Rio with the Guanabara Federation as an escape valve of sorts to help contain the violent impetus of a competitive youth prone to street-brawling and out to prove themselves by trial of fire. In the absence of *vale-tudo* fights, which were mostly illegal in the 70s and 80s in Brazil, BJJ competitions and the *confere* were welcome outlets for this aggressive youth.[224]

At any rate, what *confere* did, and *taparia* in particular, was to keep a technical lid of sorts on jiu-jitsu. By keeping the practice realistic, if not almost real, it served the purpose of a reminder of what would happen in case a practitioner's jiu-jitsu skills weren't ready for strikes to the body and head. This unique practice, even if it was also a form of fun and amusement for these men, may help explain why certain moves, such as "shin-to-shin-guard" for example, never evolved in BJJ during the *first* and *second-waves*. Simply put, anyone who tried it would get slapped in the head and never do it again.

As such, the slaps served as a buffer for anything that did not work in a real-fight. For example, imagine the consequences for placing an opponent in a "deep-half-guard" and taking a break there. Accordingly, practitioners avoided positions that would expose them to being hit in a *taparia* session and being made fun of by your fellow training partners.

---

[224] Even if many of these practitioners claimed that their skills were only for self-defense purposes, I personally find it hard to believe given the evidence available. The association between jiu-jitsu and street-brawling is so established it shouldn't even require examples. There are plenty of them in the works I cite as well as plenty of evidence from interviews in this book and elsewhere. For some entertaining videos on this, see: *"Rickson vs. Hugo Duarte – Praia"* https://www.youtube.com/watch?v=aK9oxoH5Wds ; and *"Ryan Gracie vs. Tico"* https://www.youtube.com/watch?v=MSRqGhKmsM8&t=17s . Note that the first video is from the Gracie in Action tapes used by Rorion to popularize jiu-jitsu in the USA. Rorion is also the fight's narrator. Worthy of note in the second video, is that Ryan completely bit off one of Tico's ear in the heat of battle. As Siriema tells the story, the ear was placed in a glass full of ice while the fight kept on going.

What this did, for all practical purposes, was to hinder (or at least slow down) sophistication that drifted away from the reality of combat and toward any *firula*.[225]

To put it differently, the *confere*, while keeping a reality oriented evolutionary track for jiu-jitsu open, shut down any possibility for any evolutionary track that swayed from it. Conversely, as we will see in our next chapter, this cultural trends of the 90s (in terms of what people were willing to tolerate in practice and what they weren't) shut down the more reality oriented evolutionary track while opening a whole new world of possibilities for jiu-jitsu.

Our world was changing, so naturally, jiu-jitsu adapted. And it did so rather quickly I should add, particularly when we consider jiu-jitsu's long tradition of being associated with a more warrior like approach to life and the world. Still, with all these changes and evolutions in mind and following what might indeed have been inevitable, perhaps a pertinent question is worth asking, *were all these changes beneficial?*

---

[225] Because much of this is likely to be somewhat shocking for some people, I feel compelled to add a side note here. To be clear, I am not suggesting that no one had tried any of these things before or never done any of them successfully, I am only suggesting that the *confere* worked essentially as a barrier (and a strong one at that) to deter anything that wouldn't work in a fight and played a role in hindering jiu-jitsu's technical evolution of anything that wasn't practical in a real-fight.

Chapter 23

The Americanization
of Brazilian Jiu-Jitsu
by Brazilians

*"Jiu-jitsu isn't a grocerie store where the customer is always right.
There has to be a respect for the coach and a hierarchy"*[226]

Una Proença – Carlson Gracie blue-belt

My experience with *taparia* was a brief one. When I began training
in 1998, it was already in its final days (if not already a rarety). *Why?* The
answer I believe, is a simple one: jiu-jitsu's popularization and the need
to appeal to the new ethos of the changing times.

By putting BJJ on the map, Royce Gracie drew hundreds of thousands of practitioners from outside the Carioca south-zone to the ranks
of the jiu-jitsu army. If the *third-wave* wanted to learn, the *second-wave*
wanted to teach. But was the *second-wave* intent solely on spreading
the gospel of jiu-jitsu? Or were they driven by the prospect of making a
quick dollar from fear-driven gringos willing to pay just about anything
to learn how to fight? Come to think of it, *are the two really mutually
exclusive?*

The popularization of jiu-jitsu from 1993 onward gave birth to an
entire new wave of practitioners that wanted to follow in the footsteps
of the *second-wave*. As a member of that wave, I can confirm that we
were trying to be just like them because they were our references. During

---

[226] *"Jiu-jitsu não é quitanda onde o freguês tem sempre razão. Tem que ter um respeito ao
professor e uma hierarquia."* See: *"Una Proença – Resenha PVT"* https://www.youtube.
com/watch?v=1Vf4P0jKhfs

this moment the *second-wave* had two coexisting motivations: a genuine belief and passion for jiu-jitsu and an eye on the possibility of cashing in on its popularity. An opportunity most Brazilians from the *second-wave* were unlikely to ever have in Brazil. A notion that they were all too aware of.[227]

What followed was *the Americanization of Brazilian Jiu-Jitsu by Brazilians*. The first thing that had to go was the gauntlet tradition.[228] I recall, during my first belt test in Las Vegas in 2008 when we had our recently promoted children getting whipped on their backs by their peers while their parents watched. Something I had done many times in Brazil before and with no repercussions whatsoever.

This time around, the looks on their faces were priceless and I'll never forget them. Nor did I need a reminder to never bring the tradition back. I didn't lose any students, but the look on their faces said it all, *"don't ever bring that barbaric practice back here again or we'll leave."* With that in mind, I can only imagine the reaction of most parents today if they saw a *taparia* session.[229]

Yet the changes weren't only in terms of disappearing traditions such as the gauntlet, new traditions were also quietly making their way into the *jiu-jitsusphere*. Around the same time the new jiu-jitsu craze was taking place around the world, the concept of "sand-bagging" was

---

[227] Curiously, and without mentioning names, during the boom of the mid 90s, many black-belts who had disappeared from jiu-jitsu mats for years, if not decades, decided to come back to fulfil the demands of a global audience eager to learn jiu-jitsu (demanding at once all the missed stripes on their belts). Here, we get a hint as to the two motivations and which one is the stronger one according to each individual. But again, they are not mutually exclusive.

[228] The "gauntlet" is the practice of creating a corridor of practitioners holding their belts and beating their recently promoted teammate with them. As long as the back is the aim (rather than the face or groin area), it is a harmless practice, even if noisy and shocking to uninitiates.

[229] The event also served as a revelation of sorts. It became clear to me that if I wanted to run a successful business and keep up with the changing times and the competition, I would have to concede to the demands of my students and their parents. From the Americanization of Brazilian jiu-jitsu onward, and in case the business was to be successful, it had to be acknowledged (even if unconsciously) that in reality, the paying customer was going to be in charge. In other words, the commercialization of jiu-jitsu had the downside of disrupting the hierarchy inside gyms and, in more than a few ways, placing the customer and their wants at the helm.

silently introduced for the first time in BJJ.[230] Whereas, previously in Brazil, holding your students back in rank (as well as being held back), signaled prestige and even honor to the team, coach and student alike. It was a reminder to others and to self, that rank didn't matter and that one was looking to earn everything the hardest way possible and with no rush for any rewards.

By and large, the concept and introduction of sand-bagging into BJJ serves the dual purpose of assuring that the student is rewarded rank sooner (thus pleasing him/her) as well as that, for purposes of tournaments, the student's opponents are also advanced faster than before. That way, those who are promoted faster than they previously would have been in the days prior to the introduction of sand-bagging into BJJ, increase their odds of winning by ridding themselves of the tougher competition.

The rationale goes, *"I want my child/student to win trophies, your child/student is too dominant. I don't want to hold my child/student back but want to reward them quickly instead. Can you please grade your student faster so we don't look so bad?"* The silent agreement between coaches and parents might make everyone feel good about themselves at the end, but not without first permanently weakening jiu-jitsu's intergrity and credibility in the process. This pressure of course, comes not only from other coaches and parents, but from students as well. Simply put, disguised as a practice for fairness is a practice aimed at faster rewards and easier tournament results by lowering the bar rather than elevating it.

To be fair, the cultural-trend of over-sheltering children (who would later become adults and expect the same sort of sheltering as a normal practice) was already on its way in Brazil. It is only that, in this as in so many other things, Brazilians see Americans as an older brother to be emulated. As a result of this, they largely follow Americans in much of

---

[230] Sand-bagging is meant to describe a student who is not being graded fast enough and according to their alleged skill level (real or not). Curiously, neither the term nor the concept can be translated (or explained) into Portuguese. In all fairness, the concept of sand-bagging is odd to Brazilians. Its introduction into BJJ was made by the hands of parents and American coaches.

what they do and value in life. Generally speaking, Brazilians accept what Americans first approve of (movies, music, values, politics, MMA, etc.). Even if Brazilians happen to tread a few years behind in these trends.

With all these (r)evolutions, cultural changes and commercialization rapidly taking place, the *second-wave*, was essentially split in between those who remained in Brazil and those who would travel abroad to spread the gospel of jiu-jitsu. Being responsible for training the *third-wave* in the 90s, they were also responsible for the transition from the warrior minded-model that was so befitting to their generation into the business-oriented one that the *fourth-wave* would come to see as the norm.

Nonetheless, many members of the *second-wave* resisted these changes. Many still do in fact. Nonetheless, the reality of this discussion is that those who immigrated to greener pastures saw a golden opportunity and then shrewdly adapted quickly to their clients and their wants. It could be easily argued that for purposes of growth and popularization the business model had to abide by the changing times and the expectations of parents and costumers alike. As for maintaining the courage, strength, cohesion and warrior-like ethos that made jiu-jitsu a global phenomenon in the first place, well, that is a whole different story all together (and one I will return to later). One of these two worldviews had to go, or was there another way?

A new world was emerging, something that both the *second* and *third-waves* understood perfectly well. Certainly, they love jiu-jitsu, but they are all getting older by the day and time has a way of shifting priorities. Accordingly, money became an enormous incentive for reshaping jiu-jitsu for both these waves. This was particularly true as the social, political and financial perks grew exponentially as the *third-wave* came into maturity making way for the much more populous *fourth-wave*.

For their part, not having lived or experienced the warrior culture of the south-zone in Rio and having come to maturity during the late 90s, those of us belonging to the *third-wave* conceded quite easily and adapted very quickly to the changing times. We conceded almost without a fight because we generally only knew of the warrior-ethos of the

ROBERT DRYSDALE

south-zone from videos we watched and stories we heard. Given that we all walked into jiu-jitsu when this warrior-code was already witnessing its final days.

Brazilian black-belts-turned-businessmen were set on repackaging jiu-jitsu to the preferences of their new clients, *just like their American older brothers had taught them to.*[231] Unsurprisingly, Americans who were almost exclusively part of the *third* and *fourth-waves*, were all too eager to learn and follow wherever Brazilians led them, in both technical and cultural terms.

All things considered, and perhaps predictably, Americans accepted the changes quite naturally and without even realizing anything had changed. The new business-minded-culture had been modeled after American consumerism, therefore, Americans understood it as a natural occurrence. Monetization, after all (north and south of the Equator), has become the new religion of the age. Holy in all its aspects and executions.

With the force of a rapidly changing world overwhelming even the warriors, it was time for a new jiu-jitsu. One that was no longer the brand of jiu-jitsu that brought Royce Gracie to prominence and that was perhaps best represented by Carlson's army of *casca-grossas*. The new one was modeled after the appetite of its clients. Softer, more sophisticated (yet less real), easier in some ways, harder in others, with more belts, open to all and adaptive to the clients wants (but not necessarily their needs).

Although this new model works like a charm and allows me to make a good living from it, I can't help but think that something doesn't feel right in all this. Unhappily, I concede that during this process of democratization and commercialization that jiu-jitsu has been subjected to by the *second* and *third-waves*, something valuable has also been lost along with irrational practices that should never had existed in the first place.

---

[231] An adaption not unlike the one the Japanese had undergone before them, as soon as they learned about the West's obsession with themes such as bushido, samurai and martial arts in general. The product, once again, was only being labeled according to the customer's preferences while the values also adjusted to suit.

What was lost was the kind of accountability that was demanded of the student when he lost or didn't get what he or she wanted. Hierarchies are being disrupted to honor the students tastes and wishes. While the merit-based-system and cohesion are also in decline, something that no amount of money could ever repurchase and that the further commercialization of jiu-jitsu can only continue to weaken. After all, if jiu-jitsu practitioners (now consumers) are awarded everything they want and when they want it, where does value reside?

The casualty-free cultural war between the jiu-jitsu that evolved out of the south-zone of Rio and a more democratic one led by its overcommercialization, was more of a concession and an understanding than it was an actual "war." Since wars by definition require resistance and no one was brave (foolish?) enough to fight in this one. Primarily because the world is simply too much, even for something seemingly as strong as jiu-jitsu. But also because the money was too good to bother with a battle that jiu-jitsu alone could not win anyway. It was a new environment, with new rules of engagement, new values, new characters and new challenges.

A new environment that was essentially a farewell to a dying warrior breed of men that had to go. What was left of them was only the memory of a bygone era which, after decades of work to ground the art to the reality of combat, made jiu-jitsu the most prominent martial art on the planet. But times *are a-changin*, and regardless of our feelings or wishes toward any of this, the truth of this matter is that in this new war, unlike in the wars of yester years, the Spartans didn't win.

"The middle of humanity thou never knewest, but the extremity of both ends."[232]

The final days of Carlson Gracie. Interviews with:

Carlson Gracie Jr.
Antonio Rosado (2nd half)
Murilo Bustamante (2nd half)
Wallid Ismail (2nd half)
Paulão Filho
Una Proença
Marcelo Alonso (2nd half)

---

[232] William Shakespeare - Timon of Athens, Act 4 Scene 3

Master Carlson Gracie Jr.

Carlson Gracie teaches a kids class at the Figueiredo Academy.
His son is the child with curly hair nearest the camera.
Photocred: Carlson Gracie Jr. personal archives.

"Listen, I'll tell you something, there will never be anyone like my father again. Not as a fighter, as a coach or as a person. He was born different, there is no way around it. He was open to everything, always tried to be righteous in everything he did, demanded so much of his students, always expecting excellence and loyalty from everyone because that is how he was!"

Master Carlson Gracie Jr.

Carlson Gracie Jr. is his father's only son. Today, he continues his father's legacy and works to organize their team's former students under the same banner. He teaches daily in Chicago and is an 8th degree coral-belt and was born on July 27th, 1969. Our interview took place in person after the IBJJF World Master Championships on September 4th, 2022 inside my gym in Las Vegas.

1- Your grandfather Carlos is the inception point in the split between judo and BJJ, would you say so?

The Japanese colony in Brazil is enormous. When you think about it, it should all have been judo as those guys were all judokas. Think about the influence they had in Brazilian culture with so many Japanese descendants living in Brazil. We should all be doing judo! What else do I need to say?

2- Your father left the Gracie Academy to open a gym with Ivan Gomes in 1964. Why did he do this? And what were the consequences from this?

When my father left the Gracie Academy he was termed the black-sheep of the family. People don't like to talk about this, but he left because of Uncle Helio, who had a big ego issue, especially in regards to my father. Whenever my father fought, the money earned was never his, it went to the family too. It all got worse when my father defeated Waldemar Santana [in 1956] and took the spotlight from uncle Helio. In truth, he was jealous of my father and that was something that he never really healed from. The problem is that no one ever heard Carlson's version of things. Everyone was heard, except Carlson. When you hear Carlson's version of events things change completely and everything starts to make sense. The whole family had massive egos and no one wanted to lose or give credit to anyone else, while my father had a different view of things and began to train people regardless of their last-name and he trained them well and began to defeat members of the family. But it was Uncle Helio who started all this when he began to train his students to defeat my father, and they never could. All it took was for my father to show up at the Gracie Academy and he would be challenged. Helio basically wanted my father to lose, be it himself losing or his students and my father never budged.

Helio wouldn't admit it, but he was always training those guys to beat my father. One day my father was fed up with having to be ready to fight all the time in his own academy and left. The whole thing created a weird climate, so he left and opened up his own academy and his students began to defeat those from the Gracie Academy. Things just derailed from there. Look, the Gracie family theme is very complicated. Everyone wants to shine more than the Gracie next to them, get it? Like Rickson going around telling people that he was beating Rolls... Why lie? Why even talk about that? There's no need.

3- This history, to me at least, is incredible exactly as things happened. There is no need to exaggerate or cut others out. It is such a remarkable story. But most people don't seem to see it that way. It has become highly politicized as jiu-jitsu grew.

It is interesting to me that as people get older and others are no longer here, that things are all of a sudden retold differently from how they happened. I'm quiet about most of these things, but at some point, I have to jump in and defend my father. We have all been silent over this but those who were there know. Everyone wants to give their version of events that best works for them and think that it will stay that way forever. The truth of the matter is that this history, our history never ended. It continues. Many episodes of the past were forgotten, but things keep on moving. They always do, but things need to be told accurately, the right way.

4- It is like people can't read the facts as they are. They are so concerned with their own self-interest and politics that they cannot remove themselves from these things and think objectively.

Exactly. Of course, there are things that I can't know because I wasn't there. Like I have recently heard that there is no evidence as

to whether or not Carlos trained with Maeda. How would I know
when I wasn't even born yet? But other things I was there for. Like
when Rickson came over to train with Rosado in preparation for his
fight against Zulu. Rosado was a purple-belt under my father and
was tapping Rickson when he was already a black-belt. I was there,
I saw Uncle Helio talking to Carlinho Bagana. Helio walked in late
asking, "what's happening here?" and Carlinho told him "Rickson
already trained" and Helio asked, "how did it go?" and Carlinho told
him "he got smashed." Then I saw Helio smack Rickson in the neck.
People from those days were taught not to comment on training,
there is a reason why these things were always held behind closed
doors. But since everyone is talking I will do the same. If truth be
told, the problem in the family was always Uncle Helio. No one
wants to say this, but Helio was always favoring his own children
and being biased toward them. He always clashed with my father,
and never gave Rolls enough credit, get it?

5- When did these problems with Helio and your father begin?

I think that after the fight with Waldemar. Helio was very jealous
of my father after that fight, he was very territorial and loved his
placement in the jiu-jitsu world, but my father basically came and
took that place through his own merits. When Helio was no longer the leading figure in jiu-jitsu, that created a huge rift among
the family. My father even had a column every Monday in the
newspaper called "Nota do Garotão," [Big Boy's Note] that's how
much credibility he had in Rio in those days. He was the hero then
and outshined Uncle Helio and Helio couldn't stand it. Especially
because he had the expectation that Rorion or Relson would grow
to become the next champion in the family. And then there was
Rolls. Despite Helio having raised Rolls, he never gave him the
same treatment he gave to his own children. Helio desperately
wanted Rorion to beat Rolls, but it never happened. That was also

part of the problem. And then there was Rickson who in some ways became the champion Helio wanted one of his children to be. But on the other hand, give me an elite guy that Rickson beat? There are none. My father would always say, "Rickson is very good, but he never fought the best." *He would always say that. Anyone who knew my father knows he would say that. The problem is that most people don't have the balls to say these things publicly.*

6- Your father created an army of *casca-grossas* and it could be said that this vision gave birth to a more competitive approach to jiu-jitsu. How did he do this?

My father was the one who began group classes, because he liked "rinhas" [term used to describe cock-fighting], *which didn't exist before him, it was all private lessons. That was part of the problem with Uncle Helio. Carlson wanted "rinha" and Helio didn't. He wanted private lessons, while grandpa* [Carlos Gracie] *kept out of it. It is no accident that my father's students simply dominated competitive jiu-jitsu during the late 60s, 70s, 80s and early 90s in Brazil. After that there were essentially two separate lineages in jiu-jitsu: Helio and Carlson.*

7- The written record, as far as I know it, confirms what you are saying. Carlson's guys were the most dominant ones throughout that whole era. Was there anyone who stood out from the Gracie Academy?

Rickson. He was the only one of those guys from the Gracie Academy who won in those days.

8- And how did he get so good?

Training with Rolls of course. But no one has the courage to say this, but it's the truth.

9- What about Rolls? Why did he go train with your father?

Rolls only became Rolls when he went over to train with my father. Before that he fought a guy called Cicero who was a really good guy, that was when he began to train with us. My father invited him over because Rolls' fights were starting to get harder and he needed harder training.

10- Because Rolls gave birth to such successful lineages [Gracie Barra, Alliance, etc.], he is often credited with being the father of competitive jiu-jitsu. But you seem to be saying something else. Why is it that so few people are willing to give Carlson this credit? It seems clear to me that Rolls sought your father because he knew that he had created the sort of environment that would breed excellence.

Rolls got his competitive jiu-jitsu from Carlson Gracie. Because truth be told, he showed up at the gym as a black-belt and was faced with tough competition. Training under my father he really gained a new view of jiu-jitsu. What you need to understand is that those guys were animals trying to kill each other every day. Dozens of them. An army of competitive guys going at it every day. Most people couldn't swim in that environment my father created. Most people simply weren't ready for it. When Rolls came over, he saw that the level there was completely different, so he stayed over to train with us. And I saw Rolls train with my father many times behind closed doors at the Figueiredo Academy, always closed doors. After Rolls had been training with my father for a while, Carlson would joke with Rolls, "Rolls, don't beat up Rickson too much so that Helio doesn't start to get angry at you too." That was the joke then. Everyone knows this and everyone holds great respect for Rolls, including all those from my father's lineage, because Rolls was an outstanding guy in terms of his personality. I actually took classes from him. Rolls and my father argued over who would teach me [laughs], can you imagine the privilege? And I'll tell you more, the people who are saying these things [regarding Rolls being the father of competitive jiu-jitsu] trace their lineage directly to Rolls, that's why. These guys refuse to give my father his due credit in order to strengthen their own standing and lineage. The other day I was watching a documentary and they only talked about Rolls. And I was watching it with my mother and even she took note, "what? Only Rolls? Where is your father in all this?" *In all these magazine articles and documentaries, everyone gives all the credit to Rolls, but not my father, they never talk about him, because it diminishes their own flag to place my father where he belongs. That's why I never even open my mouth. I'd rather stay quiet in my corner listening to everything to steer clear from any politics. But when they clash with me, they know the truth. I'm thinking to myself,* "nice documentary... Are you sure there is no one missing in it?" *It is all political, but they know the truth. I don't get it, there is so many egos out there. I wasn't raised like that, why is it so hard to give people the credit they deserve? Did you fight? Did you win? Did you lose? All good, because you fought! That's it. So many people in this family who never fought a day of their lives and they can't give credit to the man who was there, putting his ass on the line his whole life. The guy who dedicated all his energy into making jiu-jitsu what it is today. Everywhere you read up on these guys and they never have anything good to say about my father. Why? Are they scared? This reminds me of that movie, The Lion King. Have you seen it? Remember when the name Mufasa was mentioned and everyone just trembled in fear? That's it, it's the same with my father. And because no one ever says anything, unless I say something, no one will ever hear the truth.*

11- What you are telling me is in line with what Paquetá also said in that one interview, that Rolls had a hard time with Saraiva.

That's all true, Rolls didn't do great against my father's best students when he first got there. Look, my father liked roosters. He wanted guys with that fighting spirit and Rolls was a rooster who loved to fight. He would go at it with just about anyone ["saia na porrada com qualquer um"]. But when he went to my father's gym, it was a completely different training intensity. Those guys were all beasts ["feras"], they were the only ones that later would give Rickson a hard time. There were so many good guys, so many. We pretty much won every single division at the tournaments. It wasn't until much later where the affiliate system Carlinhos created came into play that we began to lose ground. My father simply lacked that business view of things for getting jiu-jitsu to scale. Carlinhos had that. When my father's students began to open their own gyms, he never did what Carlinhos did, he never turned all these schools into an affiliation system under one single banner. Carlson Gracie only became an affiliation team when my father died and I began to try to organize his old students under one flag. When he was alive and I tried to organize these things, he wouldn't let me or he would change everything around. I'd try to get people to pay and he'd meddle in it and stop the whole thing and wanted to do things his own way as he had always done.

12- To me it seems like the jiu-jitsu culture that took the world by storm from the mid-90s onward wasn't the culture that grew out of the original Gracie Academy. I am referring to the açaí after training, the flip-flops, the surf-culture, the relaxed and friendly manners on and off the mats, etc. All these things that became a staple of the jiu-jitsu culture that helped make it so popular around the world were born out of the Figueiredo Academy. What was that academy like?

You are right, these things weren't part of the daily life of the Gracie Academy, they had a very different environment and clientele there. To give you an idea of what things were like, the Figueiredo Academy didn't even close. You could show up there at 11pm and you would see people rolling around on the mats, going at it, trying to kill one another. It didn't stop. Speaking for myself, unless I was in school, I'd be there every night until midnight with those guys. That's how it was. That gym was a truly special place. In there you could find just about any type of person. Seriously, all types. From trouble-makers, to judges, etc. It was multicultural to the fullest, let's put it like that [laughs].

13- You were telling me earlier that Carlson hosted clandestine tournaments with Munir [Fadda student]. Can you tell us a little bit about this?

Yes, they would do this to give their guys experience because the federation wasn't hosting enough tournaments in my father's opinion. That and because it wasn't legal to hold a tournament in those days without the federation being involved. He had a good relationship with Munir, I even went there to his gym many times to train. Very good guy. So yes, they would organize tournaments among their own students because they felt that the federation wasn't doing things fast enough for jiu-jitsu to grow.

14- Your father had a stellar *vale-tudo* career. Showing only one loss to Euclides Pereira. What did your father tell you about his only loss?

This is what I was told. The fight was supposed to be 3 x 10-minute rounds or with no time limit. But when he got there, Euclides and the baianos [term to designate someone born in the state of Bahia] threatened my father and demanded the fight be 3 x 5-minute rounds instead... I mean, those guys were all armed. What could

*my father do? He had to agree to fight outside the original agree-
ment. He never fought 3 x 5-minute rounds, only in this fight with
Euclides. When the fight began, Euclides kept escaping through the
ropes and had his body covered in grease. At one point my father
even submitted him but the referee woke Euclides up and the fight
continued. The whole fight was a sham. Remember, Carlson was
the visitor and things weren't always fair in those days. I tried to
confront Euclides on this [presumably years later] but he wouldn't
talk about it. Also notice that no one was bragging about this fight
when my father was alive. What people don't know is that there
is a whole story about this that no one talks about. Did anyone
ever see a picture of my father with this face beat up? Never. Same
thing with the fight with Ivan Gomes. Everyone talks about him
getting beat up the whole fight, but look at the pictures, not a single
scratch, not to mention that my father was much lighter than Ivan.*

15-   Your father told you all this? He didn't seem like one to brag about things.

*My father? He never bragged about anything. Never talked about
the guys he beat, he always respected his opponents. So much so,
that he had a great friendship with Waldemar, even when they were
fighting each other throughout their careers. He always knew how
to differentiate personal relationships and his career in the ring, he
wasn't one to hold onto grief over such things. But he did hold a lot of
grief over the guys from BTT* [Brazilian Top Team]*, but even with all
the disagreements with Uncle Helio, he never stopped respecting him.*

16-   Your father seemed to have had a good relationship with everyone
      in the fight world in Brazil, except perhaps Helio. Even the luta-
      livre guys liked him, is that true?

*You know that event where the luta-livre guys invaded a jiu-jitsu
tournament? Those guys were all armed, they went there to cause
trouble. They went there and asked to speak to my father, you*

know why? Because he was the only person in jiu-jitsu that they all respected. And my father went into a private room with all of them, "you sons of bitches, you guys come here armed? Why are you here? You want to fight? Let's fight then, but let's do it in the ring, not here, take your guns home." That was the episode that led to the jiu-jitsu versus luta-livre challenge in 1991.

17- When *vale-tudo* came back in the 90s, your father was the most well positioned person to train everyone because he was the only one with an extensive experience fighting and preparing fighters for *vale-tudo*. During an initial moment, immediately after Royce's ascendance in the early UFC's, the best fighters in Brazil were coming out of your father's gym. Can you comment?

After Royce and the UFC, what happened was that Royce didn't make it very far because the competition got tough very quickly. And jiu-jitsu needed new representatives to fight and continue to represent it. And that was when my father's troops stepped up to the challenge as the UFC and MMA grew. Murilo, Carlão, Amaury, Vitor, etc. Those were the guys who stepped up to represent jiu-jitsu. Of course, not all of them were successful, people were catching up to our tricks, but my father's guys were there, representing and fighting because Royce had reached his limits in the early UFC's. Not taking credit from him, he was the one who opened the doors for everyone else, he was a pioneer and he had his chapter in this story, but everyone in Brazil knew that my father's students were jiu-jitsu's best representatives. And this soon became obvious to everyone who was paying attention.

18- What do you think was the role played by your cousin Carlos Gracie Jr. in all this?

He organized it, in some ways he was handed the cake ready, but he organized things. I recall once when Rickson walked up to me and told me that we had to do something because

Carlinhos was creating a monopoly over jiu-jitsu, and I told him, "what? You guys handed him everything, when he tried to have you guys run a confederation for jiu-jitsu no one wanted it, then he went and did it." Carlinhos did it because no one else wanted to do it.

19- Is it true that your father gave all the money from his fights to the family?

My friend, he never kept anything. When I tell people that he died without a dime in his bank account, they don't believe me, but it's true. He never owned anything. His gyms were never profitable, but things were as he liked them, it was his way of doing things. Everyone trained, but no one paid. The day he put me to work as the gym manager I began to charge people and got lots of shit for it. Everyone was they had to pay, they'd say "I got to pay now?" and I'd say, "yes, my father put me as gym manager and now everyone has to pay" *and they'd be angry at me.*

20- From all accounts, your father was a very giving person, his students tell me that he would take off his shoes and gift them to people in case someone complimented them.

Man, you have no idea, he was always giving his things away and always paid for everything. People would call him and ask for money and he wouldn't even ask any questions and just give them the money. I'd say something like "dad, you don't even have money for yourself, why are you giving it to people?" *and he'd go "stay out of this, stay out of this, it is my money!"*

21- What happened with BTT then? The impression I get is that after a life of giving himself to his students he came to realize late in life he had no means of taking care of himself as he aged.

THE RISE AND EVOLUTION OF BRAZILIAN JIU-JITSU

What happened was this. All the events were in the US in those days, all the big ones at least, so my father moved to the USA and was trying to bring the whole team over. These guys even lived with him when they first came over. And then there was also Pride in Japan and my father never really learned how to speak English. So those guys began signing agreements directly with Pride and without my father being involved in any negotiation. At some point my father began to speak out against this. Most people don't know this, but in 1999 AABB [Associação Atlética Banco do Brasil] was going to sponsor our team and the money was going to go to rebuild and equip the Figueiredo de Magalhães Academy. But those guys got to the AABB first and used the money for another gym at Lagoa. What followed was that everyone stopped training at the Figueiredo Academy and went over to train at Lagoa. So those guys all left without saying a word, to train at the gym at AABB Lagoa, they left to teach there and never came back to Figueiredo. So, what happened to all the fighters? They went over to Lagoa, of course. And my father would ask "why aren't you guys training at the Figueiredo Academy?" and they complain about the parking and my father would be angry at that because parking had never been an issue before. So, after that my father demanded a contract but no one would sign it. They would say that they wouldn't sign it because Carlson wasn't training them any longer. How? He had trained people his whole life, that was what he always did. You see Drysdale, when you throw money in the mix of things, everything changes.

22-   Your father died young. Was he struck by grief?

My father died of grief. As he saw it, those guys took his empire from him. He became hateful toward them. His last days were filled with hatred. When people go around saying that Carlson forgave them, none of that is true. He forgave no one, he died resenting them. I had to tolerate him complaining about them for years after. When he moved to Chicago with me, he got into his head that he was going to rebuild his army from scratch and seek revenge. He'd say things like "those guys aren't shit" and I'd say, "dad, they can't be shit, you trained them." And he'd get mad, we'd argue a lot over everything. I'd tell him "look, you need to focus on your financial stability and forget this revenge thing, because this thirst for revenge isn't doing you well." But I couldn't get this through his head, it was pointless. He was set on revenge, but he was also tired. So slowly he became sick, had issues with his kidneys, his diet wasn't healthy anymore and he slowly stopped caring. He lived with me in those days, but I was always giving him a hard time over everything [laughs] *so he got tired of me being on his case about his health and eventually moved out to live alone. But I'd visit him at his new place to give him a hard time anyway* [laughs], *and he'd say* "don't come over here, leave me alone!" [laughs]. *Listen, I'll tell you something, there will never be anyone like my father again. Not as a fighter, as a coach or as a person. He was born different, there is no way around it. He was open to everything, always tried to be righteous in everything he did, demanded so much of his students, always expecting excellence and loyalty from everyone because that is how he was! He was very possessive of his students. So much so that Renzo and those guys at one point had to choose between training with my father or Rolls. My father never went easy on anyone, not even me* [laughs]. *What he always wanted was to train these guys to prove that he was the best coach. He was very competitive with his own family to prove this. And this helped jiu-jitsu evolve because, at the end of the day, everyone had to begin training their guys with my father's vision in mind.*

Grandmaster Antonio Carlos Rosado (continued from Part 2)

Rosado and Carlson.
Photocred: Antonio Carlos Rosado personal archives.

"(...) during those days when Waldemar beat Helio, Waldemar was the man, the new king. It was Carlson who despite being so young stepped up to the mark to defend the family's name and rescue their credibility. We need to remember and respect what he did. Both for jiu-jitsu and the family. All that and at the end of his life he had nothing to show for it. I think that is what was going on in his head toward the end."

Grandmaster Antonio Carlos Rosado

1- How do you think Carlson saw the birth of CBJJ and competitive jiu-jitsu in general?

Carlson was supposed to be the guy to run it, but he had no business sense. Carlinhos did, he had a business vision for all this.

Carlson wasn't built for running federations. But today, jiu-jitsu has drifted too much from real fighting. I don't think Carlson would approve of it.

2- What about the departure of his main students to form Brazilian Top Team in the 2000s?

I don't even like to talk about it and have a more or less ambiguous stance toward all this. Both sides have their reasons and I won't venture into saying who has a stronger case. Carlson called me and wanted me to take sides, I told him I would remain neutral and that that was his fight with those guys but that I would always be loyal to him I also told him that if he were getting his butt-kicked I would jump in to take a beating with him, but that wasn't the case. As far as I can see, both sides had their reasons. What his students were asking for was fair, it could perhaps be seen as unfair if we think of everything that had been done for them all those years. But from a professional perspective they had a point.

3- You know what is confusing about that separation? Is that everyone always described Carlson as someone who didn't care about money, but toward the end of his life, he seemed to be worried about it. What changed?

Look, maybe as he got older he felt the need to have something to show for life's effort. Carlson gave all his fighting money to the Gracie Academy and when he coached, he did it for free. It is hard to say, people change. Maybe he was influenced by other voices who were living with him at the time, some people say that is what happened. Time changes things, people die, you get sick, your friends get sick and you begin to see things differently, maybe he started to think about a future in which he didn't have many options. This is a guy who never had a fixed place to live in, sometimes he slept on his own mats, sometimes at a friend's apartment. He was Carlson! If it weren't for him in his youth to give Waldemar Santana a beating, the Gracie name would have disappeared. Maybe they would have recovered down the road, but during those days when Waldemar beat Helio, Waldemar was the man, the new king. It was Carlson who despite being so young stepped up to the mark to defend the family's name and rescue their credibility. We need to remember and respect what he did. Both for jiu-jitsu and the family. All that and at the end of his life he had nothing to show for it. I think that is what was going on in his head toward the end.

4-   In a recent interview, Carlson Jr. says that his father died of sorrow. What do you have to say about this? Personally, I think of Carlson as a role model martial artist. For all his experience and results in a ring, his passion for teaching, his love for his students, for all this I think Carlson's role in the history of jiu-jitsu is very underappreciated. How can a man who gave his best years and money to his family, lived for jiu-jitsu and his students not die with a smile on his face? This is a tragedy.

This makes me very emotional just to think about it, it brings tears to my eyes... What you just said about Carlson is exactly how I feel about all this. I am even thankful and happy to hear this from you. Especially because you were never his student. So, for you to have this sort of affection for him really touches me. But I'll speak honestly here, I did my part and have a clear conscience in all this. I was his student and friend my whole life, in regards to me, he died happy. I can't speak for others, all I can say is that he died at peace with me. I know he loved me and had me as one of his favorite students, I never had any issues with him. I know we lived many good moments together, when we were here in Rio with us, he was happy. That's all I can say. Carlson was a very unique human and I will always remember him that way. But his end was very sad.

Master Murilo Bustamante (continued from Part 2)

Murilo Bustamante passing the guard.
Photocred: Murilo Bustamante personal archives.

"We were all basically working to lift his name and continue his legacy without getting paid anything to do it, we did it out of love. In my head, Carlson was just going through a passing moment and he'd come back to his senses eventually. But that wasn't the case."

Master Murilo Bustamante

1-   Can you tell us a little bit about the separation with Carlson and the formation of BTT?

Sure. Carlson was living in the USA and the previous 2 or 3 fights I had gone all the way there to train with him. But while he was there, we were no longer training in his gym, and began training at my own gym in Leblon because it was a lot easier for all of us to meet there and because parking there was also a lot easier to find. But someone put into Carlson's head that we were going to betray him because we were no longer training at his academy, even though he wasn't there. Of course, this was all made up, we were all loyal to him. Perhaps out of insecurity he drafted a new contract for us, I think it was written by one of his students. The contract basically stated that all his students had to pay 20% of all their earning from fights and sponsorships to him. Which was something we were all used to paying. This would all have been fine with me if Carlson were training us. The issue was that the contract had no obligations for Carlson to keep training us, only that we could continue to use his gym to train even though we weren't even using it anymore. While this was going on I was scheduled to fight in Japan and asked Carlson to come with me, that I would pay him the 20% even if he hadn't trained me but that I wanted to talk to him about the contract after the fight. He refused... things just deteriorated after that. The contract simply made no sense to us, so basically no one signed it and as a result Carlson kicked me off the team over the internet. It made no sense to me. I had been there for 25 years and was one of his most loyal and successful students... me and Libório basically ran the show at the academy after he left. Just to give you an idea of this, in 1998 we started the "Clube Carlson" and I was voted unanimously the president of the club. That is, except for my own vote because I voted for Delariva. We were all basically working to lift his name and continue his legacy without getting paid anything to do it, we did it out of love. In my head, Carlson was just going through a passing moment and he'd come back to his senses eventually. But that wasn't the case. Basically, Carlson created a narrative in his head that we had all abandoned him, even though I kept trying to make amends. One day I tried to shake his hand and he wouldn't shake my hand... Shortly after he offered to train Chuck Liddell to fight me in 2001 in the UFC. After that I was done. So, after I got kicked off the team, others followed me. Not because I invited them, but because they wanted to. What could I do?

2-   What is so curious about this story is that everyone always described Carlson as a guy with no financial ambition, who slept on the mats, trained people for free, fed his students and took the shoes off his own feet to gift them. What changed? I wonder if he didn't begin to regret being so giving as he got older as he also realized he had nothing material to show for his long career as a fighter and coach. I also wonder if he truly understood the content of the contract and what he was requesting from you guys. We all know he was no business man.

That is a very good question. But I did tell him, "Carlson, this contract only has rights and no obligations, why don't we write a new one that has both?" But he was set in his ways. Look, Carlson became known to the world as a coach. The best ever. How can you kick people off the team without talking to them and hearing them out first? The real problem was that Carlson never learned how to delegate. He would have made money from us for the rest of his life. None of us ever thought about cutting him out financially, we would never do this to him, never. The thought never even occurred to me. He had very loyal people around him. Maybe, had he been better at delegating and structuring, he wouldn't have had 20% from 10 fighters and instead he would have had 10% from 50... or 5% from 200 fighters. He just didn't have that sort of vision... We were even trying to transform his academy into a bigger association, organizing, buying ads... and he was the one who had the most to gain from it. We were working for his legacy... we just wanted a fair contract, that's all. And he basically ended everything with a single blow.

Master Wallid Ismail (continued from Part 2)

**Wallid Ismail after a training
session at the Figueiredo
Academy. Photocred: Wallid
Ismail personal archives.**

*"Practically all of Carlson's main students left him. Your disciples are
the ones who propagate your name."*

Master Wallid Ismail

1- I know this is a controversial topic, but what do you think happened between Carlson and the departure of his students to form
Brazilian Top Team (BTT)?

*What happened was that Carlson was a guy who always taught
for free. When he moved to the USA they formed their own team,
some more competent than others, but they formed their own*

team. *Their mistake in my view was taking so many of Carlson's students with them. Had they formed a team from scratch it would have been different. People should be able to go their own way if they choose to, but they took all of Carlson's students and stopped paying Carlson. I clashed head on with those guys and sided with Carlson, I paid him until my last fight, but I think that was their mistake. And then those guys who went over to BTT were all paying 20% just the same.*

2- Carlson's role in the history of jiu-jitsu has not been acknowledged in my view, why do you think that is?

Simple, practically all of Carlson's main students left him. Your disciples are the ones who propagate your name. That was the problem. And who is going to speak on Carlson's behalf today? Carlson Jr. and me. Of course, there are others like Cassio Cardoso, but those with any media presence are very few.

Paulo Filho

**Carlson and Paulão Filho when he was 16 years old.
Photocred: Paulo Filho personal archives.**

"The man was obsessed with competition, it bordered on a mania, something incontrollable. But this was a necessity for jiu-jitsu. Carlson was a necessity for jiu-jitsu."

Paulo Filho

Paulo Filho is one of the most successful MMA fighters of the 2000s and a known representative of Carlson Gracie's team. Our interview took place over the phone on November 8th 2022.

1- How did Carlson talk about his younger brother Rolls?

Rolls was a name that was always very present in our gym. When Carlson spoke of him it was always with a glimmer in his eyes. It was obvious that those two had a close relationship. And Rolls would often come up in the same conversations where Rickson came up. Carlson refused to compare the two. You see, Carlson was always a very merit-oriented person, I would say even in a very aggressive way which made him a misunderstood figure in some ways, and in his mind, Rickson had not done enough, he had chosen the easier path and Carlson simply couldn't respect this. He'd say "he wins because he is heavier and because he isn't fighting anyone tough." As for Rolls, he always placed Rolls on a pedestal and told us how good he was and how talented. Carlson would tell us how hard Helio was on Rickson and that despite this, Rolls would still crush him on the mats. In fact, Carlson would say that Helio was so hard on Rorion that that was why he left for the US, to get away from the pressure of being underneath the shadow of Rolls.

2- Can you comment more on his merit-based views?

He was so crazy about it that he would get mad at you if you celebrated your wins too much. To him it was a given for you to win. And he'd reprimand us too, many times I saw him do this, reprimand us for celebrating too much of our wins. He'd say "what? Were you not expecting to win? Why are you acting so surprised?" and he'd walk away angry.

3- What do you think made Carlson so special for so many people?

Carlson was different, something about him wasn't quite right, and I say this in a good way. Let's put it this way, he was a singular individual. When we went out to eat, he absolutely had to pay for everyone. He was too giving of a person, I think that that is what made him so easy to love. He never had any idea of his own greatness, he never acted that way. In some ways he was like a 10-year-old child, all while being a brute when it came to fighting and being a coach. These two sides were well balanced in Carlson. But on the other hand, that meant he was always broke. Him not caring put *him in a tough spot so I think that all of this added to his bitterness toward the end.*

4- More than that though, he was an outstanding coach, why do you think that was?

The man was obsessed with competition, it bordered on a mania, something incontrollable. But this was a necessity for jiu-jitsu. Carlson was a necessity for jiu-jitsu. The sport needed someone like him to elevate the bar competitively like in other arts and when it comes to jiu-jitsu, Carlson was that guy.

5- But his ways also put him at odds with a lot of people, especially his own family.

Carlson was the kind of guy to tell you the truth, he was like that. Even if that put him at odds with his own family. He had no tolerance for any bullshit, it didn't matter where it came from. This made him very loveable and very provocative at the same time. And this was obvious with his own family, I heard him say this on many occasions, "we don't train Gracie jiu-jitsu, Gracie jiu-jitsu is Uncle Helio's thing, I teach Carlson Gracie jiu-jitsu." So, in a sense he was waging a war against his own family and with Helio in particular. The morals of some members of the family was always a great complaint of his. Rolls was the one he always spoke highly of.

6- What happened with the BTT guys and Carlson?

Carlson never read a contract in his life. People would bring him a contract and he'd say "what, contract? I trust your word, you don't need to show me anything, I believe you." But some people, not all of them, began to take advantage of his naïve ways. They knew he wasn't going to ever read any contract so they would lie to him about how much money they made in their fights and pay him less than was promised. This happened many times and Carlson got fed up with it. This had been going on for a while, since the late 90's. People were complaining a lot too because Carlson was getting older and wasn't as active as he used to be so they began to question the percentage they had to pay him. That was it, basically many of them were dishonest with Carlson, things could have been different but instead things only deteriorated once he moved to Chicago to live and teach with his son. From that point onward, he only became more rancorous toward everyone.

Una Proença

**Una Proença and Carlson Gracie, circa Nov/Dec 1997.
Photocred: Una Proença personal archives.**

"Carlson breathed competition, he wanted it to grow beyond a practice for his family so he put his foot down to teach jiu-jitsu to everyone. He didn't want jiu-jitsu in his family's hands, he wanted to popularize it. His whole life he repeated like a mantra the need for more tournaments and to bring vale-tudo back to promote jiu-jitsu to the world."

Una Proença

Una was a close friend to Carlson and many other members of the Gracie family and jiu-jitsu community during the 90s. She also worked as both an English translator and media advisor for Carlson in the post-Royce era. She was born in 1973 and holds a blue-belt under Carlson. Una currently lives in Florida and works as an immigration consultant. Our interview took place over audios files and writing over the course of the month of October, 2022.

1- You knew Carlson well, how did your relationship with him first begin?

I used to train at the Marco Ruas gym and met Carlson through him. One day Carlson invited me to be the team's translator and media manager in exchange for a membership. This was around 1990.

2- What was he like as a person?

He respected people. He was a naive humanist in the broad sense of the word, inclusive, always bringing people together, even though he was also very agitated. Carlson loved to fight and argue but only in regards to fighting in general, not on a daily basis where he liked to please everyone. Paquetá was the one who best described him in my opinion. He would say that Carlson was explosive and would fight and argue with anyone, but in truth, he loved everyone around him. It was a side of Carlson that people didn't always see because the focus was always on him as a competitive fighter and coach.

3- What was most memorable about him?

He had so many things about him that I admired. But out of everything I experienced with him I think that the one I loved the most about him was how much he loved his roosters [talking about his students], *he treated them as if they were his children. In the moments of adrenaline and fear in the fight, in that make or break moment where you find out if the rooster is going to "mutucar" or not* ["mutucar" in cock-fighting circles is to back down before the fight], *there was no one like him. Everyone always said this, he had this way of giving the right emotional support to the fighter at the right time. Carlson was very good at feeling his fighters in that way, giving them the sort of emotional support they all needed. In that crucial moment, where those guys would be in there and it was all or nothing, that is when Carlson would show his true colors. In that regard, there was no one like him. He just felt these things, and a few words from him before the fight was worth more than the whole training camp. It was this thing, I won't call it mystical, but something very spiritual I'd say, Carlson felt his fighters.*

4-   Carlson had a troubled relationship with many members of his family, why do you think that was?

This was something he never hid from anyone. Carlson would tell this to complete strangers even. It had to do with inheritance from his father. Properties that were bought with Carlson's fighting purses. He was the one who won the most but he split it among everyone else in the family. Because in those days, the family and coach kept almost everything and he kept only some change. That was one of the reasons he was so angry at his family. He'd say, "do you know how to do math? Well then, I was the one who fought and won the most and I walked away with absolutely nothing." And that is why he would say that if it weren't for him, no one in the family would be where they are today, because all his fight money went to help take care of his family. This put him at odds with them. But also, because Carlson breathed competition, he wanted it to grow beyond a practice for his family so he put his foot down to teach jiu-jitsu to everyone. He didn't want jiu-jitsu in his family's hands, he wanted to popularize it. His whole life he repeated like a mantra the need for more tournaments and to bring vale-tudo back to promote jiu-jitsu to the world.

5-   How did Carlson perceive Royce's victories in the UFC?

Carlson couldn't believe it at first. He felt that way because he knew that his guys were more qualified to represent jiu-jitsu. It wasn't anything personal with Royce, it was just that he wanted to make sure that jiu-jitsu won. But Royce represented jiu-jitsu well. It is just that, in general, Carlson was very critical of anyone stepping into a fight and that included his own fighters, not just family members. His standards were so high and that he expected so much from everyone that he became critical of everyone all the time. He could simply not accept that others could not live up to his standards and whenever people couldn't meet that high standard, he would become very frustrated. To him it was obvious that everyone had to be at least as good as himself, but preferably better, this was all a matter of course to him. It took a long time for him to understand that people couldn't live up to his standards and I think he only understood this toward the end of his life. But this was because he was that hard on himself. Carlson would sometimes vent this frustration by going back and forth between critiquing and teasing people [laughs]. Today you can see the difficulty these guys have, fighting once a year, with all the support and technology, fighting short rounds and it is still so hard. To him what Royce did was a given, it was expected. To impress Carlson was [laughs] impossible. The most he'd say is to point out the strengths someone had, but I have never seen him call any fighter truly complete.

6- Carlson was a key figure in both jiu-jitsu and *vale-tudo*, how did he see the potential they had for growth?

As for the growth of vale-tudo and jiu-jitsu, look, this is what happened, Carlson had a vision that was so ahead of the sport, it was like he had foresight into what was going to happen next, he would tell us repeatedly how much jiu-jitsu and vale-tudo would grow across the world. This at a time when no one believed it was possible. People at best thought it was beautiful or perhaps naïve that he would daydream about its spread across the world like that. He knew what was going to happen, but no one took him seriously, but he kept saying it, from even before the first UFC all the way to his death he kept saying the same thing and no one really took him seriously. Not even Rorion fully believed in the full potential of vale-tudo and the UFC. So much so that he sold the UFC the first opportunity that he had.

7- So Carlson would talk about the potential in bringing *vale-tudo* back?

He would always say that vale-tudo and jiu-jitsu were going to take over the world. Look, Rorion had been in California since the late 70s and all he taught was jiu-jitsu, right? Carlson was the guy that kept hammering it into everyone's heads that they had to bring vale-tudo back, they had to introduce it to the world, that it would grow. And because he was the most experienced fighter and coach in the whole family, everyone listened and respected him a lot. Rorion too. Why do you think he invited Carlson over for that UFC? It was to acknowledge the execution of his dream and pay him homage. That the stage for his roosters to fight in had finally been created. Even if they never liked to admit it, deep down, they all respected and admired Carlson, he was an idol to the family so everyone listened and respected him. When they had those meetings about forming a bigger jiu-jitsu league in the early 90s, many members from the family were there. Carlson would talk about bringing vale-tudo back to promote jiu-jitsu to the world and the idea eventually reached Rorion who organized the UFC in 1993.

8- What about the foundation of CBJJ by his brother Carlinhos?

Same thing, during those meetings, they were all talking about organizing jiu-jitsu. The FJJRio [former Guanabara] was only on paper, they barely did anything. Carlson loved competition, he was addicted to it. Without a doubt he was the idealist behind all this. No one dreamed of a bigger stage for jiu-jitsu and vale-tudo more than Carlson did.

Some people thought he was crazy and a dreamer, they saw jiu-jitsu only as a hobby. It was after these meetings that Dedé [Andre Pederneiras] began to organize a National Championship in Rio in 1993. But he couldn't handle the political pressure so the following year, Carlinhos founded the CBJJ. I know all this because I used to be an intern at the Museu da Image e do Som [Sound and Image Museum] where one of these meetings took place. And they needed a neutral place to meet because no one would agree to meet at the other one's academy. Carlson spoke of 3 things in that meeting: a fighter's union, a new jiu-jitsu federation and bringing vale-tudo back. Carlinhos [Gracie], Gordo [Roberto Correa], Murilo [Bustamante], Dedé, Jacaré [Romero], Fábio [Gurgel]. They were all there.[233]

9- Can you talk a little more about his views for organizing jiu-jitsu and what this organizing ought to look like?

Carlson had a very philanthropic view on things. So much so that he was the first one in the family to open jiu-jitsu up for people who couldn't afford it. He was in favor of federations as they are in all other sports as in non-profits, rather than private and without any financial accountability. To him, a federation should be an estate of sorts, belonging to the sport and all the athletes. Today the pay is all disproportionate. Carlson defended something more balanced, he had vision for unions and other devices to organize jiu-jitsu in a way where things weren't so centralized, he wanted something more philanthropic. I can't say he wanted to organize jiu-jitsu himself, he just didn't want to be hands-on organizing the day to day things, he wanted to be the mentor of his vision. He definitely wanted jiu-jitsu in a higher place, he wanted things to be done for jiu-jitsu and not for money. Jiu-jitsu to him wasn't professional, it was personal. He saw things that way, he was jiu-jitsu and jiu-jitsu was him.

---

[233] Worthy of note here is that in 1994, Carlson founded an organization called "Liga Carioca de Jiu-Jitsu." The organization and its events never took off. See appendix for certificate.

10- I know this is a delicate topic, but what do you think happened between Carlson and the BTT guys? It seems like such a tragic ending to such a beautiful story.

I think that the world's expectation toward those guys was that they would do what they were trained to do, be Carlson's black-belts and to never let go of the office of being Carlson's lions. But this division of teams, in practice, is impossible. Because they wouldn't exist without Carlson and vice-versa, it is in their DNA. It is their fighting identity, even if they abandoned the office of being Carlson's lions, they can't abandon who they are, it is in their DNA.

11- Carlson Jr. told us that his father died of grief. It is such a sad ending for a man who, in my view at least, might have been the most important figure in the history of BJJ and MMA. If there is someone in this whole story who deserved to die with a smile on his face it was Carlson. What do you think happened at the end there?

I think Carlson was the best, look at what he did. Who can say that they won as much as he did, fought the tough guys he fought and coached the best fighters in both jiu-jitsu and MMA from his era? Who can say that? No one. As for the grief, even his black-belts knew that and would say it. Maybe some of them thought that if they all got together that Carlson would give in and agree to their terms, that they could tame a lion like him. But not even all of them together could tame that beast, they could never. Because Carlson wasn't like that, he was a rebel by nature, in a good sense, he had that restlessness that is typical of great heroes, get it? He would stand his ground, untamable and that was the best thing about him, it was his essence. He was the king of the jungle, the lion king. But you are right, he didn't die happy, with a smile on his face as he deserved and as it befitted his nature. He was a happy person, optimistic, he had always been that way, all the way to the end of his team in Rio. After that, he lost all his optimism and died a very sad person. In cold terms, it ended a verbal agreement they had where he taught them for free his whole life, not just class, he gave his life to his students and when it came time for him to receive something for his efforts, he felt underappreciated by everyone.

12- Having been in the MMA fight scene for most of my adult life, I have to admit, despite all my admiration for Carlson, that 20% of a fighter's purse is a very high sum for any trainer, most guys in the industry get paid 5% or 10% if they are lucky. Although on the other hand it is understandable considering he spent his life training so many people for free. But at the same time, I think it was exactly this that allowed Carlson to create such high expectations for his guys. What do you think?

Listen, Carlson made his stand on 20% because he already had been swindled twice on these contracts before. I was there for both these times. One day Carlson showed up at my house with someone and asked for all the documents, all contracts and bank deposits that these events were making. And that was when he figured things out. Because what were some of them doing? The events would have a contract, with the purses written on there and after the fight they would deposit the money. And because some of the fighters didn't want to pay the full 20%, some of these guys would do this: tell Carlson that they were making less than they were and then give Carlson 20% of that fabricated amount. People had been doing that for years when Carlson found out, because he never had anything written down, it was all based on trust. But what had been agreed on, wasn't being honored. You also need to remember that Carlson himself came from an era when fighters did not get to keep any of their prize money to fight, they fought for honor. For him to invert that situation and get only 20% of their purse was already very generous. Plus, for his standards, for the amount of his knowledge, and for what he had dedicated and given for free... I mean, we aren't talking about three months of free work here, we are talking about over three decades of teaching. Add that up. When Carlson found out about all this, that was when he became unmovable in that contract that no one wanted to sign. The truth of the matter is that Carlson did have his reasons. When part of the team came back with "if you want 20%, you have to come back to Brazil to train us," *in my view, they were the ones being unmovable. As far as him living in Chicago and coaching his fighters from Rio, let´s be realistic: he would continue to go to Rio often enough to train them, as well as lead the fight camps in Chicago or anywhere else, as well as being there for the actual coaching during the fights. That was already being done, accepted, and enough to justify his purse. He had already developed and donated all the knowledge to them for decades. Carlson was right in standing his ground because he had been fooled before. Twice we caught this on paper, but the other times where this might have also happened, we don't know of, we have no proof, too much time had gone by. I'm not saying that everyone did this, but everyone knows that this is what was happening. Another point was, why do you think Carlson wanted to keep all the documents at my house? Because Carlson was convinced that they were disappearing from the gym, that's why. So, when he asked me to help him get to the bottom of this matter, we only had recent contracts and paperwork, the old ones had all disappeared, so there's that too. In other words, their stance on Carlson having to move back to Brazil to train them was something that they could have perhaps worked around. Carlson's stance on the other, was unmovable and rightly so. He couldn't retreat on that stance because of what had happened. As I see it, they could have worked around the situation when considering the whole picture, having been so much younger, for being in the majority. When we take the whole picture into consideration, it fell on them to work around the situation. Carlson couldn't do more than he had already done... he was almost 70 years old when this was happening.*

13- When was the last time you spoke to him? Do you remember what you two talked about and how he was feeling?

We'd speak every week, at least twice a week for about an hour at a time, not just me but he had the habit of regularly calling some other people close to him as well. We'd laugh and talk about the most various topics, really, just about anything you can imagine. But no matter what, all our talks always ended with him being very angry, really pissed because of what happened. On his last call, before he was hospitalized, he didn't say a word about his health to me, not a single word. He had the habit of underestimating health issues too, he would never complain of being sick for example. All he felt was grief, pretty much every conversation involved this perplexity he felt in relation to his black-belts. This while everyone tried to console him, for years and years, we all tried, but there was no way, he was unmoved by any attempts at pulling him out of that place of denial. This is something that stayed with everyone who was near him toward the end, he imprinted that in our minds forever. To this day I can still hear the echoes of him complaining because it was something he did daily.

14- Do you think Carlson's history has been underappreciated?

Yes, absolutely. Firstly, because Brazil does not have a tradition of preserving cultural heritage. It is a country that in cultural terms has always been and remains colonized. Secondly, because Carlson was responsible for many good movements in BJJ and vale-tudo if you take into consideration that the understanding of jiu-jitsu that people have today was a product of his mind. He was the one who injected so much into the sport when it took form in the 90s. This explains that explosion in Rio that echoed in a spiral to the whole world. It was his energy, his belief, his view and his knowledge that raised the bar for the other teams to follow and conquer the world.

Marcelo Alonso (continued from Part 2)

"But in that moment, if [Carlson] had had a little more flexibility this wouldn't have happened. Those guys did not want to leave Carlson. I was there when Libório cried, Murilo was really upset too (...) Carlson lacked the ability to navigate the changing times as things were becoming more professional"

Marcelo Alonso

1- When Carlson's cousin Royce came out victorious in the first UFC, what was Carlson's reaction?

It was something very curious. The rivalry between Helio Gracie and Carlson came from a distant era. Watching Royce win had the opposite effect one would expect. Instead of being a climate of celebration, it became a climate of exactly what he had been telling his students all along. Basically, wondering how Royce was up there instead of one of his guys. It wasn't a climate of "awesome, my cousin won!" Never. To the contrary, Carlson deep down was always like "it is us versus them." This was clear to me. On the other hand, Rorion brings Carlson over to help Royce later.

2- And how did Carlson react to the foundation of the CBJJ [later IBJJF] in 1994?

Carlinhos was brilliant in that moment. You need to understand the family's internal dynamics. Carlinhos was a much younger brother to Carlson, who just wasn't respected. Up to then, he was a no one inside the family. He wasn't a respected champion like Carlson was and nobody ever expected Carlinhos to grow into so much political power. Robson [Gracie] was the president of the State federation and was older than Carlinhos too. But Carlinhos came in unexpectedly and started a much bigger and nationwide organization, having the political tact to unite everyone, get it? And Carlson, in reality, was a weak link in these developments. His bellicose spirit of constantly pitching people against one another and being so combative at tournaments was very divisive and was not what jiu-jitsu needed then. Carlinhos was the guy who had the vision and common sense to unite everyone and began to bring Carlson near him and the CBJJ tournaments. At first Carlson wasn't too happy about this, he'd get mad. But slowly, Carlinhos brought him in. There is even a funny story where Carlinhos was absolutely brilliant. He thought, "who better than Carlson to be head of security? I'm going to pay Carlson to be head of security for the World Championships [Mundial] and I'll solve half my problems in one single stroke." *This was in 1998 I think, when Saulo [Ribeiro] defeated [Fabio] Gurgel. Carlson as head of security was truly hilarious. At some point that day he went and grabbed Saulo by his pants [laughs] I had a lot of fun watching all this. It was a genius move by Carlinhos, he gave Carlson just enough to shut him up, keep him happy and be supportive at the same time.*

3- How did you see the departure of Carlson's main students to form Brazilian Top Team?

I was in the eye of the hurricane when this was all happening. Carlson you know, he was great in all but he could be fiercely stubborn too. Was it true that he never charged students? Yes. Was he giving with his money? Yes. But in that moment, if he had had a little more flexibility this wouldn't have happened. Those guys did not want to leave Carlson. I was there when Libório cried, Murilo was really upset too. To summarize, there were many students that were never really part of the core of the team that were influencing Carlson because they knew that if the big names left, they would automatically move up the ranks. Carlson lacked the ability to navigate the changing times as things were becoming more professional. Also, during a moment where he was living in the USA and distanced himself from his headquarters gym in Rio. It was a moment where Carlson should have accepted less because he was no longer there, he could have accepted a smaller fee and let those guys run the business for him in Rio. When Carlson finally put himself together, he was so full of anger in all this and came up with an ultimatum "you will all have to sign this contract for 20% or you're out!" *And it really wasn't the right moment for that. But of course, that's a view from someone who didn't live the daily routine in the academy when Carlson formed all those guys from white to black-belt. Perhaps those guys were a bit stubborn too and were fed up with Carlson as well. I was there and saw the whole thing and frankly, the situation was much more complex than it seems. That's why I get bothered when I hear people simply call those guys traitors. It was an unfortunate situation where communication wasn't great and things could perhaps have been avoided if everyone cooled down a bit. It was really sad to see Carlson so unhappy and living his last 6 years only to* "avenge against the creontes." *I have no doubt that this resentment killed him little by little. In 30 years working as a martial arts journalist this is one of the most upsetting moments of my life. Especially because I remained so close to both sides in the following years. Having seen up close Carlson being consumed by sadness due to what he considered the greatest treason by the students he loved so much and on the other hand, watching all those dissidents continue to love their master unconditionally, remembering him and telling stories of him, all their conquests together, every trip, every meeting with friends. The love those guys had for Carlson is something so genuine that I am sure that if they could go back in time, they would give Carlson what he wanted. Truly a shame what happened.*

Chapter 24

Carlson... Truly as
Real as it Gets

Carlson and his army. From left to right standing:
Pinduka, Vitor Belfort, Carlson, Carlão Barreto,
Bustamante, Zé Mario. Knees: Libório, Bebeo,
Amaury Bitetti and Marcelo "Playmobil".
Photocred: Fernando Pinduka.

*"Carlson was different, something about him wasn't quite right, and I
say this in a good way. Let's put it this way, he was a singular individual. When we went out to eat, he absolutely had to pay for everyone. He
was too giving of a person, I think that that is what made him so easy
to love. He never had any idea of his own greatness, he never acted that
way. In some ways he was like a 10-year-old child, all while being a
brute when it came to fighting and being a coach. These two sides were
well balanced in Carlson."*

Paulo Filho

Evolution is much less a product of individual genius than it is the
result of the problems brought forth by competition and the need to

solve them under pressure. Since a genius without problems is nothing but a promise. As for the execution of the promise, it requires more than genetic luck to sharpen itself, it requires resistance, struggle, war... or, in jiu-jitsu lingo, it requires *porrada*.

As the saying goes, *a chain is only as strong as its weakest link...* and the same can be said about any environment with its eyes set on performance. With this in mind, for the individual to be strong the group must also be strong. And how do we foster an environment that is optimal for evolution? Simple. Carlson had the answer: *"Se quiser ser um leão, você tem que treinar com leões"* (If you want to be a lion, you must train with lions). That is the coach's ultimate struggle, to keep the room hot for long periods of time in order to ensure that iron continues to sharpen iron so evolution can take place. The rest is only a matter of time, space and numbers.

In case the reader agrees with me that the formula above is what a group needs in order to excel, then I am correct in calling Carlson a revolutionary coach. Because in terms of the criteria outlined above, no one did more than Carlson. Nonetheless, perhaps what makes Carlson even more endearing to us is that he did all this with a complete disregard for money, notoriety, political power, race, class or surname.[234] All this while sporting infinite levels of courage, passion, commitment and charisma.

According to all those who knew him well, off the mats Carlson was the cool Uncle everyone wanted to be around for a good laugh. A bit of a womanizer (a trait he undoubtedly learned from his father and Uncle if not for simply being Brazilian), lover of music and a fanatic about cock-fighting and soccer. Carlson was in many ways your typical Carioca. What wasn't typical about him in the least was that not only could he fight, but that he made a life commitment

---

[234] To be clear, I am not glorifying financial martyrdom. I only stress Carlson's disregard for money in order to highlight his obsession with jiu-jitsu and competition as ends in themselves. Regardless of any potential rewards.

to the evolution of jiu-jitsu above his own well-being and financial future.[235]

To be fair, and according to all accounts, Carlson was uniquely awful with managing his own personal finances. A fact reflected on his borderline refusal to charge his students for a membership. But why did he do this? *Why would he prioritize his students above his own financial security?* My guess is that he valued being close to those he loved and keeping his mats competitive more than he valued money. If letting the warriors train for free was the price to be paid to keep the room highly competitive, then so be it. Anything for jiu-jitsu.

Carlson's way of thinking and being were much like his jiu-jitsu. They were simple, pure, to the point and *firula* free. Having no grand vision for himself beyond teaching jiu-jitsu, he was freer to be himself and bypass all the pretense and posturing from those who so eagerly aspire to project themselves socially, financially and politically.

His love for jiu-jitsu, competition and results were what set him apart from others and what made him the central figure in the history of BJJ. Nobody did a greater job of embodying, in terms of personality or methodology, the brand of jiu-jitsu that captivated the world than Carlson did. Not surprisingly perhaps, since the brand had been modeled after his own personality, methods and aspirations:

> *"When he opened his gym, he began to print the Carlson way of being into his teaching of jiu-jitsu. He subverted the order of things in jiu-jitsu. Whereas before the interest was aimed at teaching those who had financial means to pay, Carlson*

---

[235] Once, 2x Absolute IBJJF World Champion Rodrigo "Comprido," told me that, shortly before Carlson's death, they were making friendly conversation at a tournament in Chicago. Comprido, who had recently acquired an apartment in Rio, decided to share the good news with Carlson. Comprido told me of Carlson's silent and reflective reaction to this news. Carlson, the eldest son of the founder of the Gracie dynasty, the man who alone and inside the ring carried the family's name on his back for over a decade and who is arguably the most successful coach in the history of both BJJ and MMA, went onto confide to Comprido that even in advanced age, he had never owned an apartment.

put money as a third priority. Above all, he wanted to train champions."[236]

A commitment that certainly didn't come without its costs. He showed his "roosters" the sort of disinterested commitment that I have no doubts were exploited by many of them. Perhaps he was even a bit naïve in regards to his blind faith in human reciprocity. Carlson was like that throughout his life, and when it came to teaching, he remained selfless to the fullest even if it was to his own detriment during his final years.

On the other hand, his big heart and reputation made him a unique figure in jiu-jitsu circles. Few were left untouched by his immense heart and fewer still can say that they were as loved and respected. Even his opponents paid the man the respect he earned during the course of a life in the vanguard. Not simply commanding the troops, or leading from afar, but leading them in battle and by example and against the greatest challenges available to him during his prime. All while exulting those brave enough to follow him and continue to carry forward the banner and its call to arms.

Yet, even the fiercest of warriors have their weaknesses and their limits and considering I only met Carlson once (briefly) I can't comment with any authority. Nonetheless, I think I know his biography well enough to assert that his main weakness was having a heart too big for a world too cunning to pay him back in kind. As for his limits, he reached them when the grief he felt over losing his roosters took hold of him. It is one thing to fight the monster that was Ivan Gomes, it is a very different matter altogether to lose overnight the army you spent a life training.

The diaspora of Carlson Gracie's team is a controversial topic and I am nowhere near the most qualified person to comment on it. For that, I reached out to the people whom I felt were best qualified to give a more informed take on the matter. What seems obvious to me was that Carlson was loving, but also fiercely stubborn and set in his ways. Also, while he

---

[236] Marcelo Alonso: *"Carlson Gracie – Reportagem – Sensei SporTV – 2009"* https://www. youtube.com/watch?v=JOWeCDAoi7Q

was unquestionably giving, his expectations that others ought to meet his high-standards (on and off the mats) and be as giving as he was strikes me as naïve.

Having inhabited the MMA ecosystem for my entire adult life, I speak from experience when I say that 20% of a fighter's purse is off market value.[237] With that said, I am not Carlson, nor did I lead the evolution of competitive jiu-jitsu through the 60s, 70s, 80s and early 90s in Brazil. I also didn't train hundreds of people for free during decades, nor did I train the largest army of MMA fighters (from small regional tournaments all the way to modern colosseums) the world is yet to see.

When all of the above is considered and bearing in mind his advanced age, 20% seems less unrealistic. Conversely, demanding a percentage that is so unusual in MMA while simultaneously expecting your students to travel to Chicago from Rio to be trained by you, makes Carlson's stance more difficult to defend. With that said, no matter how I think this over, I can't help but think that guys like Bustamante (whom I consider to be a reference in the art as well as a sensible man) were not wrong either. No one was "wrong." It was a simply an unfortunate sequence of events.

From a safe (and perhaps ignorant) distance, it seems clear to me that the combination between Carlson moving to the USA and poor communication was what led to the rift. It was an ill-fated and tragic end to what I consider to be one of the greatest episodes in the history of jiu-jitsu.

One can only wonder, but it is my view that had Carlson remained in Rio it is unlikely that even the financial promises of the burgeoning MMA scene would have severed the relationship he had with his troops. As we know, the only thing that can break a frontline of warriors is the distance between its members.

---

[237] Speaking for myself and having trained more than a few fighters winning hefty purses for their fights, I was content (and surprised) whenever I received 5% of their prize money.

Chapter 25

The Tragic End of a Hero

Carlson throws a right hand at Waldemar who
changes levels. Photocred: Agência O Globo.

*"Carlson was a very unique human and I will always remember him
that way. But his end was very sad."*

Grandmaster Antonio Carlos Rosado

In February 2006, after a life dedicated to jiu-jitsu and its evolution,
Carlson drew his final breath. The official cause of death was heart failure. The true cause we all know to have been a different one: Carslon was
tired and in grief. After a life in the ring, teaching and giving himself to

jiu-jitsu and *vale-tudo*, his body finally gave in. As it turns out, even the heart of a great man has its limits.[238]

Despite his centrality to the history of jiu-jitsu, his memory is at risk of being buried one day along his remaining students. While Carlson may not have left a legacy of many children or an empire to be passed down to them, he left us something else, something of much greater worth.

To all his "roosters," he left the recipe for what we now refer to as *"Brazilian Jiu-Jitsu"* but could just as well be called *"Carlson Gracie Jiu-Jitsu."* Not because he invented a martial art (no one did, not Kano, not Carlos, not Helio, not Carlson), but because the lead role in carving the space for the brand of jiu-jitsu we all practice today to even exist, in technical and cultural terms, was his. That legacy, even if unacknowledged by a highly politicized jiu-jitsu community (whose financial success tends to further politicize it), lives on through all of us, every time we welcome a friend or family member into jiu-jitsu and incite them to roll with us at our local academy, *"galo contra galo"* (rooster vs. rooster).

In some ways, I think of Carlson as a figure transcending his own family name in a way that no other Gracie can. Carlos *is* Gracie, Helio *is* Gracie, Royce *is* Gracie. Carlson is, well... *Carlson is Carlson.* His accomplishments stand on their own and do not require a strong family name with a firm and long tradition to be well placed at the center of BJJ history. His merits speak for themselves, and if up to recently it has not seemed that way, then it is only due to our misguided perception of a very poorly told history. Because again, despite the facts of the matter, *the role of marketing has always been a stronger force in human affairs than the role of merit.* As the saying goes, *it is what it is.* The human experience is inextricably bound to our political, social and financial standing. That will never change.

---

[238] Jorge Pereira and Carlson Jr. comment respectively: *"He died out of distaste. That's what no one talks about;"* and *"He was very upset. He got to a point of sadness that is hard to explain. The sorrow he felt was a very deep one. The truth is, he never forgave anyone."* See: *"Jorge Pereira Fala do Sentimento de Mágoa e Desgosto que o GM Carlson Carregou até a Morte!!"* https://www.youtube.com/watch?v=I2MU89W3Qhw ; and *"Filho de Carlson fala de mágoa que o consumiu nos últimos anos de vida."* https://www.youtube.com/watch?v=T8fY9s1Ja4s

Unsurprisingly, those who *control the present, control the past, while those who control the past, control the future.* It is unfortunate, but when it comes to people's understandings of events and history, narratives matter more than facts do.

Luckily for those who care, the facts remain, recorded in time, proving the nay-sayers wrong with a straight and consistent record: Carlson fought the best pool of fighters available to him in his prime, trained the best jiu-jitsu and *vale-tudo* fighters during his era, does not have a single street-fight on his record, was loved and respected by all, and perhaps what makes him even more endearing, he had a heart of gold, *can anyone from the first, second, third or fourth-wave comfortably say that they have accomplished more than Carlson as a fighter and coach? In either BJJ or MMA?* Certainly no one I can think of.

Moreover, he never busied himself with self-promotion or marketing in order to create a legacy for himself. His efforts and passion lay elsewhere, in training champions and beginning the process of setting the foundation for the spread of jiu-jitsu around the world. On top of all this, Carlson was a giving person. When it came to jiu-jitsu, it was clear where his priorities were.

Carlson's financial generosity is well known. According to himself in the testimony he gave his sister Reila in her book, all his purse money from his fight career was always given to his family.[239] To add insult to injury, when his father Carlos passed, his siblings kept the inheritance. Could all these events combined perhaps help explain his distancing from the rest of his family and his bitterness toward his former students later in life? I think so.

The relationship with his family was always a complicated one. His willingness (indeed, eagerness) to teach anyone the secrets of "real jiu-jitsu" left a bad taste in the mouth of an entire generation of Gracies who didn't quite understand what they (erroneously) perceived as a lack of loyalty to the family name. Yet here lies another reason why Carlson

---

[239] *"It was always that way. Out of 50 thousand dollars, I'd keep one."* See: Gracie, 2008 pg. 371.

stands out in this history: What we need to understand is that Carlson's loyalty was never to fame, money or even his family's name. *Above all, Carlson's allegiance was always to jiu-jitsu and its evolution.*

In some ways, he really does stand outside his own family, doing things his own way long enough to prove, through results, that his methods were indeed superior. Eventually, almost everyone conceded that Carlson had been right all along, even if they refused to acknowledge it publicly and found it more politically convenient to grant Rolls the credit instead. Even if for that to happen, they had to ignore that it was Rolls who sought Carlson and his roosters out, because he was competitive and intelligent enough to understand that the only path to high-performance is through high-level competition.

Which is not to discredit the efforts of others. Still, rank is rank, it exists it is real and it ought to be acknowledged and respected in a truthful manner. Not for reasons of personality-cult or adulation but to remind ourselves and those who we are responsible for teaching of this rank and of the qualities that we must nurture if we are to remain in a state of personal growth.

All these characters matter and have their place in this history. But what made jiu-jitsu and *vale-tudo* special to millions of people around the world wasn't vision, ambition, obsessively strong leaders, or even Herculean marketing efforts (although these were all vital in getting us this far). We all fell in love with jiu-jitsu because it *worked* inside a cage and because Carlson proved to the martial arts world that we could all be *casca-grossas* while simultaneously smiling and laughing at every opportunity.

So why isn't Carlson's remembered as one of the founding pillars of both BJJ and *vale-tudo*? Simple, marketing, or more precisely, *lack of marketing*. Carlson never had a Rorion to handle his publicity. This coupled with the highly politicized environment jiu-jitsu grew out of from the south-zone and into the world where most of those who had held the historical pen saw Carlson as their opposition. Electing to promote and favor their own lineages instead. All while ignoring that the father of the competitive brand of jiu-jitsu that most of us practice today, is Carlson, not Rolls.[240]

On another note, I am fully aware that this book brings up and questions the sensitive topic that is jiu-jitsu's hierarchy, *who is the patriarch of jiu-jitsu in Brazil?* Carlos? Helio? Carlson? Lineages are arbitrary, no matter how we choose to organize them. Carlos was undoubtedly the inception point in the divorce of jiu-jitsu from the judo matrix. While his younger brother Helio was the indispensible political leader jiu-jitsu needed during a specific era. Especially at a time when their practice was under serious threat of being either reabsorbed back into judo or of dying, still as an embryo of what one day it had the potential to become.

Despite Helio being a vital piece in this history, could it be that the same stubbornness that made him the iconic figure squaring up against the rise of judo in the 40s, 50s and 60s in Brazil, was a problem later on?[241] Namely that, had it not been for Carlson democratization, that Helio's orthodoxy and reluctance to sufficiently open jiu-jitsu up and delegate would have kept jiu-jitsu without an outlet for evolution?[242] Could the jiu-jitsu taught as private lessons at the original Gracie Academy have conquered the world as the one that Carlson taught at the Figueiredo Academy did? The consistency of team results throughout the life of the Guanabara Federation as well as how most of us practice jiu-jitsu today seem to answer both these questions.

---

[240] Interestingly, and perhaps revealing of the depth of the influence of jiu-jitsu politics shaping its history, no one seems to have a problem giving Bob Anderson (the wrestler) or Oswaldo Alves (the judoka), credit for having influenced Rolls' jiu-jitsu. Despite Bob only having spent a few weeks with Rolls in Rio and the extent of his apprenticeship in judo being unclear. Yet when it comes to the far more significant role played by Carlson in influencing Rolls, we get almost absolute silence. Perhaps the silence itself tells us everything we need to learn about the depth of political leanings contaminating history.

[241] In regards to Rolls seeking knowledge from other styles at least, Carlinhos Gracie claims that Helio was completely against it. See: Drysdale 2020, pg. 71.

[242] Worth mentioning here, is that Kano had similar concerns regarding the spread of techniques beyond the control of the Kodokan. Beginning in 1882, Kano required his students to make promises signed in blood. In the oath, the promise not to reveal or instruct the secrets of judo without authorization. See: Pedreira 2018, pg. 108-109.

What Helio and Carlson had in common was that they both wanted and expected diehard loyalty. Where the two generals differed was in terms of their approach to teaching, who they taught and why they taught them. Whereas Helio ruled by exercising the sort of authority that established respect, Carlson did so by showing the love that earned him respect. Not surprisingly, such different personalities, methodologies and worldviews led to very different results.

These were the vital differences between the two and the reason why I believe that Carlson, ultimately, was the victor in their civil war. Because at the end of the day, it was his view of *what jiu-jitsu is* that held the greater appeal to the world. Acknowledged or not.

It was Machiavelli who famously remarked that it is better to be feared *and* loved but, if one had to choose between the two, that *it is better to be feared than to be loved*, for love vanishes sooner than fear. And while I share with Machiavelli the cynical life experience that inclines me to think that he was right, in Carlson's final victory, I find a thread of hope that perhaps he wasn't.

PART 4

The Fourth-Wave and The Internet Era (2007-Present)

"This view of jiu-jitsu as a business, and everyone thinking only of making money and making jiu-jitsu for everyone really changed jiu-jitsu a lot. In some ways for the better, in others not so much."

Grandmaster Orlando Saraiva

Chapter 26

The Rise and Fall of
Jiu-Jitsu in MMA

"The whole thing became too soft in my opinion. And these guys want to get into the Olympics? What Olympics man? Forget that. Every fighting style has its own essence, Kano wanted 'the way,' the polite, the Olympic, you see... But that's not us."

Master Otávio Peixotinho

On November 11th, 1993, a lean and non-threatening Brazilian man sent shock waves through the martial arts world. He did this by reviving a style of combat that had largely disappeared from the minds of movie enthusiasts and martial artists around the world. It was a revival, because there was nothing new about it. Submission-grappling had never been really dead. It had survived in the West in pro-wrestling as well as in other arts such as judo and wrestling. It was just that few looked at grappling as being akin to something efficient for real-fighting. So why was Royce Gracie's performances in 1993 such a mental jolt? If submission-grappling and its efficiency had never really left the world stage, why the shock?

The issue was that between Hollywood movies and comic books, the popular understanding of what a real fight looked like was framed by the need to sell movies, comics or tickets. It wasn't the first or last time this has happened, but reality would have to take a backseat to entertainment and ticket sales, at least for the time being.

After Royce brought reality back to the center-stage, fighting, real-fighting would never be the same and for a minute, what the world was calling Gracie or Brazilian jiu-jitsu seemed invincible. Of course, the minute was only that, a short-lived moment of invincibility because it didn't take long for wrestlers to learn how to defend an armbar or a triangle and for strikers to learn how to sprawl and stand back-up with or without the fence. The co-evolutionary arms-race had leveled the playing field and the dominance of jiu-jitsu's representatives in the cages of the world had become merely a distant and nostalgic memory.

Nostalgic for some at least, mostly the old-timers who liked the idea of practicing combat as realistically as possible and knowing how to win in a real situation. That generation would have welcomed absorbing new tricks to keep up in the arms-race that cage-fighting had become. But the jiu-jitsu practitioners from younger generations, the ones that would have been responsible for remaining faithful to a more realistic evolutionary track, simply don't care about reality. They are perfectly happy practicing jiu-jitsu for what it was becoming: fun, sportive, entertaining and trendy. An attitude that was essentially a farewell decree to the days where jiu-jitsu seemed invincible. A reality we would all have to come to terms with, including those who cared and those who cared so little that they didn't even notice the decline.

So, what of jiu-jitsu in MMA today? Is it dead like some claim? Is there no more room for an almost absolute domination like in the old days? I'll begin by stating the obvious: no one other than the most dogmatic and fanatical has ever suggested that grappling ought to stand alone in a fight. A strategy that might have worked in the past (as well as help promote jiu-jitsu), but times were changing quickly and it didn't take much to get left behind.

Carlson Gracie understood and tackled this problem well before jiu-jitsu lost its supremacy in the cage and well before his cousin Royce was shining in one. To him, the assimilation of anything that worked was a given, fittingly, he made sure his students learned it. Some, like Vitor Belfort for example, even became known for their boxing rather than for jiu-jitsu.

Had Carlson's open-minded and reality oriented vision been the dominant force in jiu-jitsu's evolution, things might have turned out differently. But that wasn't the case, the dominant force was shifting from Carlson's *vale-tudo* oriented views toward a new standard definition of *what jiu-jitsu is*. The sport-oriented practice quickly became the dominant definition of jiu-jitsu, overwhelming the reality leaning one. From then onward, *who cared if jiu-jitsu won in a cage or not?*

Another obvious factor is that it wasn't grappling in MMA that was dead, but rather the shift of focus in the kind of jiu-jitsu that was combat-oriented toward one that was geared toward a practice for the masses, something MMA was unlikely to accomplish due to its gruesome nature. Which isn't a new problem... If you want big numbers, you will have to water down the product to reach the greatest number of practitioners possible. And so, it went with jiu-jitsu, as it slowly lost exactly what had set it apart from other arts while it gained the commercial prominence it enjoys today. A prestige that was essentially built upon the back of this more Spartan like approach to combat which was now being neglected by the commercial demands of its growth and popularization.

Dominance in a cage through grappling had never been dead; however, it was no longer exclusive to jiu-jitsu. Wrestlers, became the best representatives of grappling in MMA. In fact, one could easily argue that they have become the dominant force in MMA today.[243] The Dagestani Khabib Nurmagomedov being the best example of this dominance, with an astounding record of 29-0. The times have changed jiu-jitsu, which facilitated the displacement of its representatives as the most dominant grapplers in MMA. These days, that role belongs to wrestlers, our old-time rivals. So where does jiu-jitsu stand in all this today?

The reality is that jiu-jitsu survives in MMA less through the hands of those who officially represent it and more through the hands of those who borrow from it. A good example of this is Khabib's last victory in the UFC over Justin Gaethje via mounted triangle. A move that is ille-

---

[243] Although to be fair, the fact that the UFC is an American organization may help explain the larger number of American fighters. Keeping in mind that wrestling in the USA has a pool of young and competitive talent to pull from that is infinitely greater than in any other martial art it competes with. Which makes their dominance in MMA, less surprising.

gal in both sambo and wrestling, the styles which Khabib traces back his foundation as a fighter (that and wrestling bear cubs as a child of course...).[244]

Other fighters absorbed from jiu-jitsu instructors that which their style's arsenal did not offer them. All without losing their foundation. A combination that has proven to be incredibly successful, particularly for wrestlers. Because in many ways, jiu-jitsu offered wrestlers the tools they were lacked. This basically meant that wrestlers didn't just learn how to defend armbars and triangles coming from their opponent's guard, but they now also knew how to take the back and apply kimuras and guillotines from just about any position. That and whatever else they felt didn't compromise their wrestling foundation of being on top no matter what.

Needless to say that there are exceptions to this. There are still many jiu-jitsu representatives who fare well in MMA. It is just that their numbers dwindle when compared to the overall growth of the art around the world. Which is to say that despite the worldwide growth of jiu-jitsu, this growth is largely centered around the sportive sphere, in which successful competitors can make a comfortable living through jiu-jitsu and without MMA as their only outlet. Today jiu-jitsu practitioners have a bourgeoning professional circuit, online instructionals, schools, private lessons and seminars from which they (we) are all making a comfortable living from. *Vale-tudo* is no longer the only financial option on the table. Therefore, the vast majority of its most competitive representatives go through their careers without even considering MMA as an option. As a result of this, jiu-jitsu became underrepresented in the cages of the world.

This coupled with the evolution of jiu-jitsu in a direction that has less and less to do with the reality of combat, has made jiu-jitsu a bubble

---

[244] While the triangle (or *sankaku-jime*) is known in judo circles and legal in combat-sambo, I find it hard to believe that its mounted version descended from either art. What is more likely to have been the case, is that Khabib over the years became exposed to variations and other possibilities for the triangle that are uncommon in both judo and combat-sambo. The mounted triangle he applied in his last fight is likely influenced by BJJ and the influence it has had in the grappling world since the first UFC.

completely independent from the same *vale-tudo* that launched it into prominence. The results of all this were basically the lack of results inside cages. Hence the accusations that jiu-jitsu is dead. To be fair to the gentle-art, the rules in MMA don't favor it: short rounds, resets on the ground and untrained judges certainly don't help. And by "untrained" I mean exactly that, many MMA judges have no previous fight experience.[245]

For its part, the crowd is generally speaking too uneducated in terms of grappling and favors a knockout over a tight choke, or an exchange of punches over an exchange of grappling sequences. Logically, the organizations as well as the athletic commissions that give structural support to MMA, follow the money and allow the customers and their wants to dictate the future of the art.

However, that's not all, there is also the bias and resentment against jiu-jitsu and its popularity. Primarily coming from wrestlers themselves who, despite being overall better trained athletes and for the most part more dominant in the cage, resent their efforts normally leading to nothing after college (unless they succeed in MMA or as high-school or college coaches, essentially the only financial outlets for retired wrestlers). Conversely, jiu-jitsu coaches, however unsuccessful and incompetent as they may be, have the luxury of opening a school and watching a flood of students walk through their doors with virtually no effort due to the current jiu-jitsu fad.

It is this sort of resentment toward the financial success and growth of jiu-jitsu that leads people to say things like *"jiu-jitsu is dead in MMA."* Ignoring perhaps that the act of defending an armbar or triangle is in itself an act of successful use of jiu-jitsu. Normaly learnt by training with BJJ coaches and practitioners. But there is more.

---

[245] Once a commission judge gave a seminar at Xtreme Couture where I was training at the time. I asked him if a near submission counted as much as a near knockout, a proposition that made him laugh, as he explained to me that even a nice takedown was worth more in the eyes of the judges than a near submission. Despite a near submission, from an objective perspective, being the exact same thing as a knockout in the sense that it almost finishes the fight. Albeit, a near knockout normally has a long-term effect in a fight that a submission rarely has (except in the event of a torn ligament after a near submission for example).

Interestingly, critics of jiu-jitsu often use its representative's inability to win via submission in a fight as the fault of the art. Perhaps ignoring the amount of right hands and left-hooks that are thrown and missed in a fight. Are we to apply the same standard and say that right hands and left-hooks are no longer efficient? Or admit to a double-standard instead? As the saying goes in Brazil, *"pau que bate em Chico, também bate em Francisco..."* (a stick that beats Chico, must also beat Francisco).

There is no doubt that the days when jiu-jitsu was single handedly the largest force in MMA are long gone. Was there any other way? Probably not. As Carlson himself well knew, a fighter needed to be complete in order to qualify for the kind of combat whose name is literally "anything goes." Perhaps the failure, hasn't been of jiu-jitsu after all. Perhaps the greatest failure has been in how jiu-jitsu is seen, taught and trained in the midst of the same popularity that gives it its financial edge over traditional martial arts and wrestling.

Have we become what we once criticized? Have the true to the core strikers and wrestlers remained loyal to the reality of fighting while jiu-jitsu has lost that same reality-oriented spirit it used to represent and which was perhaps best embodied by Carlson's views on jiu-jitsu?

It is a curious feature of this whole discussion that the MMA world has learned more from jiu-jitsu than jiu-jitsu has learned from it. The respect for jiu-jitsu, despite claims to the contrary, is so obvious that few MMA fighters would venture inside a cage without a fundamental understanding of it. What about jiu-jitsu? Does it still watch MMA as closely as MMA fighters are watching and learning jiu-jitsu? I doubt it. Most jiu-jitsu practitioners have completely abandoned their interest in real-combat.

The reasons for the rise and fall of jiu-jitsu in MMA are complex and much of the discussion in this chapter is simplistic and arbitrary. What seems obvious is that by watering down the intensity and the quality of the product (in terms of realism) in order to please commercial demands, jiu-jitsu became a viable financial reality for thousands of instructors like myself. While at the same time steering jiu-jitsu away from what made it special and brought it to prominence in the first place. The days of a jiu-jitsu *"raiz"* might be over, but the days of the *raiz* use of jiu-jitsu are far from over.

Jiu-jitsu, once the most dominant art inside a cage, will survive no matter what. Just not by the hands of its official representatives.

Chapter 27

What Should Guide Jiu-Jitsu's Evolution: Efficient and Simple or Entertaining and Sophisticated?

"[Carlson] *was trying to make the techniques shorter. He was good with his hands but he never wanted to make the techniques too long for vale-tudo purposes. And when you think about it 80% of the jiu-jitsu we learn in the gym we wouldn't use in MMA. Which makes me think that Carlson did have a specific view on this, as if thinking, 'I know I won't use all this, I have fought, I know what I need.' And I think his ring experience led him to say 'hey short! Short! We are not going to use all that!' and looking at it all today, he was right.*"

Master Jean-Jacques Machado

Any martial artist will have no problem coming up with a list of reasons why they train and how their training has benefited them. But at the bottom of it all, if truth be told, the real reason (or at least the most common reason) people begin their training is because they want to learn how to fight efficiently. It is as simple as that.

Sure, there are other motivations that may follow or coexist with this, and may at some point, even become more important than the want or need for self-defense. At any rate, regardless of these overlapping reasons and all the benefits that come along with the effort, if we are going to learn how to fight, we might as well learn how to do it as efficiently as possible and *keep it as real as it can get.*

The revolution ignited by Royce inside the octagon in 1993 was more than a reminder of what reality looked like beyond Hollywood's need to impress, entertain and sell. It was the assurance that from then onward, as long as the UFC existed, the reality of combat would have an arena it could attend. Naturally, others wanted to join in on the revolution and martial arts enthusiasts either conceded that they had been wrong all along, assimilated that which the revolution brought with it or, in some cases, they simply jumped ship and embraced jiu-jitsu's flag. Indeed, BJJ shook the foundations of the combat world.

During mid to late 90s when jiu-jitsu's credibility in terms of the reality of combat was at its height. In time however, wrestling would come to not only rival jiu-jitsu but eventually outdo it in terms of their dominance inside the cage. But how did that happen? How was BJJ growing so rapidly, while simultaneously becoming less and less representative in the cages that jiu-jitsu itself had introduced to the world? And perhaps more importantly, *why did wrestling become the most dominant style in MMA today?*

The brand of jiu-jitsu displayed by Royce inside that cage was designed to control the range, strike to clinch, get the opponent to the ground, control position and strike his way into submitting his opponent. It was the classical method of the Gracie fighting system at its best and at the moment it mattered the most, because if the world wasn't watching yet, it would soon tune in. Simple, elegant and to the point. It was an efficient combination of grappling with strikes that accomplished the goal of placing the spotlight on what had been brewing in Brazil for decades.

Despite the stunning performances, and with all due respect to Royce and the admiration I hold for him as a hero of my youth, the record states clearly that Royce was not the best representative of jiu-jitsu in those days. With the exception of perhaps Royce's brother Rickson, it was obvious that in terms of *vale-tudo* the sharpest tools in the jiu-jitsu shed could be found on the Figueiredo de Magalhães Street, inside Carlson's gym. But why were Carlson's guys so dominant and what was the difference between their approach to Royce's?

Even though both traced their roots back to the original Gracie fighting system, the two systems differed in that thanks to Carlson's experience and obsession for a competitive teaching methodology, he had greatly expanded and improved on their original system. The differences between these two systems weren't small, neither in terms of methodology, skills nor in terms of results. What they did have in common however was their simplicity in terms of approach to combat. In both these methods (Carlson's and the original Gracie fighting system), fighting was about results, not impressing or selling tickets.

Punch or kick your way into the clinch, get the fight to the ground, strike some more, submit. Carlson's methods were different from Royce's methods only that they were evolved in every sense. So much so that as Carlson Jr. observed, when Royce reached his technical limits inside the UFC, it was Carlson's army who stepped up to represent jiu-jitsu against the biggest challenges it had ahead. Which in those days was mainly American wrestling.

Worthy of note here, is that Carlson's team wrote its history on the mats of the Guanabara Federation and their jiu-jitsu tournaments. Throughout this era of evolution of competitive jiu-jitsu, the practice had not yet drifted too far from the reality of a fight. A preference for reality that, despite their civil war and disagreements, Helio and Carlson certainly agreed on.

In between the assurance of jiu-jitsu's leadership that reality remained the cornerstone of their practice, the *confere* with its reminder of what *real* looked like and a tough-love approach to training, jiu-jitsu remained largely grounded (even in a sportive format) in the *reality of combat*. This, while it was safely in the hands of the Gracie family, democratization would change all that.

What followed was a whole new world of possibilities in which evolution meant sophistication. And where the simplicity that had been the hallmark of jiu-jitsu for *vale-tudo* prior to democratization, was left aside by an audience with a preference for novelty and no patience, attention span or discipline, to actually master anything before they moved to the next trend.

Entertainment, coolness, fads, sophistication and *firula* had come to replace the reality, efficiency and simplicity that had been the winning recipe for jiu-jitsu up to recently. The *jiu-jitsusphere* had grown immensely, so much in fact that it no longer needed *vale-tudo* to sustain itself. From its rise in popularity and democratization onward, jiu-jitsu was a universe of its own. Realistic or not.

Who replaced them in the cages of the world? Their long arch-nemesis, wrestling. How did they do this? Simple, they remained *simple.*

The sophistication led by the explosion of new techniques in the 90s and early 2000s brought infinite possibilities and tools to jiu-jitsu's arsenal. So many in fact that students didn't even bother actually mastering any of them. For these students, the act of entertaining themselves watching the novelties was enough. The thirst for "knowledge" was quenched, and now they could move on to the next trend. Forget reality, discipline and performance.

Conversely, while this may have augmented competitive jiu-jitsu in many ways, the change in perception of *what jiu-jitsu is* coupled with the lack of slaps to remind people of what worked and what didn't, set in motion an evolutionary track that continuously drifted away from reality. The outcome, unsurprisingly perhaps, was a decrease in credibility and results inside the cage. This, despite the numbers of practitioners having grown tremendously, the successful representation inside cages has decreased in diametrical opposition to the art's growth in popularity.

Wrestling however kept it simple, grounded in reality and, in some ways was even closer to Carlson's vision (in terms of tough-love values) than what was coming out of the competitive scene in jiu-jitsu during its democratization phase. Even if in terms of the possibilities of what the wrestling ruleset allows for, wrestling happens to be relatively simple in comparison to jiu-jitsu.

By remaining simple, objective, to the point and *firula-free*, wrestling essentially took over the same stage that jiu-jitsu (and the Gracie family in particular) had spent over half a century in Brazil building for themselves. The jungle had a new breed of kings and while its tools might have been remarkably simple, the results speak for themselves. *Was there any other way?*

Sticking to the mark of the reality of combat, simple does not equate easy or inefficient. In fact, at least in terms of fighting, simplicity might be more readily associated with *efficiency* than sophistication is (think the simplicity of boxing and wrestling). Furthermore, simplicity leaves far less room for error. The add-ons, however appealing, create more opportunities for things to go wrong, especially in an environment in which, while you are working on the add-ons, your opponent is raining down strikes on you.

The "center," as I refer to the group of techniques that are at the core of the reality of combat (rear-naked-choke, guillotine, kimura, head-and-arm, triangle, etc), was beginning to share the stage with an excessiveness of trendy add-ons.[246] Who I should say in passing, were often added more to impress and to give an air of novelty in order to sell, then they were to actually improve on jiu-jitsu's overall efficiency.

Of course, the problem is not with complexity itself. Much of this sophistication and evolution set in motion by the expansion of the competitive landscape brought with it many welcome additions that were somewhat sophisticated but still grounded in the reality of combat (the evolution of back-takes, kimura set-ups, arm-triangles and guillotines for example), others not so much (lapel-guards and berimbolos for example). The bigger issue is that complexity, in many ways, has become an end in itself for the average practitioner. Which is to say, the metric to be pursued here isn't whether a move is *old* or *new*, *simple* or *sophisticated*, *cool* or *uncool*. The only valid question is, *does it work in a fight*

My personal preference is that whatever shape jiu-jitsu takes moving forward, it should be steered toward the reality of combat while still evolving in a competitive format. In this sense, the original Gracie self-defense methodology, was limited in that it lacked a competitive arena to

---

[246] On a side note, it would be a mistake to frame these central moves as "old-school" and, hence, inadequate. This is to presume there is no more room for their evolution in case they are set as a priority and that their potential, as of now, are fully explored.

evolve in. Which kept it "original," in the sense that it was deprived of any evolutionary outlet. Competitive jiu-jitsu on the other hand (as it is currently practiced today at least), by not being guided by a more reality-oriented ruleset, is in the hands of competitors instead. Who in turn are leading our practice too far from what would actually work in the streets or in a cage. The solution? Guide the evolution with a ruleset that favors reality, while banning that which drifts from it.[247]

How do we know what is fit for reality and what isn't? I believe the answer to this is quite obvious. We can begin by taking a look back into where we came from in terms of our thinking, back into the beginnings of our own history and, once again, leave entertainment behind in favor of efficiency. Back into pursuing *victory under the trials of reality*. Or, and perhaps less ambitious, by pursuing *victory with our eyes on reality*.

Needless to say, I am only giving voice to my own views here and things won't change anytime soon. Additionally, it goes without saying that people are free to train in anyway they see fit. In the democratic era, there is no such thing as "real jiu-jitsu," only the kind of jiu-jitsu that keeps you coming back to the gym for more. *That is the best jiu-jitsu.*

My concern here is over the issue of jiu-jitsu's credibility in case it moves too far from the reality that set it into prominence and that held it together for so long. My opinions are only a reminder that despite our preferences, we have a long, rich and spectacular history that made efficiency, not entertainment its cornerstone. It was this premise that kept jiu-jitsu cohesive and credible under the direction of the first two waves of jiu-jitsu practitioners led primarily by the Gracie family. From the democratization phase onward, the cornerstone upholding jiu-jitsu

---

[247] Worthy of note here, is that the nature of internet algorithms is to elevate the "cool" for entertainment's sake. This because under this frame, the hierarchy of what is relevant is not established by experience, but rather by the coding of the algorithm that levels all "clicks" and "likes" as equal and doesn't screen for expertise. Which seems harmless on the surface, but has the effect of confusing the student as to where priorities ought to lie while making the coach's job a difficult one. Should the coach submit to the trends and give his customer what he *wants*? Or should he/she stand his/her ground and teach them what they *need* and according to their experience? Even if this approach harms their business? The future and credibility of jiu-jitsu depends on how we address these questions.

seems to be in the hands of what pleases the greatest number of paying customers. Whatever that happens to be that particular week.

Fads and practitioners come and go. But the reality of combat? It is not so capricious and will outlast all trends and eras. As for jiu-jitsu, its integrity, cohesion, longevity and credibility are best served when fads and agents deliberately submit to the certainty of reality.

Chapter 28

The Americanization of Brazilian Jiu-Jitsu by Americans

"...it's all judo" Georges Mehdi in 1999 in regards to judo and jiu-jitsu.[248]

"...it's all jiu-jitsu" Romero *"Jacaré"* Cavalcanti in 2022, in regards to BJJ and AJJ.[249]

The 2019 edition of the ADCC event was unique in the history of jiu-jitsu, but not due to the evolution of competitors and their techniques. Since technical evolution in relation to previous events, isn't an anomaly, but rather the norm in all high-level competition. What was so unusual was that for the first time in the history of jiu-jitsu there was an attempt at creating a rift between practitioners from different countries. The attempt at division was obvious for everyone to see and hear, and what had always been a cohesive effort in the name of jiu-jitsu, was now being crafted into a game of "us" vs. "them."

At some point during the event, a chant began that I have never heard before in any jiu-jitsu event. A small group of people in the stands were chanting *"USA! USA! USA!"* in what to them might have felt like a display of their patriotism, but that in fact left most of the arena stunned. After all, no one in jiu-jitsu had ever heard this before, certainly no one in Brazil or Europe chanted their respective countries during a jiu-jitsu

---

[248] Pedreira 2013, pg. 141

[249] See Romero Cavalcanti interview.

event. Jiu-jitsu up to recently was a gigantic family free of identity politics, ethnicity, nationalism, gender, religion, etc. In fact, it had up to recently always been mostly free of anything that wasn't unifying.

On the mats, the only distinction is that of skill and experience, excluding those two, any other differences have never been an issue of concern to anyone. For most practitioners, jiu-jitsu was "us" (all of jiu-jitsu), vs. "them" (anyone who didn't train jiu-jitsu but who we were trying to bring in). Yet something was changing in the *jiu-jitsusphere*, perhaps as a result of its growth and the inevitable commercialization that followed the growth. Regardless of the motive, the 2019 ADCC showcased this transformation and made it obvious for everyone to see. From then on, there was a coordinated effort to frame jiu-jitsu in terms of "us" vs. "them," from now on, it was *AJJ vs. BJJ*.

While the growing rift might have been noticeable only recently; its wake has been long in the making... In reality, this wasn't even the first time in which personal ambition had recruited nationalism to disguise itself. But what is underneath this disguise? It seems to me that we are witnessing a coordinated effort to split jiu-jitsu. *But why?*

From a young age, it was always apparent to me through interactions with people from the USA and Brazil, that the relationship between the two countries was a hierarchical one. Everything that was American or that came from the USA was automatically superior. It didn't matter that political correctness restrained people from saying this out loud, because the silence did nothing to change the belief in the hierarchy. This order of rank is clear if you look at it closely; one held the superior seat in every way, while the other was somewhat submissive in this relationship. A cultural dominance that Brazilians, for the most part, concede to. Whether Brazilians accept this or not, Brazil is and remains submissive to the USA in cultural terms, if not in geo-political and economic terms as well.

An observation always reinforced whenever I hear Brazilians speak of Americans and of how Americans speak of everything south of the *Rio Grande*. It is also an observation to which I am remitted to whenever I have to explain to perplexed Americans why was it that my parents chose to raise me and my sister in Brazil rather than in the USA, as if wondering, *"why would you trade the best for something subpar?"*

As a child, none of this made any sense, since if the two countries were more or less of the same size (which is how I measured power in those days), why was the relationship so off balanced? Why was it that it was taken for granted that everything made and done in the USA was immediately and scrutiny-free accepted as the "best?" And when America isn't the "best" at something, it was because we didn't care about those sports that others around the world felt were important to them (say, Formula 1 and soccer for example).

It is all as simple as that, *"everything that is American is automatically better"* and as testimony to this obvious truism, we have the efforts of thousands of immigrants from all over the world who desperately want to raise their families here. The riddle is solved, no more questions asked, *"we are number 1,"* case closed.

A point that isn't without its merits. If life in the USA were not on average more convenient, comfortable, and promising than it is in other nations, then how do we explain the mass immigration from these less economically fortunate nations? Though I don't agree with the statement that *"everything that is American is better"* (which I would prefer to rephrase as *"life in the US, in general terms, is better for a lot of people including myself"*) the fact that I choose to live here, speaks volumes about where I consider life to be more promising. Being born in the USA is a privilege that Americans are born into, something all of its citizens ought to be aware of. I know I am.

Yet the ranking paradigm between the USA and the rest of the world, doesn't only affect the relationship and perceptions between both countries and their respective lifestyles. More than this, the rank goes well beyond it and succeeds in establishing itself in parallel to other arenas such as values, habits, know-how, culture and people in general. Which is to say, woven within the fabric of this dynamic was an assertive insistence that with this economic rank between nations, the people that inhabited these lands were framed alongside these other arenas and were also "better" or "worse" according to which country they so happened to be born into.

While it has always been somewhat obvious to me that, in general, we Americans are extremely successful in the sports that matter to us, it is a bit of a stretch to extend this into believing we are always "number one." Even though few are willing to admit in public that this is indeed the case, I vouch that this is in fact the case. That this belief in superiority permeates not only the USA, but the Anglo world in general. Albeit not a belief that is spoken out in the open, but that is rather veiled in attitudes toward this hierarchy and those who belong to it.

In my observations, having spent my entire life between two different cultures and having traveled significant portions of the rest of the world, despite these environments differing dramatically in many ways, people themselves, all peoples, are on average not so different. Some simply try harder, while others have it harder... But on average, I don't believe we are so different.

Nevertheless, the belief and certainty in this rigid hierarchy remains intact. Additionally, the American confidence and sense of a higher-purpose (or "Manifest Destiny") is one of the countries most endearing qualities, but also a major blind-spot. Especially when confidence turns into over-confidence, or even worse, when it sets itself onto the task of reframing reality and facts to suit the pre-established confidence instead of the other way around.

Right about now, you the reader, might be asking what does any of this has to do with jiu-jitsu, or more specifically, with "American jiu-jitsu"? The answer is *everything*. If we pay close attention, there is a common thread between my simplified generalizations of the social-cultural dynamic of the USA and Brazil and the current debate between AJJ and BJJ.

I first became aware of this connection when a friend, over a couple of beers and perhaps forgetting that I had been raised in Brazil, asked me perplexed: *"But how Rob, how can they* [Brazilians] *be so good at jiu-jitsu?"* The question seemed so strange to me that at first it caught me completely off-guard. My immediate answer was what to me remains the only and obvious one, "*people improve in proportion to their efforts and talents.*" Which didn't satisfy my friend in the least. The answer, must lie elsewhere... Or at least that is what I gathered by his reaction to my answer.

It took me a few days to actually digest what my friend had actually meant by his question. Upon reflection, this is what I think his thought process looked like, to him, it was inconceivable that Brazilians were so dominant at something that mattered so much to Americans. Since, unlike Formula 1 and soccer, Americans fell in love with jiu-jitsu, and because it matters to us, *how can we be number two?* To my friend, the number of high-level practitioners coming out of Brazil simply made no sense. The belief in the fixed hierarchy was so ingrained that he couldn't even fathom any answer to his question that didn't fit the pre-established belief.

So how exactly is anyone to explain this to someone who is steadfast in their belief in this fixed hierarchy and for who being number one is a God-given truism? The explanation must lie elsewhere. Perhaps it is because Brazilians take more steroids? Or perhaps there is a conspiracy of referees that are favoring Brazilians. There must be an explanation... But what is it? Anything will do, as long as it can bypass the obvious answer that *being skilled at jiu-jitsu has absolutely nothing to do with nationality or geography* and everything to do with effort, environment and genetic talent.

But in case the cognitive dissonance remains, in other words, if the belief cannot readjust itself to reality, then perhaps doing the opposite might just do the trick, *perhaps it is reality that needs a little tweaking.* If, a) we Americans fell in love with jiu-jitsu; and b) we Americans are better at everything that matters to us, then the high-proportion of Brazilians winning tournaments needs to be addressed differently. *Enter American jiu-jitsu.*

I first heard the term "American jiu-jitsu" or simply "AJJ" fairly recently, but had in fact been aware of its first movements well before jiu-jitsu became a worldwide phenom. Back in the day where the *Joe Moreira Invitational* and *Cleber Luciano's Copa Pacifica*, were still the largest tournaments in the land, *circa* 1999. Even then, the division was already becoming apparent. In those days, two of the most common questions that jiu-jitsu *aficionados* asked were, *"when will vale-tudo* ("NHB" in those days) *surpass boxing in terms of popularity?"* and *"when will Americans outdo Brazilians at jiu-jitsu?"*[250]

There are no easy answers to any of this, the motivation behind these movements are multi-faceted and complex. They may hide behind a veil of nationalism (which is an easy and almost certain way to gain patriotic followers to your side), but does any of this really have anything to do with patriotism? Personally, I don't think so, and I have a hard time believing that Thomas Jefferson himself would be impressed with this discussion...

More importantly, what is AJJ after all? There are two answers to this question. The standard one that is relentlessly repeated and that more or less takes the shape of the assertion that 1) *"Americans are now innovating the art of jiu-jitsu and taking it to the next level"* and 2) what I believe AJJ actually is. We will address both of these answers one at a time.

1- Americans are taking jiu-jitsu to the next level

To begin with, there are two different AJJ movements that contradict one another. One wears a gi and claims the acronym "AJJ" while the other is a no-gi movement and strategically claims no acronym but that is in fact, the real movement of dissent. Given the differences in terms of reach and marketing, the rest of this text will

---

[250] For the record here, is it really so surprising that there is an attempt at replacing "BJJ" with "AJJ" when the effort had already been made, and later accomplished, by eliminating the words *"vale-tudo"* and replacing them with "MMA" instead? Perhaps for contemporary fans, MMA didn't begin in 1933 when George Gracie fought Tico Soledade in a "anything goes" match... Not even when Rorion and Royce forever revolutionized fighting exactly 60 years later. Perhaps for some fans, MMA really began when Dana White took over the wheel.

be concerned exclusively with the second no-gi variant, since the gi version does not deviate in any significant way from the IBJJF sphere of influence other than in replacing the letter "B" with the letter "A."

The AJJ we are discussing in this chapter isn't exclusively "American" either, but is rather "Anglo" in nature. Because this movement of dissent isn't exclusive to the USA, but is rather a larger global movement centered around the English-speaking world. Keeping in mind that the Anglo world doesn't only share the English language, but also the belief in a "Manifest Destiny" of sorts.

Despite this no-gi version of AJJ not differing from BJJ in technical terms, for the justification for a departure to work, it must justify itself to its audience somehow. Which is to say, the narrative must be constructed in a way to adjust reality according to convenience and preferences. Below are a few common attempts at shaping the narrative:

a) **Americans are leading the technical innovation of the sport**

Innovation has nothing to do with nationalism and everything to do with a competitive environment in the Darwinian sense. Which essentially means that through the process of selection the best techniques get passed on to further generations while the less efficient ones are either adapted or eliminated from the curriculum. The more competitive the environment, the higher the need for technical innovation, in an arms-race sort of fashion. And while it is certainly true that many techniques are developed daily in the US, this is the case in every country where the art is practiced competitively, no exceptions. Although to be fair, wherever there is more high-level competition, there will be more innovations. Unsurprisingly, more innovations are coming from countries with a great number of high-level competitions, namely Brazil and the USA.

It is true that many innovations in terms of leg-attacks have been developed in the Anglo world in recent years. Nonetheless, I do find it odd that this observation somehow completely misses that when Brazilians were leading innovation in terms of spider-guard, delariva-guard, back-takes, half-guard, butterfly-guard, closed-guard, etc., I never heard any of them say that the innovation took place because they were Brazilians, or because they took place in Brazil. The innovations were for all to use, who cares who invented them? Better yet, who cares where they were invented as long as they work?

b)   No-gi is more realistic for true combat

I won't address the gi vs. no-gi debate here but there is a lot of truth in the claim that no-gi is more realistic, at least in terms of transitioning to vale-tudo/MMA.[251] The problem here is the belief that the "sub-only" (which AJJ commonly uses) is representative of this approach to reality. When in fact, it is less realistic than the IBJJF ruleset, since it consists of a game that largely neglects positioning (so fundamental for real-combat) focusing instead on "submissions only." As if a fight were "all about submissions," as those who have never been hit in the face often claim.

By not rewarding controlling top position, competitors naturally neglect it. The result is a festival of butt-scooting (penalty free), sacrifice submissions (the ones that relinquish superior position, something very risky in a real-fight) and people not bothering to defend takedowns or sweeps (both terrible ideas in a real fight). Not to mention the overtime tie-breaker, in which contestants begin the tie-breaker very near a submission and whoever escapes the submission or finishes the opponent faster wins the prize. A highly problematic thing to teach because it reinforces a strategy of stalling and not losing (which isn't the same as winning) for the entire match and only choosing to actually try to win during the over time. Nonetheless, this is a reasonable strategy considering the ruleset.

---

[251] See Drysdale 2022a for a discussion on the mertis of training with and without the gi.

It is worth reminding ourselves here that the whole point of jiu-jitsu is to get to the submission while dominating your opponent (which doesn't mean that submission can't sometimes precede position), not win by escaping them quickly; or starting very close to submitting in a completely arbitrary and artificial overtime that has no grounds in the reality of combat.

Interestingly, its advoctes often make the case that sub-only tournaments are more fun to watch ("beauty" they say, "is in the eye of the beholder"). What is striking in this discussion and flies over most people's heads, is that these advocates, perhaps without fully understanding what it is that they are supporting, uphold a vision of jiu-jitsu that has entertainment in the driver's seat. Driving toward this destination, the reality of combat can comfortably take the back seat.

c) Brazilians referees are corrupt and biased against non-Brazilians

There may not be a single American who has competed in Brazil more than I have. In fact, almost all of my competition experience took place in that country. Although I wouldn't call myself an outsider (among my close friends at least, who always treated me fairly and as one of their own), I didn't exactly fit in either.

The vast majority of referees in my matches in Brazil didn't know me, and given my more than gringo name and looks, immediately singled me out as a foreigner. Yet, despite all this, I never felt like I received unfair treatment by any referee or organization during my decade long training and competing in Brazil. I can recall many instances where the calls didn't go my way, but I cannot believe that these mistakes were intentional or that they had anything to do with the fact that I was American. If truth be told, I can also recall many times the referees favored me during those decisions.

And here lies the crux of the conspiracy theory of Brazilian referees acting against non-Brazilian grapplers: this belief is nothing but
a perfect example of the good old confirmation bias. In other words,
ignore the times where the iffy calls favor you and hyper focus on the
ones in which they favor your opponent.[252]

d) **"We were ignoring half-the body" (in relation to the recent
surge in leg attacks)**

From the first time I heard this one it always seemed strange to
me. Especially since leg-attacks have always been part of jiu-jitsu's
arsenal. Judokas were using them early in the 20th century; Carlson
won a tournament with one in 1950;[253] Rodrigo Comprido won an
IBJJF Absolute World Title with a toe-hold in 1999 against Roleta.
So what changed? Simple, heel-hooks have been made legal in recent
years and that has significantly expanded the arsenal of leg-attacks.

Which points us to the misleading belief that the welcomed additions to the arsenal has something to do with jiu-jitsu reaching the
anglosphere for the innovations to have taken place. Accidentally
implying that others could not have done it themselves. When in
fact, the ban of heel-hooks and their more recent acceptance has
nothing to do with innovation being exclusive to the anglosphere.
But may well have something to do with the advances in modern
medicine and its ability to repair torn ligaments.

Reminding ourselves here that a total reconstruction of the
knee was not a technological possibility only a few decades ago. At
at time when, depending on the damage inflicted by the heel-hook,
the practitioner could well become crippled for life. Something technology has remedied in the 21st century allowing heel-hooks to be

---

[252] A side note makes itself necessary here. Bias toward friends and teammates has been a
real issue in the past but has, to a large extent, been remedied. Furthermore, the shrewd
use of *"malandragem"* by Brazilians might help explain their success on the mats. Lastly,
claims such as bias for or against peoples due to their nationality need to be made with
evidence in hand.

[253] Serrano 2014b, pg. 473

permitted in competition. Thus, creating the incentive to practice them competitively which is what lead to innovation.

Long story short, the change is more likely to be more of an issue of advances in technology than one of geography. Furthermore, even if it were true that leg-attacks and AJJ were revolutionizing jiu-jitsu, in what way does this justify a rift? Unless, of course, we apply the same rule to all countries, which would leave us with hundreds of different acronyms (and even more division) to essentially describe the same thing.

e) **AJJ is bringing more eyes to the sport**

One of the most common justifications for the AJJ movement's drift apart from the rest of BJJ is that it is more business minded and that by pushing for ticket sales, marketing, self-promotion and sensationalism in general, jiu-jitsu will attract more viewers/practitioners. A claim that has some merit to it, if more people are watching, doesn't that mean more money? It certainly does, however, the problem is twofold here. Firstly, commercialization isn't necessarily the best direction for the art in my opinion. Secondly, the claim that show business in general is leading the growth of jiu-jitsu worldwide is absolutely false. Let me explain.

Regarding ticket sales and show business, one can also think of extravagant ways of selling tickets, say, by pitching a mud-wrestling match between the Russian internet sensation Hasbullah and Paris Hilton; or Tom Cruise versus Justin Bieber, etc. Get it? My point here isn't to banalize the discussion, but to demonstrate that the placement of ticket sales and viewership in the driver's seat is already in itself an act of banalization of jiu-jitsu. Especially if we follow through with sensationalist tactics. In that case, worst-case scenario we take fighting back to the circus from whence it came. And best-case scenario, we will become more like boxing, which wouldn't be bad for the athletes themselves (in financial terms at least), but would it be a sport for the masses like jiu-jitsu is now? Hard to say.

Show business does have its advantages. It just also comes with many bad practices, the most obvious one being prioritizing what is financially best for the athlete and or organization. While maintaining what is best for the longevity and credibility of the art becomes a secondary force and only in case it happens to be a side-effect of the primary force (money).

Just to make sure that I am not being misunderstood here, a side note becomes necessary. My point here isn't to question profiting or to attempt to eliminate it (of course I like money too). What I am trying to say here is that the jiu-jitsu community would do well to rethink the direction of the art and if placing profit in the driver's seat is what is best for the art in the long run. That perhaps, these profiting tactics only benefit selected individuals, at the cost of transforming jiu-jitsu into a business first and foremost.

Morever, the notion that these sort of promotional tactics (slander, self-promotion, show business, personality cult and other sensationalist marketing practices in general) are responsible for the growth of jiu-jitsu can't be taken seriously. If we were to go to any jiu-jitsu event (gi or no-gi, professional or amateur, north or south of the equator), the result would be the same, the vast majority of the people in the arena are practitioners that are well within the jiu-jitsu competition circuit. While the rest of those attending are family members supporting them. Jiu-jitsu has no "fans" (not that we can't or shouldn't change that) in the traditional sense of the word. What jiu-jitsu has is a plethora of practitioners in love with the art. Which I should add in passing, is not a small difference.

As for the "new eyes" that are being introduced to the sport, they are in reality not "new" at all, but rather the same people that go to every local jiu-jitsu event. Simply put, the attendance and viewership of the new wave of professional events is to the credit of the organizations and their promotion efforts only in a secondary way.

Whereas in reality, the two greatest forces behind the growth of jiu-jitsu around the world today are the IBJJF and Joe Rogan respectively. IBJJF due to their organization and systems that grants jiu-jitsu the platform necessary for continuous and steady growth. While Joe Rogan's voice, combined with the voices of other celebrities embracing jiu-jitsu, has been single handedly the greatest marketing tool for the expansion of jiu-jitsu at least since Royce Gracie.

Yet these power houses are far from being alone in their efforts to popularize jiu-jitsu. They run in parallel to the hundreds of smaller leagues organizing tournaments and the thousands of gyms teaching BJJ around the world. In short, the growth of jiu-jitsu is a collective effort made by hundreds of thousands of individuals over many decades who have always worked hard to popularize the art.

2- What I believe AJJ really is

In reality, AJJ began the day jiu-jitsu landed in the USA. From that point onward, it was bound to transform itself. Jiu-jitsu was brought here on the wings of an almost extinct tradition called vale-tudo and destined to continue its long tradition of change.

It could easily be argued that these initial changes for the establishment of BJJ as a credible and profitable martial art business (structured classes, curriculums, belt tests, uniforms, classes starting on time, etc.) were extremely necessary for the scalable grown of the gentle art. Simply put, the initial changes that took BJJ from a sub-culture that blended fighting typical Latino machismo and the surf-culture of Rio de Janeiro, were necessary and, for the most part, beneficial to everyone (excepting rival martial arts instructors of course).

With that being said, the business minded shift didn't stop at improving organization and good business practices, both of which were lacking in Brazil when the sport was beginning to take off there. The changes were also in terms of the values that guided the growth of jiu-jitsu and how the art was to be practiced henceforth. Jiu-jitsu now had an entrepreneurial mindset that, coupled with the rise of social media, dramatically altered the interpretation of the art and its landscape.

The cultural shift becomes wider and more obvious as the art grows in popularity. As an example, insults like "marqueteiro" (marketer) *or Carlson Gracie's favorite* "poderoso" (almighty or all powerful) don't translate well into English, at least not as insults... In Carlson's days, the behavior of self-promotion was not only frowned upon, it was also an embarrassment to yourself and your school. In this old-school mindset, recognition of any kind was necessarily a byproduct of merit achieved through your efforts on the mats, not of shrewd marketing practices. Whereas today, such practices aren't perceived as bad, in fact, they are even taught and reinforced by many leaders and organizations in the community as being desirable and good.

These cultural trends, while certainly a drift from the merit-based system so defining of the second-wave of practitioners, drift even further when compared to the Japanese cultural matrix so common to judo (if not always in practice, at least so in theory):

"Kimura: *Then, you know, like, we were just mobbed by fans. People lined up. They wanted autographs. I was more popular than Obina Den. Like you are, now. Judo was extremely popular. Anywhere I went, people offered to buy me drinks and meals. I didn't need money. I started to believe the hype about me. I became a bit arrogant. If you get arrogant, your skills level will drop. If you are a 5-dan, you'll be a 4-dan. If you are a 4-dan, you'll be a 3-dan. When you go to Kodokan, you won't be able to execute even the basic techniques. It isn't just a temporary 'slump.' Your real ability is actually declining. That's what happens when you're overconfident. [...] Praise is a problem. People will say, like, 'Oh, you're strong.' That's no good. You should always think of yourself as weak. Think of yourself as a perpetual sho-dan, always in*

need of improvement. Avoid people who tell you how good you are.
That's very important."[254]

While it is indeed a cliché to say that money corrupts everything, in some ways, the commercialization and popularization of jiu-jitsu are doing exactly that. An observation that is less finger pointing than it is analyzing of the reality of our daily practice and culture. But isn't profiting from jiu-jitsu good?

As discussed above, it certainly is, but only as a secondary force and remaining behind the healthy growth of the art (by healthy I mean practices that actually teach children good behavioral values and teaching them how to win medals at the same time), not as its guiding principle. A lesson we should have all learned when we allowed vital services such as health and education to be corrupted by this sort of business orientation. By normalizing such business-oriented practices and mentality, we invert our hierarchy of priorities, by placing what ought to be a side-effect in the driver-seat instead.

Ultimately, what AJJ is attempting at doing to BJJ is remarkably similar to what the Gracie brothers did to judo beginning in the 1930s. Of course, there was nothing invented by Brazilians. What Brazilians did was to modify judo, add a few moves from other styles, replace the Kodokan hierarchy with an entirely new one in which they stood at the top and modify the culture in which the art was practiced to suit their own internal beliefs and values.

Moreover, if you believe you deserve a higher standing in the world, but still can't defeat your rivals at their game (and in case your belief and ambition don't match reality), then change the game (by creating a new reality, or in this case a new set of rules and culture nurtured by an entirely new narrative). Which is to say, modify the rules, market yourself and your favorites relentlessly, rewrite history while ignoring inconvenient facts and use (pseudo) patriotic lingo to justify and camouflage your true intentions. All while insisting that your jiu-jitsu is the "real"

---

[254] See: *"Masahiko Kimura Discusses Judo and Life with Yasuhiro Yamashita"* http://global-training-report.com/Kimura_Masahiko_interview.htm

one, while the mothership is suddenly inadequate somehow. *Can you see the similarities?* It's an old method. This time around with new protagonists coupled with the snow-balling effect of social media algorithms. That's it.

But to justify the division, AJJ has to continue to ignore all this, insisting that they have something new and better to replace the old and inadequate and finally confirming that the fixed-hierarchy between "them" and "us" was right all along. It was only due to a fluke of what "real Jiu-jitsu" looked like that the hierarchy has somehow been flipped on its head. Temporarily of course, since now it is back on its way to where it rightfully belongs.

Which naturally points us to the question, if what the Gracie brothers did to judo worked for them and now we all have this new modified version of judo that we now call jiu-jitsu (or BJJ, or whatever), doesn't that mean that if the same thing happens again it will also be an improvement?

First, the notion that BJJ is an improvement from judo can only be made on technical grounds by the sheer fact that BJJ allows for more techniques, since the cultural cohesion in judo is something BJJ (AJJ being even less cohesive since its cultural cloth is made out of even more individualistic and less cohesive strategies) lags well behind. Keeping in mind that judo is at least 140 years old. While BJJ, if we count its founding in 1967 or 1975, is still around half-a-century in age. Whereas throughout most of its life it was a practice limited to the south-zone of Rio de Janeiro and a few even smaller centers across Brazil.

Second, the issue of a split being beneficial must be analyzed on its own merits and not with historical background to be used as justification for it. The background is, at best, a reference to help think about these events, not evidence or a justification for what should (or will) happen next. Which raises the following questions, is it beneficial for jiu-jitsu to go in this new direction- for show business, money, viewership and ticket sales to be placed in the driver's seat? Or should we maintain the course of growth that has worked remarkably well so far by doing what is best for the growth of the art, with its commercialization as a side-effect or secondary force? The bigger difference I am trying to draw here is the differences between these two different cultural approaches (judo's *jita kyoei* vs. the boxing show business mentality) and how they best instruct the future of jiu-jitsu.

The Gracie brothers drifted away from judo as it was becoming increasingly more sport and less reality oriented. But does the same apply to AJJ today? Is BJJ more sport oriented than the AJJ nogi sub-only style? Hardly so, considering the complete lack of concern for positioning and the strategical practice of butt-scooting and suicidal submission attempts that are perfectly tactically sound in a sub-only format.

What about the culture, where the Gracie's abandoned the judo tradition in favor of a mixture of a Spartan like ethos mixed with surf-culture and remnants of Japanese manners? What are we replacing that with? Is the replacement more beneficial in cultural terms or for the longevity of jiu-jitsu? I don't think they are. People are free to disagree of course.

So, what is AJJ after all? *AJJ is in reality, a copy of a copy of a copy.* In martial arts, much like in nature, nothing is created, everything is transformed. Judo itself was heavily influenced by wrestling, sumo and the other two *jū-jutsu* styles that influenced kano: *tenjinshinyo-ryu* and *kito-ryu*. Who in turn may have been influenced by a 17th century Dutch style of grappling.[255] This is just the way these things evolve and I don't think there is much that can be done. Because, at the end of the day, the art is still growing worldwide, changing the lives of millions, and at least in terms of popularity, is far from losing momentum. What will come next is nothing but food for imagination.

To finish, I would like to end this chapter by completing my story of the 2019 edition of the ADCC.

The chanting of *"USA! USA!"* made itself heard a few times during the show but was never overwhelming or a unanimous chant. What was

---

[255] There is circumstantial evidence that grappling techniques may have made their way into Japan through Dutch travelers, in a book from 1674 by Nicolaes Petter called *"The Art of Wrestling."* See Pedreira 2021, pg. 122 for details.

overwhelming was what happened next in what was, looking back now, the highlight of the event (to me at least).

Fabricio Werdum and Braulio Estima, in midst of the chants began to urge the crowd to perform the traditional "Mexican wave" that is so common in games held in sports arenas all over the world. Besides being a spectacle for all who attended, it also had the added benefit of bonding the entire crowd into one single body which produces the wave in harmonic unison.

I remember taking a moment to think about that wave and what it actually meant for jiu-jitsu and its future. I also took note that some did not participate in it and were not on board with the ecstatic energy that the wave was producing in the arena. Some, a small minority, were sitting down while the wave went full circle, perhaps thinking about their own identity and place within jiu-jitsu or their feelings toward what the collective reality of what the wave actually represented. Or, perhaps, beyond this, they were already dreaming of a new reality instead...

It was a truly remarkable moment, as if reminding all in the crowd that we are all one. That what is best for jiu-jitsu in the long run, might not be what is best for a small group of individuals. At the end of the day, *fighting is a team sport* and we can't do it alone because we can't grow alone and the more of us there are, the better the competition. And how do we grow without the friction of competition? Besides, doesn't jiu-jitsu teach that when faced with hardship we should embrace it wholeheartedly? That when there is a problem we ought to confront it head on? Or do we look away and create a new, easier and more gratifying reality instead?

Beyond dominant narratives, the wave was symbolic and spoke volumes about who the viewership of jiu-jitsu truly is and what they really want. All manifested in that moment of interaction that was as much electrifying as it was unifying. An interaction that reminded spectators supporting various players that, even if on opposite sides of the arena, we are all one in the passion we share.

Conclusion – Where to Next?

"Men are not born equal in themselves, so I think it beneath a man to postulate that they are. If I thought myself as good as Sokrates I should be a fool; and if, not really believing it, I asked you to make me happy by assuring me of it, you would rightly despise me. So why should I insult my fellow-citizens by treating them as fools and cowards? A man who thinks himself as good as everyone else will be at no pains to grow better. On the other hand, I might think myself as good as Sokrates, and even persuade other fools to agree with me; but under a democracy, Sokrates is there in the Agora to prove me wrong. I want a city where I can find my equals and respect my betters, whoever they are; and where no one can tell me to swallow a lie because it is expedient, or some other man's will."

Mary Renault, The Last of the Wine chp. 20

The 17th century Italian historian, Gianbattista Vico, in his seminal work, *The New Science*, proposes a cycle of three ages to which the classical world was held to. The three ages were meant as symbols of the dominant ethos in each of these eras, struggling with one another in cyclical motion from one to the next. They were specific worldviews in fields such as jurisprudence, art, culture, politics and philosophy where each in turn, despite coexisting with the other two, would hold preeminence over them in the various arenas where these modes of thinking acted.

First, was the *theocratic age*, meant to represent a hierarchically cohesive and rigid worldview centered around an absolutist stance toward society and the world in general. Next, the *aristocratic age*, representing an age of heroes and a less rigid hierarchy that urged humanity to outdo its neighbors by emulating their superiors. Finally, the *democratic age*, where all cohesion and hierarchy undergo dispersion and where mere existence levels achievements and rank into a state of ultimate equality.

Which in essence meant a coordinated move toward the dissolution of any sense of rank, merit and authority.

The democratic age, according to Vico, had the effect of leading into a moment of chaos in terms of values, ideas and events. The chaos, presumably a consequence of the social fragmentation derived from the excesses (misunderstandings?) of democratic thinking. Perhaps the chaos is not so surprising, since the weakening of the social fabric that leads to it is likely due to a loss of accountability (if we are all equally accountable, then we can just as well be equally unaccountable). At which point Vico suggests that social disorder urges society to regroup itself, back into order and cohesion, reigniting the cycle at once.

Carlos and Helio Gracie are points of inception in the history of jiu-jitsu in Brazil. Despite not having invented anything, they did what every other martial art style before them had also done: borrow and adapt to your own preferences or understanding of what "real" means. Or, in our more specific case here, of *what jiu-jitsu is*.

The Gracie brothers had the cunning and ambition to carve a style of their own out of judo while meshing it with elements of *vale-tudo*. They did all this without abandoning the personal values they already embodied well before judo or *vale-tudo* came into their lives: their *patrician-ethos*, Brazilian *machismo* as well as a militaristic and fiercely hierarchical worldview that fit in with Helio's personality like a hand in glove.

For this unusual combination to stick they needed glue, and lots of it. They managed this feat, by virtually making a religion out of their custom-made interpretation of jiu-jitsu. To them, jiu-jitsu was whatever they said it was, end of story. It could change, it could adapt, it could even contradict itself in terms of how it was meant to be practiced, as long as everyone followed along and their views came out on top at the end. As they saw it, it was all for the greater good.

Outsiders were quick to spot the inconsistencies, distortions and contradictions. But none of this mattered, because at the end of the day, they created and controlled their own narrative by an enforced policy of zero tolerance toward anyone who dared to question it. The ones who did question it, could always be barked at and even physically attacked in case they went too far, and their questions began to make sense. While students could always be convinced and coerced by the confident demeanor, and body language (as well as in the fervent belief in what they were saying, true or not) that works so well on those who don't care enough to form an educated opinion on the matter. Accordingly, they are easily convinced of anything (then and now).

Confidence, real confidence, can't be faked. And when it is real, it doesn't matter if it is grounded in facts, logic and an ethical stance, or if it is untrue, makes no sense at all and is unethical. Because being uninformed leaves us vulnerable to be drawn toward conclusions that are solely based on the speaker's ability to relay that information in a convincing manner. In other words, it is a human trait to often allow our emotions to make these decisions for us because emotional decision making is quick, effortless and normally makes us feel good too. To make matters worse, emotionally derived judgements are often accurate, which has the undesired effect of reinforcing our reliance on them. Exactly why they are so dangerous.

Rational decision making on the other hand, is exhausting, requires knowledge, reading, evidence, cross-referencing, experience, lots of critical-thinking and lots of looking for your own contradictions and intentions in regards to *what you believe and why you believe it.* But if someone comes along and gives us all these answers with unmatched confidence, then it is easy to see why that particular narrative carries with it the risk of becoming our own. Since the confidence serves the purpose of granting the narrative an air of infallibility and truthfulness. Verified or not.

The gift (if we can call it that) of passing this infallible confidence on to others is the kind of faith that transforms that which seemed illogical into a new forming reality that is palpable enough for others to believe it because others have already pre-approved it. And *great numbers cannot ever be wrong, can they?*

It is right around this time that the belief system becomes a self-propelling mechanism and blind faith, rather than critical thinking, is the one that begins to craft an entirely new reality from an older one. At best, out of scattered truths and fragments of whatever evidence so happens to be in tune with the preferred narrative. At worst, we end up with fabrications out of thin air.

Long story short, irrational or unfounded beliefs are nothing but a game of winning numbers over to your narrative. From that point onward, facts no longer matter (did they ever?). Which doesn't mean that any given narrative can't do some good in the future. On the contrary, it often does. The problem here is that in this case our bedrock is porous and isn't as solid as we once thought or wished it to be. In this case, the premise is false and can good things be built on false premises?

So again, I ask, *does the end justify the means?* And again, I don't think it does. However, this *post-hoc* line of arguing does seem like an outstanding (self) deceptive tool to camouflage just about any sort of action or behavior and the intentions lying beneath it. Truly, the *"but it will do some good in the future,"* sounds like the sort of deception to justify any sort of misconduct . History at least, well beyond our favorite pajama game, teaches that it *can* and that it *does* justify just about anything.

If something is good, does it require anything but blunt reality to sustain itself? If a narrative has good intentions and is not self-interested at all, does it require anything but facts, the truth, honesty and logic to win the day? What if the narrative is self-serving, wouldn't that mean that it requires the opposite?

Controlling the narrative is key. Those who frame it well (and are consistent enough with it that many others come to believe it themselves), escape the scrutiny of facts and logic. All while crafting from the blind faith of others in them, the reality they had envisioned from the start. *Has anything changed? Will it ever?*

One of my favorite exercises is to try to discover the reasons why we, as people, simply can't identify these inconsistencies as they are happening. Clearly, we do not lack the historical precedent to justify our skepticism. The lessons are all there, that is, if we care enough to actually learn them.

Yet, if we don't lack precedent, and we have more access to information than ever before, and we pride ourselves on being nature's greatest achievement, then why does it keep happening? Over and over again? Why do we keep allowing the narrative to be kidnapped and reframed according to convenience and self-gain rather than the facts of the matter, especially when these are available? Or do we concede that by default the news we so happen to prefer and that appeals to our preconceived notions and biases is "real," whereas the news we don't like is "fake." Are our feelings and personal preferences the ablest criteria for determining objective reality?

Of course, we could all just simply say that *"I don't know and won't until I give the topic some serious time."* And of course, we don't always follow the skeptic's path even when we know we should. What I am saying here is that blind faith isn't something to be proud of.

Reading about happenings of decades or centuries past is troubling enough, but watching falsehoods being spoken outloud, right in front of our eyes is something else completely. Many times, I have wondered why those who saw clearly what was happening didn't alert others of the incongruities they were witnessing. Then I would read that they did, only to be ignored (or worse). Because again, once the narrative takes over, nothing else matters, while challenging it is akin to an act of war to be dealt with in a war-like manner.

Others, perhaps because they were envisioning things differently while finding gratification in simply living life and doing what they love, had different goals in sight. Correspondingly, their accomplishments and acknowledgements differ in proportion to where these life efforts were placed from the start. Some spend their lives doing the heavy lifting of carving the bedrock until it takes its current shape, others (then and now) spend their life patting themselves on the back and selling it as if all the work was their own. The public, for our part, once again dispenses with reason and places whatever historical remembrance we are capable of in accordance with our personal preferences (political, emotional or financial).

For his part, Carlson is a fork in the road that is the history of jiu-jitsu because he escaped the need for any narrative. His was carved through a consistent track record of victory, world class coaching and a heart of gold. He is placed at the center regardless of any narrative, because in terms of fighting and coaching, he did more and he did it better than any other before or after him. And whether we are prepared to acknowledge this or not, the greatest effort for the creation of the bedrock for an entire community to stand on, was his. Even if that community has no idea they have been standing on it all along.

While those with a sharper eye for business and self-promotion, gladly and cunningly took much of the credit for themselves, well beyond their due share. With this in mind, while intentions might be difficult to determine, sometimes glimpses of who is in the driver's seat can be found here and there. And I think the fact that Carlson so altruistically gave his life to jiu-jitsu speaks volumes about where his heart had been all along.

Yet some forces are beyond any efforts we may be capable of, however genuine the efforts may be. Approaching his final years, the world was changing and reshaping itself as it always does. This time, according to popular demand and into a new worldview where *casca-grossas* were no longer the dominant core of the jiu-jitsu population, and nor was the *casca-grossa* worldview the dominant one either.

The process of democratization started by Carlson with the help of Rolls inside the Figueiredo Academy was destined to grow. For their gospel to become a worldwide one, all it needed was a giant billboard called the UFC. That, and a plethora of missionaries standing ready to quickly supply the demand given rise by the final triumph of their faith by the hands of Royce. This time around with an ethos that was less warrior-like, and instead one that agreed with the consumer's appetite and into yet another definition of *what jiu-jitsu is.*

Without a doubt, the popularization was a home run and few can question the astounding success jiu-jitsu enjoys as a martial art in the world today. Nevertheless, while I benefit, appreciate and enjoy the moment myself, I can't help but wonder if the continuous fragmentation of hierarchy isn't already signaling what comes next.

Or perhaps I am overthinking and overdramatizing all this. Perhaps things are exactly as they should be and no one cares either way. Jiu-jitsu will fragment, the technical center won't hold, and no one cares about either learning how to fight realistically or about upholding any sense of merit and rank. I don't like it, but I concede that this far in the game, this may well be the case. Still, at least as a matter of curiosity, I wonder what would happen if a blue-belt under Helio showed up inside the original Gracie Academy with their own logo on their gi one day, or if someone decided to play a shin-to-shin guard during a *taparia* session with Carlson or Rolls...

Beyond our nerdy *jiu-jitsusphere*, I also wonder if some of these forces that shape the world around us, don't mirror and signal the deterioration of other more relevant spheres of human coexistence. That our mini-universe is a reflection of a much larger and more significant stage. Hard to say, and while I admit that much of this discussion is abstract, I think this is indeed the case and the signs are all there if we pay close attention.

Recently, a student of mine brought to my attention that a popular grappling event created the equivalent of baseball trading cards with its competitors on them. The cards, much like baseball cards, had the player's stats and overall achievements written on them. Among the measurements of achievements, and next to the players other stats, was a new criteria or "accomplishment" to be measured—*popularity*.

It is no secret that people enjoy being acknowledged. Something that no amount of humility or nobility of character can mask, because social approval is an integral part of our biological blue-print. Expressed or not.

There is no doubt that popularity has its benefits, and I have made a living from whatever little popularity I have enjoyed through and because of jiu-jitsu. It matters, since it is financially promising and money grants us security, comfort and (potentially) free time. And who has ever said that these things aren't important? Yet when popularity becomes the measurement and very symbol of success (in the example above, not replacing merit, but standing right next to it, on *equal* grounds), then what's next? Can it be that next it will be placed in the driver's seat above all other goals to be pursued? A youtuber fighting Floyd Mayweather (arguably the greatest boxer of all time), seems to confirm that we seem to be headed that way indeed.

If that is the case, then what? Well, then I suppose popularity becomes a measurement to be pursued in and of itself. Free of the higher standards of scrutiny, logic, ethics or merit. Jokingly, someone recently suggested to me that if this is the direction we are headed, then fans will soon be voting to decide who the next world-champion is.[256] Unsurprisingly, there is confusion and a complete loss of any track of what metrics we ought to pursue. Side effects, I suppose, of the fragmentation derived from the inversion of values of strength and merit toward one of comfort, cheap-rewards and that insists on leveling all opinions as equally valid (regardless of expertise). Which, like everything else in history, isn't new at all.

In ancient Greece, there was a specific way of thinking that had its maximum expression in the invention of the Olympics. It was a worldview that Vico would have identified as an aristocratic set of values, one that urged a young and competitive youth to compete with one another in open contest. Propelled by the thought of glory to self and to the victor's *polis*. It was a world crafted in noble fashion, requiring of its contestants (at least those who were allowed to compete), the strength and courage necessary to be crowned in victory and gain prestige that way.

Greeks called it the *Agon* and it was associated with the *Paraestra*, the gym or academy where the young and competitive wrestled each

---

[256] A few months back, I drew some statistics on who the top 40 most successful competitors of all time are. It didn't receive much attention but a few readers wrote me voicing their opinion that they felt "this name or that name" should have been on that list. The fact that the conclusions were drawn based on numbers and facts escaped entirely the questioner's opinions and feelings. See: Drysdale 2022f.

other daily, preparing themselves for a hard life by simulating war. Naturally, its rise and public acceptance led to immense popularity for the warriors. Which had the downside of becoming a criterion in itself and to be pursued as a measurement of success, rather than being merely a side-effect of victory in the arena.

The end of the *agonal age*, as Jakob Burckhardt called it, was brought forth by the rise of Athenian democracy. A moment where a merit-oriented worldview was being replaced by one that called for equality of everything and everywhere instead. One where indulging in a craze for fame at any cost took the wheel. It was a moment where burning buildings and assassinating despised politicians became a worthy medium to achieve the desired goal. One that previously would have required winning an olive crown for yourself and your *polis* by outdoing your peers in brotherly-rivalry. Again, nothing new here, only that this time around the confusion is more tech savvy.

Though the larger issue here isn't that popularity in itself is bad (or good). Looming above this is the matter that by becoming an achievement to be so forcefully pursued, the craze for attention bypasses the necessary qualities that struggling ought to teach us through hard lessons. Something that the avoidance of any hardship and the granting of participation trophies to shelter hurt feelings, simply cannot teach. The result of this is a civilization marked by softness, ignorance, arrogance and desperation when it isn't awarded everything it feels entitled to.

When culture isn't subjected to a binding belief system with high standards of merit, but rather becomes subjected to the whims of the majority (whatever that happens to be that particular week), a tool for political power is born. What follows is that factual reality becomes the victim of those who best manipulate public opinion by giving and telling the public everything they want to have and hear.

Besides, if we concede that we are all potentially corruptible and vulnerable to wrongful purposes, then not having firmly held high standards is no better than not being able to participate in decision making. In other words, without high standards and beliefs, the democratization of jiu-jitsu (or anything else for that matter) is in reality nothing but the massification of low standards.

Add to this the business logic of maximizing profits at any cost and you have a recipe for aiming for high numbers, rather than cohesion and the integrity the glue was meant for in the first place. The one that got us this far and that, presumably, is still necessary if jiu-jitsu is to survive intact the chaos that the internet has become.

If the majority wants more in exchange for less, who can deny them? If the white-belts want their own logo and they are in the majority, who can deny them? If the white-belt expects equal say in the class and its format, and they are the paying customer, then clearly the voice of the majority must be heard and obeyed, *right*?

Moreover, if the white-belt wants more belts, more trophies and more rewards with less work and less effort then, in that case, what sane business person would deny that the majority of consumers decide the fate of the direction his business ought to take? The message is clear and straight-forward, either indulge or go out of business. *Are we really so sure that financial success is the highest achievement on the horizon?*

Perhaps turning jiu-jitsu into a mega-business was good for us as individuals, but what about jiu-jitsu itself? Can it be said that its commercialization doesn't bring about the fragmentation of exactly what made it cohesive, strong and oriented toward a merit base hierarchy in the first place? After all, it is one thing to have the freedom to have and give your opinion, it is a more complex matter to grant all opinions equal standing. Because in that case, what do we do if the majority decides to believe that the Earth is flat? In that case, should we modify our school curriculums to accommodate to people's opinions?

What if it is collectively decided that Helio Gracie invented the guard position and that scientists don't know what they are talking about (and since they have already given us Google and Facebook, we are doing just fine without them)? Should white-belts determine what they ought to learn in class and how it ought to be taught? In an environment prone to believe that all opinions (or "clicks") are equally qualified, these are very important questions we need to answer.

Here lies our problem. If people truly cared enough to inform themselves properly, the hustlers would be out of business or at least not be able to shape the narrative according to their own convenience. Having the power to choose is a blessing if and when we are well informed and the bedrock of our beliefs isn't a hustle. It is a blessing when the beliefs happen to reinforce the cohesion rather than indulge the individual. After all, aren't empires built on the collective faith of their founders? And isn't the absence of this same faith that which leads these empires to their decline and eventual fall? (The American Republic comes to mind here...).

Having an opinion, of course, entails the responsibility of understanding what the collective format of this opinion will determine. Hence, the gathering and growing power of poorly informed stances is just as terrifying as the thought of not being allowed to voice any stance. Having the power to so quickly voice and share our views and wants is an enormous technological and political achievement. Which is exactly why it carries with it an equally great level of responsibility for acquiring the wisdom to match this power.

Not that the white-belts aren't welcome to improve their rank. That was the whole point of Carlson's initial process of democratization. But the standards then were high and equality meant having the opportunity to enter the arena and rise to its challenges. It meant the white-belt surviving the jungle among lions long enough to be awarded rank and the earned privilege of one day having your name and brand on your own gym's front door. Consequently, to avoid complete anarchy, the most pressing task is to elevate all standards from white to black, not lower the standards in order to comfort the entitled expectations of those who demand more in exchange for less.

I sincerely hope that I don't come across as overly critical, or despising the moment I am living. While I am critical of it (being a coach compels me to be this way), I do acknowledge the many advantages of the current age. As Saraiva remarked, the changes brought good and bad. Something we all hold a degree of responsibility for.

There is no contradiction here. Growth is desirable, but so is the maintenance of the standards and values that brought jiu-jitsu into prominence. Condemning jiu-jitsu's disorderly and hooligan ways does not prevent me from admiring their loyalty, unity and adherence to a worldview of accountability, humility, merit and strength. Nor does it make me a hypocrite to applaud the end of their feudal wars over turf.

To clarify my stance here, the greater issue is with the long-term damage to the art's credibility that placing the customer in charge will cause. Leading to the inevitable replacement of cohesiveness for individualism; hierarchy for its dissolution; reality for entertainment; merit with marketing; and accountability for entitlement. I stand by the view that the jiu-jitsu's movements should be in the opposite direction.

All these worldviews have the potential to carry positive as well as negative implications within their DNA. It is up to us to distinguish between them and select, uphold, or veto according to our beliefs and vision moving forward.

***

The end of the Carlson Era wasn't the loss of his army or even his death. The end was a much slower one. It ended when the war was won and jiu-jitsu began to enjoy the level of popularity its troops had spent decades fighting for in almost total obscurity in Brazil. It was nothing new, jiu-jitsu was once again merely adapting to the times, values, wants and narratives written on the fly. Again, according to the season and taste of those who held the historical pen.

Perhaps because I have always romanticized jiu-jitsu as belonging to a culturally unique enclave of the world, I am more aware of these changes than others are. The values of the *second-wave* are the ones I reminisce of. Not because things were perfect in those days or because I believe Carlson was some kind of saint. But rather because the absence of any financial rewards made their motivations purer. Nonetheless, while I am thankful for what the *third-wave* brought forth, I worry that my generation was the one responsible for shaping jiu-jitsu further away from the cultural matrix I learned to view as the pinnacle of strength, loyalty, accountability and cohesion.

Jiu-jitsu will survive of course, but it will stay true to its long trajectory of continuously changing as time goes by. I worry that by placing the customer in the driver's seat and allowing them to determine the direction of jiu-jitsu's future is a short to medium-term strategy. One that has already harmed jiu-jitsu's credibility in the martial art landscape.

How do I know this? Having navigated both the MMA and BJJ worlds for my entire life, I am aware that the MMA crowd makes fun of BJJ techniques. Much like the members from the *second-wave* made fun of other traditional martial arts breaking thin wood-boards. Simply put, whether we care to admit it or not, we have become what we once criticized and the ogres are not really extinct after all. They only migrated, to more realistic pastures, or better yet, more realistic cages. Which, I should say in passing would be an ideal solution to our problem here if it weren't for the fact that MMA has such awful culture. Undeniably, BJJ has better culture than MMA. It is friendlier, happier, more respectful, open to all and its mats have a homely feel to them. By ridding itself of the ogres (or most of them at least), it became a truly more inclusive environment open to all.

In regards to this growth, the IBJJF needs to be credited more than any other organization or individual. It is my view that they will continue to be jiu-jitsu's leading body in the foreseeable future. Something that no amount of hustle, work-ethic or steering the narrative can alter. Because credibility (in today's world at least), can be easily bought. Logistics, organization and know-how can be easily outsourced. But game plan? That requires vision, high-standards, cohesion, glue and superior metrics aimed at longevity, rather than quick rewards and ticket sales. Those with the clearest vision for the future will continue to shape jiu-jitsu and right now that is the IBJJF.

This, of course, if we can agree that we are all moving toward the same goal. Which I am inclined to think that we are not. That in fact, we have already departed and splintered beyond reparation. Soon beyond technical compatibility as jiu-jitsu branches off into various organizations with various rules, internal cultures and target demographics with their various purposes.

Much like in the past, where ambition, cunning and controlling the narrative have splintered a group, and however beneficial this all may have been to many of us, *the end*, in my view, *still does not justify the means*. With that being said, it is easier said than done and accusing from afar is cheap. Those who live daily in the heat of battle have a right to see things from a different point of view. Which I respect.

Jiu-jitsu is now for everyone, and no longer exclusive to those who could afford private lessons inside the original Gracie Academy, or even for *casca-grossas* who could survive Carlson and Rolls intense and competitive jungle. Their legacies survive in the growing geographic pockets of competitive jiu-jitsu spread across the world. They meet regularly at tournaments such as IBJJF, NAGA, Grappling Industries, JJWL, ADCC, Abu-Dhabi Pro, ACBJJ, AGF, CBJJE and a plethora of other smaller organizations, gyms and instructors leading the effort to bring new troops into the art. This much, no one can deny.

On the other hand, knowing what I know from yester years of merit, reality based-combat and group cohesion, I am tempted to self-deprecate my own life and standing in jiu-jitsu and note that the lions have lost their mane and despite still having teeth they are no longer sharp. I fear we are losing our appetite and the courage for a real hunt in the name of money, popularity, softness and trendy moves that have no place in a real fight.

What jiu-jitsu's leadership (coaches and organizations) needs to keep in mind, and what this book is attempting to remind us of here, is that which made jiu-jitsu popular in the first place. To remind us that decisions are made daily and making it perfectly clear who is and who isn't in the driver's seat will determine our destination. To be clear, far be it from me to call back the ogres. They need to either be tamed or expelled. Conversely, and as far as the non-casca-grossas go, they won't step up to the mark themselves, it is up to jiu-jitsu's leadership to urge them to do so.

With that being said, my view is that jiu-jitsu rulesets (all of them), need to be gradually revised and steered back toward the reality of combat and away from fads and cool moves. Lest we continue to drift from reality with our butt-scooting and lapel-guards and into becoming the equivalent of the nerdy kid in the 80s watching kung-fu movies while hitting himself in the head with a set of nunchuks. Come to think of it, in some ways, I think we are already there. Whereas our culture needs to be more clearly defined so it isn't subjected to the trends and standards of the internet. These, I am learning, are increasingly low.

Lastly, if there is one thing I have learned in the last five years, I have made a modest effort to understand the history of martial arts, it is this, *what goes around comes around*. Ticket sales, fads, coolness, *firula's* and everything else brought forth by popular demand, are just as quick to come as they are to go. What is consistent during any time period, from ancient Greece all the way to the present, is *what will remain at the end, with or without jiu-jitsu, the reality of combat*. At the end, reality remains and those who are responsible, or care about longevity, bear the responsibility to place reality back in the driver's seat and keep it there once and for all.

At any rate, I am fully aware that this is only the idealist in me speaking out loud (impotent or not). And there is not much else he has to say on this matter. His cynical twin reminds him that there isn't much to be done other than to help register the moment. On the other hand, if the twin has taught us anything, he has taught us that there is *nothing new under the sun* and *what goes around comes around*. More than this, from instruction we have learned that streams, despite always flowing into the sea, descend from mountain tops.

Come to think of it, the twin's cynicism carries with it a spark of hope, grounded in the same history he so cynically observes. Because since time immemorial, *"All streams flow into the sea, yet the sea is never full. To the place the streams come from, there they return again."*[257]

---

[257] Ecclesiastes 1:7

Epilogue

"Daddy, why do people train jiu-jitsu?"

C. Drysdale

Children don't need a lesson in Socratic methods to pin adults down. Their innate curiosity is enough to catch us off guard with the simplest of questions. What do you mean *"why do people train??"* Isn't it obvious? We train for health reasons and to learn how to defend ourselves... *Don't we?*

In general, I always try to answer any questions my daughters ask as truthfully as I can. I do this to build trust so that I have it when it matters the most. That and because replying to good questions with cookie-cutter replies doesn't do a good question any justice. And her question was a good one... So, *why do we train jiu-jitsu?*

The simplicity of the question set me to think of my own motivations. After 25 years on the mats, I can't say I can answer her question in a fully satisfactory way. The argument for physical health seems so laughable to me it doesn't even merit serious thought. How can an art that causes its practitioners to suffer from multiple cases of arthritis before they hit 40 be *healthy*? Unless of course, by health we are referring to mental health, which in that case, I couldn't agree more. But that is not how jiu-jitsu is sold, is it?

As for the self-defense argument, I find it slightly less than a good reason to dedicate your life to jiu-jitsu. Sure, much of what is in the jiu-jitsu curriculum works in a fight. I even used it once successfully. But considering all the work done and the price to be paid, I can hardly find it justifiable to dedicate a life to something you may only use once in a lifetime.

On top of that, fighting (at least as the *second-wave* understood it) is no longer acceptable (even if sometimes I wish it were). Additionally, there are too many people carrying guns around which significantly diminishes any possibility for any well-informed reaction (regardless of your preferred brand of self-defense) to an attacker. Not to mention an attack by multiple assailants.

But why then? Why did we begin and continue this journey? Is it to learn how to fight and win medals? Vanity? Ambition? The search for an identity in order to simply belong somewhere? My daughter's question got me thinking beyond the cookie-cutter answers we tell ourselves and our students daily. It got me thinking about what is the underlying motive that pushes so many people to leave their comfort zone and habitually beat themselves up for no apparent reason.

Whether we care to admit it or not, the world around us isn't shaped by our *wants* or by our *needs*, but the other way around. Challenges and opponents come to us in currents that exist as a series of circumstances that are, more often than not, beyond our strength to shape, so they shape us instead.

For our part, all we can do is to fight back as best we can, stay the course that we believe to be the right one and not allow ourselves to be overwhelmed by any current. At some point during this journey, and despite our best efforts, we come to the realization that our *wants* are merely the innocence of our feeble selves speaking out loud, always falling short of its own ambition.

As for our *needs*, those aren't negotiable. *Needs* lack the sort of luxury that innocence enjoys so freely, demanding instead that we fight back. Even if fighting is more about failing than it is about having your hand raised at the end. After all, what would be the significance of having our hands raised if we didn't learn the hard way that things don't always go according to plan? In fact, that they rarely do. It is for this reason that I have always thought the ungifted to be fortunate, even if in a strange way. Since for those who lack any talent, the distance between failure and having your hand raised, is much longer and filled with far more lessons... Filled with far more perspective.

Jiu-jitsu has taught me a thing or two about getting beat up, falling and the perspectives that follow these beatings and falls. It taught me to accept outcomes that are beyond my reach and in whatever shape they happen to come in. It has also taught me that the promise of a new perspective is sufficient to warrant the risk of falling again. Because in failure lies the kind of perspective that victory is too arrogant to ever witness up close. And after a life on the mats, I'll take the perspective gained from my wins and losses over any reward jiu-jitsu could ever offer me. Which brings me back to the answer I still owed my daughter.

Thinking all this too complex and abstract for a child, I settled on bringing the issue around to her own world.

-Hey baby, you remember when you asked Daddy why people trained jiu-jitsu?

-Yeah.

-I think I know why.

My daughter put a pause to her task of coloring her book and looked up, ready the hear my answer to her question.

-You know how you like to draw and redraw your favorite cartoon characters?

-Yes.

-Why do you keep redrawing them?

-Well, sometimes I draw their legs too skinny and sometimes too fat and then I want to draw them all over again.

-But why?

She paused for a second, touching her temple with her pencil as if to help her think.

-Because I want to make it beautiful...

-That's it my love. That is all there is to it.

I like to think that our little exchange won the day, because without saying a word, she put her head down and got back to work.

Bibliography

Cairus, José Tufy (2012a) *The Gracie Clan and the Making of Brazilian Jiu-jitsu: National Identity, Culture and Performances, 1905-2003*

Cairus, José Tufy (2012b) *Modernization, Nationalism and the Elite: The Genesis of Brazilian Jiu-jitsu, 1905-1920*

Drysdale, Robert (2020) *Opening Closed Guard: The Origins of Jiu-Jitsu in Brazil - The Story Behind the Film*

Drysdale, Robert (2022a) *To gi or not to gi*; http://www.global-training-report.com/drysdale42722_giornogi.htm

Drysdale, Robert (2022b) *Creonte: Loyalty versus Self-Perfection in Jiu-jitsu*; http://www.global-training-report.com/Drysdale_Creonte.htm

Drysdale, Robert (2022c) *How to Win at Jiu-jitsu while Keeping it Real*; http://www.global-training-report.com/Drysdale_6522_IBJJF.htm

Drysdale, Robert (2022d) *The ADCC Blind-Spot*; http://www.global-training-report.com/Drysdale_61722_ADCC.htm

Drysdale, Robert (2022e) *The Fallacy of Submission Only;* http://www.global-training-report.com/Drysdale_Subonly.htm

Drysdale, Robert (2022f) *Who are the BJJ Top 40 Goats?;* http://www.global-training-report.com/Drysdale_top40.htm

Gracie, Reila (2008) *Carlos Gracie: O Criador de uma Dinastia*

Gracie, Rickson and Maguire, Peter (2021) *Breathe: A Life in Flow*

Pedreira, Roberto (2013) *Jiu-jitsu in the South Zone 1997-2008, 3rd ed.*

Pedreira, Roberto (2015a) *Choque: The Untold Story of Jiu-jitsu in Brazil, vol 1: 1854-1949,* 2nd ed.

Pedreira, Roberto (2015b) *Choque: The Untold Story of Jiu-jitsu in Brazil, vol 2: 1950-1960*

Pedreira, Roberto (2015c) *Choque: The Untold Story of Jiu-jitsu in Brazil, vol 3: 1961-1999*

Pedreira, Roberto (2018) *Craze: The Life and Times of Jiu-jitsu, vol 1: 1854-1904*

Pedreira, Roberto (2019) *Craze: The Life and Times of Jiu-jitsu, vol 2: 1905-1914*

Pedreira, Roberto (2021) *Craze: The Life and Times of Jiu-jitsu, vol 1: 1915-1934*

Serrano, Marcial (2013) *O Livro Proibido do Jiu-jitsu, vol 1*

Serrano, Marcial (2014a) *O Livro Proibido do Jiu-jitsu, vol 2*

Serrano, Marcial (2014b) *O Livro Proibido do Jiu-jitsu, vol 3*

Serrano, Marcial (2016) *O Livro Proibido do Jiu-jitsu, vol 6*

Serrano, Marcial (2016b) *O Livro Proibido do Jiu-jitsu, vol 7*

Serrano, Marcial (2021) *O Tunel do Tempo, vol 3*

Appendix:

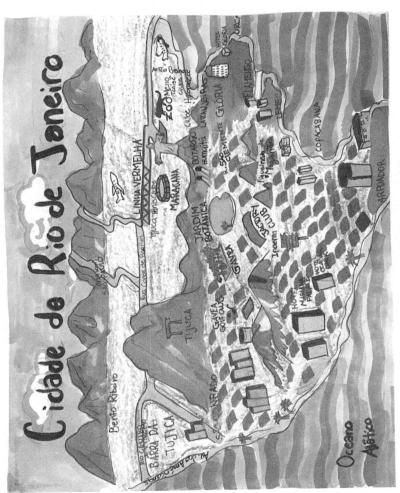

A map of the city of Rio de Janeiro.
Can you spot some of the places we discussed in
the book?
Artcred: A. and C. Drysdale.

Group of early Kodokan graduates that helped spread judo/
jiu-jitsu in Brazil in the 1910s and 20s. From left to right:
Akitaro Ono, Shoshihiro Satake, Tokugoro Ito and Mitsuyo
Maeda (a.k.a. "Count Koma") Photocred: Unknown.

Jacyntho Ferro (left) sits next to Mitsuyo Maeda. Photocred:
Gustavo Goulart via Kano Society Bulletin #56.

Jacyntho (on the right), the man who learned from Mitsuyo
Maeda and taught Carlos Gracie and Donato Pires dos
Reis in the Amazon. Photocred: Revista Tiro e Sport.

Before he became a judo/jiu-jitsu practitioner, Jacyntho
Ferro was already a marksman, cyclist, weight-lifter and
overall well known athlete in the state of Pará in the Brazilian
Amazon. Photocred: Brazilian National Library.

Geo Omori, one of the most
important figures for the
development of judo, BJJ and
vale-tudo in Brazil. Photocred:
Brazilian National Library.

Geo Omori (left) in a
rare photograph.
Source: Unknown.

Carlos Gracie in 1931 wearing the pre-1907 short-sleeve and pants judo uniform.
Photocred: Brazilian National Library.

Helio in 1932 before his match against Namiki. According to his own testimony, Helio had never heard of jiu-jitsu prior to 1929. Photocred: Brazilian National Library.

The Academia de Jiu-Jitsu" founded by Donato, later rebranded "Academia Gracie de Jiu-Jitsu" on the Marques de Abrantes street. Photocred: Author's personal archives.

George Gracie e Geo Omori

George Gracie (left) and Geo Omori (right) worked as partners for many years together. Photocred: Brazilian National Library.

Geo Omori and George Gracie.
Photocred: Brazilian National Library.

Helio with Capoeira practitioners. Photocred:
Brazilian National Library.

Ono demonstrates a move in 1935 shortly before
his first match agains Helio Gracie (O Globo Sportivo,
December, 5th, 1935). Photocred: Acervo O Globo.

**Eduardo Gracie: *"I also want to
be a champion one day."*
Photocred: Brazilian National Library.**

**The book published in 1949 by the Argentinian nutritionist that
inspired the "Gracie Diet." Photocred: Author's personal
archives via Daniel Alfano.**

**Helio teaches a throw to a female student in 1951.
Photocred: Brazilian National Library.**

Kimura shortly after finishing Helio with a "kimura shoulder-lock." Notice that the caption on the bottom reads that the move Kimura defeated Helio with was the "chave Americana." Considering the article is from 1951, this challenges the assertion that Rolls Gracie named any shoulder-lock in Bob Anderson's honor. Photocred: Brazilian National Library.

Passarito: one of Carlson's most challenging opponents. The caption reads: *"Passarito is not scared of Carlson."* Photocred: Brazilian National Library.

Carlson applies an "omoplata" shoulder-lock on Passarito in 1954. They fought one of the longest vale-tudo's in history. The caption reads: "(...) *The fight showed exceptional violence from both contenders, but the Gracie superiority was flagrant.*"

Carlson applies a takedown on Waldemar Santana at the original
Gracie Academy when they were still training partners. In
the background, notice the original logo from the *"Academia
Gracie."* Photocred: Brazilian National Library.

Waldemar lifts Helio off the ground.
Photocred: Brazilian National Library.

Waldemar Santana battles Helio Gracie.
Photocred: Brazilian National Library.

Waldemar celebrates victory over Helio
Photocred: Brazilian National Library.

After his victory over Helio, Waldemar became a superstar in Rio.
Photocred: Brazilian National Library.

Waldemar Santana, the "Black Leopard."
Photocred: Brazilian National Library.

Waldemar Santana, the former janitor and student turned nemesis. Photocred: Brazilian National Library.

Carlson battles Waldemar, this time under vale-tudo rules. Photocred: Brazilian National Library.

Waldemar and Carlson fall outside the ring. Photocred: Brazilian National Library.

Carlson mounts Waldemar.
Photocred: Brazilian National Library.

Carlson drops elbows on Waldemar. The caption reads: *"Carlson avenged the Gracies!"* **Photocred: Brazilian National Library.**

Carlson is lifted up in the air after his victory over Waldemar.
Photocred: Brazilian National Library.

A bloody vale-tudo battle between two jiu-jitsu
representatives in 1956: Guanair Vial and
Moacir Ferraz. Photocred: Brazilian National Library.

Carlson demolishs the much heavier Leão de Portugal
(Lion from Portugal) in 1957. Photocred: Brazilian National Library.

Helio runs for office in 1959 for the "Partido Social Democrata."
Photocred: Brazilian National Library.

Ivan Gomes (top) and Carlson engage in a legendary fight.
Photocred: Cléa Cordeiro Rodrigues personal archives.

Ivan attempts to take Carlson down.
Photocred: Cléa Cordeiro Rodrigues personal archives.

Carlson with some head-movement.
Photocred: Cléa Cordeiro Rodrigues personal archives.

Carlson and Ivan Gomes fight to a draw.
Photocred: Cléa Cordeiro Rodrigues personal archives.

Ivan Gomes and Euclides Pereira go to war.
Photocred: Cléa Cordeiro Rodrigues personal archives.

Ivan and Euclides exchange blows from the "50/50" position.
Photocred: Cléa Cordeiro Rodrigues personal archives.

Ivan attacks Euclides' back.
Photocred: Cléa Cordeiro Rodrigues personal archives.

Ivan Gomes fights Euclides Pereira to another draw.
Photocred: Cléa Cordeiro Rodrigues personal archives.

Ivan after a bloody battle. Photocred:
Cléa Cordeiro Rodrigues personal archives.

Ivan continues his reign of terror in the rings.
Here he is seen applying a "kimura" shoulder-lock.
Photocred: Cléa Cordeiro Rodrigues personal archives.

Ivan Gomes and Carlson Gracie.
Photocred: Cléa Cordeiro Rodrigues personal archives.

Ivan and Carlson partner up to open a gym in Copacabana in 1964.
Here, Carlson is seen applying a *seoi-otoshi* throw on Ivan.
Photocred: Cléa Cordeiro Rodrigues personal archives.

Georges Mehdi goes to Japan and meets Masahiko Kimura. Photocred: Mehdi Academy.

Georges Mehdi and Carlson often trained together. Photocred: Mehdi Academy.

Carlson teaching jiu-jitsu. The top caption reads: *"I hate drawing blood from my opponents."* **The bottom one reads:** *"Substituting his Uncle Helio, Carlson became the most famous member of the Gracie family. Since he began his career as a luta-livre professional Carlson has not tasted bitter defeat."* **Photocred: Brazilian National Library.**

**Carlos and Helio receive official approval for the Guanabara Federation in 1973.
Photocred: Brazilian National Library.**

**Rolls has his hand raised at a tournament.
Photocred: Brazilian National Library via Elton Silva.**

**Document showing that Orlando Saraiva was a hired instructor at Carlson Gracie's
Academy. Photocred: Orlando and Henrique Saraiva personal archives.**

**Paquetá (left) and Orlando Saraiva (right). Photocred:
Orlando and Henrique Saraiva personal archives.**

**Helio visits the founding fathers of jiu-jitsu in São Paulo. From left
to right: Orlando Saraiva, Oswaldo Carnivalle, Otávio de Almeida,
Pedro Hemetério and Helio Gracie at an event in São Paulo in 1976.
Photocred: Orlando and Henrique Saraiva personal archives.**

**Rosada winning a match with a strained shoulder in 1976. Rorian Gracie
is the referee. Photocred: Antonio Carlos Rosado personal archives.**

Oswaldo Fadda (on the right) with one of his black-belts.
Photocred: Master Guedes via Marcial Serrano.

Two Fadda students practice kicks.
Photocred: Master Guedes via Marcial Serrano.

Romero "Jacaré" Cavalcanti plays guard at a tournament.
Photocred: Romero Cavalcanti personal archives.

Rorion holds his son Ryron in a gi among some of his first students in the US. Richard Bresler is standing to the far right. Circa 1982. Photocred: Richard Bresler personal archives.

Pinduka in wrestling gear. Photocred: Fernando Pinduka personal archives.

Pinduka (far right) plays beach soccer in Rio. Photocred: Fernando Pinduka personal archives.

Carlinhos with his team in 1984. Fron left to right standing: Crolin Gracie, Zé Beleza, Carlinhos Gracie Jr., Rigan Machado, Rilion Gracie and Carlos Machado. From left to right kneeling: Roger Machado, John Machado, Paulo Negão, Renzo Gracie, Nelson Monteiro and Jean Jacques Machado. Photocred: Carlos Gracie Jr. personal archives.

Peixotinho loses to Rickson. Helio Gracie is the referee. Photocred: Otávio Peixotinho personal archives.

Peixotinho wins the brown-belt open at the Rio State Championships. Notice that in the diploma he is representing "Clube: Academia Carlson." Photocred: Otávio Peixotinho personal archives.

Richard Bresler and Helio Gracie in 1983. Photocred: Richard Bresler personal archives.

Standing, from left to right: Peixotinho, Marco Kuhner, Carlson and Rosado. Bottom, Paulo Mamão and Bebeto at the Leblon academy where Rosado taught in the early 90s. Photocred: Otávio Peixotinho personal archives.

Rosado and his family.
Photocred: Antonio Carlos Rosado personal archives.

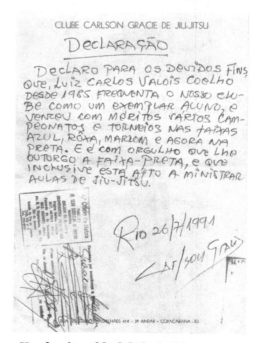

Hand written black-belt certificate from
Carlson to Luis Carlos Valois.
Photocred: Luis Carlos Valois personal archives.

Bustamante wins a match refereed by Rickson Gracie. Photocred: Murilo Bustamante personal archives.

1991 document bringing the federations from Rio (under Robson Gracie), Minas Gerais (under Adair Alves de Oliveira) and São Paulo (under Paulo Pirondi and Moisés Muradi) together in order to attempt to combine forces to form a national Confederation. Photocred: Master Guedes via Marcial Serrano.

The "Copa Brasileira Mameluc de Jiu-Jitsu" originally meant to take place in 1991 but only realized in 1993. This tournament gave a push for the foundation of the CBJJ, later IBJJF, in 1994. From left to right: Henrique China, Alexandre das Dores, Carlos Pedro, André Pederneiras, Abelardo Guimarães and Luís Amigo. Photocred: André Pederneiras personal archives.

Gracie Barra's headquarters in the early 90s.
Photocred: Carlos Gracie Jr. personal archives.

Renzo squares up with Wallid before their match in 1993.
Photocred: Marcelo Alonso personal archives.

Cover of the 1994 CBJJ ruleset.
Photocred: Master Guedes via Marcial Serrano.

Richard Bresler and Helio Gracie hold the 50,000 dollar check won by Royce in the first UFC. Photocred: Richard Bresler personal archives.

**Pinduka and Helio Gracie.
Photocred: Fernando Pinduka personal archives.**

A back dated black-belt diploma from Carlson's "Liga Carioca de Jiu-Jitsu," belonging to Peixotinho. Photocred: Otávio Peixotinho personal archives.

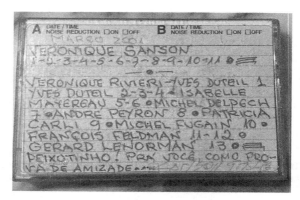

**Tape gifted by Carlson to Peixotinho
with some of his favorite songs on it.
Photocred: Otávio Peixotinho personal archives.**

**Carlinhos Gracie Jr. has his hand raised at the first "Masters International in
1999 at the Tijuca Tenis Clube. Photocred: Carlos Gracie Jr. personal archives.**

**Carlos Gracie Jr. would go on to become not only one of the most successful
coaches in the history of art, but also its all time leading political figure.
Photocred: IBJJF via Marcelo Siriema.**

Carlson is held up in the air by Vitor Belfort next to Wallid Ismail,
Rodrigo Medeiros and others during celebration for the 1996 Pans.
Photocred: Marcelo Alonso personal archives.

Carlson is lifted in the air by his students after Murilo Bustamante defeats
Jerry Bohlander in 1997. Photocred: Marcelo Alonso personal archives.

Carlson holds trophy after Carlão Barreto defeats Paul Varelans in 1997.
Photocred: Marcelo Alonso personal archives.

**Carlson is raised in the air by Carlão Barreto, Ricardo Libório
and Mario "Maresia" in 1998 after Wallid's victory over Royce.
Photocred: Marcelo Alonso personal archives.**

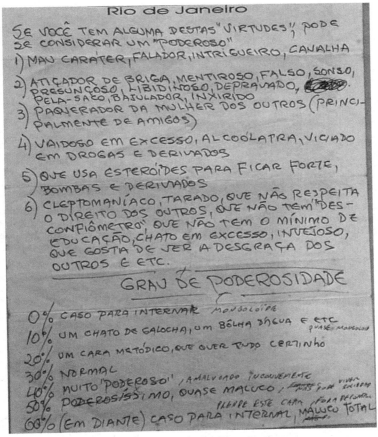

Rio de Janeiro

SE VOCÊ TEM ALGUMA DESTAS "VIRTUDES", PODE SE CONSIDERAR UM "PODEROSO"

1) MAU CARÁTER, FALADOR, INTRIGUEIRO, CANALHA

2) ATIÇADOR DE BRIGA, MENTIROSO, FALSO, SONSO, PRESUNÇOSO, LIBIDINOSO, DEPRAVADO, ██████. PELA-SACO, BAJULADOR, INXIRIDO

3) PAQUERADOR DA MULHER DOS OUTROS (PRINCIPALMENTE DE AMIGOS)

4) VAIDOSO EM EXCESSO, ALCOÓLATRA, VICIADO EM DROGAS E DERIVADOS

5) QUE USA ESTERÓIDES PARA FICAR FORTE, BOMBAS E DERIVADOS

6) CLEPTOMANÍACO, TARADO, QUE NÃO RESPEITA O DIREITO DOS OUTROS, QUE NÃO TEM "DESCONFIÔMETRO", QUE NÃO TEM O MÍNIMO DE EDUCAÇÃO, CHATO EM EXCESSO, INVEJOSO, QUE GOSTA DE VER A DESGRAÇA DOS OUTROS E ETC.

GRAU DE PODEROSIDADE

0% CASO PARA INTERNAR, MONGOLÓIDE

10% UM CHATO DE GALOCHA, UM BOLHA D'ÁGUA E ETC QUASE MONGOLÓIDE

20% UM CARA METÓDICO, QUE QUER TUDO CERTINHO

30% NORMAL

40% MUITO "PODEROSO", AMALUCADO, INCONVENIENTE

50% PODEROSÍSSIMO, QUASE MALUCO, ████ QUE NÃO VIVEM ████ PERDE ESTE CARA FORA DISTO...

60% (EM DIANTE) CASO PARA INTERNAR, MALUCO TOTAL

Carlson's famous *"teste de poderosidade"* ("powerful," or "almightiness" test), was half-joking way of keeping culture under control. It consisted of a lighthearted insult of sorts meant to remind students of a code of behavior they ought to follow on and off the mats: Below is the translation: "If you have any of these "virtues," you may consider yourself to be a *"poderoso."* 1) bad character, talks too much, looks to cause problems, jerk; 2) instigates fights, liar, false, dumb, presumptuous, libidinous, depraved, *"pela-saco"* (annoying), flatterer, nosy; 3) hits on someone else's girl (especially a friend's girl); 4) excessively vain, alcoholic, addicted to drugs and derivatives; 5) takes steroids, *"bomba"* and derivatives to get strong; 6) cleptomaniac, sex-addict, does not respect other people's rights, has no *"desconfiômetro"* (measurement of suspiciousness), has no minimal level of education, excessively annoying, jealous, who likes to watch other's in disgrace, etc. LEVEL OF PODEROSIDADE: 0%) case for hospitalization, mongoloid; 10%) very annoying, a water bubble, etc. Almost a mongoloid; 20%) A methodical person who wants everything to be right; 30%) normal; 40%) very "poderoso", tawny, inconvenient; 50%) ultra powerful, almost crazy, cannot live in society; 60% and over) must be hospitalized, totally crazy. Photocred: Paulo Filho personal archives.

The unending war. Carlson extends his arm to shake Helio's hand, Helio recoils and João Alberto Barreto extends his arm out to shake Carlson's hand in order not to leave him hanging. Photocred: Marcelo Alonso personal archives.

Joe Silva (on the right) the man who coined the term "as real as it gets," next to Carlson, the man who lived by that motto. Photocred: Joe Silva personal archives.

The author and Carlson Gracie at a tournament in Southern California in 1999. Photocred: Author's personal archives.

Carlson Gracie.
Photocred: Luca Atalla personal archives.

Senator Arthur Virgilio receives an honor at the "Bitetti Combat."
Photocred: Arthur Virgilio personal archives.

Sergio Malibu next to a cut out of Rolls Gracie.
Photocred: Sergio Malibu personal archives.

Euclides Pereira (left) makes a surprise appearance at one of Rosado's seminars in Brasilia on July 2016. Photocred: Antonio Carlos Rosado personal archives.

Royler, Carlinhos and Carlson Jr. Photocred: IBJJF archives via Marcelo Siriema.

Carlinhos Gracie Jr. and Roger Gracie on the mats. Roger is widely considered the most dominant jiu-jitsu practitioner of all time. Photocred: Carlos Gracie Jr. personal archives.

Carlinhos and his eldest son and IBJJF 2010 Pan champ, Kayron Gracie.
Photocred: Carlos Gracie Jr. personal archives.

Romero "Jacaré" Cavalcanti, founder of Alliance.
Photocred: Romero Cavalcanti personal archives.

IBJJF 2016 World Championships in Long Beach, California.
BJJ takes over the world. Photocred: IBJJF via Jon Medina.

Carlos Gracie, Marcelo Siriema, Carlos Gracie Jr., the author, André Fernandes and Helio Gracie at the IBJJF HQ in Irvine, California, June 2022. Photocred: Author's personal archives.

Sign at the IBJJF HQ in Irvine California reads: *"Make Jiu-Jitsu the Most Practiced Martial Art in the World."* Photocred: Author's personal archives.

Carlson is raised into the air by his students after (allegedly) winning the 1996 Pans in Los Angeles. Photocred: Marcelo Alonso personal archives.

"For heroes have the whole earth for their tomb; and in lands far from their own, where the column with its epitaph declares it, there is enshrined in every breast a record unwritten with no tablet to preserve it, except that of the heart. These take as your model."

Thucydides, "The History of the Peloponnesian War," Chapter 6.

Made in the USA
Middletown, DE
30 September 2023